IMPERIAL PERIPHERIES IN THE
NEO-ASSYRIAN PERIOD

IMPERIAL PERIPHERIES IN THE NEO-ASSYRIAN PERIOD

Edited by
CRAIG W. TYSON *and*
VIRGINIA R. HERRMANN

UNIVERSITY PRESS OF COLORADO
Louisville

© 2018 by University Press of Colorado

Published by University Press of Colorado
245 Century Circle, Suite 202
Louisville, Colorado 80027

All rights reserved

 The University Press of Colorado is a proud member of the Association of University Presses.

The University Press of Colorado is a cooperative publishing enterprise supported, in part, by Adams State University, Colorado State University, Fort Lewis College, Metropolitan State University of Denver, Regis University, University of Colorado, University of Northern Colorado, Utah State University, and Western State Colorado University.

ISBN: 978-1-60732-822-3 (cloth)
ISBN: 978-1-60732-991-6 (paperback)
ISBN: 978-1-60732-823-0 (ebook)
DOI: https://doi.org/10.5876/9781607328230

Library of Congress Cataloging-in-Publication Data

Names: Tyson, Craig W. (Craig William), 1976– editor. | Herrmann, Virginia Rimmer, editor.

Title: Imperial peripheries in the Neo-Assyrian period / edited by Craig W. Tyson, Virginia R. Herrmann.

Description: Boulder : University Press of Colorado, [2018] | Includes bibliographical references and index.

Identifiers: LCCN 2018034661| ISBN 9781607328223 (cloth) | ISBN 9781607328230 (ebook)| ISBN 9781607328916 (paperback)

Subjects: LCSH: Assyria—Politics and government. | Imperialism—History—To 1500. | Assyria—History. | Assyria—Antiquities.

Classification: LCC DS73.7 .I47 2018 | DDC 935/.03—dc23

LC record available at https://lccn.loc.gov/2018034661

Cover illustrations: courtesy, Metropolitan Museum of Art, New York City, 74.51.4557 (*front, top*); courtesy, Hebrew University of Jerusalem (*front, bottom*); © Metropolitan Museum of Art (*back*).

In Memory of Bradley J. Parker

A rare and enthusiastic scholar equally at home
in Old and New World Archaeology

Contents

List of Illustrations ix
List of Tables xiii
Preface and Acknowledgments xv
Abbreviations xvii
Chronology of the Ancient Near East xxi
Map—Expansion of the Neo-Assyrian Empire 1

1. Introduction: The Construction of the Imperial Periphery in Neo-Assyrian Studies
   Virginia R. Herrmann (Universität Tübingen) and Craig W. Tyson (D'Youville College) 3

2. At the Root of the Matter: The Middle Assyrian Prelude to Empire
   Bleda S. Düring (Leiden University) 41

3. Empire of Conflict, Empire of Compromise: The Middle and Neo-Assyrian Landscape and Interaction with the Local Communities of the Upper Tigris Borderland
   Guido Guarducci (CAMNES; University of Reading) 65

4. The Southern Levant under the Neo-Assyrian Empire: A Comparative Perspective
   Avraham Faust (Bar-Ilan University) 97

5. Reaction, Reliance, Resistance? Judean Pillar Figurines in the Neo-Assyrian Levant
    Erin Darby (University of Tennessee)   *128*

6. Dining under Assyrian Rule: Foodways in Iron Age Edom
    Stephanie H. Brown (University of California, Berkeley)   *150*

7. Peripheral Elite as Imperial Collaborators
    Craig W. Tyson (D'Youville College)   *177*

8. East of Assyria? Hasanlu and the Problem of Assyrianization
    Megan Cifarelli (Manhattanville College)   *210*

9. In the Middle of the Sea of the Setting Sun: The Neo-Assyrian Empire and Cyprus—Economic and Political Perspectives
    Anna Cannavò (CNRS, UMR 5189 HiSoMA, MOM, Lyon)   *240*

10. Neo-Pericentrics
    Bradley J. Parker[†] (University of Utah)   *265*

    About the Contributors   *283*
    Index   *287*

Illustrations

0.1	Map—Expansion of the Neo-Assyrian Empire	1
2.1.	Juxtaposition of the extent of the Assyrian Empire in the Middle Assyrian Period and the early part of the Neo-Assyrian Period	43
2.2.	Late Bronze Age occupation at Tell Sabi Abyad in level 6A	54
2.3.	Map of the Middle Assyrian Empire with various repertoires of rule used by Assyria indicated	55
3.1.	Upper Tigris Borderland with main Iron Age sites and modern cities indicated	66
3.2.	Diagram of pottery productions and influence dynamics within the Upper Tigris Borderland	74
3.3.	The Middle Assyrian network-empire and its settlement types and the Neo-Assyrian territorial empire and its main contexts	79
3.4.	Upper Tigris River Valley settlement increase from the Early Iron Age to the Middle Iron Age	82
3.5.	Middle and Late Assyrian number of sites recorded from selected survey areas	83
4.1.	Map of sites mentioned in the text	99
4.2.	Assyrian destruction layer at Tel 'Eton	101
4.3.	Integrated economic system of the south in the seventh century BCE	108

4.4.	One of eighth-century BCE olive presses at Beit Aryeh	111
4.5.	Distribution of olive oil production centers in time and space	112
5.1.	Molded head figurine from the City of David	129
5.2.	Pinched head figurine from the City of David	129
5.3.	JPF body from the City of David	129
6.1.	Map of southern Jordan and the Negev in the Iron Age	151
6.2.	Excavated areas at Busayra	157
6.3.	Oakeshott's Bowl K	162
6.4.	Buildings DD001 and DD002	164
6.5.	Storage vessels from Busayra	166
6.6.	Cooking vessels from Busayra	167
6.7.	Serving vessels from Busayra	168
6.8.	Percentage of vessel types from Buildings DD001 and DD002 by function	169
6.9.	Frequency of painted and fine-ware sherds from Buildings DD001 and DD002	169
6.10.	Frequency of Imitation Assyrian Palace Ware	169
7.1.	Map of Ammon	179
7.2.	Increase in number of identified sites from the Late Bronze Age/Iron Age I transition through Iron Age IIC	182
7.3.	Assyrian-style pottery from Ammon	189
7.4.	Seal illustrating Mesopotamian-style iconography with an Ammonite inscription: "Belonging to Shub'el"	191
7.5.	Relief from Rujm al-Kursi showing local adaptation of the standard of Sîn of Harran	191

7.6.	Statue of Yaraḥ ʿazar illustrating a mix of iconographic styles	191
8.1.	Excavation photograph of Period IVb destruction in Temple BBII	211
8.2.	Hasanlu citadel, Period IVb	214
8.3.	Contour plan of Hasanlu, Iran, with burial excavations in the northeast quadrant	217
8.4.	Excavation drawing Burial SK493a, young male	219
8.5.	Map of the region	222
8.6.	Excavation photograph of the Gold Bowl	225
8.7.	Excavation photograph of the Silver Beaker	226
8.8.	Copper alloy belt from Burial SK493	228
9.1.	Sargon II stele from Larnaca, 707 BCE, with a detail of the left side	243
9.2.	Lulî of Tyre escaping the Assyrians, 701 BCE	245
9.3.	Esarhaddon prism from Nineveh, 673 BCE	246
9.4.	Map of Cyprus, showing the main Archaic and Classical centers	249
9.5.	Map of Cyprus, showing the area of cultural influence of each kingdom according to terracotta stylistic analysis	250
9.6.	Silver bowl with incised decoration and Cypro-Syllabic inscription, said to be from Kourion, late eighth–seventh centuries BCE	251
9.7.	Limestone colossal head from Golgoi, late seventh–sixth centuries BCE	252
9.8.	Phoenician dedication to Baal of Lebanon by the *skn* of Qarthadasht, found in Cyprus, 739–730 BCE	254

Tables

2.1.	Overview of hardware type repertoires of rule in the Middle and Neo-Assyrian Empires	46
2.2.	Overview of software type repertoires of rule in the Middle and Neo-Assyrian Empires	48
7.1.	Transjordanian chronology	183
9.1.	Cypriot chronology	241
9.2.	Cypriot kings named in the parallel lists of Esarhaddon (673–672 BCE) and Ashurbanipal (after 664 BCE)	247

Preface and Acknowledgments

Our interest in the peripheries of the Neo-Assyrian Empire stems from research on two regions that had sustained interactions with Assyrian power. In Craig's case it is the area around Amman, Jordan, that was home to the ancient Ammonites. In Virginia's case it is the site of Zincirli in southern Turkey. In both cases our studies led us to consider carefully the interactions between empires and the smaller societies surrounding them. This shared interest was what led us to organize sessions on imperial peripheries at three consecutive annual meetings of the American Schools of Oriental Research (2011–13). A core group of scholars from those sessions joined us in proposing this volume, and we brought together several others to broaden its geographical scope. The resulting volume brings together eleven scholars from five countries to reconsider and reconceive interactions between the Neo-Assyrian Empire and its peripheries.

We would like to thank Darrin Pratt, director of the University Press of Colorado, for his initial idea for the book, as well as Jessica d'Arbonne (former acquisitions editor) and the rest of the University Press of Colorado staff for shepherding us through the process of producing this book. Our thanks to three anonymous reviewers whose comments and critiques strengthened many of the book's chapters as well as the overall clarity. We would also like to thank our contributors, who have been responsive to our feedback and requests. It has been a pleasure to work with all of you.

Unfortunately, shortly after the book went to production, Bradley Parker died unexpectedly. He was very generous with his time, advice, and encouragement for this volume, which is better because of it. Those who are familiar with Bradley's scholarly interests—which are broad and comparative—will see them on display in his contribution to this volume. Bradley was among a small group of scholars who published on Old and New World Archaeology. Several months before his death he had been awarded a three-year grant from the National Endowment for the Humanities for fieldwork on Inca and Wari imperialism in Peru. His voice will be missed.

Craig Tyson would like to thank the D'Youville College Faculty Research Committee for its support of several trips to Jordan for research and also the Montante Family Library staff for additions to the library collections that support my research. The inter-library loan staff has been an indispensable part of my research as well, obtaining books and articles that go far off the beaten path. As always, I thank my family for their love and support along the way.

Virginia Herrmann thanks the supporters of her dissertation research on Neo-Assyrian imperialism at Zincirli that sparked the development of this book: the Neubauer Family Foundation, the Whiting Foundation, and the Helen Rich Memorial Fund. She, too, sends her heartfelt gratitude to her family for their support and patience.

Abbreviations

AA	*American Anthropologist*
ABull	*Art Bulletin*
AD	*Archaeological Dialogues*
ADAJ	*Annual of the Department of Antiquities of Jordan*
AJA	*American Journal of Archaeology*
AMI	*Archäologische Mitteilungen aus Iran*
AMIT	*Archäologische Mitteilungen aus Iran und Turan*
ANES	*Ancient Near Eastern Studies*
AnIr	*Ancient Iran*
AnSt	*Anatolian Studies*
AoF	*Altorientalische Forschungen*
ARA	*Annual Review of Archaeology*
BA	*Biblical Archaeologist*
BAIAS	*Bulletin of the Anglo-Israel Archaeological Society*
BAR	*Biblical Archaeology Review*
BASOR	*Bulletin of the American Schools of Oriental Research*
BCH	*Bulletin de Correspondance Hellénique*
BCSMS	*Bulletin of the Canadian Society for Mesopotamian Studies*
BMM	*Metropolitan Museum of Art Bulletin*
BO	*Bibliotheca Orientalis*

BSOAS	Bulletin of the School of Oriental and African Studies
CA	Current Anthropology
CANE	Civilizations of the Ancient Near East (edited by Jack Sasson, 4 vols., New York: Scribners, 1995)
CCEC	Cahier du Centre d'Études Chypriotes
CCR	Comparative Civilizations Review
CRAIBL	Comptes rendus de l'Académie des inscriptions et belles-lettres
DNWSI	Dictionary of the North-West Semitic Inscriptions (by J. Hoftijzer and K. Jongeling, 2 vols., Leiden: Brill, 1995)
EJA	European Journal of Archaeology
ErIsr	Eretz-Israel
ESI	Excavations and Surveys in Israel
Hen	Henoch
HJSR	Humboldt Journal of Social Relations
IEJ	Israel Exploration Journal
IrAnt	Iranica Antiqua
JAA	Journal of Anthropological Archaeology
JAAS	Journal of Assyrian Academic Studies
JANER	Journal of Ancient Near Eastern Religions
JAOS	Journal of the American Oriental Society
JAR	Journal of Anthropological Research
JAS	Journal of Archaeological Science
JBL	Journal of Biblical Literature
JCS	Journal of Cuneiform Studies
JEOL	Jaarbericht Ex Oriente Lux
JESHO	Journal of the Economic and Social History of the Orient
JFA	Journal of Field Archaeology
JHS	Journal of Hebrew Scriptures
JMA	Journal of Mediterranean Archaeology
JNES	Journal of Near Eastern Studies
JRA	Journal of Roman Archaeology
JRAS	Journal of the Royal Asiatic Society
JRitSt	Journal of Ritual Studies

JSOT	*Journal for the Study of the Old Testament*
KTEMA	*KTEMA: Civilisations de l'Orient, de la Grèce et du Rome antiques*
NABU	*Nouvelles assyriologiques bréves et utilitaires*
NEA	*Near Eastern Archaeology*
OLZ	*Orientalistische Literaturzeitung*
Or	*Orientalia (NS)*
PBA	*Proceedings of the British Academy*
PEFA	*Palestine Exploration Fund Annual*
PEQ	*Palestine Exploration Quarterly*
PNA	*Prosopography of the Neo-Assyrian Empire*
Qad	*Qadmoniot*
QDAP	*Quarterly of the Department of Antiquities of Palestine*
RA	*Revue d'assyriologie et d'archéologie orientale*
RAnt	*Res Antiquae*
RB	*Revue biblique*
RDAC	*Report of the Department of Antiquities, Cyprus*
REA	*Research in Economic Anthropology*
RSF	*Rivista di Studi Fenici*
SAAB	*State Archives of Assyria Bulletin*
SCCNH	*Studies on the Civilization and Culture of Nuzi and the Hurrians*
SEL	*Studi Epigrafici e Linguistici sul Vicino Oriente antico*
SHAJ	*Studies in the History and Archaeology of Jordan*
SSR	*Social Science Research*
Syria	*Syria: Revue d'art oriental et d'archéologie*
TA	*Tel Aviv*
Topoi	*Topoi Orient-Occident*
Transeu	*Transeuphratène*
UF	*Ugarit Forschungen*
WA	*World Archaeology*
ZA	*Zeitschrift für Assyriologie*
ZAH	*Zeitschrift für Althebraistik*
ZDPV	*Zeitschrift des deutschen Palästina-Vereins*

*Chronology of the
Ancient Near East*

ARCHAEOLOGICAL PERIODS

LATE BRONZE AGE	1550–1200
IRON AGE I	1200–1000
IRON AGE II	1000–586
Iron Age IIA	1000–900
Iron Age IIB	900–700
Iron Age IIC	700–586

POLITICAL CHRONOLOGY[*]

MIDDLE ASSYRIAN PERIOD	1366–1208
Assur-uballit I	1366–1330
Adad-nirari I	1307–1275
Shalmaneser I	1274–1245
Tukulti-Ninurta I	1244–1208
PERIOD OF WEAKNESS IN ASSYRIA	1207–935
Tiglath-pileser I	1115–1077
NEO-ASSYRIAN PERIOD	*934–612*
Assur-dan II	934–912
Adad-nirari II	911–891
Tukulti-Ninurta II	890–884
Ashurnasirpal II	883–859
Shalmaneser III	858–823
Shamshi-Adad V	823–811
Adad-nirari III	810–783
Tiglath-pileser III	744–727
Shalmaneser V	726–722

---

[*] Dates follow those in *CANE* II, 818–19.

Sargon II	721–705
Sennacherib	704–681
Esarhaddon	680–669
Ashurbanipal	668–627
Fall of Nineveh	612
NEO-BABYLONIAN EMPIRE	*612–539*

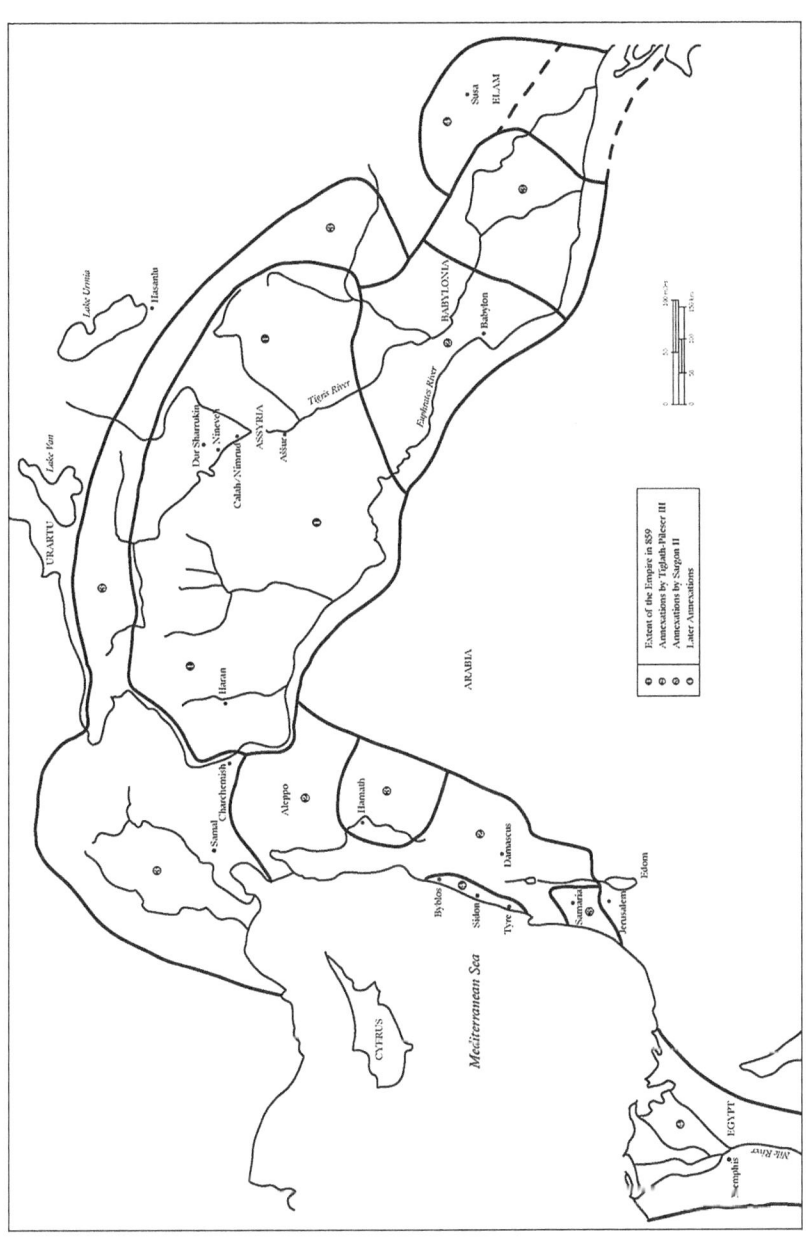

FIGURE 0.1. *Map—Expansion of the Neo-Assyrian Empire*

1

Introduction

The Construction of the Imperial Periphery in Neo-Assyrian Studies

VIRGINIA R. HERRMANN
(UNIVERSITÄT TÜBINGEN)
AND
CRAIG W. TYSON
(D'YOUVILLE COLLEGE)

At its height, the Neo-Assyrian Empire was the largest state the world had yet seen, uniting and administering disparate peoples and landscapes across the Near East for 300 years (934–612 BCE). From its heartland on the Tigris River, Assyria expanded to incorporate territories from western Iran to the Nile Valley, from the Persian Gulf to the Mediterranean Sea, and from the Taurus Mountains to the Arabian Desert, inhabited by millions of people of myriad tongues, ethnicities, lifestyles, and gods, with ripple effects on millions more beyond its borders. Its royal dynasty, unbroken for a thousand years, expressed a vision of universal kingship under the national god Aššur through propagandistic inscriptions and the construction of fantastically sculptured royal palaces and enormous imperial capitals, annual campaigns of conquest and subjugation, and the deportation and resettlement of countless of the conquered. Over the century and a half since the rediscovery of the Assyrian royal capitals, a great wealth of epigraphic, iconographic, and archaeological material from the period of Neo-Assyrian domination has been recovered in the cities and plains of the heartland, as well as the imperial provinces, vassal kingdoms, and peripheral adversaries.[1]

The rich textual and archaeological record of Assyria, the prototypical world-empire, has great potential to contribute to cross-cultural study of the imperial political form and its motives, methods, and consequences. However, its size, diversity, and longevity tend

DOI: 10.5876/9781607328230.c001

to frustrate attempts at synoptic comprehension and description of a key topic in the study of imperialism: the relationship between the imperial center and its shifting periphery. Was Neo-Assyrian territorial expansion driven primarily by defensive reactionism, politico-religious ideology, or the quest for wealth? What direct and indirect methods of control and administration were used by the Assyrian authorities, and to what factors can we attribute regional variation in the development of subject territories? What were the short- and long-term social, economic, and cultural effects of Assyrian subjugation and contact on peripheral societies? And how might Assyrian motives and methods have evolved as the imperial domain spilled over from its historical Upper Mesopotamian limits to include ever more foreign lands and peoples?

This chapter reviews efforts old and new to answer these questions and get to the heart of Neo-Assyrian imperialism. Shifting contemporary values have undoubtedly played and continue to play an influential role on the field of Neo-Assyrian studies, as have periodic surges in the quantity and diversity of available archaeological and textual evidence. Equally important has been the influence of a comparative approach that has attempted to comprehend modern and ancient imperialism alike through general principles, models, and typologies that take a panoramic view of these empires from the center (e.g., Ekholm and Friedman 1979; Eisenstadt 1963, 1979; D'Altroy 1992; see Sinopoli 1994; Steinmetz 2014). Despite the heuristic value of this approach that has motivated much groundbreaking analysis, unitary models of the definition and relations of imperial core and periphery have often been criticized as reductionist, centrist, static, or anachronistic (Alcock 1997; Morrison 2001; Sinopoli 2001a; Stein 2002; Schreiber 2006; Goldstone and Haldon 2009). However, the lasting legacy of this perspective is the widespread recognition that the interaction between imperial centers and their provinces and peripheries is crucial for understanding developmental processes in each.

The more recent turn in imperial studies toward a kaleidoscopic perspective that embraces themes of diversity, complexity, and negotiation (see Sinopoli 2001a; Stein 2002) aims at closer approximation of the contingent experiences of imperial subjects and administrators in lieu of universal explanatory and predictive frameworks. Recent comparative work on ancient empires has often concentrated on the meso- or micro-level of the strategies, processes, and types of actors identified in imperial societies.[2] A related development influenced by postcolonial and subaltern studies has been a shift of analytical focus toward the societies of subjugated areas and non-elite subjects that rejects the idea of the "passive periphery," recognizes imperial center and periphery as mutually constituted, and decenters our idea of what empires are and do.[3]

The nine contributions that make up this book, outgrowths from three sessions (2011–13) at the annual meetings of the American Schools of Oriental Research (ASOR) titled "Imperial Peripheries: Archaeology, History, and Society on the Edge of Empires," form part of this ongoing dialogue, casting a fresh look at the Assyrian Empire with new evidence and syntheses from its periphery.

INTRODUCTION TO THE NEO-ASSYRIAN EMPIRE

After a period of relative weakness in Assyria, the Neo-Assyrian Empire emerged during the reign of Assur-dan II (934–912 BCE), who set out to reconquer old Assyrian holdings in Upper Mesopotamia (see Düring, this volume). His successors, Adad-nirari II (911–891 BCE) and Tukulti-Ninurta II (890–884 BCE), continued this activity into the early ninth century and gained a firm grasp on Upper Mesopotamia but without establishing a foothold west of the Euphrates. Ashurnasirpal II (883–859 BCE) and Shalmaneser III (858–823 BCE) continued to strengthen Assyria's hold in the north and east and maintained control of areas in the west to the Euphrates. Following their reigns there was a period of relative weakness (823–745 BCE) without new conquests (Kuhrt 1995, 478–93; Van De Mieroop 2007, 238–45). It was the reign of Tiglath-pileser III (744–727 BCE) that brought the Neo-Assyrian Empire to its classic shape. Tiglath-pileser III and his successors launched a series of campaigns that would bring much of the ancient Near East under their control, either as provinces or as vassals (Kuhrt 1995, 493–501; Van De Mieroop 2007, 247–58). It was not until more than a century later that Neo-Assyrian power gave way to the Neo-Babylonian Empire.

THE ASSYRIAN HEARTLAND

The kings of Assyria made a significant imprint on the Assyrian heartland. Successive kings embarked on massive projects to rebuild old cities or found new capitals. The size of these building projects, especially the newly founded capitals with their elaborate palaces and temples, were fitting symbols of the power of the Assyrian monarch. One of the best-known examples is the building of Calah/Nimrud as a capital by Ashurnasirpal II (883–859 BCE). The city of 360 ha was enclosed by a city wall 7.5 km long and included several palaces and temples, including a large ziggurat (stepped pyramid temple) (Oates and Oates 2001, 27). The famous "Banquet Stele" found in the Northwest Palace lists Ashurnasirpal's accomplishments, especially construction, and commemorates the completion of the palace, including details about a massive party held to celebrate it. Full of pomp, Ashurnasirpal claims:

> (20b–31) Aššur, the great lord, cast his eyes upon me and my authority (and) my power came forth by his holy command. Ashurnasirpal, the king whose strength is praiseworthy, with my cunning which the god Ea, king of the *apsû*, extensively wise, gave to me, the city Calah I took in hand for renovation. I cleared away the old ruin hill (and) dug down to water level. From water level to the top, (a depth of) 120 layers of brick, I filled in the terrace. I founded therein a palace of boxwood, *meskannu*-wood, cedar, cypress, terebinth, tamarisk, *meḫru*-wood, eight palace (area)s as my royal residence (and) for my lordly leisure (and) decorated (them) in a splendid fashion. I fastened with bronze bands doors of cedar, cypress, *daprānu*-juniper, boxwood, (and) *meskannu*-wood (and) hung (them) in their doorways. I surrounded them with knobbed nails of bronze. I depicted in greenish glaze on their walls my heroic praises, in that I had gone right across highlands, lands, (and) seas, (and) the conquest of all lands . . .
>
> (36b–40) I dug out a canal from the Upper Zab, cutting through a mountain at its peak, (and) called it Patti-hegalli. I irrigated the meadows of the Tigris (and) planted orchards with all kinds of fruit trees in its environs. I pressed wine (and) offered first-fruit offerings to Aššur, my lord, and the temples of my land. I dedicated this city to Aššur, my lord . . .
>
> (53–55) In the city Calah, the centre of my dominion, temples which had previously not existed . . . I founded . . . (60–68) I established in them the seats of the gods, my lords. I decorated them in a splendid fashion. I installed over them cedar beams (and) made high cedar doors. I fastened (them) with bronze bands (and) hung (them) in their doorways. I stationed holy bronze images in their doorways. I made (the images of) their great divinity resplendent with red gold and sparkling stones. I gave to them gold jewellery, many possessions which I had captured . . .
>
> (140–154) when I consecrated the palace of Calah, 47,074 men (and) women who were invited from every part of my land, 5,000 dignitaries (and) envoys of the people of the lands Suhu, Hindānu, Patinu, Hatti, (145) Tyre, Sidon, Gurgumu, Malidu, Hubušku, Gilzānu, Kummu, (and) Musasiru, 16,000 people of Calah, (and) 1,500 *zarīqū* of my palace, all of them—altogether 69,574 (including) those summoned from all lands and the people of Calah—for ten days I gave them food, I gave them drink, I had them bathed, I had them anointed. (Thus) did I honour them (and) send them back to their lands in peace and joy. (Grayson 1991a, 289–93)

In his turn, Sargon II (721–705 BCE) began work on a completely new capital city called Dur-Sharrukin, "fortress of Sargon," at the modern site of Khorsabad. Sargon II's successor, Sennacherib (704–681 BCE), subsequently rebuilt the city of Nineveh (near modern Mosul), including his elaborately decorated "Palace without rival," whose carved and inscribed orthostats reveal Assyrian royal ideology in its grandest fashion (Russell 1992). In addition to building cities, the kings of Assyria demonstrated other interests. They collected exotic animals, planted gardens with exotic plants, built libraries (Black and Tait 1995, 2206), worked to assure an adequate food supply (Altaweel 2008), and more generally presented themselves as making the land fruitful (Radner 2000). Each Assyrian monarch thus sought to display his power over the world, his devotion to the gods, and his beneficence to the people he ruled.[4]

MAJOR COMPETITOR STATES

In their bid for influence and control of the ancient Near East, several powerful adversaries played recurring roles in the expansion and eventual demise of the Neo-Assyrian Empire. North of the Assyrian heartland, in what is now southeastern Turkey and northwestern Iran, the Urartian state, entrenched in mountain fortresses, was a powerful enemy. While its history is obscure, we find Shalmaneser III clashing with Urartu in the mid-ninth century. Undeterred, by about 800 BCE the Urartians had expanded toward Lake Urmia in the southeast and expanded westward toward the Mediterranean Sea, giving them access to important trade routes (Kuhrt 1995, 554–57; Zimansky 1995, 1138–39). It was only with the concerted military efforts of Tiglath-pileser III and Sargon II that Assyria was able to subdue, but not eradicate, Urartu, which continued to have diplomatic relations with Assyria (Kuhrt 1995, 557–58; Zimansky 1995, 1139–40; Melville 2016, 116–40).

The relationship with Babylonia to the south would remain Assyria's most troublesome sphere of influence. With its long heritage and entrenched political interests, Babylonia did not take easily to external control. In the mid-ninth century, relations between Assyria and Babylonia were stabilized by treaty. The relationship continued in this way until the reign of Shamshi-Adad V (823–811 BCE), who campaigned in Babylonia to deal with unspecified political problems (Kuhrt 1995, 557).

As with much of the rest of Neo-Assyrian history, it was Tiglath-pileser III who, with his major military campaigns, settled matters with Babylonia for a time. He defeated the Chaldean ruler of the area and took up dual kingship of Assyria and Babylonia. This state of affairs eventually crumbled, and the next hundred years or so would see a periodic changeover in the ruler of Babylon, alternating between local rulers and the Assyrian monarch (Oates 1986, 113–23).

Often allied with the Babylonians in the struggle against Assyria were the Elamites, who lived in the region to the east and southeast of Babylon, an area later occupied by the Persians. This state, centered on the city of Susa, figured most prominently in the late eighth and seventh centuries, in some cases helping the Babylonians repel Assyrian attacks on Babylonia and in other cases repelling Assyrian incursions into Elamite territory. The last of these incursions was in 646 BCE when Ashurbanipal defeated Susa, bringing an end to the Elamite state (Brentjes 1995, 1013–15).

Egypt was of perennial interest to the Assyrians as a source of wealth, especially gold. Egypt's distance from Assyria, however, made subjugating it a difficult proposition. Nonetheless, as Tiglath-pileser III and his successors pressed into the southern Levant in the late eighth century, an invasion of Egypt became more possible. An actual invasion of Egypt, however, did not take place until the reign of Esarhaddon, who mounted a failed attempt in 674 BCE and a successful attempt in 671 BCE. He conquered the Nile Delta and the area upstream to Memphis, appointed a series of petty kings from among the local population to fragment political power, and installed various other officials to keep an eye on them (Leichty 2011, 186). This was an unstable state of affairs that Ashurbanipal had to deal with in 667 and 664, when rebellion broke out in Egypt led by Kushite kings from the south. The Assyrians defeated the rebels in both cases but maintained a local dynast to rule Egypt from the Nile Delta city of Sais, a situation that inaugurated the twenty-sixth Saite dynasty (Kuhrt 1995, 634–38). The precise path the Assyrian-Egyptian relationship took from there is not clear, especially as Assyrian power waned in the Levant after about 640 BCE. Nonetheless, Egyptian forces appear alongside the Assyrians as they fought desperately to hold off the Babylonians in the late seventh century (Kuhrt 1995, 544–45, 590), suggesting that an alliance between these two powers was still in effect.

NEO-ASSYRIAN IMPERIAL SUBJECTS AND PRACTICE

Alongside the large states surveyed above were many smaller groups with whom the Neo-Assyrian Empire interacted. Not surprisingly, these smaller groups often resisted Assyrian attempts to control them, sometimes gathering in military coalitions to beat back the Assyrian army, in other cases capitulating. In the case of nomadic groups such as the Arabs, their movement and lack of significant settled populations meant that evasion was often the most effective form of resistance.

The Assyrians used a full complement of hegemonic tactics to coerce and control these subjects (see Düring, this volume). These included military force, deportations (Oded 1979), conscription of personnel from provinces and vassals (Postgate 1974b, 59–60), and the use of garrisons in peripheral lands (Saggs 2001, 156-57; Grayson and Novotny 2012, 180, no. 22 iv 54–60). In the realm of administration, the Assyrians divided the lands they controlled into provinces, which were directly controlled by Assyrian personnel, and vassals,[5] which remained under local leadership that was then bound the to the Assyrian king by a variety of means. Provinces were described as part of "the land of Aššur," the land owned by the Assyrian state god Aššur. Vassals, in contrast, bore "the yoke of Aššur," which is to say they were subject to the control of Aššur (Postgate 1992, 251–55). Vassal rulers were required to swear oaths that stipulated loyalty to the Assyrian king and his dynasty, including coordination of foreign policy, approval for local changes in rulers, provision of laborers and supplies for building projects, and aid to the Assyrian army in the form of intelligence, supplies, and troops (Machinist 1992, 70; Parker 2001, 250–51; for texts, see Parpola and Watanabe 1988). Vassals delivered various kinds of tribute and gifts—perhaps on an annual basis—to the imperial palace from whence they were distributed to the royal court. These trips to the imperial capital probably included a renewal of vassal oaths, thus serving as a central act of ongoing loyalty and incorporating vassals into an empire-wide elite class (Postgate 1974b, 121–27). In return for their submission and faithful remittance of tribute, vassals retained a level of autonomy with which to govern their lands.

The Assyrians employed several kinds of officials to monitor military, economic, and political activity throughout the empire. We hear of the *pīḫatu*, *šaknu*, and *šāpiru* officials, all of whom could rule and administer lands under Assyrian control (CAD P/12, 360–69; CAD Š/17.1, 180–92, 453–58).[6] There was also the *rab kāri*, "port inspector," who oversaw trading stations and could collect taxes and tribute. The *qīpu* officials seem to have monitored Assyrian vassal rulers, in some cases embedded in or near vassal courts. For example, Tiglath-pileser III installed a *qīpu* over Samsi, "the queen of the Arabs," after having defeated her in 733 (Tadmor and Yamada 2011, 106–7, no. 42:19'–26').

The Assyrians also built an ideological system that legitimated Assyrian rule and integrated vassal rulers and their gods into what Bedford (2009, 60) calls a "symbolic universe." The Assyrian king was seen as the agent of the divine world engaged in a process of ordering the earthly world to reflect the divine preeminence of the god Aššur (Bedford 2009, 48–55). This ideology was expressed in the vassal oaths that invoked Assyrian and local gods such that when a vassal rebelled, the Assyrian king was obliged to impose order by punishing the rebel (Bedford 2009, 54–55). The removal of cult statues from rebellious territories reinforced this by portraying local deities as abandoning their people because of the latter's evil actions (Cogan 1974, 9–21). This ideology shaped an elite identity in which vassals could participate (Bedford 2009, 60–61). Put another way, the vassal elite—along with the provincial elite and royal court—were "the actors that spread the king's power to the rest of the empire" (Parker 2011, 371).

THE PERIPHERY IN NEO-ASSYRIAN STUDIES
Rediscovery of Ancient Assyria in an Age of Empire

Before the rediscovery of ancient Mesopotamian civilizations in the nineteenth century by European adventurers such as Layard and Botta and the decipherment of cuneiform (described in Larsen 1996), nearly all that was known of the Assyrian Empire derived from the Hebrew Bible, in which Assyria plays the arch-villain and rod of divine anger. The "fascinated horror" (Machinist 1993, 78 n. 2) with which this foundational text of Western civilization regarded the Assyrians was borne out by the newly discovered palace reliefs, which showcased love of war and seemingly endless cruelty toward opponents.

While the Roman Empire was considered by many a model to be emulated by European imperialists, this was generally not the case when it came to the empires of the Near East. Liverani (2005, 224–25; cf. Frahm 2006) points out that despite the European-American perception of a *translatio imperii* from the Assyrian, Babylonian, and Persian Empires to the Greeks and thence to the Romans and modern Western empires,[7] the empires of Asia were at the same time viewed as incarnations of Oriental despotism, the true prototypes of the contemporary Ottoman Empire.[8] The biblical fear and loathing of Assyria thus harmonized with this image of a totalitarian and immoral state that embodied "the negative values of despotism, generalized slavery, centralized economy, magic, stagnation, lust and sadistic cruelty" (Liverani 2005, 225–26; see also Holloway 2006; Frahm 2006). To its conquered periphery, the irresistible force of Assyria brought devastation in place of governance[9] and monomaniacal proselytism of Aššur (a stand-in for Islam; [see Holloway 2002, 33–34]) in place of civilization.

By the turn of the twentieth century, study of Assyrian royal inscriptions and archival texts had progressed to the point where Assyriologists could begin to define not only Assyria's political history but also the organization and administration of its empire (e.g., Johns 1901; Olmstead 1918; Forrer 1920). This began to erode the impression that the Assyrians had been merely militaristic predators, not bothering to administer or improve their holdings once they had taken the booty they desired. Admiration for Assyrian art and literary and religious texts vied with their (often anti-Semitic) dismissal (Frahm 2006, 79–85). At the same time, the atrocities of colonial empires and the horrors of the world wars began to evoke ambivalence toward imperialism in general, whether Western or Eastern, overturning the formerly positive valuation of "bellicosity, imperial ambitions, and autocratic political system" (Frahm 2006, 86–87).

NEO-ASSYRIAN STUDIES IN THE POSTCOLONIAL PERIOD

Neo-Assyrian studies flourished in the period after World War II, kicked off by the resumption of archaeological work and the discovery of new texts in the Assyrian heartland, particularly at the renewed British excavations at Nimrud (see Reade 1982; Cifarelli, this volume). But advances in Assyriology and authoritative new editions of royal inscriptions, letters, and administrative and legal documents[10] were accompanied by a new interest, influenced by the postcolonial academic climate, in deconstructing imperial ideology and social and economic history (cf. Liverani 2005, 230).

Tadmor, Liverani, and others analyzed the royal inscriptions to explore the Assyrian semiotic system, issues of access and audience, and the propagandistic shaping and masking of relationships with rivals, vassals, and victims (e.g., Liverani 1979; Fales 1981; Tadmor 1997). The iconography of the palace reliefs, rock monuments, and royal steles, known for a century, was investigated anew for the creation in these monuments of an ideological program complementing that in the texts (e.g., Reade 1979; Winter 1983; Porter 2000). The study of Assyrian religion and its relationship with imperialism also developed considerably (e.g., Cogan 1974; Pongratz-Leisten 1994; Holloway 2002; Vera Chamaza 2002). Meanwhile, the publication of archival texts provided fodder for a host of studies illuminating the operation of the Neo-Assyrian Empire and its economic and social structure (e.g., the synthetic studies of Diakonoff [1969] and Postgate [1979]. Assyriologists have wrestled with and debated thorny questions regarding the palatial and provincial administration and bureaucracy (see Radner 2006), taxation and royal service (e.g., Fales 1973; Postgate 1974b), foreign tribute (e.g., Elat 1982; Bär 1996), the deportation system (e.g., Oded 1979), land tenure (e.g., van Driel 1970; Postgate 1974a; Fales

1984a; Liverani 1984), labor (e.g., Zabłocka 1972; Postgate 1987; Fales 1997), long-distance trade (e.g., Oppenheim 1967; Fales 1984b; Elat 1991; Radner 1999), money and prices (e.g., Müller 1997; Radner 1999), the social and legal status of the population (e.g., Jacobson 1969; Garelli 1972; Galil 2007), and its ethnic and linguistic composition (e.g., Tadmor 1978; Zadok 1995; Zehnder 2007).

During this revival of Neo-Assyrian studies in the late twentieth century, Lenin's (1939) thesis of imperialism as the "highest stage of capitalism" and its successors, dependency theory (Frank 1966) and world-systems theory (Wallerstein 1974), were deeply influential on contemporary understanding of the newly decolonized world. This perspective inspired ancient historians and archaeologists to seek evidence in the peripheries of ancient colonial systems and empires—including Assyria—for structural transformation and economic, social, and cultural destruction comparable to contemporary Third World poverty and turmoil. The "criminalization" of Assyria as an "evil empire" thus took a new turn (Liverani 2005, 226; cf. Frahm 2006, 86–87). The democratic critique overlay, but did not entirely replace, a palimpsest of orientalist and biblical images of Assyrian rapacity and omnipotence. Mann (1986, 237) found it safe to say that "uniquely among the major ancient empires, Assyria has been looked back upon fondly by no one."[11]

In concert with this new attraction to interregional explanatory models, the postcolonial shift of attention toward areas outside the imperial metropoles also found expression in Neo-Assyrian studies. While Assyria had always loomed large for historians of the biblical lands, this new systemic approach, combined with new textual and archaeological evidence, led to a resurgence of work on this period in the southern Levant, making the provinces and vassal kingdoms of this region the first intensively studied part of the Assyrian periphery (see references in Faust, this volume; Brown, this volume.). In the 1980s and 1990s, the new interest in imperial peripheries dovetailed with changing archaeological opportunities. Salvage initiatives necessitated by the construction of dams in Iraq, Syria, and Turkey encouraged regional survey and excavation of Neo-Assyrian provincial sites of all sizes, even as work in the capital cities of the Assyrian heartland in Iraq became politically more difficult (see Wilkinson et al. 2005; MacGinnis, Wicke, and Greenfield 2016; Düring, this volume; Guarducci, this volume).

The Influence of World-Systems Theory

World-systems theory answered a need in Neo-Assyrian studies for a large-scale interregional explanatory framework to comprehend this mass of new textual and archaeological data, and it became the dominant paradigm (together with related core-periphery perspectives) in theoretical and synthetic scholarship on the Neo-Assyrian Period for several decades. Wallerstein sought to explain the rise of the modern "world-system," that is, a multi-polity system (a "world") linked together largely by economic rather than political relations. He distinguished this "world-economy" from earlier "world-empires" in which one polity dominated others through military means. While world-empires appropriate surpluses through tribute and taxation, dominant core states in the modern world-economy profit by securing monopolistic rights for their businesses in the periphery (Wallerstein 1974, 15–16). The key element of this world-economy is the division of labor between core states, where high-skill occupations and capital are concentrated, and the periphery, which provides labor for the production of raw or semi-finished materials that are moved in bulk to the core (Wallerstein 1974, 349–51).[12]

Despite Wallerstein's (1974, 15–16, 1991) conviction that the modern world-economy was a unique historical phenomenon, ancient historians and archaeologists have found his analysis and terminology—as well as Frank's (1966) dependency theory and *longue durée* adaptation of world-systems theory (Frank 1993)—attractive, regardless of whether they explicitly embrace world-systems theory. One appeal is that the broadened scale of analysis requires the evaluation of localized changes within a larger network of interactions or world-system (Rowlands 1987, 3; Stein 1999, 176), allowing evidence from disparate sources and a wide geographical spread to be understood within a single cohesive framework. The focus on long-term material flows and interregional power asymmetries is also well suited to archaeological data (D'Altroy 1992, 13–14).

Notwithstanding the obvious technological, social, economic, and cultural differences of the Neo-Assyrian Empire, an analogy could be made with the modern European imperialist and colonialist world-system on the assumption that the driving force of expansion and consolidation was the economic exploitation of the periphery for the benefit of the core. A dichotomy of political status justified the creation of an interregional but intra-imperial division of labor between core and periphery. The Assyrians subjugated their neighbors to access raw materials and luxury goods unavailable in Assyria itself. When indirect control through local vassals eventually proved troublesome, they annexed these territories as provinces to enable their more efficient exploitation (e.g., Diakonoff 1969, 29; Grayson 1995, 964; Bedford 2009, 42, 44).

Congruent with Wallerstein's (1974, 15) distinction between past *tributary* "world-empires" and the *capitalist* "world-economy," most considered the mode of "suction" in the Assyrian Empire to have been the traditional, parasitic system of annual tribute of luxury goods from vassal states and taxation in the form of staples and labor from provinces (see Postgate 1979). The depredations of Assyrian conquest and deportation, followed by "the exorbitant extortions of the imperial tax system" (Grayson 1995, 967) and only halfhearted measures to rebuild and repopulate in an effort to maintain control (Larsen 1979, 96; Grayson 1991b, 216–17), were thought to have resulted in the economic devastation of subjugated territories, a state of "underdevelopment" (Diakonoff 1969, 29; Elat 1982, 245; Lamprichs 1995, 382; Allen 1997, 140). Furthermore, several studies of Neo-Assyrian documents argued for the transition to a "slave mode of production" during this period, as the king's family and high officials acquired enormous, discontinuous agricultural estates from newly conquered lands, cultivated mainly by "un-free" deportee peasants (e.g., Diakonoff 1969, 30; Fales 1973; Fales 1984a). By eroding to nothing the sector of communally owned village lands worked by free peasants,[13] a vast "internal periphery" was created and controlled by a small class of Assyrian nobles and officials.

Accumulating archaeological evidence from new excavations and surveys in peripheral regions of the empire soon challenged the image of a uniformly depopulated, depressed, and ruralized Assyrian hinterland. While the expected depopulation was found in some parts of the southern Levant (see Na'aman 1993; Faust, this volume), elsewhere the evidence showed a demographic and economic boom. Surveys in the rain-fed agricultural lands and steppe between the Tigris and Euphrates Rivers showed a massive increase in small, dispersed settlements during the ninth through seventh centuries BCE, including in agriculturally marginal areas that had never before been settled (see Wilkinson et al. 2005). A similar new agricultural settlement was found in the Assyrian vassal kingdoms of the southern Levant (see Na'aman 1993; Gitin 1997; Faust, this volume). Urbanism expanded as well in the Neo-Assyrian Period. Provincial capitals of the Jazirah such as Tell Sheikh Hamad, Tell Ahmar, and Ziyaret Tepe were large, densely inhabited, and prosperous (see Kühne 1995; Barbanes 2003). Vassal capitals of the southern Levant such as Ekron and Jerusalem expanded enormously in size and population and showed evidence of extensive production and trade (see Gitin 1997; Faust and Weiss 2005; Faust, this volume).

This new evidence of economic and demographic transformation encouraged some toward more explicit use of world-systems theory and comparison with modern colonial empires. Alongside the traditional tributary methods of wealth extraction, the Neo-Assyrian Empire was suggested to have innovated new *proto-capitalistic* methods for the creation of wealth. At the same time, the uneven development of different parts of the Assyrian periphery required an explanation that was not inherent in the world-systems model.

One solution was offered by Parker (2001), who applied the Territorial-Hegemonic Model[14] to his study area in the Upper Tigris River Valley. According to this model, empires employed a continuum of strategies ranging from intensive control at high cost (*territorial* control, i.e., annexation and colonization) to loose control at low cost (*hegemonic* control, i.e., vassal treaties and punitive campaigns), depending on a calculation of the "cost of that control and the amount of income the core can extract from its subject territories" (Parker 2001, 14; similarly, Berlejung 2012; Bagg 2013). In areas of little economic or strategic value, the empire made the minimum investment necessary for pacification, while in areas of high value an intensive effort was applied to control and restructure local economies and settlement systems. Contrary to the model of the purely parasitic empire, Parker (2001, 252, 2003, 540–41) argued for much more *active* interventions in provincial economies to create and extract more wealth for the Assyrian core, including state-controlled agricultural colonization and the centralization and monopolization of ceramic, metal, and wool production. The provinces of Upper Mesopotamia were developed as an immense breadbasket, feeding the capital cities of the Assyrian heartland (Parker 2001, 252, 2003, 541).

Gitin (1997) and Allen (1997) applied a world-systems or "center-periphery" model to the southern Levant under Assyrian rule. Like Parker, they proposed a flexible Assyrian policy of "selective economic development" (Allen 1997, 156) adapted to local potential, although with opposite results. Here it was the southern Assyrian vassals whose economies were "targeted for growth" in production and trade (Gitin 1997, 84), while any area such as the northern kingdom of Israel that was "not a desirable zone for furthering Assyrian interests in accumulating and centralizing resources" (Allen 1997, 155) was conquered and looted, depopulated through deportations, and reconstituted as a province with a bare-bones administration; it was thus pacified but not developed.

Distance from the imperial core and economic specialization could account for the different strategy applied to the Levant. From the fact that some Levantine vassal kingdoms that were heavily involved in long-distance trade were left semi-autonomous despite repeated rebellions, it has often been argued that the Assyrians were reluctant to take direct control of them. As the Assyrians were unprepared to mount their own maritime expeditions or desert caravans, it was more lucrative to skim off part of the profits of local trade and run the risk of another rebellion (Elat 1978, 20–21, 34, 1991, 24–25;

Allen 1997, 1–2; Radner 2004, 157; Berlejung 2012). Some have argued that the imposition of heavy Assyrian tribute demands for precious metals and exotic goods forced Phoenician port cities to expand their trading activities into the western Mediterranean in search of new sources of silver (Frankenstein 1979; Sherratt and Sherratt 1993, 370) and required southern Levantine vassal kingdoms to intensify and commercialize their agricultural production, especially of "cash crops," and monetize their economies to participate in the Arabian caravan trade (Allen 1997, 155, 306; Gitin 1997,84; Byrne 2003; Routledge 2004, 207). Allen (1997, 135–36, 144, 201–7, 225, 293, 324) suggested that the Assyrian administration had an even more direct role in planning and directing the economies of the Philistine city-states toward intensified production and trade. Allen (1997, 42) used the world-systems concept of the semi-periphery—"both exploiter and exploited"—to classify the Levantine vassal kingdoms that profited from this relationship.

Analogies with the cultural and religious imperialism of later empires have been less frequent, though questions of both "Assyrianization" (Parpola 2004, 9–10) (on the model of "Romanization" or "Westernization") and "deculturation" (Liverani 1979, 300; Zehnder 2005, 548; Mazzoni 2014, 697–99) have sometimes been raised. It was once a common view that the worship of the Assyrian national god Aššur was imposed on conquered territories (e.g., Olmstead 1908, 171; Spieckermann 1982). By contrast, Holloway's (2002) more recent take on Assyrian religious imperialism considers both the positive and negative treatment of local cults to be part of the empire's hegemonic project.

RECENT RESPONSES AND ALTERNATIVES TO WORLD-SYSTEMS THEORY

The widespread influence of world-systems and other core-periphery theories on the study of the Neo-Assyrian Empire and other ancient empires and interaction spheres has had several salutary effects. It has broadened the scale of analysis, encouraged consideration of the long-term structural influence of interregional interaction on local societies, and expanded the focus of archaeological research from the cultural products of the ruling elite to wider regional and socioeconomic perspectives. However, the generality and simplicity of these models that gives them their analytical and comparative power also requires homogenizing significant social and cultural differences, making them vulnerable to criticism as reductionist, anachronistic, centrist, and static.

Pre-Modern Economic Systems

A particular problem has been the application of world-systems theory to the economic systems and technological conditions of pre-modern societies. Such applications of world-systems theory have necessitated dropping or modifying the role Wallerstein assigned to the capitalist mode of production that is dependent on an axial division of labor and deemphasizing the role of the long-distance exchange of bulk goods (Rowlands, Larsen, and Kristiansen 1987; Chase-Dunn and Hall 1991, 10–12; Algaze 2005). The role of the exchange of bulk goods is especially problematic in pre-modern periods with prohibitively high overland transportation costs (Adams 1974) and where the frictional effects of distance and easily transferable technologies (Kohl 1987) limit the ability of cores to achieve long-term dominance over peripheries (Stein 1999). Schneider's (1977) now classic critique of world-systems theory argues that the exchange of luxury or prestige goods (especially metals, cloth, and exotic items) is more important for interdependencies among (pre-capitalist and even capitalist) societies than Wallerstein was ready to admit. However, in many contexts, prestige goods did not function as fungible means of exchange but instead as sources of "symbolic capital" in a web of personalized social relations (Schloen 2001, 87, 200).

Furthermore, the difference between the military and political means of domination characteristic of world-empires and the economic dependencies created by market-based asymmetric exchange in the world-economy cannot be dismissed as epiphenomenal (see Schloen 2001, 88–89). When core dominance is achieved through military superiority (world-empire) rather than significant advantages in technology, organizational structure, or economic power (world-economy), the potential for deep structural transformation, long-term dependency in the periphery, and the overwhelming dominance and benefit of the core is limited. This is demonstrated by the rapid shifting of imperial cores in the first millennium BCE Near East from Assyria to Babylonia and then to Persia, Greece, Rome, and Parthia. In the end, when the adaptation of world-systems theory to pre-modern settings requires the evisceration of its most characteristic features, namely, "core dominance, asymmetric exchange, and long-distance exchange as the prime mover of social change," Stein (1999, 25, 42–43) argues that the model becomes so general that it is no longer of real analytical use.

Nevertheless, some continue to argue for the effectiveness of world-systems analysis even in pre-modern societies under a revised, cross-cultural definition of world-systems. For example, Chase-Dunn and Hall (1991, 7) define a world-system as "intersocietal networks in which the interaction (trade, warfare, intermarriage, etc.) is an important condition of the reproduction of the internal structures of the composite units and importantly affects changes which occur in these local structures" (see also Frank 1993, 387). They retain the focus on the "world" unit of analysis and an interest in the ways the interactions between societies within the system drive observed changes in its constituent parts, considering, for example, the forces of the core on the periphery to be endogenous (to the system) rather than exogenous (to the study area).

Allen's (2005) more recent contribution on the Neo-Assyrian Empire is representative of this nuanced application of world-systems terminology and theory. He describes how the Neo-Assyrian world-empire (in Wallersteinian terms) over time moved in the direction of a world-economy as it incorporated more and more territory into its area of influence (Allen 2005, 76). Once its expansion exceeded the practical limits of territorial incorporation and management of imperial lands, the Assyrians developed new strategies to profit from their dominance over distant Levantine vassals: cultivating local elites as Assyrian proxies, levying taxes at key ports of trade, placing officials to keep an eye on vassal rulers, and depending on Arab, Phoenician, and Philistine traders to acquire the resources of a wide periphery—Cyprus, Spain, Arabia, Nubia, and Afghanistan—over which the empire had no direct control or influence (Allen 2005, 80–85). The great size of the empire particularly increased the demand for and importance of silver as a fungible resource that attained near currency status (Allen 2005, 85–86; see Jursa 2010 for the subsequent Neo-Babylonian Period). While the drivers of the system remain exclusively economic, Allen's model not only accounts for the limits of ancient technologies invoked by critics of world-systems theory but also incorporates temporal development and plays down core dominance, two further common threads in recent imperial studies.

Time and Process

Recent models of empire have called for greater attention to temporal processes in imperial histories. Significant differences are cited between the motives and methods of the expansion and consolidation phases of past empires. "Young" empires that never attempt or never succeed at consolidating their territories are best described as parasitic conquest states (Goldstone and Haldon 2009, 17; cf. Münkler 2005), while "mature" or "world" empires pass a temporal and organizational "Augustan threshold" (Doyle 1986, 93–97) beyond which generations of "state embedding" (Goldstone and Haldon 2009, 17) create a unified state with a homogeneous administrative system and a common identity. In keeping with these perspectives, one expects the goals, means, and constraints of Assyrian expansion and consolidation to have evolved considerably across space and time. With Allen (2005), it seems important to distinguish among the period of reclamation of the territories formerly held by the Middle Assyrian kingdom (the "expanded core" of Upper Mesopotamia between the Tigris and Euphrates Rivers) in the tenth and early ninth centuries, the subordination of the perimeter of this zone through annual campaigns and tributary relationships beginning in the mid-ninth century, and the annexation and consolidation of this perimeter (coupled with increasing clashes with powerful and distant enemies) from the mid-eighth through seventh centuries. By the seventh century BCE the Neo-Assyrian Empire passed the Augustan threshold in a large swathe of its territory (Bagg 2013, contra Münkler 2005).

Another strain in the study of ancient empires argues that theories that hypostatize empires as coherent entities or systems and propose grand narratives and strategies are inherently misleading. "Empire" is a mental template imposed by past participants and present-day analysts on a set of phenomena empirically composed of the myriad actions of motivated social actors over a long period (Barrett 1997; Schloen 2001, 49–50; Sinopoli 2001a, 451; Morrison 2001, 258). The characterization of the decisions of imperial authorities as general "policies" or part of a grand strategic plan misconstrues what was experienced as ad hoc or "reactionist" responses to inherently unpredictable local conditions, contingent external and internal events, and the goals and abilities of individual rulers and administrators (Mann 1986, 169; Sinopoli 2001a, 448–50; cf. Morrison 2001; Goldstone and Haldon 2009, 25). While in hindsight we might perceive trends and strategic or economic advantages in the way Assyrian territorial expansion proceeded, in practice each campaign and annexation was an unpredictable, situational response to a complex mosaic of local, historical, and personal factors (Herrmann 2011a, 153–55). Similarly, while we abstract a coherent dual strategy of indirect rule through tributary vassals and direct rule through provincial governors, with a routine and inexorable progression from one to the other in most areas, Cogan (1993, 412) writes that "no single paradigm can explain the mosaic of political and social relationships that developed between Assyria and its dependents." He complains of the "tyranny of a construct" (Cogan 1993, 410), which is unable to explain the mixed, shifting, and sometimes ambiguous political impositions placed on polities and tribes at the edges of the empire that blurred the distinction between vassal/client state and province.

PERIPHERAL AGENCY

Allied with the idea that imperial functioning was often ad hoc is a critique of the top-down and centrist bias of global interaction models, which tend to treat "all power and control [as] emanating from the imperial core" (Sinopoli 2001a, 465) and unrealistically depict imperial authorities as highly knowledgeable, rational, and effective in all situations (see also Alcock 1997; Morrison 2001; Schreiber 2006; Goldstone and Haldon 2009, 21). This idea of a "passive periphery," the periphery as a powerless recipient of the imperial will and imperial culture, has been seriously questioned (Stein 2002).

In Neo-Assyrian studies, one fruitful area of research along these lines has been the replacement of the idea of unidirectional "Assyrianization" with a recognition of the *mutual interpenetration* of the cultural practices of imperial core and periphery. Through the intensive interaction between Assyria and particularly its western and southern neighbors, an "Assyro-Aramaic *koine*" gradually emerged; permeated the empire's language, religion, architecture, art, dress, and administrative and commercial practices (Tadmor 1975, 1978; Winter 1982; Lumsden 2001); and existed alongside persistent local practices in every area. Instead of coercive or automatic acculturation to the norms of the dominant power, postcolonial theories of selective consumption and hybridization (Dietler 2010) seem to better describe the limited and variable Assyrian influence seen in the material culture of provinces and vassal states (Berlejung 2012; Bagg 2013), where identification with a distant power could be used to enhance local status (Lumsden 2001, 40–41; Tyson 2014a, 492–94; Tyson, this volume). Meanwhile, the adoption of foreign practices and material culture at the imperial center was made acceptable and even desirable by the universalistic politico-religious ideology of Assyrian sovereignty, in which the royal capital and palace "take on the form of a microcosm, which sums up the elements of the whole world" (Liverani 1979, 314).

Rather than closed concepts, "Assyria" and "Assyrian" were open ones capable of profound change over time. As the empire expanded, the original ethnic and geographical meaning of these terms came to exist in tension with their new political definition as "the region and people that manifest the required obedience" (Machinist 1993, 89) to the king as the representative of the god Aššur (Oded 1979, 86; Lumsden 2001, 39; Fales 2009–10; Richardson 2016).[15] The lack of a persistent "rule of difference" (Chatterjee 1993, cited in Steinmetz 2014, 80) that presented barriers to the attainment of high political position and the cultural trappings of "Assyrianness" by the conquered population is a significant and often overlooked[16] distinction between the Neo-Assyrian Empire and modern European colonialism and imperialism.[17] In the Neo-Assyrian

Empire there were non-Assyrians, presumably former deportees, in positions at every level of the Assyrian army and administration and also as merchants and influential scholars (Tadmor 1978; Oded 1979, 104–9).

Other areas of discussion that accord greater power and agency to subject populations are the *limits of coercion* and the *integrative processes* that promote imperial stability. These discussions recognize that to maintain control beyond an initial period of conquest, imperial rulers had to cultivate the support of different groups in both the core and the periphery through the provision of real benefits that supported their ideological legitimacy (e.g., Sinopoli 2001a, 451–56; Goldstone and Haldon 2009, 9; Tyson 2014a, 499; Tyson, this volume). In this view, ancient empires are negotiated entities. Factionalism and the diversity of agendas play an important role, as supporters and opponents of the imperial project were to be found in both the core and peripheral territories (cf. Brumfiel and Fox 1994).[18] As a result, the co-option of local elites seems to have been a particularly important strategy to administer subject territories and maintain the continuity of local forms of legitimation (Mann 1986, 170; Mattingly 1997; Alcock 1997; Sinopoli 2001a, 454–55; Elson and Covey 2006; Dusinberre 2013; Lavan, Payne, and Weisweiler 2016). In the Neo-Assyrian Empire, loyal vassals were rewarded with material and ideological benefits, including grants of additional territory, removal of rivals and support for their claim on the throne, granting of higher dignities, and (in the case of Sargon II) even the gift of the king's daughter in marriage (Lanfranchi 1997, 82–85, 2009; Dion 2006). Recognizing the enabling "synergies" of imperial expansion and imperial interests, Tyson (2014a, 482, 2014b) argues that the real agents of striking socioeconomic change in Iron Age IIC Ammon were the local elite, describing how they profited as "imperial collaborators, actively pursuing their own gain while fulfilling imperial expectations."

Beyond the support of vassal rulers and their courts, imperial annexation frequently also provided avenues of social mobility for military, craft, and ritual specialists who could come to identify their interests with those of the empire (Sinopoli 2001a, 455). Soldiers in the armies of conquered territories and skilled craftsmen were frequently co-opted by conscription into the Assyrian army, and some were promoted into the king's cohort (Lanfranchi 1997, 84; Lumsden 2001, 41). Furthermore, Lanfranchi (1997, 84, 86) argues that the support of merchants in both client kingdoms and new provinces was sought by the removal of commercial blockades. The royal patronage of temples within Assyria proper and in other parts of the empire (see Pongratz-Leisten 1994; Holloway 2002) must also have been aimed in part at winning the support of temple personnel. Even the populations of entire territories or cities could be courted, for example, by granting tax and service exemption (*kidinnūtu*) and debt remission (*andurāru*) in the Babylonian cities (Holloway 2002), by restoring those exiled by Assyria's enemies to their homes (Lanfranchi 1997, 84), and by "speaking kindly" to or negotiating with foreign and client kings as well as representatives of various cities and provinces (Fales 2009).

Challenges to the "passive periphery" paradigm also attempt to distinguish between "*bottom-up processes*" (defined as "local and individual responses to incorporation into larger political, economic, and prestige networks") and the "top-down" manipulations of imperial administrators (Sinopoli 1994, 171, 2001a, 445) in influencing provincial development and generating long-term transformations. Thus, greater analytical weight is granted to the agency of provincial subjects, who can be responsible for "internal adaptations" to the demands and opportunities created by imperial annexation (Alcock 1993, 1997; cf. Schreiber 2006). Bottom-up adaptation to major shifts in political, economic, and social boundaries could have unpredictable and unintended consequences and affect the long-term continuity of the political system. The addition of household archaeology and other high-resolution studies in provincial settings to the discussion of agency promises to help identify the agents of change in imperial contexts with even greater precision, whether top-down or bottom-up (Herrmann 2011a, 2011b).

Bottom-up perspectives allow the transformations of Assyria's subject territories to be viewed in a new light. The spate of new settlement in previously depopulated parts of Upper Mesopotamia conceived in world-systems terms as proto-capitalistic investment aimed at surplus extraction can be re-envisioned as an amalgam of imperially directed attempts to stabilize and pacify the region, with bottom-up sedentarization in a context of renewed political and economic integration. According to Harmanşah (2012, 61), "Assyrian elites appropriated this [existing] settlement trend and developed an elaborate rhetoric of regional development as a policy of territorial organization, labor investment, colonization, and political control." Likewise, Faust (this volume) and others (Schloen 2001, 141–47; Na'aman 2003) argue that the new intensification and integration shown in Assyria's southern Levantine vassals was hardly Assyrian policy but rather an unintended by-product of the Pax Assyriaca[19] from which both sides benefited. Alongside concerted imperial strategies—conquest, destruction, deportation, resettlement, reconstruction, urbanization, diplomacy, trade, tribute, and taxation; unforeseen responses to the waxing and waning of conflict; the creation of vast new social, economic, and political networks; and the construction of new identities and the breaking of old ones had equal potential to produce structural transformation in Assyria's shadow (see Lumsden 2001, 39–43; Herrmann 2011a, 506–9, 2011b, 317–18).

THE PERSPECTIVES OF THIS BOOK

Contributors to the ASOR sessions on which this volume is based were asked to reflect on the role the Neo-Assyrian Empire played in societal change and transformation in its subject territories and beyond, taking into account not only top-down imperial impositions but also local responses to imperial encounters. Taken together, the resulting papers demonstrated the variability and complexity of outcomes—intended and unintended, destructive and constructive—accompanying Assyria's interaction with other lands, as well as the influence of investigators' assumptions and paradigms. The papers published here are consistent with the fragmented, multi-scalar set of approaches, eschewing monolithic frameworks, that characterizes much recent work on ancient empires.

Five of the chapters (Düring, Guarducci, Faust, Tyson, and Cannavò) take a regional perspective, summarizing the evidence for changes in settlement and economy and the extent and nature of Assyrian interventions in different parts of the empire and its "periphery." Although they describe locally consistent patterns and often significant restructuring of subject territories, all of these authors give recognition to the limitations of Assyrian power and the impact of different localities and histories on the Assyrian approach. Three others (Darby, Brown, and Cifarelli) focus on a particular site or category of material culture. Their contextual approaches, informed by theories of consumption and communication in intercultural settings, emphasize the mutual interaction of local choices with the enabling connectivity of empire over the hegemonic imposition of imperial culture.

Two chapters, by Bleda S. Düring and Guido Guarducci, take a long-term perspective on Assyrian rule of the provinces found between the Tigris and Euphrates Rivers. In chapter 2 Düring shows that nearly all of the territorial control and integration strategies used in the Neo-Assyrian Empire (up to the turning point of the new phase of expansion begun by Tiglath-pileser III) already originated in the Middle Assyrian Period. Viewed from a local perspective, however, this top-down "repertoire of rule" appears as a patchwork of different strategies and intensities applied unpredictably according to local conditions and historical circumstances. Düring finds that a self-consciously superior Assyrian cultural identity was also important for the consolidation of rule in both periods but was ultimately an open and selectively used category.

Like Düring, Guarducci compares the imperial strategies of the Middle and Neo-Assyrian periods, using the Upper Tigris region as a well-documented case study (chapter 3). His analysis reveals the limits of coercion, showing that the Middle Assyrian approach of constant conflict and minimal interaction with local communities resulted in precarious and less fruitful control, while later Neo-Assyrian efforts at compromise with local communities in multiple social fields were much more successful. Indigenous sociopolitical changes in this region during the intervening period of Assyrian retrenchment seem to have been an important factor in the change in Assyrian strategy.

The next chapters, by Faust, Darby, Brown, and Tyson, turn to the southern Levant, the outer edge of the Neo-Assyrian Empire where a number of vassal kingdoms persisted down to the empire's fall. Avraham Faust's review of settlement, demography, and economic activity in different areas (chapter 4) upholds and further supports the stark dichotomy in the development of the northern provinces versus the southern vassal kingdoms previously described by Gitin and Allen. However, he challenges their attribution of these dramatic changes to a concerted Assyrian policy of economic maximization. Rather, the Assyrian devastation and lack of reconstruction in the northern kingdom of Israel appears economically short-sighted and irrational, especially given the evidence Faust cites for the earlier prosperity of this region, including in olive oil production that was subsequently so strongly developed in the kingdom of Ekron.

In a contextual study of Judean pillar figurines (chapter 5), Erin Darby also resists a prevalent impulse to connect all changes evident in the periphery directly to the effects of imperial domination. Against a move to understand the rise of this figurine style (and other regional Levantine figurine types) during the Neo-Assyrian imperial period as a mode of resistance through local identity consolidation, she puts forward a more complex explanation in which greater connectivity throughout the empire enabled the spread and local adaptation of magico-medical rituals that used figurines.

Stephanie H. Brown (chapter 6) reviews interpretations of either direct Assyrian influence or indirect influence through co-opted local elites on the settlement and subsistence shift in the Transjordanian kingdom of Edom that began in the eighth century BCE. Her discussion of new evidence for Edomite serving vessels shows that in both elite and non-elite contexts, cultural capital was expressed by Levantine forms and decorations, with only generalized Assyrian influence in a small minority of vessels, suggesting that both theories may have overstated the case for Assyrianization.

Chapter 7 republishes, in slightly modified form, a paper originally presented at ASOR and subsequently published in the *Journal of Anthropological*

Research (Tyson 2014a). In it, Tyson considers one of the patterns societies on the periphery of empires experience as a result of their interaction with or incorporation into empires: sociopolitical and economic intensification that becomes visible at roughly the same time as the onset of imperial rule. Through a diachronic study of multiple categories of cultural artifacts from the Ammonites—who lived in and around modern Amman, Jordan—Tyson argues that the elite of this small, tribally organized society were actively involved in the processes of intensification. In this sense they were imperial collaborators, taking advantage of their mediating position between these empires and the local context to improve their own status, wealth, and power.

The following chapters, by Megan Cifarelli and Anna Cannavò, provide perspectives from two areas at, respectively, the eastern and western ends of the Neo-Assyrian Empire that are typically considered part of the imperial periphery. By giving careful attention to the contexts in which Assyrian objects were and were *not* found at the site of Hasanlu in northwestern Iran, Cifarelli shows in chapter 8 that the numerical and social significance of these objects has long been exaggerated. She argues that an Assyrocentric bias in the scholarship on Hasanlu that reproduces propagandistic claims of broad imperial supremacy has wrongly constructed a core-periphery relationship between Assyria and this region in the ninth century BCE, despite evidence to the contrary.

Cannovò's chapter (chapter 9) also questions whether all polities of lesser size and power that were in contact with Assyria can properly be construed as "peripheries" in a world-systems sense. Despite Assyrian claims of Cypriot submission, there is no evidence that economic exchange between the empire and the island was asymmetrical, and it is only through the intermediary of the Phoenician vassal cities that the Neo-Assyrian Empire had a (diffuse and indirect) effect on the economic and political organization of Cyprus.

Finally, in chapter 10, Bradley J. Parker moves from the particulars of these cases studies to a broader discussion of the theoretical and methodological questions raised by the study of imperial peripheries. Parker argues that a productive way forward in the study of peripheries and empires is a pericentric approach that focuses on the peripheries as an important source of the forces propelling imperialism. He suggests that such an approach should take into account pathways of power (political, social, and economic) and the relationships by which those pathways operate. This combination of a pericentric approach with the consideration of pathways of power and relationships is what Parker terms "Neo-pericentrics."

The contributions to this book add new perspectives and evidence to the growing body of research on the lands subjected to and in contact with the

Neo-Assyrian Empire. They align with the recent movement in imperial studies to replace global, top-down materialist models with theories of contingency, local agency, and bottom-up processes. The impact of the unprecedented expansion and astounding success of the Neo-Assyrian Empire on nearly every aspect of ancient Near Eastern society can hardly be overstated. New evidence and local and contextual studies are increasingly demonstrating how the periphery shaped the empire in turn.

NOTES

1. This chapter does not attempt to provide a comprehensive bibliography of Neo-Assyrian studies but rather selected examples to illustrate trends in research on this period. For recent overviews of the history and archaeology of the Neo-Assyrian Empire in English, see Pedde 2012; Parker 2012; Radner 2015. For extensive bibliographies of Neo-Assyrian studies since World War II, see Hämeen-Anttila 1987; Deller 1988; Mattila and Radner 1997; Brinkman 1997; Luukko and Gaspa 2008; Gaspa 2011.

2. Examples include Mann 1986; Alcock et al. 2001; Sinopoli 2001a, 2001b; Elson and Covey 2006; Burbank and Cooper 2010; Areshian 2013; Steinmetz 2014; Lavan, Payne, and Weisweiler 2016.

3. For example, Alcock 1993; Mattingly 1997; D'Altroy and Hastorf 2001; Morrison 2001; Sinopoli 2001a; Stein 2002; Schreiber 2006; Mattingly 2011; Khatchadourian 2013; Dusinberre 2013.

4. On the parallels between Middle Assyrian and Neo-Assyrian building and efforts at modifying the landscape, see Düring, this volume.

5. It is standard practice in ancient Near Eastern scholarship to use the terms *suzerain* and *vassal* to speak of the more powerful and weaker parties, respectively, in international diplomacy, which normally established tributary relations. This language is used here and more broadly in the scholarship of the ancient Near East without any reference to or adaptation of concepts from the use of these terms in other areas of study (e.g., the Ottoman Empire or European feudalism).

6. These titles, *pīḫatu*, *šaknu*, and *šāpiru*, respectively "governor," "commander," and "manager," were used differently over time. From the way they are used, it appears that there is much overlap in their roles.

7. This idea is depicted in the tympanum over the entrance to the Oriental Institute of the University of Chicago, dedicated in 1931, in which knowledge is passed from East (including a king of Assyria) to West (described in Abt 2012, 349–53).

8. As Larsen (1994, 29) writes, the Near Eastern empires were considered simultaneously as "origin and contrast" for the modern West.

9. "As far as [the Assyrian] extended his empire, he ruled but he did not govern; his appetites were without limit. In him is incarnate, to the highest degree, the defects and vices of Asiatic political systems" (de Morgan 1909, 340; trans. in Olmstead 1923, 645).

10. See especially the series Royal Inscriptions of Mesopotamia, Royal Inscriptions of the Neo-Assyrian Period, and State Archives of Assyria.

11. See, however, Frahm's (2006, 89–94) identification and critique of a "neo-diffusionist" trend in recent Assyrian cultural and religious studies that neglects the darker side of Assyrian history.

12. The "semi-periphery" is conceived as an area standing midway between core and periphery in its political integration and occupational skills that "partially deflects the political pressures which groups primarily located in peripheral areas might otherwise direct against core-states" (Wallerstein 1974, 350).

13. This was presumed to have existed in balance with the "slave sector" (state dependents) in the Marxian "Asiatic mode of production" (see Zaccagnini 1989; Schloen 2001, 189–94).

14. This model was first developed by Luttwak (1976), Hassig (1985), and D'Altroy (1992) for (respectively) the Roman, Aztec, and Inka Empires.

15. Assyrian royal inscriptions from Tiglath-pileser I down to Sargon II say of deportees who settled both in the imperial heartland and in the outlying provinces, "I counted them with the people of the land of Assyria" (*itti nišē* KUR *Aššur amnūšunūti*), and Tiglath-pileser III and Sargon II claim that "tribute and tax I imposed upon them as Assyrians" (*biltu maddattu ki ša Aššuri ēmissunūti*) (Liverani 1979, 312; Oded 1979, 81–86; Machinist 1993, 86). This political definition of Assyria and Assyrian was open to continual reinterpretation and reevaluation and need not have been universally held. Alternative, more exclusive Assyrian and peripheral identities could be defined against the background of this creeping cosmopolitanism. This is demonstrated by the prophecies against Assyria in the Hebrew Bible (Weinfeld 1986) and perhaps also by the "hardening" of imperial rhetoric concerning newly conquered territories found in royal inscriptions of the seventh century, which use the phrase "to account (them) as captives/booty" (*šallatiš/ana šallati manû*) (Oded 1979, 83, 89; Machinist 1993, 93–95). Richardson (2016) argues that the maintenance of local elite identities was essential to uphold the credibility of Assyrian rule through vassals and provincial officials and that a self-conscious imperial elite identity was nascent only in the Neo-Assyrian Empire.

16. Such assumptions of a dichotomy of political status based on nationalism and ethnocentrism are often only implicit in analyses of the Neo-Assyrian Empire but are sometimes given explicit voice (e.g., Mann 1986, 235; Liverani 2005, 233; Bedford 2009, 61; cf. Goldstone and Haldon 2009, 24).

17. In the absence of this "rule of difference," some analysts would not consider such an expanding state to be a true "empire" at all (Steinmetz 2014, 81).

18. On pro- and anti-Assyrian factions in Neo-Assyrian vassal kingdoms, see Lanfranchi 1997, 84; Lumsden 2001, 40–41.

19. The reduction in regional conflict and opening of previously closed borders, especially in the late eighth and seventh centuries (see Fales 2008).

WORKS CITED

Abt, Jeffrey. 2012. *American Egyptologist: The Life of James Henry Breasted and the Creation of His Oriental Institute*. Chicago: University of Chicago Press.

Adams, Robert McC. 1974. "Anthropological Perspectives on Ancient Trade." *CA* 15: 239–58.

Alcock, Susan E. 1993. *Graecia Capta: The Landscapes of Roman Greece*. Cambridge: Cambridge University.

Alcock, Susan E. 1997. "Greece: A Landscape of Resistance." In *Dialogues in Roman Imperialism: Power, Discourse, and Discrepant Experiences in the Roman Empire*, ed. David J. Mattingly, 103–15. Portsmouth, RI: Journal of Roman Archaeology.

Alcock, Susan E., Terence N. D'Altroy, Kathleen D. Morrison, and Carla M. Sinopoli, eds. 2001. *Empires: Perspectives from Archaeology and History*. Cambridge: Cambridge University Press.

Algaze, Guillermo. 2005. *The Uruk World System: The Dynamics of Expansion of Early Mesopotamian Civilization*. Chicago: University of Chicago Press.

Allen, Mitchell. 1997. "Contested Peripheries: Philistia in the Neo-Assyrian World-System." PhD dissertation, University of California, Los Angeles.

Allen, Mitchell. 2005. "Power Is in the Details: Administrative Technology and the Growth of Ancient Near Eastern Cores." In *The Historical Evolution of World-Systems*, ed. Christopher Chase-Dunn and E. N. Anderson, 75–91. New York: Palgrave Macmillan. https://doi.org/10.1057/9781403980526_4.

Altaweel, Mark. 2008. *The Imperial Landscape of Ashur: Settlement and Land Use in the Assyrian Heartland*. Heidelberg: Heidelberger Orientverlag.

Areshian, Gregory, ed. 2013. *Empires and Diversity: On the Crossroads of Archaeology, Anthropology, and History*. Los Angeles: Cotsen Institute of Archaeology.

Bagg, Ariel M. 2013. "Palestine under Assyrian Rule: A New Look at the Assyrian Imperial Policy in the West." *JAOS* 133 (1): 119–44.

Bär, Jürgen. 1996. *Der assyrische Tribut und seine Darstellung: Eine Untersuchung zur imperialien Ideologie im neuassyrischen Reich*. Neukirchen-Vluyn, Germany: Neukirchener Verlag.

Barbanes, Eleanor. 2003. "Planning an Empire: City and Settlement in the Neo-Assyrian Period." *BCSMS* 38: 15–22.

Barrett, John C. 1997. "Romanization: A Critical Comment." In *Dialogues in Roman Imperialism: Power, Discourse, and Discrepant Experiences in the Roman Empire*, ed. David J. Mattingly, 51–64. Portsmouth, RI: Journal of Roman Archaeology.

Bedford, Peter R. 2009. "The Neo-Assyrian Empire." In *The Dynamics of Ancient Empires: State Power from Assyria to Byzantium*, ed. Ian Morris and Walter Scheidel, 30–65. Oxford: Oxford University Press.

Berlejung, Angelika. 2012. "The Assyrians in the West: Assyrianization, Colonialism, Indifference, or Development Policy?" In *Congress Volume Helsinki 2010*, ed. Martti Nissinen, 21–60. Leiden: Brill. https://doi.org/10.1163/9789004221130_003.

Black, Jeremy A., and W. J. Tait. 1995. "Archives and Libraries in the Ancient Near East." In *CANE*, 2197–2209.

Brentjes, Burchard. 1995. "The History of Elam and Achaemenid Persia: An Overview." In *CANE*, 1001–21.

Brinkman, John A. 1997. "Unfolding the Drama of the Assyrian Empire." In *Assyria 1995: Proceedings of the 10th Anniversary Symposium of the Neo-Assyrian Text Corpus Project, Helsinki, September 7–11, 1995*, ed. Simo Parpola and Robert M. Whiting, 1–16. Helsinki: Neo-Assyrian Text Corpus Project.

Brumfiel, Elizabeth M., and John W. Fox, eds. 1994. *Factional Competition and Political Development in the New World*. Cambridge: Cambridge University Press. https://doi.org/10.1017/CBO9780511598401.

Burbank, Jane, and Frederick Cooper. 2010. "Imperial Trajectories." In *Empires in World History: Power and the Politics of Difference*, ed. Jane Burbank and Frederick Cooper, 1–22. Princeton, NJ: Princeton University Press.

Byrne, Ryan. 2003. "Early Assyrian Contacts with Arabs and the Impact on Levantine Vassal Tribute." *BASOR* 331: 11–25.

Chase-Dunn, Christopher, and Thomas D. Hall, eds. 1991. *Core/Periphery Relations in Precapitalist Worlds*. Boulder: Westview.

Chatterjee, Partha. 1993. *The Nation and Its Fragments: Colonial and Postcolonial Histories*. Princeton, NJ: Princeton University Press.

Cogan, Mordechai [Morton]. 1974. *Imperialism and Religion: Assyria, Judah, and Israel in the Eighth and Seventh Centuries* BCE. Missoula, MT: Scholar's Press.

Cogan, Mordechai. 1993. "Judah under Assyrian Hegemony: A Reexamination of Imperialism and Religion." *JBL* 112: 403–14.

D'Altroy, Terence N. 1992. *Provincial Power in the Inka Empire*. Washington, DC: Smithsonian Institution Press.

D'Altroy, Terence N., and Christine A. Hastorf, eds. 2001. *Empire and Domestic Economy*. New York: Kluwer/Plenum Academic.

Deller, Karlheinz. 1988. "Bibliography of Neo-Assyrian—1988 and Updates." *SAAB* 2: 130–35.

de Morgan, Jacques. 1909. *Les premières civilisations: Études sur la préhistoire et l'histoire jusqu'à la fin de l'empire macédonien.* Paris: E. Leroux.

Diakonoff, Igor M. 1969. "Main Features of the Economy in the Monarchies of Ancient Western Asia." In *Troisième conférence internationale d'histoire économique: The Ancient Empires and the Economy*, ed. Moses Finley, 13–32. Paris: Mouton.

Dietler, Michael. 2010. *Archaeologies of Colonialism: Consumption, Entanglement, and Violence in Ancient Mediterranean France.* Berkeley: University of California Press. https://doi.org/10.1525/california/9780520265516.003.0002.

Dion, Paul. 2006. "Ahaz and Other Willing Servants of Assyria." In *From Babel to Babylon: Essays on Biblical History and Literature in Honour of Brian Peckham*, ed. Joyce Rillett Wood, John E. Harvey, and Mark Leuchter, 133–45. New York: T&T Clark.

Doyle, Michael W. 1986. *Empires.* Ithaca, NY: Cornell University Press.

Dusinberre, Elspeth R.M. 2013. *Empire, Authority, and Autonomy in Achaemenid Anatolia.* Cambridge: Cambridge University Press. https://doi.org/10.1017/CBO9781139087551.

Eisenstadt, Shmuel N. 1963. *The Political Systems of Empires.* London: Collier-Macmillan.

Eisenstadt, Shmuel N. 1979. "Observations and Queries about Sociological Aspects of Imperialism in the Ancient World." In *Power and Propaganda: A Symposium on Ancient Empires*, ed. Mogens T. Larsen, 21–34. Copenhagen: Akademisk Forlag.

Ekholm, Kajsa, and Jonathan Friedman. 1979. "'Capital' Imperialism and Exploitation in Ancient World Systems." In *Power and Propaganda: A Symposium on Ancient Empires*, ed. Mogens T. Larsen, 41–58. Copenhagen: Akademisk Forlag.

Elat, Moshe. 1978. "The Economic Relations of the Neo-Assyrian Empire with Egypt." *JAOS* 98: 30–32.

Elat, Moshe. 1982. "The Impact of Tribute and Booty on Countries and Peoples within the Assyrian Empire." In *Vorträge gehalten auf der 28: Rencontre Assyriologique Internationale in Wien 6–10 Juli 1981*, ed. Hans Hirsch and H. Hunger, 245–51. Horn, Austria: Verlag Ferdinand Berger.

Elat, Moshe. 1991. "Phoenician Overland Trade within the Mesopotamian Empires." In *Ah, Assyria . . . : Studies in Assyrian History and Ancient Near Eastern Historiography Presented to Hayim Tadmor*, ed. Morton Cogan and Israel Eph'al, 21–35. Jerusalem: Magnes.

Elson, Christina M., and R. Alan Covey, eds. 2006. *Intermediate Elites in Pre-Columbian States and Empires.* Tucson: University of Arizona Press.

Fales, Frederick M. 1973. *Censimenti e catasti di epoca neo-Assira.* Rome: Centro per le Antichità e la Storia dell'Arte del Vicino Oriente.

Fales, Frederick M., ed. 1981. *Assyrian Royal Inscriptions: New Horizons in Literary, Ideological, and Historical Analysis*. Papers of a Symposium Held in Cetona (Siena), June 26–28, 1980. Rome: Centro per le Antichità e la Storia dell'Arte del Vicino Oriente.

Fales, Frederick M. 1984a. "A Survey of Neo-Assyrian Land Sales." In *Land Tenure and Social Transformation in the Middle East*, ed. Tarif Khalidi, 1–13. Beirut: American University of Beirut.

Fales, Frederick M. 1984b. "The Neo-Assyrian Period." In *Circulation of Goods in Non-Palatial Context in the Ancient Near East*, ed. Alfonso Archi, 207–20. Rome: Edizioni dell'Ateneo.

Fales, Frederick M. 1997. "People and Professions in Neo-Assyrian Assur." In *Assyrien im Wandel der Zeiten: XXXIXe Rencontre Assyriologique Internationale, Heidelberg, 6.–10. Juli 1992*, ed. Hartmut Waetzoldt and Harald Hauptmann, 33–40. Heidelberg: Heidelberger Orientverlag.

Fales, Frederick M. 2008. "On Pax Assyriaca in the 8th–7th Centuries BC and Its Implications." In *Isaiah's Vision of Peace in Biblical and Modern International Relations*, ed. Raymond Cohen and Raymond Westbrook, 17–35. New York: Palgrave Macmillan. https://doi.org/10.1007/978-1-137-10442-7_2.

Fales, Frederick M. 2009. "'To Speak Kindly to Him/Them' as Item of Assyrian Political Discourse." In *Of God(s), Trees, Kings, and Scholars: Neo-Assyrian and Related Studies in Honour of Simo Parpola*, ed. Mikko Luukko, S. Svärd, and Raija Mattila, 27–40. Helsinki: Finnish Oriental Society.

Fales, Frederick M. 2009–10 [2015]. "Ethnicity in the Neo-Assyrian Empire: A View from the *Nisbe* (II): 'Assyrians.'" In *Homenaje a Mario Liverani, fundador de una ciencia nueva*, ed. Maria Giovanna Biga, Joaquín M. Cordoba, Carmen del Cerro, and Elena Torres, 183–204. ISIMU 11–12. Madrid: PUBLICEP.

Faust, Avraham, and Ehud Weiss. 2005. "Judah, Philistia, and the World: Reconstructing the Seventh Century BCE Economic System." *BASOR* 338: 71–92.

Forrer, Emil. 1920. *Die Provinzeinteilung des assyrischen Reiches*. Leipzig: J. C. Hinrichs.

Frahm, Eckart. 2006. "Images of Assyria in Nineteenth- and Twentieth-Century Western Scholarship." In *Orientalism, Assyriology, and the Bible*, ed. Steven W. Holloway, 74–94. Sheffield, UK: Sheffield Phoenix.

Frank, André Gunder. 1966. "The Development of Underdevelopment." *Monthly Review* 18 (4): 17–31. https://doi.org/10.14452/MR-018-04-1966-08_3.

Frank, André Gunder. 1993. "Bronze Age World System Cycles." *CA* 34: 383–429.

Frankenstein, Susan. 1979. "The Phoenicians in the Far West: A Function of Neo-Assyrian Imperialism." In *Power and Propaganda: A Symposium on Ancient Empires*, ed. Mogens T. Larsen, 263–94. Copenhagen: Akademisk Forlag.

Galil, Gershon. 2007. *The Lower-Stratum Families in the Neo-Assyrian Period*. Leiden: Brill. https://doi.org/10.1163/ej.9789004155121.i-406.

Garelli, Paul. 1972. "Problèmes de stratification sociale dans l'empire assyrien." In *Gesellschaftsklassen im alten Zweistromland und in den angrenzenden Gebieten*, ed. Dietz O. Edzard, 73–80. Munich: Verlag des Bayerischen Akademie der Wissenschaften.

Gaspa, Salvatore. 2011. "A Bibliography of Neo-Assyrian Studies (2007–2012)." *SAAB* 19: 279–328.

Gitin, Seymour. 1997. "The Neo-Assyrian Empire and Its Western Periphery: The Levant, with a Focus on Philistine Ekron." In *Assyria 1995: Proceedings of the 10th Anniversary Symposium of the Neo-Assyrian Text Corpus Project, Helsinki, September 7–11, 1995*, ed. Simo Parpola and Robert M. Whiting, 77–103. Helsinki: Neo-Assyrian Text Corpus Project.

Goldstone, Jack A., and John F. Haldon. 2009. "Ancient States, Empires, and Exploitation: Problems and Perspectives." In *The Dynamics of Ancient Empires: State Power from Assyria to Byzantium*, ed. Ian Morris and Walter Scheidel, 3–29. Oxford: Oxford University Press.

Grayson, A. Kirk. 1991a. *Assyrian Rulers of the Early First Millennium BC I (1114–859 BC)*. Toronto: University of Toronto Press.

Grayson, A. Kirk. 1991b. "Assyrian Civilization." In The Cambridge Ancient History III/2: The Assyrian and Babylonian Empires and Other States of the Near East, from the Eighth to the Sixth Centuries BC., ed. John Boardman, I.E.S. Edwards, E. Sollberger, and N.G.L. Hammond, 194–228. Cambridge: Cambridge University Press.

Grayson, A. Kirk. 1995. "Assyrian Rule of Conquered Territory in Ancient Western Asia." In *Civilizations of the Ancient Near East*, ed. Jack M. Sasson, 2:959–68. New York: Scribners.

Grayson, A. Kirk, and Jamie Novotny. 2012. *The Royal Inscriptions of Sennacherib, King of Assyria (704–681 BC), Part 1*. Winona Lake, IN: Eisenbrauns.

Hämeen-Anttila, Jaakko. 1987. "Bibliography of Neo-Assyrian (Post-War Period)." *SAAB* 1 (2): 73–92.

Harmanşah, Ömür. 2012. "Beyond Assur: New Cities and the Assyrian Politics of Landscape." *BASOR* 365: 53–77.

Hassig, Ross. 1985. *Trade, Tribute, and Transportation: The Sixteenth-Century Political Economy of the Valley of Mexico*. Norman: University of Oklahoma Press.

Herrmann, Virginia R. 2011a. "Society and Economy under Empire at Iron Age Sam'al (Zincirli Höyük, Turkey)." PhD dissertation, University of Chicago, Chicago.

Herrmann, Virginia R. 2011b. "The Empire in the House, the House in the Empire: Toward a Household Archaeology Perspective on the Assyrian Empire in the Levant." In *Household Archaeology in Ancient Israel and Beyond*, ed. Assaf Yasur-Landau, Jennie R. Ebeling, and Laura B. Mazow, 303–20. Leiden: Brill. https://doi.org/10.1163/ej.9789004206250.i-452.92.

Holloway, Steven W. 2002. *Aššur Is King! Aššur Is King! Religion in the Exercise of Power in the Neo-Assyrian Empire*. Leiden: Brill.

Holloway, Steven W., ed. 2006. *Orientalism, Assyriology, and the Bible*. Sheffield, UK: Sheffield Phoenix.

Jacobson, V. A. 1969. "The Social Structure of the Neo-Assyrian Empire." In *Ancient Mesopotamia, Socio-Economic History: A Collection of Studies by Soviet Scholars*, ed. Igor M. Diakonoff, 277–95. Moscow: Nauka Publishing House.

Johns, C.H.W. 1901. *An Assyrian Doomsday Book*. Leipzig: J. C. Hinrichs.

Jursa, Michael. 2010. *Aspects of the Economic History of Babylonia in the First Millennium BC: Economic Geography, Economic Mentalities, Agriculture, the Use of Money, and the Problem of Economic Growth*. Münster, Germany: Ugarit Verlag.

Khatchadourian, Lori. 2013. "An Archaeology of Hegemony: The Achaemenid Empire and the Remaking of the Fortress in the Armenian Highlands." In *Empires and Diversity: On the Crossroads of Archaeology, Anthropology, and History*, ed. Gregory Areshian, 108–45. Los Angeles: Cotsen Institute of Archaeology.

Kohl, Philip L. 1987. "The Ancient Economy, Transferable Technologies, and the Bronze Age World-System: A View from the Northeastern Frontier of the Ancient Near East." In *Centre and Periphery in the Ancient World*, ed. Michael Rowlands, Mogens T. Larsen, and Kristian Kriastiansen, 13–24. Cambridge: Cambridge University Press.

Kühne, Hartmut. 1995. "The Assyrians on the Middle Euphrates and the Habur." In *Neo-Assyrian Geography*, ed. Mario Liverani, 69–85. Rome: Università di Roma "La Sapienza."

Lamprichs, Roland. 1995. *Die Westexpansion des neuassyrischen Reiches: Eine Strukturanalyse*. Neukirchen-Vluyn, Germany: Neukirchener Verlag.

Lanfranchi, Giovanni B. 1997. "Consensus to Empire: Some Aspects of Sargon II's Foreign Policy." In *Assyrien im Wandel der Zeiten: XXXIXe Rencontre Assyriologique Internationale, Heidelberg 6–10 Juli 1992*, ed. Hartmut Waetzoldt and Harald Hauptmann, 81–87. Heidelberg: Heidelberger Orientverlag.

Lanfranchi, Giovanni B. 2009. "A Happy Son of the King of Assyria: Warikas and the Çineköy Bilingual (Cilicia)." In *Of God(s), Trees, Kings, and Scholars: Neo-Assyrian and Related Studies in Honour of Simo Parpola*, ed. Mikko Luukko, Saana Svärd, and Raija Mattila, 127–50. Helsinki: Finnish Oriental Society.

Larsen, Mogens T. 1979. "The Tradition of Empire in Mesopotamia." In *Power and Propaganda: A Symposium on Ancient Empires*, ed. Mogens T. Larsen, 75–102. Copenhagen: Akademisk Forlag.

Larsen, Mogens T. 1994. "The Appropriation of the Near Eastern Past: Contrasts and Contradictions." In *The East and the Meaning of History: International Conference (23–27 November 1992)*, ed. Giovanni Garbini, Biancamaria Scarcia Amoretti, and Piero Corradini 29–51. Rome: Bardi Editore.

Larsen, Mogens T. 1996. *The Conquest of Assyria: Excavations in an Antique Land, 1840–1860*. New York: Routledge.

Lavan, Myles, Richard Payne, and John Weisweiler, eds. 2016. *Cosmopolitanism and Empire: Universal Rulers, Local Elites, and Cultural Integration in the Ancient Near East and Mediterranean*. Oxford: Oxford University Press. https://doi.org/10.1093/acprof:oso/9780190465667.001.0001.

Leichty, Erle. 2011. *The Royal Inscriptions of Esarhaddon, King of Assyria (680–669 BC)*. Winona Lake, IN: Eisenbrauns.

Lenin, Vladimir I. 1939. *Imperialism, the Highest Stage of Capitalism*. New York: International Publishers.

Liverani, Mario. 1979. "The Ideology of the Assyrian Empire." In *Power and Propaganda: A Symposium on Ancient Empires*, ed. Mogens T. Larsen, 297–317. Copenhagen: Akademisk Forlag.

Liverani, Mario. 1984. "Land Tenure and Inheritance in the Ancient Near East: The Interaction between 'Palace' and 'Family' Sectors." In *Land Tenure and Social Transformation in the Middle East*, ed. Tarif Khalidi, 33–44. Beirut: American University of Beirut.

Liverani, Mario. 2005. "Imperialism." In *Archaeologies of the Middle East: Critical Perspectives*, ed. Susan Pollock and Reinhard Bernbeck, 223–43. Malden, MA: Blackwell.

Lumsden, Stephen. 2001. "Power and Identity in the Neo-Assyrian World." In *The Royal Palace Institution in the First Millennium BC: Regional Development and Cultural Interchange between East and West*, ed. Inge Nielson, 33–51. Aarhus, Denmark: Aarhus University Press.

Luttwak, Edward N. 1976. *The Grand Strategy of the Roman Empire from the First Century AD to the Third*. Baltimore: Johns Hopkins University Press.

Luukko, Mikko, and Salvatore Gaspa. 2008. "A Bibliography of Neo-Assyrian Studies (1998–2006)." *SAAB* 17: 189–257.

MacGinnis, John, Dirk Wicke, and Tina L. Greenfield, eds. 2016. *The Provincial Archaeology of the Assyrian Empire*. Cambridge: McDonald Institute for Archaeological Research.

Machinist, Peter. 1992. "Palestine, Administration of (Assyro-Babylonian)." In *The Anchor Bible Dictionary*, ed. David Noel Freedman, 5:69–81. New York: Doubleday.

Machinist, Peter. 1993. "Assyrians on Assyria in the First Millennium BC." In *Anfänge politischen Denkens in der Antike: Die nahöstlichen Kulturen und die Griechen*, ed. Kurt A. Raaflaub, 77–104. Munich: Oldenbourg. https://doi.org/10.1524/97834 86595734.77.

Mann, Michael. 1986. *A History of Power from the Beginning to AD 1760*, vol. 1: *The Sources of Social Power*. Cambridge: Cambridge University Press.

Mattila, Raija, and Karen Radner. 1997. "A Bibliography of Neo-Assyrian Studies (1988–1997)." *SAAB* 11: 115–37.

Mattingly, David J., ed. 1997. *Dialogues in Roman Imperialism: Power, Discourse, and Discrepant Experiences in the Roman Empire*. Portsmouth, RI: Journal of Roman Archaeology.

Mattingly, David J. 2011. *Imperialism, Power, and Identity: Experiencing the Roman Empire*. Princeton, NJ: Princeton University Press.

Mazzoni, Stefania. 2014. "The Aramean States during the Iron Age II–III Periods." In *The Oxford Handbook of the Archaeology of the Levant c. 8000–332 BCE*, ed. Margreet L. Steiner and Ann E. Killebrew, 683–705. Oxford: Oxford University Press.

Melville, Sarah C. 2016. *The Campaigns of Sargon II, King of Assyria, 721–705 BC*. Norman: University of Oklahoma Press.

Morrison, Kathleen D. 2001. "Coercion, Resistance, and Hierarchy: Local Processes and Imperial Strategies in the Vijayanagara Empire." In *Empires: Perspectives from Archaeology and History*, ed. Susan E. Alcock, Terence N. D'Altroy, Kathleen D. Morrison, and Carla M. Sinopoli, 252–77. Cambridge: Cambridge University Press.

Müller, Gerfrid W. 1997. "Gedanken zur neuassyrischen Geldwirtschaft." In *Assyrien im Wandel der Zeiten: XXXIXe Rencontre Assyriologique Internationale, Heidelberg, 6–10 Juli 1992*, ed. Hartmut Waetzoldt and Harald Hauptman, 115–22. Heidelberg: Heidelberger Orientverlag.

Münkler, Herfried. 2005. *Imperien: Die Logik der Weltherrschaft—vom alten Rom bis zu den Vereinigten Staaten*. Berlin: Rohwolt.

Na'aman, Nadav. 1993. "Population Changes in Palestine Following Assyrian Deportations." *TA* 20: 104–24.

Na'aman, Nadav. 2003. "Ekron under the Assyrian and Egyptian Empires." *BASOR* 332: 81–91.

Oates, Joan. 1986. *Babylon*, rev. ed. London: Thames and Hudson.

Oates, Joan, and David Oates. 2001. *Nimrud: An Assyrian Imperial City Revealed*. London: British School of Archaeology in Iraq.

Oded, Bustenay. 1979. *Mass Deportations and Deportees in the Neo-Assyrian Empire*. Wiesbaden: Dr. Ludwig Reichert Verlag.

Olmstead, A. T. 1908. *Western Asia in the Days of Sargon of Assyria, 722–705 BC: A Study in Oriental History*. New York: Henry Holt.

Olmstead, A. T. 1918. "Assyrian Government of Dependencies." *American Political Science Review* 12 (1): 63–77. https://doi.org/10.2307/1946342.

Olmstead, A. T. 1923. *History of Assyria*. New York: Charles Scribner's Sons.

Oppenheim, A. Leo. 1967. "Essay on Overland Trade in the First Millennium BC." *JCS* 21: 236–54.

Parker, Bradley J. 2001. *The Mechanics of Empire: The Northern Frontier of Assyria as a Case Study in Imperial Dynamics*. Helsinki: Neo-Assyrian Text Corpus Project.

Parker, Bradley J. 2003. "Archaeological Manifestations of Empire: Assyria's Imprint on Southeastern Anatolia." *AJA* 107 (4): 525–57. https://doi.org/10.3764/aja.107.4.525.

Parker, Bradley J. 2011. "The Construction and Performance of Kingship in the Neo-Assyrian Empire." *JAR* 67: 357–86.

Parker, Bradley J. 2012. "The Assyrians Abroad." In *A Companion to the Archaeology of the Ancient Near East*, ed. Daniel T. Potts, 867–76. Malden, MA: Wiley-Blackwell. https://doi.org/10.1002/9781444360790.ch46.

Parpola, Simo. 2004. "National and Ethnic Identity in the Neo-Assyrian Empire and Assyrian Identity in Post-Empire Times." *Journal of Assyrian Academic Studies* 18 (2): 5–22.

Parpola, Simo, and Kazuko Watanabe. 1988. *Neo-Assyrian Treaties and Loyalty Oaths*. Helsinki: Helsinki University Press.

Pedde, Friedhelm. 2012. "The Assyrian Heartland." In *A Companion to the Archaeology of the Ancient Near East*, ed. Daniel T. Potts, 851–66. Malden, MA: Wiley-Blackwell. https://doi.org/10.1002/9781444360790.ch45.

Pongratz-Leisten, Beate. 1994. *Ina šulmi īrub: Die kulttopographische und ideologische Programmatik der akītu-Prozession in Babylonien und Assyrien im I. Jahrtausend v. Chr*. Mainz am Rhein: Philipp von Zabern.

Porter, Barbara N. 2000. "Assyrian Propaganda for the West: Esarhaddon's Stelae for Til Barsip and Sam'al." In *Essays on Syria in the Iron Age*, ed. Guy Bunnens, 143–76. Louvain, Belgium: Peeters.

Postgate, J. Nicholas. 1974a. "Some Remarks on Conditions in the Assyrian Countryside." *JESHO* 17: 225–43.

Postgate, J. Nicholas. 1974b. *Taxation and Conscription in the Assyrian Empire*. Rome: Biblical Institute Press.

Postgate, J. Nicholas. 1979. "The Economic Structure of the Assyrian Empire." In *Power and Propaganda: A Symposium on Ancient Empires*, ed. Mogens T. Larsen, 193–222. Copenhagen: Akademisk Forlag.

Postgate, J. Nicholas. 1987. "Employer, Employee, and Employment in the Neo-Assyrian Empire." In *Labor in the Ancient Near East*, ed. Marvin A. Powell, 257–70. New Haven, CT: American Oriental Society.

Postgate, J. Nicholas. 1992. "The Land of Assur and the Yoke of Assur." *WA* 23: 247–63.

Radner, Karen. 1999. "Money in the Neo-Assyrian Empire." In *Trade and Finance in Ancient Mesopotamia*, ed. Jan G. Dercksen, 127–58. Leiden: Nederlands Historisch-Archeologisch Instituut te Istanbul.

Radner, Karen. 2000. "How Did the Neo-Assyrian King Perceive His Land and Its Resources?" In *Rainfall and Agriculture in Northern Mesopotamia*, ed. R. M. Jas, 233–46. Leiden: Nederlands Instituut voor het Nabije Oosten.

Radner, Karen. 2004. "Assyrische Handelspolitik: die Symbiose mit unabhängigen Handelszentren und ihre Kontrolle durch Assyrien." In *Commerce and Monetary Systems in the Ancient World, Means of Transmission and Cultural Interaction: Proceedings of the Fifth Annual Symposium of the Assyrian and Babylonian Intellectual Heritage Project, Held in Innsbruck, Austria, October 3rd–8th 2002*, ed. Robert Rollinger, Christoph Ulf, and Kordula Schnegg, 152–69. Stuttgart: Franz Steiner Verlag.

Radner, Karen. 2006. "Provinz. C. Assyrien." In *Reallexikon der Assyriologie und vorderasiatischen Archäologie* 11.1–2:42–68. Berlin: Walter de Gruyter.

Radner, Karen. 2015. *Ancient Assyria: A Very Short Introduction*. Oxford: Oxford University Press.

Reade, Julian. 1979. "Ideology and Propaganda in Assyrian Art." In *Power and Propaganda: A Symposium on Ancient Empires*, ed. Mogens T. Larsen, 329–43. Copenhagen: Akademisk Forlag.

Reade, Julian. 1982. "Nimrud." In *Fifty Years of Mesopotamian Discovery: The Work of the British School of Archaeology in Iraq, 1932–1982*, ed. John E. Curtis, 99–112. London: British School of Archaeology in Iraq.

Richardson, Seth. 2016. "Getting Confident: The Assyrian Development of Elite Recognition Ethics." In *Cosmopolitanism and Empire: Universal Rulers, Local Elites, and Cultural Integration in the Ancient Near East and Mediterranean*, ed. Myles Lavan, Richard Payne, and John Weisweiler, 29–64. Oxford: Oxford University Press. https://doi.org/10.1093/acprof:oso/9780190465667.003.0002.

Routledge, Bruce E. 2004. *Moab in the Iron Age: Hegemony, Polity, Archaeology*. Philadelphia: University of Pennsylvania Press.

Rowlands, Michael. 1987. "Centre and Periphery: A Review of a Concept." In *Centre and Periphery in the Ancient World*, ed. Michael Rowlands, Mogens T. Larsen, and Kristian Kristiansen, 1–11. Cambridge: Cambridge University Press.

Rowlands, Michael, Mogens T. Larsen, and Kristian Kristiansen, eds. 1987. *Centre and Periphery in the Ancient World*. Cambridge: Cambridge University Press.

Russell, John Malcolm. 1992. *Sennacherib's Palace without Rival at Nineveh*. Chicago: University of Chicago Press.

Saggs, H.W.F. 2001. *The Nimrud Letters, 1952*. Trowbridge: British School of Archaeology in Iraq.

Schloen, J. David. 2001. *The House of the Father as Fact and Symbol: Patrimonialism in Ugarit and the Ancient Near East*. Winona Lake, IN: Eisenbrauns.

Schneider, Jane. 1977. "Was There a Pre-Capitalist World System?" *Peasant Studies* 6: 20–29.

Schreiber, Katharina J. 2006. "Imperial Agendas and Local Agency: Wari Colonial Strategies." In *The Archaeology of Colonial Encounters: Comparative Perspectives*, ed. Gil J. Stein, 237–62. Santa Fe, NM: School of American Research Press.

Sherratt, Susan, and Andrew Sherratt. 1993. "The Growth of the Mediterranean Economy in the Early First Millennium BC." *WA* 24: 361–78.

Sinopoli, Carla M. 1994. "The Archaeology of Empires." *Annual Review of Anthropology* 23 (1): 159–80. https://doi.org/10.1146/annurev.an.23.100194.001111.

Sinopoli, Carla M. 2001a. "Empires." In *Archaeology at the Millennium: A Source Book*, ed. Gary Feinman and T. Douglas Price, 439–71. New York: Kluwer/Plenum Academic. https://doi.org/10.1007/978-0-387-72611-3_13.

Sinopoli, Carla M. 2001b. "Imperial Integration and Imperial Subjects." In *Empires: Perspectives from Archaeology and History*, ed. Susan E. Alcock, Terence N. D'Altroy, Kathleen D. Morrison, and Carla M. Sinopoli, 195–200. Cambridge: Cambridge University Press.

Spieckermann, H. 1982. *Juda unter Assur in der Sargonidenzeit*. Göttingen: Vandenhoeck and Ruprecht. https://doi.org/10.13109/9783666538001.

Stein, Gil J. 1999. *Rethinking World Systems: Diasporas, Colonies, and Interaction in Uruk Mesopotamia*. Tucson: University of Arizona Press.

Stein, Gil J. 2002. "From Passive Periphery to Active Agents: Emerging Perspectives in the Archaeology of Interregional Interaction." *American Anthropologist* 104 (3): 903–16. https://doi.org/10.1525/aa.2002.104.3.903.

Steinmetz, George. 2014. "The Sociology of Empires, Colonies, and Postcolonialism." *Annual Review of Sociology* 40 (1): 77–103. https://doi.org/10.1146/annurev-soc-071913-043131.

Tadmor, Hayim. 1975. "Assyria and the West: The Ninth Century and Its Aftermath." In *Unity and Diversity: Essays in the History, Literature, and Religion of the Ancient Near East*, ed. Hans Goedicke and J.J.M. Roberts, 36–48. Baltimore: Johns Hopkins University Press.

Tadmor, Hayim. 1978. "The Aramaization of Assyria." In *Mesopotamien und seine Nachbarn: politische und kulturelle Wechselbeziehungen im alten Vorderasien vom 4.*

bis 1, Jahrtausend v. Chr, ed. Hans J. Nissen and Johannes Renger, 449–59. Berlin: Reimer.

Tadmor, Hayim. 1997. "Propaganda, Literature, Historiography: Cracking the Code of the Assyrian Royal Inscriptions." In *Assyria 1995: Proceedings of the 10th Anniversary Symposium of the Neo-Assyrian Text Corpus Project, Helsinki, September 7–11, 1995*, ed. Simo Parpola and Robert M. Whiting, 325–38. Helsinki: Neo-Assyrian Text Corpus Project.

Tadmor, Hayim, and Shigeo Yamada. 2011. *The Royal Inscriptions of Tiglath-Pileser II (744–727 BC) and Shalmaneser V (726–722 BC), Kings of Assyria*. Winona Lake, IN: Eisenbrauns.

Tyson, Craig. 2014a. "Peripheral Elite as Imperial Collaborators." *JAR* 70 (4): 481–509.

Tyson, Craig. 2014b. *The Ammonites: Elites, Empires, and Sociopolitical Change (1000–500 BCE)*. London: Bloomsbury T&T Clark.

Van De Mieroop, Marc. 2007. *A History of the Ancient Near East ca. 3000–323 BC*. 2nd ed. Malden, MA: Blackwell.

van Driel, Govert. 1970. "Land and People in Assyria: Some Remarks." *BO* 27: 168–75.

Vera Chamaza, Galo W. 2002. *Die Omnipotenz Assurs: Entwicklungen in der Assur-Theologie unter den Sargoniden Sargon II, Sanherib, und Asarhaddon*. Münster, Germany: Ugarit Verlag.

Wallerstein, Immanuel. 1974. *The Modern World System I: Capitalist Agriculture and the Origins of the European World-Economy in the Sixteenth Century*. San Diego: Academic.

Wallerstein, Immanuel. 1991. "World System versus World-Systems: A Critique." *Critique of Anthropology* 11 (2): 189–94. https://doi.org/10.1177/0308275X9101100207.

Weinfeld, Moshe. 1986. "The Protest against Imperialism in Ancient Israelite Prophecy." In *The Origins and Diversity of Axial Age Civilizations*, ed. Shmuel N. Eisenstadt, 169–82. Albany: State University of New York Press.

Wilkinson, Tony J., Eleanor Barbanes Wilkinson, Jason Ur, and Mark Altaweel. 2005. "Landscape and Settlement in the Neo-Assyrian Empire." *BASOR* 340: 23–56.

Winter, Irene J. 1982. "Art as Evidence for Interaction: Relations between the Assyrian Empire and North Syria." In *Mesopotamien und seine Nachbarn: politische und kulturelle Wechselbeziehungen im alten Vorderasien vom 4, bis 1, Jahrtausend v. Chr*, ed. Hans J. Nissen and Johannes Renger, 355–82. Berlin: Reimer.

Winter, Irene J. 1983. "The Program of the Throneroom of Assurnasirpal II." In *Essays on Near Eastern Art and Archaeology in Honor of Charles Kyrle Wilkinson*, ed. Prudence O. Harper and Holly Pittman, 15–31. New York: Metropolitan Museum of Art.

Zabłocka, Julia. 1972. "Landarbeiter im Reich der Sargoniden." In *Gesellschaftsklassen im Alten Zweistromland und in den angrezenden Gebeiten XVIII: Rencontre assyriologique internationale, München, 29. Juni bis 3.* Juli 1970, ed. Dietz O. Edzard, 209–16. Munich: Verlag der Bayerischen Akadamie der Wissenschaft.

Zaccagnini, Carlo. 1989. "Asiatic Mode of Production and Ancient Near East: Notes towards a Discussion." In *Production and Consumption in the Ancient Near East*, ed. Carlo Zaccagnini, 1–126. Budapest: University of Budapest.

Zadok, Ran. 1995. "The Ethno-Linguistic Character of the Jezireh and Adjacent Regions in the 9th–7th Centuries (Assyria Proper vs. Periphery)." In *Neo-Assyrian Geography*, ed. Mario Liverani, 217–82. Rome: Università di Roma "La Sapienza."

Zehnder, Markus. 2005. Umgang mit Fremden in Israel und Assyrien: Ein Beitrag zur Anthropologie des "Fremden" im Licht antiker Quellen. Stuttgart: Kohlhammer.

Zehnder, Markus. 2007. "Die 'Aramaisierung' Assyriens als Folge der Expansion des assyrischen Reiches." In *In . . . der seine Lust hat am Wort des Herrn! Festschrift für Ernst Jenni zum 80: Geburtstag*, ed. Jürg Luchsinger, Hans-Peter Mathys, and Markus Saur, 417–39. Münster, Germany: Ugarit Verlag.

Zimansky, Paul E. 1995. "The Kingdom of Urartu in Eastern Anatolia." In *CANE*, 1135–46.

2

At the Root of the Matter

The Middle Assyrian Prelude to Empire

BLEDA S. DÜRING
(LEIDEN UNIVERSITY)

The Neo-Assyrian Empire, arguably the first world-empire, is often presented by scholars as a fundamentally new phenomenon. Here, I will argue that the foundations of Neo-Assyrian success reach back in part into the short-lived preceding Middle Assyrian imperial state. This continuity can be seen in a range of imperial practices in conquered territories and in a "culture of empire" that has its roots in the Late Bronze Age. Other components of the Neo-Assyrian repertoires of rules were first developed in the Iron Age, however. This chapter will bring into sharper focus how the Neo-Assyrian Empire can be understood in its historical context to better understand its remarkable success.

CONCEPTUALIZING THE MIDDLE TO NEO-ASSYRIAN TRANSITION

The idea that the Neo-Assyrian Period is separate and distinct in character from the preceding Middle Assyrian Period is found in many studies (Roaf 1990; Bedford 2009; Cline and Graham 2011; Herrmann and Tyson, this volume). Arguments for drawing such a distinction between the two periods can indeed be found in both philological and archaeological data sets. In particular, textual data are plentiful in the twelfth century BCE and from the ninth–sixth centuries BCE but are much less abundant in the intervening period (Postgate 1992; Radner 2004, 53). Likewise, in many

DOI: 10.5876/9781607328230.c002

regions in Upper Mesopotamia, the archaeological sequence shows a gap separating Middle Assyrian and Neo-Assyrian occupation. This is true, for example, for the Upper Tigris region, the Balikh Valley, and parts of the Khabur Triangle (Parker 2001; Szuchman 2007; Tenu 2009; Matney 2010).

At the same time, we now have many archaeological sequences that suggest a greater degree of continuity from the Middle Assyrian Period to the Neo-Assyrian Period than previously thought in much of the Assyrian heartland and the central and southern Habur region, at sites such as Tell Sheikh Hamad, Tell Barri, and Tell Taban (D'Agostino 2009; Kühne 2013; D'Agostino 2015). Further north and west, in the Upper Habur, the Upper Tigris, and the Balikh, there is some evidence from sites such as Tell Fekheriye and Tell Halaf that Assyrian material culture continued deep into the Iron Age and was used by groups who would self-identify as Arameans as late as the tenth century BCE (Novak 2013).

Furthermore, the *dunnu* (a privately owned agricultural estate, the owners of which usually lived elsewhere and used the proceeds as a source of income) of Giricano had Assyrian texts dating to between 1073 and 1056 BCE, more than a century after the Late Bronze Age "collapse" of ca. 1180 BCE (Cline 2014). There is little to suggest unstable conditions at Giricano, and the transactions the estate was involved in point to business as usual (Radner 2004, 73). Giricano, at least, evidences continuity of Middle Assyrian traditions of the Late Bronze Age on into the Iron Age.

Eventually, the Upper Tigris, Upper Habur, and the Balikh were lost to Assyria for about two centuries, during which period regional states dominated these areas (Szuchman 2007). The memory of these lost former Middle Assyrian territories seems to have been an important *topos* in Assyria in the Iron Age, and the initial wars of conquest in the Neo-Assyrian Period were presented as a *reconquista* in which Assyrian lands and Assyrian communities were liberated from their oppressors (Liverani 1988; Postgate 1992; Fales 2012). So from an Assyrian perspective, the Middle Assyrian Period was perceived as an ideal representing the essence of the Assyrian project rather than a qualitatively distinctive period in history.

To most scholars who argue for a disjunction between the Middle and Neo-Assyrian Periods, the crux of the matter appears to be that the Neo-Assyrian state qualifies as an empire—because it was an expansive state that dominated a large number of vassal states that were not provincialized—whereas the Middle Assyrian state was much smaller in scale and as a rule converted conquered territories into provinces (Postgate 2010, 20; Koliński 2015; Kühne 2015, 59). However, the real disjunction between Assyria as a relatively small

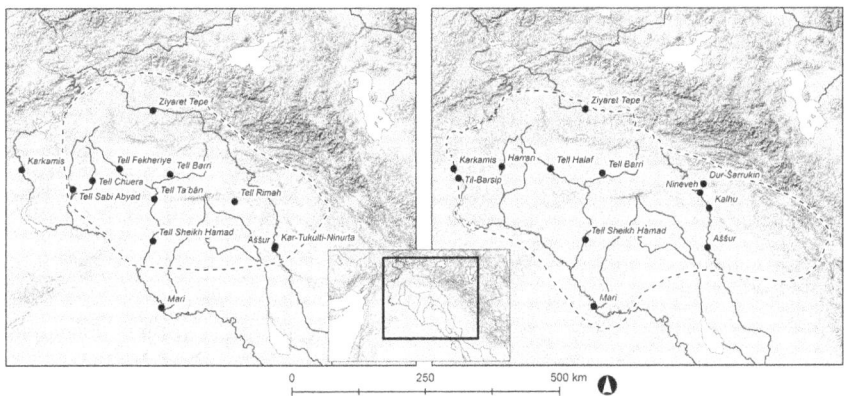

FIGURE 2.1. *Juxtaposition of the extent of the Assyrian Empire in the Middle Assyrian Period and the early part of the Neo-Assyrian Period. Produced by Tijm Lanjouw.*

state and its expansion into the first world-empire arguably took place within the Neo-Assyrian Period, starting with the reign of Tiglath-pileser III from 744 BCE and lasting until 612 BCE, when the Neo-Assyrian Empire finally fell (Postgate 1992; Kühne 2015). From a historical perspective one could therefore argue that the early Neo-Assyrian state—that is, before the expansion under Tiglath-pileser III—was not only consciously modeled on its Middle Assyrian predecessor but also very similar in its scale and aspirations (figure 2.1).

In the end, the assessment of the degree to which the Middle Assyrian state is perceived as similar to or different from the succeeding Neo-Assyrian state depends on both the data set one focuses on and the phenomena one is interested in. In this chapter the focus is the Assyrian "repertoires of rule" in both periods and the degree to which they are different or similar. "Repertoires of rule" (Burbank and Cooper 2010, 6) are the practices applied by imperial states in conquered territories to create and maintain their dominance. Are there, then, specific repertoires of rule that appear first in the Middle Assyrian imperial state which might explain the remarkable longevity and success of the Assyrian state in the Late Bronze and Iron Ages?

COMPARING REPERTOIRES OF RULE IN THE MIDDLE AND NEO-ASSYRIAN PERIODS

In the long-term perspective of ancient Near Eastern history, the Assyrian Empire, ca. 1350–612 BCE, appears to represent a decisive turning point.

Whereas earlier empires were relatively short-lived, here a state emerged that lasted for about seven centuries, rose from humble origins, and ultimately came to dominate much of the ancient Near East. How, then, did the Assyrian state become so successful, and in what ways did it differ from other polities in the ancient Near East?

If one were to compare Assyrian repertoires of rule with those of contemporary empires of the ancient Near East, such as those of Mitanni, the Kassites, the Hittites, and the Egyptians, the most striking differences are not to be found in the core areas or metropolitan regions (Doyle 1986). All of these empires invested heavily in the construction of large monumental capitals, developed elaborate courts, and undertook considerable efforts toward the development of an imperial ideology. The Assyrians stand out, however, for how they dealt with conquered territories and how they transformed provinces and peripheries. Thus, while other empires in the ancient Near East operated in a hegemonic fashion (Higginbotham 2000; Glatz 2009, 2013; Heinz 2012; Von Dassow 2014), ruling a series of vassals through a system of indirect rule, the Assyrians used a territorial system of domination (Parker 2001; Koliński 2015), annexing neighboring regions as provinces. While it is possible to qualify this distinction, for example, Egypt also used territorial repertoires of rule in Nubia (Smith 2003; 2013) and the Hittites appear to have done the same in their heartland (Glatz 2009, 2013), the systematic way territorial repertoires of rule were put to use by the Assyrians is quite exceptional in the ancient Near East.

So how did the Assyrian Empire achieve and maintain its control over the conquered territories? To what degree are repertoires of rule continuous from the Middle to the Neo-Assyrian Period? To facilitate this discussion, it is useful to distinguish between "hardware" and "software" types of hegemonic practices. These categories are for heuristic purposes only and are not intended as a new interpretive framework.

Hardware refers to changes in infrastructure, landscapes, and societies that were effected to serve the (perceived) needs of the empire (table 2.1). These include:

1. Development of the imperial core through policies of agricultural development, settlement of populations, and the creation of monumental capitals
2. Modification of existing settlement systems, including the destruction of some cities, the modification of others, the foundation of new cities, and the construction of forts and fortification systems, to facilitate the control of alien territories and to control access to imperial lands

3. Agricultural development of regions previously little cultivated by means such as the establishment of agricultural estates, agricultural colonization, and the construction of (complex) irrigation systems
4. Demographic policies in which existing population centers are in part replaced by new ones and populations are broken up through deportation and colonization policies that frustrate the cultural capacities of conquered populations to form an alternative to the imperial system
5. Construction of an imperial road and relay system to facilitate communications, trade, and military campaigns

Software refers to changes in culture promoted by the empire and the practices of government that help consolidate imperial hegemony. These include:

1. Techniques of administration, such as the development of a homogeneous system of administration that facilitates control by the imperial core and the deployment of administrators throughout the imperial lands
2. Organization of the imperial elite
3. Use of a vassal system
4. An ideology that legitimized imperial domination to both the dominators and the dominated, and investment in propaganda media
5. A policy of co-opting local elites into the interests of empire by providing them with clear incentives for collaboration
6. A *culture of empire* in which the imperial culture is distinguished from and considered superior to that of dominated societies. In this system there are possibilities and incentives for outsiders to opt into imperial culture and associate with the empire.[1]

The "hardware" repertoires of rule for the Middle and Neo-Assyrian Periods are remarkably similar. In both periods we can document the development of the imperial core region through the construction of large canals for agricultural development and the foundation of new capitals (Bagg 2000; Wilkinson et al. 2005; Mühl 2015). The construction of the large new capital of Kar-Tukulti-Ninurta in the Middle Assyrian Period, estimated to have measured ca. 480 hectares (Dittmann 2011) and for which major canals were constructed, has striking similarities to later construction of the capitals of Kalhu (which in fact seems to have had a Middle Assyrian predecessor [Bagg 2000, 311]) and Dur-Sharrukin in the Neo-Assyrian Period (Bagg 2000; Wilkinson et al. 2005; Altaweel 2008).

Moving beyond the core region, in both periods we can document Assyrian efforts to modify existing settlement systems, for example, through the

TABLE 2.1. Overview of hardware type repertoires of rule in the Middle and Neo-Assyrian Empires

Repertoires of rule—hardware	Middle Assyrian	Neo-Assyrian
Development of imperial core	√	√
Destruction of cities	√	√
Modification of cities	√	√
Foundation of cities	√	√
Creation of rural settlements	√	√
Agricultural colonization	√	√
Deportations	√	√
Road networks	√	√

destruction or abandonment of major existing settlements, such as Tell Brak in the Middle Assyrian Period and Babylon in the Neo-Assyrian Period, and the creation or redevelopment of new centers, such as Dur-Katlimmu and Kulushinas (Tell Amuda) and Tušhan (Ziyaret Tepe) in Middle Assyrian times and cities such as Nineveh and Till Barsip in the Neo-Assyrian Period (Wilkinson et al. 2005; Szuchman 2007; Tenu 2009, 2015; Harmanşah 2012; Kühne 2013). In both the Middle and Neo-Assyrian Periods we can document the creation of a series of forts along the frontiers and in the newly occupied territories (Parker 1997; Tenu, Fenollós, and Caramelo 2012; Tenu 2015).

For both periods we can document significant investments in the agricultural development of previously marginal or uncultivated territories. Major canals for irrigation purposes were built in the Middle and Neo-Assyrian Periods (Bagg 2000; Wilkinson et al. 2005; Kühne 2015), and this is true even if one excludes the controversial Lower Habur canal from consideration. Further, we have clear data for agricultural colonization in both periods, for example, along the Balikh and in the Upper Tigris (Wiggermann 2000; Parker 2001, 2003; Radner 2004). Although the scale of the "infilling of the landscape" was much more pronounced in the Neo-Assyrian than in the Middle Assyrian Period (Wilkinson et al. 2005), the same process can be documented in the area close to the capital in the Middle Assyrian Period (Postgate 1982, 308; Mühl 2013).

The deportation of populations from one part of the empire to another is well attested in both the Middle and Neo-Assyrian Periods (Wiggermann 2000; Postgate 2013) and can be regarded as one of the key Assyrian strategies. While deportations are often portrayed as repressive, divide-and-rule policies (Na'aman 1993, 117), it is also possible that at least some of these population movements consisted of voluntary colonizations in which groups were provided with clear incentives (Parker 2001, 2003; Düring, Visser, and Akkermans 2015). For example, at Tell Sabi Abyad the migrants included both *siluhlu* (serfs, probably predominantly Hurrians) and *alaju* (free men with Assyrian names), and the latter were free to move elsewhere (Wiggermann 2000). While the *siluhlu* did not have this freedom, it is possible that at least some of them regarded agricultural colonization as an attractive opportunity. In any case, the demographic policies of the Assyrians were clearly an instrument to change realities on the ground in specific regions.

Finally, an imperial road system, complete with relay stations, seems to have been created first in the Middle Assyrian Period and been further expanded in the Neo-Assyrian Period (Pfälzner 1993; Kessler 1997; Faist 2006; Kühne 2013). For any empire the construction of such a road system, facilitating fast sharing of information over large distances and the swift transport of military personnel, is essential to maintain control over large territories (Taagepera 1978; Colburn 2013).

In all these "hardware" repertoires of rule, we can draw clear parallels between the Middle and Neo-Assyrian Empires, displaying strong continuity. Further, the similarities are not of the generic type—in that any empire would make use of these repertoires of rule—but they are specific to Assyria. Here, for example, we could compare Mitanni and Middle Assyrian repertoires of rule to illustrate this point. Unlike the Assyrian state, the Mitanni state appears to have preferred to rule through indirect means. Most of Mitanni's territory consisted of a series of vassal polities that were ruled by either a king or a council. Only in exceptional cases did the Mitanni state convert conquered territories into provinces, for example, when a vassal proved unreliable, as was the case with the polity of Aleppo (Von Dassow 2014, 20–22). The Mitanni state did not have a standardized bureaucracy; instead, rather different recording procedures were used in Ugarit and Arrapha (Postgate 2015). Institutions such as the *dimtu* (a privately owned agricultural estate, the owners of which usually lived elsewhere and used the proceeds as a source of income) denoted radically different forms of estates in the empire; in Nuzi they were owned by wealthy absentee families, but in Ugarit they were royal estates owned by the local dynasty (Koliński 2001). Thus, the Mitanni state had a diversity of political forms and institutions across its territories, lacked an overarching state system, and was not engaged in practices such as deportation, agricultural colonization, or the creation of new cities. Similar arrangements seem to have characterized Hittite and Egyptian repertoires of rule in the Levant, as well as those of the Kassites in Babylonia. In short, the Assyrian

TABLE 2.2. Overview of software type repertoires of rule in the Middle and Neo-Assyrian Empires

Repertoires of rule—software	Middle Assyrian	Neo-Assyrian
Provincial system	√	√
Great families	√	—
Vassal system	√	√
Incorporation into the land and cult of Aššur	√	√
Co-optation of local elites	√	√
Culture of empire	√	√
Ideological propaganda	—	√

repertoires of rule were exceptional in the degree to which landscapes and societies were actively reengineered. In part, these social engineering practices explain Assyrian successes.

For the "software" repertoires of rule, the situation is somewhat different (table 2.2). Some of the elements are present in both the Middle and Neo-Assyrian Periods, but in others we see clear transformations. The creation of the provincial system starts in the Middle Assyrian Period and continues into the Neo-Assyrian Period (Llop 2011). At least in the areas conquered in the Middle Assyrian Period, the standard policy was to provincialize the occupied territories rather than to rule by indirect means (Koliński 2015). Largely the same region was ruled through the provincial system in the Neo-Assyrian Empire, except for its final stages, when it was expanded far beyond (Bedford 2009; Barjamovic 2013, 148). These provinces were also symbolically incorporated into the land and cult of Aššur, as demonstrated by the Aššur temple offerings, which were brought from all provinces (Postgate 1992). However, as Pongratz-Leisten (2011) has argued, there was no homogeneous religious system across the Assyrian provinces, and local religious practices remained dominant in most places. In her view there was a significant accommodation to local religious systems by the Assyrians, an accommodation that is not evident from the official state propaganda.

In both periods small vassal kingdoms were tolerated by the Assyrians within and between their provinces, as exemplified by the examples of the Land of Mari in the Middle Assyrian Period and Guzana in the Neo-Assyrian Period (Novak 2013; Shibata 2015). The prevailing consensus on Assyrian tolerance toward these vassals in the land of Aššur is that the local dynasties switched allegiance to Aššur at critical moments in history and were rewarded for their continuing loyalty. Local dynasties appear to have been linked to the royal house through marriages (Shibata 2015), and in the Neo-Assyrian Period local elites were co-opted through ideological means and through incentives for the improvement of their positions and careers (Parker 2011; Pongratz-Leisten 2013).

From the beginning of the Middle Assyrian Period, the Assyrian repertoires of rule include something that for want of a better word I will call a "culture of empire," by which I mean something different from state propaganda and its ideological justification. Instead, the focus is on a cultural framework that would have operated at a less discursive (or subconscious) level and structured social interaction between Assyrians and with others. At the core of this is a distinction between an Assyrian "high" culture, on the one hand, and vernacular traditions, on the other, which was culturally elaborated. This normative distinction contributed enormously to the legitimation of the empire. The association among an empire, a cultural idiom, and concepts of civilization is well-known from many empires (Zimansky 1995; Stein 2005; Mattingly 2011).

In administrative and legal documents, being Assyrian was a clearly demarcated status that entitled the person in question to certain rights and entailed obligations that set the individual apart from non-Assyrians (Postgate 2013, 12–27). In the newly conquered territories in the west, Assyrians were usually free men and non-Assyrians were often serfs (Wiggermann 2000, 174). Assyrian status seems to have been independent of class. Apart from Assyrian administrators there is evidence for Assyrian agricultural colonists in the western territories, as at Tell Sabi Abyad, where 100 Assyrian farmers settled with their families (Wiggermann 2000), and at Tell Chuera, where there were similarly designated settlers (Jakob 2009, 98). These latter Assyrians might have included both poorer members of Assyrian society and groups that had gradually opted into an Assyrian identity (Postgate 2013, 38). The fact that this "opting in" occurs suggests that being Assyrian was considered a desirable status in contemporary society.

With the emergence of the Middle Assyrian Empire, we can also document the spread of a particular type of material culture. This includes Middle Assyrian pottery (Pfälzner 1997; D'Agostino 2008, 2015; Tenu 2013; Duistermaat 2015), house forms (Bartl and Bonatz 2013; Akkermans and Wiggermann 2015), and burial traditions (Sauvage 2005; D'Agostino 2008; Tenu 2009; Bonatz 2013; Düring, Visser, and Akkermans 2015). These "Assyrian" types co-occur with vernacular ceramic repertoires, burial traditions, and house forms (Sauvage 2005; Tenu 2013; Düring, Visser, and Akkermans 2015; D'Agostino 2015; Jakob 2015).

The spread of Assyrian artifacts and traditions can be most convincingly linked to the presence of Assyrian colonists across the Middle Assyrian Empire. In part, the spread of Assyrian artifacts and customs was a function of necessity, especially where empty landscapes were colonized, but it should also be explained in part by the desire of Assyrians to distinguish themselves in how they lived, cooked, ate, and buried their dead, and through the style of the artifacts they used.

Assyrian-style artifacts and practices might have been associated with and important to Assyrian elites in particular, who occupied the key positions in the conquered lands of Hanigalbat (Harrak 1987, 195–205). Indeed, typically Assyrian material culture seems to have been concentrated mainly in administrative centers where the elite tended to settle (Tenu 2013; D'Agostino 2015; Jakob 2015).

This does not mean the entire elite of the Assyrian Empire consisted of people from Assyrian stock, but it entails that in their official capacity they would have needed to present themselves as Assyrians. Interestingly, we have some evidence for non-Assyrian elites taking up Assyrian names and practices (Shibata 2015) and for Assyrian elites who buried themselves in decidedly non-Assyrian fashion (Wicke 2013; Düring, Visser, and Akkermans 2015). In contrast, non-elite Assyrians demonstrably adhered to Assyrian ways in how they ate, dressed, and were buried (Wicke 2013; Düring, Visser, and Akkermans 2015).

The concept of a "culture of empire" might help explain why Assyrians felt it was legitimate to reengineer conquered territories and societies and what motivated participants to contribute to this project. Further, by giving poor members of Assyrian society and even non-Assyrians the possibility to associate with and benefit from the Assyrian project, the allegiance of such groups could be obtained.

In contrast to these patterns of continuity, the role of great families appears to have changed significantly. Whereas in the Middle Assyrian Period the execution of government was delegated largely to the major Assyrian houses, in the Neo-Assyrian Period the king assumed a much more central position, and the military apparatus was used to create a state administration in which written bureaucracy was less important (Postgate 2007a). The attempt to eliminate alternative powerful lineages seems to have been largely successful and to have led to a situation in which the collapse of the court equaled the collapse of the empire (Liverani 2001).

Another significant difference between the Middle and Neo-Assyrian repertoires of rule is in the realm of state propaganda. Neo-Assyrian elites went to great efforts to communicate imperial ideology through visible means such as victory stelae, rock monuments, statues, and elaborately carved and inscribed palace decor. They may also have used other means to communicate imperial ideology, such as processions and proclamations (Parker 2011, 2015; Harmanşah 2012, 2013; Pongratz-Leisten 2013).

One can ask, however, what the efficacy of this imagery and associated practices was, who the target audiences were, and whether we can even qualify them as propaganda. Much of the imagery was placed within the palace and was accessible only to a small segment of Assyrian society, that is, the elite and palace personnel. It is an open question whether elite visitors would have had the possibility or the inclination to take in the rich totality of images and understand the messages they were meant to convey. In all likelihood, few of these visitors would have been able to read the inscriptions placed on the orthostats. This is best illustrated by the famous boast of King Ashurbanipal that he could read and write (which was probably true [Livingstone 2007]). The boast suggests that such skills were exceptional among the Assyrian elite. Likewise, the efficacy of Assyrian rock art monuments—often in extremely remote locations—as propaganda statements can be questioned. Whatever our interpretation of the efficacy of the Neo-Assyrian visual programs, this type of investment in visual imagery is almost completely absent in the Middle Assyrian Period (Pittman 1996, 350–53), and this difference is significant.

In conclusion, in the "software" repertoires of rule, there is some continuity as well as a number of transformations and innovations within the Assyrian tradition. Nonetheless, the overarching picture is that of a historical development in a continuous Assyrian tradition rather than a fundamentally new development in the Neo-Assyrian Period.

DEALING WITH DIVERSITY

In the discussion so far, I have argued, first, that most of the repertoires of rule found in the Neo-Assyrian Period have clear antecedents in the Middle Assyrian Period and, second, that there were a number of innovations in the Neo-Assyrian period. To structure this discussion, I have followed a checklist approach, noting whether particular repertoires of rule are present or absent. The danger of such an approach is that we might reduce imperial systems to a list of blanket strategies. In this section I would like to highlight (1) the heterogeneity of the Assyrian Empire in both the Late Bronze Age and the Iron Age and (2) the parallels between the patchwork solutions used in both periods.

Recent studies of European colonial empires—the Ottoman, Habsburg, and Russian Empires and that of ancient Rome—have demonstrated that empires were not administrated homogeneously (Maier 2006; Burbank and Cooper 2010; Bang and Bayly 2011; Mattingly 2011). Instead, they were constituted by a patchwork of institutions and personnel that differed greatly from one part of the empire to the next. The particular situation in any region was the result of specific historical circumstances and was determined in part by the activities of key individuals. Thus, while it appears that these empires had a homogeneous system of administration, there were great differences in the forms imperial government took on the ground as a result of local factors (also Herrmann and Tyson, this volume).

Thirty years ago, Liverani (1988, 86) stated that the Assyrian Empire was "not a spread of land, but a network of communications over which material goods are carried." Liverani envisaged the empire as consisting of a series of Assyrian strongholds in essentially alien landscapes and populations, and he argued that military campaigns were primarily undertaken to support and expand this network of Assyrian settlements. In a very similar vein, Bernbeck (2010) has recently compared the Assyrian Empire to that of the United States, arguing that both are systems in which military bases were instrumental in controlling alien territories. By contrast, Postgate (1992) responded to Liverani's characterization by arguing that the area of Hanigalbat was under the direct territorial control of the Assyrians and was considered part of the land of Aššur, unlike the regions beyond, which were controlled through vassals. Postgate argued that while Assyrian presence was necessarily concentrated in certain nodes, the provinces were homogeneously administered.[2] Since Liverani and Postgate formulated their ideas, a massive amount of new data has become available and many systematic studies dealing with Assyria have appeared (Parker 2001; Szuchman 2007; Tenu 2009; Postgate 2007b, 2013; Düring 2015). As a result, we are in a much better position to evaluate how homogeneous or heterogeneous Assyrian repertoires of rule were in conquered provinces and peripheries.

For the Neo-Assyrian Period we have a number of archaeological studies that investigate the variable impact of the Assyrian Empire in provincial and peripheral regions. Parker (2001, 2003, 2015) has argued for a modified version of Luttwak's *hegemonic empire* in which regions brought under the direct control of the Assyrians need not have been spatially contiguous. For example, the Assyrians imposed direct territorial control over the Upper Tigris and the northern Habur and Balikh, but the intervening Tur Abdin Mountains remained outside the effective control of the Assyrians, for reasons that were in part strategic, in part logistic, and in part economic.

Parker's work in the Upper Tigris region was based primarily on data obtained in the extensive reconnaissance survey undertaken by Algaze and colleagues (2012) ahead of dam construction projects. In subsequent years, much additional research has been done at a range of sites, such as Ziyaret Tepe, Üçtepe, Kavuşan Höyük, Giricano, Boztepe, Salat Tepe, Kenan Tepe, Gre Dimse, Müslümantepe, Hirbemerdon, and Hakemi Use. As a result, Matney (2010), building on earlier work by Parker (2003, 2006), recently reconstructed the configuration of the Neo-Assyrian Empire in the Upper Tigris, showing a coexistence of Assyrian-dominated urban settlement with small Assyrian agricultural colonies—probably consisting mostly of deportees—and local farming and pastoral communities that were incorporated into the Assyrian economy. Matney's reconstruction suggests that this Assyrian province was a multiethnic society and that the hegemony of the Assyrian state was precarious (also Wicke 2013).

A similar situation of a precarious hegemony can be documented in the Middle Assyrian Empire. As mentioned, Pongratz-Leisten (2011) has demonstrated that Middle Assyrian religious practices and iconographic conventions in the provinces did not follow mainstream Assyrian standards and that local gods remained important. Jakob (2015, 180–82) has recently illustrated how precarious Assyrian control in the western provinces really was at that time by discussing a number of letters from Ḫarbe (Tell Chuera). These letters describe the repeated attacks of enemy troops descending from the mountains to the north on the cities of Ḫarbe and Niḫrija and the Assyrian official Sîn-muddameq without troops to halt them. These raiding troops from the mountains also plundered trading caravans when the opportunity presented itself. In these ways they posed a real threat to the power of local Assyrian officials.

Interestingly, the evidence of patchy control coexists with evidence for formidable changes in settlement and demography in specific regions. In the Balikh Valley, for example, significant changes in the settlement pattern have been subjected to a detailed analysis by Lyon (2000; also Koliński 2015). In the Mitanni Period (ca. 1500–1350 BCE), there were a substantial number of settlements in the valley. At some point in the Late Bronze Age, most of the sites appear to have been abandoned. When the Middle Assyrian state took control of the area, many of the sites in the southern Balikh were not reoccupied. It is possible that the southern Balikh functioned as a buffer zone with the Hittites, who were entrenched further west along the Euphrates (Luciani 1999–2001; Lyon 2000).[3] In the northern Balikh Valley, where rain-fed agriculture is possible, there were clear shifts in the settlement system: many large "urban" sites were not reoccupied, and new settlements were mostly small rural places (Lyon 2000).

One clear example of an important rural settlement is the Tell Sabi Abyad *dunnu* (figure 2.2). This was an agricultural estate to which 900 people were

FIGURE 2.2. *Late Bronze Age occupation at Tell Sabi Abyad in level 6A (ca. 1200–1184 BCE)*

attached, only a few of whom lived in the central settlement (Wiggermann 2000). From the *dunnu* a large landholding was farmed, measuring about 36 km² and producing about 300 tons of barley per annum. Thus, large-scale farming took place for surplus production in a landscape previously little cultivated. This was made possible through the deployment of a large labor force and the investment of substantial resources. The cultural landscape was profoundly altered. The existing settlement system was reshuffled. Large numbers of people were brought into the area, creating a new demographic reality, and large-scale farming estates were established. Given that Tell Sabi Abyad was only one of a series of *dunnu* estates established in the valley—although probably the largest—what happened can best be described as social and landscape engineering.

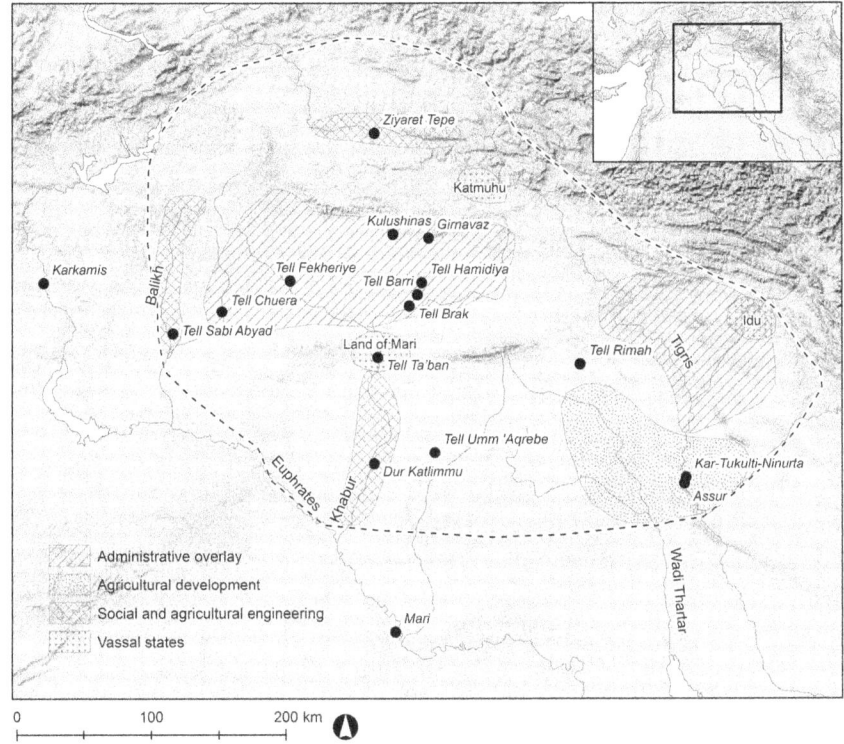

FIGURE 2.3. *Map of the Middle Assyrian Empire with various repertoires of rule used by Assyria indicated*

The Balikh is not, however, representative of the broader situation in the western provinces (compare Koliński 2015) (figure 2.3). In some areas, such as the Balikh and the Lower Habur—at Dur-Katlimmu—the Assyrians went to great efforts to develop agricultural surpluses and settlements in previously marginal territories (Kühne 2015). In areas such as the Upper Habur, the Assyrians largely superimposed their administration upon the existing settlements and agricultural practices (Szuchman 2007; Tenu 2009, 2015). As a result, settlement continuity can be shown for sites such as Tell Barri and Tell Fekheriye (D'Agostino 2008; Tenu 2009; Bonatz 2013). The Assyrians even incorporated previously independent polities, such as "the Land of Mari," centering on Tell Taban, with a local dynasty serving under the Assyrian king (Shibata 2015). Finally, in the Assyrian heartland, there appears to have been expansion or intensification of agricultural production, with the construction

AT THE ROOT OF THE MATTER 55

of new canals and the foundation of new settlements (Miglus 2011; Mühl 2015).

The Assyrian repertoires of rule outlined here suggest that neither Liverani nor Postgate was right because both argued that Assyrian repertoires of rule were relatively standardized. More recent data and syntheses point to a flexible approach toward controlling conquered territories, in which what happened on the ground depended on a range of practical and strategic considerations. In both the Middle and Neo-Assyrian Periods we can see similar patterns: first, with heavy investments in the (agricultural) development of the Assyrian heartland, including the construction of major canals that enabled the cultivation of previously little-cultivated zones, facilitating a more densely populated imperial core; second, the development of peripheries with agricultural potential, such as the Balikh in the Middle Assyrian Period and the Upper Tigris in the Neo-Assyrian Period; third, the depopulation or neglect of peripheral or buffer zones at the edge of empire, as was the case initially in the Balikh in the Middle Assyrian Period, in the Neo-Assyrisan Period in the northern part of the southern Levant (Faust, this volume), and in buffer zones such as the Garzan and Bohtan River Valleys (Parker 2001). Finally, in some regions the Assyrian administrators accommodated preexisting densely populated and productive regions and intervened relatively little, as in the Upper Khabur in the Middle Assyrian Period or the Levantine Phoenician cities in the Neo-Assyrian Period (Bagg 2011, 281–94). Thus, although we see heterogeneous effects of Assyrian domination in both the Middle and Neo-Assyrian Periods, this heterogeneity is spatially distributed (what repertoires of rule are applied where) similarly.

DISCUSSION AND CONCLUSION

To what degree can we trace the origins of the highly successful Neo-Assyrian Empire back to its more obscure predecessor in the Late Bronze Age? In this chapter I have argued that if we focus on the repertoires of rule used by the Assyrians in the Middle Assyrian Period and the Neo-Assyrian Period, we can document clear continuities in changes effected on the ground, including elements such as the destruction of cities, the modification of cities, the foundation of new settlements, agricultural development of previously uncultivated regions, deportations, the construction of road networks, and the development of relay systems. Likewise, the ways in which the administration was organized were parallel in many respects, including institutions such as the provincial system; the occasional use of vassals; the cultic incorporation of conquered territories into the land of Aššur, symbolized in food offerings to the Aššur temple; and the co-opting of local elites. An important ingredient of Assyrian imperialism consisted of a normative distinction between Assyrian culture, on the one hand, and normative traditions, on the other, that we find expressed in things such as burial habits and legal statuses in both the Late Bronze Age and the Iron Age. There are also some differences in the repertoires of rule between these two periods. The role of great families was reduced in the Neo-Assyrian Empire, and (investment in) propaganda became much more significant in the Neo-Assyrian Empire. Nonetheless, there is strong continuity between the practices of the Middle Assyrian Empire and the Neo-Assyrian Empire.

The Assyrian Empire was not a homogeneously administered territorial empire, nor was it a network empire. Instead, it is better described as a patchwork, in which repertoires of rule were applied in a flexible manner (Sinopoli 1994; Burbank and Cooper 2010), depending on a range of strategic, logistical, and economic considerations, as well as the nature of the preexisting society and economy and how well they could be made to serve the needs of the empire. Importantly, the manner in which the repertoires of rules were applied in different parts of the empire is structured in ways that are very similar in the Middle and Neo-Assyrian Periods. I argue, then, that the imperial practices that generated the unprecedented Neo-Assyrian territorial expansion and consolidation are rooted in an Assyrian cultural-political repertoire that first took shape in the fourteenth century BCE.

NOTES

I would like to thank Craig Tyson and Virginia Herrmann for the opportunity to contribute to this book, and I thank the two anonymous reviewers for their feedback. The research presented here was part of the ERC-funded project (282785) Consolidating Empire: Reconstructing Hegemonic Practices of the Middle Assyrian Empire at the Late Bronze Age Fortified Estate of Tell Sabi Abyad, Syria, ca. 1230–1180 BCE at Leiden University.

1. Some of the elements mentioned here also occur in Smith and Montiel (2001), but in a different ordering.

2. Postgate's model, in which a distinction is made among a core territory that is incorporated into the metropolitan state, the land of Aššur, and an outer zone under the yoke of Aššur, mirrors an influential distinction between territorial and hegemonic rule put forward by Luttwak (1976).

3. Although it is possible that Tutul/Tell Bi'a was under Assyrian control for some time (Tenu 2015).

WORKS CITED

Akkermans, Peter M.M.G., and Frans A.M. Wiggermann. 2015. "West of Aššur: The Life and Times of the Middle Assyrian *Dunnu* at Tell Sabi Abyad." In *Understanding Hegemonic Practices of the Early Assyrian Empire*, ed. Bleda S. Düring, 89–124. Leiden: Nederlands Instituut voor het Nabije Oosten.

Algaze, Guillermo, Emily Hammer, and Bradley J. Parker. 2012. "The Tigris-Euphrates Archaeological Reconnaissance Project: Final Report of the Cizre Dam and Cizre-Silopi Plain Survey Areas." *Anatolica* 38: 1–115.

Altaweel, Marc. 2008. *The Imperial Landscape of Ashur: Settlement and Land Use in the Assyrian Heartland*. Heidelberg: Heidelberger Orientverlag.

Bagg, Ariel M. 2000. "Irrigation in Northern Mesopotamia: Water for the Assyrian Capitals (12th–7th Centuries BC)." *Irrigation and Drainage Systems* 14 (4): 301–24. https://doi.org/10.1023/A:1006421000423.

Bagg, Ariel M. 2011. *Die Assyrer und das Westland*. Leuven, Belgium: Peeters.

Bang, Peter F., and Christopher A. Bayly. 2011. *Tributary Empires in Global History*. Basinstoke, UK: Palgrave. https://doi.org/10.1057/9780230307674.

Barjamovic, Gojko. 2013. "Mesopotamian Empires." In *The State in the Ancient Near East and Mediterranean*, ed. Peter F. Bang and Walter Scheidel, 120–60. Oxford: Oxford University Press.

Bartl, Peter V., and Dominik Bonatz. 2013. "Across Assyria's Northern Frontier: Tell Fekheriye at the End of the Late Bronze Age." In *Across the Border: Late Bronze–Iron Age Relations between Syria and Anatolia*, ed. K. Aslihan Yener, 263–92. Leuven, Belgium: Peeters.

Bedford, Peter R. 2009. "The Neo-Assyrian Empire." In *The Dynamics of Ancient Empires*, ed. Ian Morris and Walter Scheidel, 30–65. Oxford: Oxford University Press.

Bernbeck, Reinhard. 2010. "Imperialist Networks: Ancient Assyria and the United States." *Present Pasts* 2 (1): 30–52. https://doi.org/10.5334/pp.30.

Bonatz, Dominik. 2013. "Tell Fekheriye—Renewed Excavations at the Head of the Spring." In *In 100 Jahre archäologische Feldforschungen in Nordost-Syrien—eine Bilanz*, ed. Dominik Bonatz and Lutz Martin, 209–34. Wiesbaden: Harrasowitz.

Burbank, Jane, and Frederick Cooper. 2010. *Empires in World History: Power and the Politics of Difference*. Princeton, NJ: Princeton University Press.

Cline, Eric H. 2014. *1177 BC: The Year Civilization Collapsed*. Princeton, NJ: Princeton University Press. https://doi.org/10.1515/9781400849987.

Cline, Eric H., and Mark W. Graham. 2011. *Ancient Empires: From Mesopotamia to the Rise of Islam*. Cambridge: Cambridge University Press.

Colburn, Henry P. 2013. "Connectivity and Communication in the Achaemenid Empire." *JESHO* 56: 29–52.

D'Agostino, Anacleto. 2008. "Between Mitannians and Middle-Assyrians: Changes and Links in Ceramic Culture at Tell Barri and in Syrian Jezirah during the End of the 2nd Millenium BC." In *Proceedings of the 5th International Congress on the Archaeology of the Ancient Near East*, ed. Joaquín M. Córdoba, Miquel Molist, M. Carmen Pérez, Isabel Rubio, and Sergio Martínez, 525–47. Madrid: Centro Superior de Estudios sobre el Oriente Próximo y Egipto.

D'Agostino, Anacleto. 2009. "The Assyrian-Aramean Interaction in the Upper Khabur: The Archaeological Evidence from Tell Barri Iron Age Layers." *Syria* 86 (86): 17–41. https://doi.org/10.4000/syria.507.

D'Agostino, Anacleto. 2015. "The Rise and Consolidation of Assyrian Control on the Northwestern Territories." In *Understanding Hegemonic Practices of the Early Assyrian Empire*, ed. Bleda S. Düring, 33–44. Leiden: Nederlands Instituut voor het Nabije Oosten.

Dittmann, Reinhard. 2011. "Kar-Tukulti-Ninurta through the Ages: A Short Note." In *Between the Cultures: The Central Tigris Region from the 3rd to the 1st Millennium BC*, ed. Peter A. Miglus and Simone Mühl, 165–78. Heidelberg: Heidelberger Orientverlag.

Doyle, Michael W. 1986. *Empires*. Ithaca, NY: Cornell University Press.

Duistermaat, Kim. 2015. "The Pots of Assur in the Land of Hanigalbat: The Organization of Pottery Production in the Far West of the Middle Assyrian Empire." In *Understanding Hegemonic Practices of the Early Assyrian Empire*, ed. Bleda S. Düring, 125–52. Leiden: Nederlands Instituut voor het Nabije Oosten.

Düring, Bleda S., ed. 2015. *Understanding Hegemonic Practices of the Early Assyrian Empire*. Leiden: Nederlands Instituut voor het Nabije Oosten.

Düring, Bleda S., Eva Visser, and Peter M.M.G. Akkermans. 2015. "Skeletons in the Fortress: The Late Bronze Age Burials of Tell Sabi Abyad, Syria." *Levant* 47 (1): 30–50. https://doi.org/10.1179/0075891415Z.00000000056.

Faist, Bettina. 2006. "Itineraries and Travellers in the Middle Assyrian Period." *SAAB* 15: 147–60.

Fales, F. Mario. 2012. "'Hanigalbat' in Early Neo-Assyrian Royal Inscriptions: A Retrospective View." In *The Ancient Near East in the 12th–10th Centuries BCE: Culture and History*, ed. Gershon Galil, Ayelet Gilboa, Aren M. Maeir, and Kahn Dan'el, 99–120. Münster: Ugarit Verlag.

Glatz, Claudia. 2009. "Empire as Network: Spheres of Material Interaction in Late Bronze Age Anatolia." *JAA* 28: 127–41.

Glatz, Claudia. 2013. "Negotiating Empire: A Comparative Investigation into the Responses to Hittite Imperialism by the Vassal State of Ugarit and the Kaska Peoples of Pontic Anatolia." In *Empires and Diversity: On the Crossroads of Archaeology,*

Anthropology, and History, ed. Gregory E. Areshian, 21–56. Los Angeles: Cotsen Institute of Archaeology.

Harmanşah, Ömür. 2012. "Beyond Assur: New Cities and the Assyrian Politics of Landscape." *BASOR* 365: 53–77.

Harmanşah, Ömür. 2013. *Cities and the Shaping of Memory in the Ancient Near East*. Cambridge: Cambridge University Press. https://doi.org/10.1017/CBO9781139227216.

Harrak, Amir. 1987. *Assyria and Hannigalbat*. Hildesheim, Germany: Georg Olms Verlag.

Heinz, Marlies. 2012. "The Ur III, Old Babylonian, and Kassite Empires." In *A Companion to the Archaeology of the Ancient Near East*, ed. Daniel T. Potts, 706–21. Oxford: Oxford University Press. https://doi.org/10.1002/9781444360790.ch37.

Higginbotham, Carolyn R. 2000. *Egyptianization and Elite Emulation in Ramesside Palestine: Governance and Accommodation on the Imperial Periphery*. Leiden: Brill.

Jakob, Stefan. 2009. *Die mittelassyrischen Texte aus Tell Chuera in Nordost-Syrien*. Wiesbaden: Harrasowitz.

Jakob, Stefan. 2015. "Daily Life in the Wild West of Assyria." In *Understanding Hegemonic Practices of the Early Assyrian Empire*, ed. Bleda S. Düring, 177–87. Leiden: Nederlands Instituut voor het Nabije Oosten.

Kessler, Karlheinz. 1997. "'Royal Roads' and Other Questions of the Neo-Assyrian Communication System." *SAAB* 1: 129–36.

Koliński, Rafal. 2001. *Mesopotamian Dimātu of the Second Millennium BC*. Oxford: Archaeopress.

Koliński, Rafal. 2015. "Making Mittani Assyrian: The Hegemonic Practices of the Middle Assyrian Empire in Context." In *Understanding Hegemonic Practices of the Early Assyrian Empire*, ed. Bleda S. Düring, 9–32. Leiden: Nederlands Instituut voor het Nabije Oosten.

Kühne, Hartmut. 2013. "Tell Sheikh Hamad—the Assyrian-Aramean Centre of Dur-Katlimmu/Magdalu." In *In 100 Jahre archäologische Feldforschungen in Nordost-Syrien—eine Bilanz*, ed. Dominik Bonatz and Lutz Martin, 235–58. Wiesbaden: Harrasowitz.

Kühne, Hartmut. 2015. "Core and Periphery in the Assyrian State: The View from Dur-Katlimmu." In *Understanding Hegemonic Practices of the Early Assyrian Empire*, ed. Bleda S. Düring, 59–74. Leiden: Nederlands Instituut voor het Nabije Oosten.

Liverani, Mario. 1988. "The Growth of the Assyrian Empire in the Habur/Middle Euphrates Area: A New Paradigm." *SAAB* 2: 81–98.

Liverani, Mario. 2001. "The Fall of the Assyrian Empire: Ancient and Modern Interpretations." In *Empires, Perspectives from Archaeology and History*, ed. Susan

E. Alcock, Terrence N. D'Altroy, Kathleen D. Morrison, and Carla M. Sinopoli, 374–91. Cambridge: Cambridge University Press.

Livingstone, Alistair. 2007. "Ashurbanipal: Literate or Not?" *ZA* 97 (1): 98–118. https://doi.org/10.1515/ZA.2007.005.

Llop, Jaume. 2011. "The Creation of the Middle Assyrian Provinces." *JAOS* 131: 591–603.

Luciani, Marta. 1999–2001. "On Assyrian Frontiers and the Middle Euphrates." *SAAB* 13: 87–114.

Luttwak, Edward N. 1976. *The Grand Strategy of the Roman Empire.* Baltimore: Johns Hopkins University Press.

Lyon, Jerry D. 2000. "Middle Assyrian Expansion and Settlement Development in the Syrian Jezira: The View from the Balikh Valley." In *Rainfall and Agriculture in Northern Mesopotamia*, ed. Remco M. Jas, 89–126. Leiden: Nederlands Instituut voor het Nabije Oosten.

Maier, Charles S. 2006. *Among Empires: American Ascendancy and Its Predecessors.* Cambridge, MA: Harvard University Press. https://doi.org/10.4159/9780674040458.

Matney, Timothy. 2010. "Material Culture and Identity: Assyrians, Aramaeans, and the Indigenous People of Iron Age Southeastern Anatolia." In *Agency and Identity in the Ancient Near East: New Paths Forward*, ed. Sharon R. Steadman and Jennifer C. Ross, 129–47. London: Equinox.

Mattingly, David J. 2011. *Imperialism, Power, and Identity: Experiencing the Roman Empire.* Princeton, NJ: Princeton University Press.

Miglus, Peter A. 2011. "Middle Assyrian Settlements in the South." In *Between the Cultures: The Central Tigris Region from the 3rd to the 1st Millennium BC*, ed. Peter A. Miglus and Simone Mühl, 217–25. Heidelberg: Heidelberger Orientverlag.

Mühl, Simone. 2013. *Siedlungsgeschichte im mittleren Osttigrisgebiet: Vom Neolithikum bis in die neuassyrische Zeit.* Wiesbaden: Harrasowitz.

Mühl, Simone. 2015. "Middle Assyrian Territorial Practices in the Region of Ashur." In *Understanding Hegemonic Practices of the Early Assyrian Empire*, ed. Bleda S. Düring, 45–58. Leiden: Nederlands Instituut voor het Nabije Oosten.

Na'aman, Nadav. 1993. "Population Changes in Populations following Assyrian Deportations." *TA* 20: 104–24.

Novak, Mirko. 2013. "Gozan and Guzana: Anatolian, Aramaeans, and Assyrian in Tell Halaf." In *In 100 Jahre archäologische Feldforschungen in Nordost-Syrien—eine Bilanz*, ed. Dominik Bonatz and Lutz Martin, 259–80. Wiesbaden: Harrasowitz.

Parker, Bradley J. 1997. "Garrisoning the Empire: Aspects of the Construction and Maintenance of Forts on the Assyrian Frontier." *Iraq* 59: 77–87. https://doi.org/10.1017/S0021088900003363.

Parker, Bradley J. 2001. *The Mechanics of Empire: The Northern Frontier of Assyria as a Case Study in Imperial Dynamics*. Helsinki: Neo-Assyrian Text Corpus Project.

Parker, Bradley J. 2003. "Archaeological Manifestations of Empire: Assyria's Imprint on Southeastern Anatolia." *AJA* 107 (4): 525–57. https://doi.org/10.3764/aja.107.4.525.

Parker, Bradley J. 2006. "Toward an Understanding of Borderland Processes." *American Antiquity* 71 (1): 77–100. https://doi.org/10.2307/40035322.

Parker, Bradley J. 2011. "The Construction and Performance of Kingship in the Neo-Assyrian Empire." *JAR* 67: 357–86.

Parker, Bradley J. 2015. "Power, Hegemony, and the Use of Force in the Neo-Assyrian Empire." In *Understanding Hegemonic Practices of the Early Assyrian Empire*, ed. Bleda S. Düring, 287–97. Leiden: Nederlands Instituut voor het Nabije Oosten.

Pfälzner, Peter. 1993. "Die Späte Bronzezeit: Tell Umm 'Aqrebe." In *Steppe als Kültürlandschaft*, ed. Reinhard Bernbeck, 70–96. Berlin: Dietrich Reimer Verlag.

Pfälzner, Peter. 1997. "Keramikproduktion und Provinzverwaltung im mittelassyrischen Reich." In *Assyrien im Wandel der Zeiten: 39 Rencontre Assyriologique Internationale*, ed. Hartmut Waetzoldt and Harald Hauptmann, 337–45. Heidelberg: Heidelberger Orientverlag.

Pittman, Holly. 1996. "The White Obelisk and the Problem of Historical Narrative in the Art of Assyria." *ABull* 78: 334–55.

Pongratz-Leisten, Beate. 2011. "Assyrian Royal Discourse between Local and Imperial Traditions at the Habur." *RA* 105: 109–28.

Pongratz-Leisten, Beate. 2013. "All the King's Men: Authority, Kingship, and the Rise of the Elites in Assyria." In *Experiencing Power, Generating Authority: Cosmos, Politics, and the Ideology of Kingship in Ancient Egypt and Mesopotamia*, ed. Jane A. Hill, Philip Jones, and Antonio J. Morales, 285–309. Philadelphia: University of Pennsylvania Museum of Archaeology and Anthropology.

Postgate, J. Nicholas. 1982. "*Ilku* and Land Tenure in the Middle Assyrian Kingdom, a Second Attempt." In *Societies and Languages of the Ancient Near East: Studies in Honour of I. M. Diakonoff*, ed. Mohammed A. Dandamayev, Ilya Gershevitch, Horst Klengel, G. Komoróczy, Morgens T. Larsen, and J. Nicholas Postgate, 304–13. Warminster: Aris and Phillips.

Postgate, J. Nicholas. 1992. "The Land of Assur and the Yoke of Assur." *WA* 23: 247–63.

Postgate, J. Nicholas. 2007a. "The Invisible Hierarchy: Assyrian Military and Civilian Administration in the 8th and 7th Centuries BC." In *The Land of Assur and the Yoke of Assur: Studies on Assyria 1971–2005*, ed. J. Nicholas Postgate, 331–60. Oxford: Oxbow Books.

Postgate, J. Nicholas. 2007b. *The Land of Assur and the Yoke of Assur: Studies on Assyria 1971–2005*. Oxford: Oxbow Books.

Postgate, J. Nicholas. 2010. "The Debris of Government: Reconstructing the Middle Assyrian State Apparatus from Tablets and Potsherds." *Iraq* 72: 19–37. https://doi.org/10.1017/S0021088900000577.

Postgate, J. Nicholas. 2013. *Bronze Age Bureaucracy: Writing and the Practices of Government in Assyria*. Cambridge: Cambridge University Press. https://doi.org/10.1017/CBO9781107338937.

Postgate, J. Nicholas. 2015. "Government Recording Practices in Assyria and Her Neighbours and Contemporaries." In *Understanding Hegemonic Practices of the Early Assyrian Empire*, ed. Bleda S. Düring, 275–85. Leiden: Nederlands Instituut voor het Nabije Oosten.

Radner, Karen. 2004. *Das Mittelassyrische Tontafelarchiv von Giricano/Dunna-Ša-Uzibi*. Turnhout, Belgium: Brepols.

Roaf, Michael. 1990. *Cultural Atlas of Mesopotamia and the Ancient Near East*. New York: Facts on File.

Sauvage, Martin. 2005. "Incinération et inhumation à l'époque médio-assyrienne (XIIIe–XIIe s. av. J.-C.): le cas de Tell Mohammed Diyab (Syrie du Nord-Est)." *KTEMA* 30: 47–54.

Shibata, Daisuke. 2015. "Dynastic Marriages in Assyria during the Late Second Millennium BC." In *Understanding Hegemonic Practices of the Early Assyrian Empire*, ed. Bleda S. Düring, 235–42. Leiden: Nederlands Instituut voor het Nabije Oosten.

Sinopoli, Carla M. 1994. "The Archaeology of Empires." *ARA* 23: 159–80.

Smith, Michael E., and Lisa Montiel. 2001. "The Archaeological Study of Empires and Imperialism in Pre-Hispanic Central Mexico." *JAA* 20: 245–84.

Smith, Stuart T. 2003. *Wretched Kush: Ethnic Identities and Boundaries in Egypt's Nubian Empire*. London: Routledge.

Smith, Stuart T. 2013. "Revenge of the Kushites: Assimilation and Resistance in Egypt's New Kingdom Empire and Nubian Ascendancy over Egypt." In *Empires and Diversity: On the Crossroads of Archaeology, Anthropology, and History*, ed. Gregory E. Areshian, 84–107. Los Angeles: Cotsen Institute of Archaeology.

Stein, Gil J., ed. 2005. *The Archaeology of Colonial Encounters: Comparative Perspectives*. Santa Fe, NM: School of American Research Press.

Szuchman, Jeffrey J. 2007. "Prelude to Empire: Middle Assyrian Hanigalbat and the Rise of the Arameans." PhD dissertation, University of California, Los Angeles.

Taagepera, Rein. 1978. "Size and Duration of Empires: Systematics of Size." *SSR* 7: 108–27.

Tenu, Aline. 2009. *L'expansion Medio-Assyrienne: Approche archéologique*. Oxford: Archeopress.

Tenu, Aline. 2013. "Imperial Culture: Some Reflections on Middle Assyrian Settlements." In *Time and History in the Ancient Near East: Proceedings of the 56th*

Recontre Assyriologique Internationale, ed. Lluis Feliu, Jaume Llop, Adelina Millet Albà, and Joaquín Sanmartin, 575–84. Winona Lake, IN: Eisenbrauns.

Tenu, Aline. 2015. "Building the Empire: Settlement Patterns in the Middle Assyrian Empire." In *Understanding Hegemonic Practices of the Early Assyrian Empire*, ed. Bleda S. Düring, 75–87. Leiden: Nederlands Instituut voor het Nabije Oosten.

Tenu, Aline, Jean-Louis Montero Fenollós, and Francisco Caramelo. 2012. "L'empire Assyrien au XIIIe siècle av. J.-C.: Tell Qabr Abu al-'Atiq sur le Moyen Euphrate." In *Du Village Néolithique à la Ville Syro-Mésopotamienne*, ed. Jean-Louis Monterro Fenollós, 143–61. Ferrol, Spain: Sociedad Luso-Gallega de Estudios Mesopotámicos.

Von Dassow, Eva. 2014. "Levantine Polities under Mittanian Hegemony." In *Constituent, Confederate, and Conquered Space: The Emergence of the Mittani State*, ed. Eva Cancik-Kirschbaum, Nicole Brisch, and Jesper Eidem, 11–32. Berlin: De Gruyter. https://doi.org/10.1515/9783110266412.11.

Wicke, Dirk. 2013. "*Iti nisekur Assur* Amusunuti: Zu den Leuten Assyriens zählte Ich Sie: Beobachtungen zum kulturellen Austausch am Oberen Tigris in neuassyrischer Zeit." In *Patterns of Urban Societies*, ed. Thomas R. Kämmerer and Sabine Rogge, 233–54. Münster: Ugarit Verlag.

Wiggermann, Frans A.M. 2000. "Agriculture in the Northern Balikh Valley: The Case of Middle Assyrian Tell Sabi Abyad." In *Rainfall and Agriculture in Northern Mesopotamia*, ed. Remco M. Jas, 171–232. Leiden: Nederlands Instituut voor het Nabije Oosten.

Wilkinson, Tony J., Jason Ur, Eleanor Wilkinson, and Marc Altaweel. 2005. "Landscape and Settlement in the Neo-Assyrian Empire." *BASOR* 340: 23–56.

Zimansky, Paul. 1995. "Urartian Material Culture as State Assemblage: An Anomaly in the Archaeology of Empire." *BASOR* 299–300: 103–15.

3

Empire of Conflict, Empire of Compromise

The Middle and Neo-Assyrian Landscape and Interaction with the Local Communities of the Upper Tigris Borderland

Guido Guarducci (CAMNES; University of Reading)

This study discusses the characteristics and behavior of the Assyrian Empire in the Upper Tigris Borderland (figure 3.1) and the relationship established with the local communities of the region.[1] This relationship commenced at an early stage of the imperial growth. Therefore, this chapter will also take into account the Middle Assyrian Period (MAP) (ca. fourteenth–tenth centuries BCE) in addition to the Late or Neo-Assyrian Period (NAP) (ca. tenth–seventh centuries BCE).

The interaction between the Assyrians and the local population is divided into two main approaches, one of conflict and one of compromise. These two strategies do not necessarily form a chronological sequence, since both sides will adopt one or the other repeatedly during the centuries under examination, with constant negotiation between harsh conflicts and solutions of compromise. Nevertheless, at a macroscopic level it is possible to classify the time frame starting from the end of the Middle Assyrian Period to the beginning of the Neo-Assyrian Period as a phase of violent conflict between the empire and the local groups of the Upper Tigris Borderland while classifying the rest of the Neo-Assyrian Period as a phase of compromise between these two parties. Using the conflict and compromise approaches as general frameworks, the chapter aims first to analyze the specific spheres and dynamics of interaction established between the Assyrians and local communities as well as with the Upper Tigris Borderland territory. Second, once delineated, this relationship is

DOI: 10.5876/9781607328230.c003

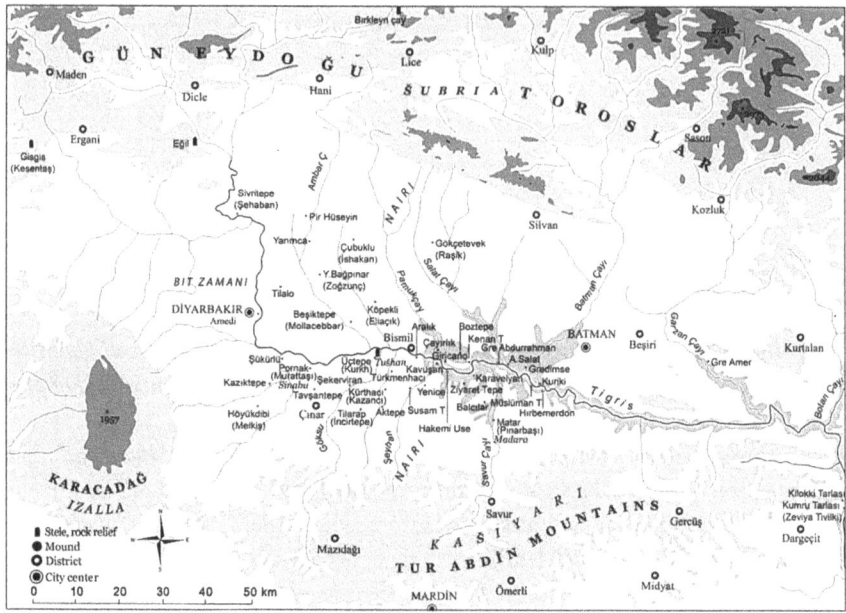

FIGURE 3.1. *Upper Tigris Borderland with the main Iron Age sites and modern cities indicated (after Köroğlu 2015)*

used to assess the Upper Tigris borderland socioeconomic landscape and the differences between the Middle and Neo-Assyrian imperial systems.

If we can consider borderlands the external edges of periphery—in our case, the periphery of an empire—before proceeding, it is important to make clear what the term *borderland* involves in this study. Parker's (2006, 80) definition is rather fitting: borderlands "are regions around or between political or cultural entities where geographic, political, demographic, cultural and economic circumstances or processes may interact to create borders or frontiers." In addition, we can claim that after a minimum period of contact, borderlands in most cases display overlapping of a variable number of these circumstances or processes. This overlapping introduces the concept of interaction and its complex nuances. In most cases the result of this overlapping is an osmosis, which goes beyond physical borders and conceptual frontiers by merging the original circumstances and processes and forging new versions of them. This process is very similar to that of White's (1991) "middle ground" theory, also cited by Parker (2006, 86). This reciprocal influence is in some cases reflected in the material culture and textual sources of the borderlands in which it takes place.

Nevertheless, we must bear in mind that only a small fraction of this complex process is detectable and understandable through this type of data. The circumstances and processes of reciprocal influence in the Upper Tigris take place in specific spheres and with distinctive dynamics of interaction, with the result of forging the new socioeconomic landscapes explored below.

SPHERES AND DYNAMICS OF INTERACTION

To expand its power structures and satisfy its growing demands, the Assyrian Empire during its Middle and Late Periods required large amounts of arable land and resources. The Upper Tigris region offered all of this, leading the empire to collide with its local communities. To better understand the relationship established between the Assyrians and local communities and, subsequently, to trace a profile of the borderland socioeconomic system, we must first focus on the processes and collateral effects underlying the Assyrian and local interaction, which can be observed through five main spheres: warfare, commodities, symbolic landscape, agriculture, and material culture.

Warfare

The Assyrians began to interact consistently with the Upper Tigris under Adad-nirari I (1305–1275 BCE) and Shalmaneser I (1274–1245 BCE). The Upper Tigris region was part of a wider area the Assyrians referred to as the Nairi lands[2] (see Radner and Schachner 2001, 761–65; Salvini 1967). The first mention of Nairi appears in an inscription from Aššur of Tukulti-Ninurta I (1244–1208 BCE; Grayson 1987, 237). We know this area was not under Assyrian control because of its exceptionally broad extension. Only a few regions in the south were intermittently controlled, as suggested by the frequent military campaigns conducted there. During this period, the texts record the first important episodes of contact with the local population. The result was a series of large-scale conflicts. Toward the end of the thirteenth century BCE, forty "kings"[3] of Nairi formed a coalition against Tukulti Ninurta I (Grayson 1987, 266). A similar scene was repeated a century later when twenty-three "kings" of Nairi, soon growing to sixty, joined in battle against Tiglath-pileser I (1115–1077 BCE; Grayson 1991, 21). These large coalitions reveal an unexpected level of networking and organization among the communities of the Nairi lands. The Assyrian threat perhaps enhanced the local cohesiveness but does not explain such a vast phenomenon and the degree of its coordination (see Guarducci 2011).

These episodes of conflict belong mainly to the MAP, which came to an end with the increasing loss of control over the conquered areas and the subsequent retraction of the imperial boundaries as a result of the issues raised by the collapse of the Late Bronze Age power networks. For about 200 years the yoke of Aššur drastically diminished its weight on the Upper Tigris, giving local communities the chance to emerge, expand, and develop. It was during this particular moment—the end of the Late Bronze Age (LBA) (ca. fourteenth–thirteenth centuries BCE) and the Early Iron Age (EIA) (ca. twelfth–tenth centuries BCE)—that local material culture production flourished in the Upper Tigris Borderland and the rest of eastern Anatolia.

As part of this complex social framework, we must include the Aramaean communities that were originally pastoral nomadic tribes (*aḫlamû*) as the majority of the Upper Tigris Borderland local communities. At the end of the MAP, the Aramaeans were able to settle and organize their own polities in various parts of Mesopotamia, becoming true states during the first millennium BCE. The main local polity of the Upper Tigris Borderland was Bīt-Zamāni, with its capital at Amīdu, modern Diyarbakır. Starting at the beginning of the thirteenth century BCE, this community is mentioned in the texts (Finkelstein 1953, 116–17), in which we learn that the territory was under the influence of Aššur through a local governor. In the early stages of their emergence, Aramaean tribes, as well as the following Iron Age dynastic states, appear to have seldom been influenced by external ethnicities and cultures, as confirmed by the strong and widespread presence of Aramaean polities rooted in their tribal lineage—probably a necessary approach to maintain intact their identity and "Houses." In a later phase the Syrian Aramaean polities lost their tribal kinship character, which was replaced by a geographical affiliation and identification with a city-state or kingdom that was also expressed through its architecture (Kühn 2014, 40). Kühn (2014, 40) claims that in this later phase there was no need for ethnic or tribal links to become a member of the *bīt* (House) in order to guarantee the loyalty of indigenous non-Aramaean groups. If this were true, it would demonstrate a sophisticated strategy to maintain a degree of identity in response to the growing Assyrian control over a specific territory, the Upper Tigris Borderland in our case, and at the same time the acceptance by local groups within their polity to increase their power.

Unfortunately, we do not know the modalities and level of interaction between local populations and Bīt-Zamāni; nor do we have an idea of the latter's material culture. Nevertheless, by examining the texts and the other Aramaean political organizations, it is plausible to think of a one-way influence process toward Bīt-Zamāni, meaning that the Aramaean community did not affect the Upper Tigris Borderland indigenous culture, which instead became part of Bīt-Zamāni. In fact, Szuchman (2009a, 64) reaches the conclusion that Aramaean polities did not produce their own pottery, since they adopted the ceramic tradition of the local communities. Moreover, the early Assyrian domination of the territory of Bīt-Zamāni and its integration within the Assyrian system, which must be read not as a disruption of its identity but as a compromise to maintain it, made interaction with other local groups even more difficult. Bīt-Zamāni did not easily accept the subjugation and the heavy tribute inflicted by Aššur. In the following centuries a few episodes of conflict are reported in the Assyrian annals, alternating with an equal number of treaties (see Szuchman 2009a; Radner and Schachner 2001). These agreements offer a good example of compromise reached by the two sides, usually in terms of autonomy and tribute for the Aramaeans and aid against third-party enemies for Assyria (Szuchman 2009a, 57).

During the Neo-Assyrian Period, Ashurnasirpal II (883–859 BCE), Shalmaneser III (858–823 BCE), Tiglath-pileser III (744–727 BCE), and Sargon II (721–705 BCE) dedicated a substantial part of their military campaigns against the people of Nairi. There is no mention of local coalitions or large conflicts as in the past, but there was a constant effort to gain control of key sites along the Tigris Borderland such as Tušhan, Tidu, Sinabu, Damdamusa—the buffer states of Bīt-Zamāni—and, in particular, Šubria, an indigenous polity with a strong ethnic admixture worth exploring in further detail.

The kingdom of Šubria was north of the Tigris at the end of the EIA and during the MIA. The extension of its territories appears to have been rather broad, remaining oddly independent until the final phase of the Neo-Assyrian Period. Two realms belonging to the city-states of Uppumu and Kullimeri, possibly the modern sites of Fum and Gre Migro (Kessler 1995, 57), formed this kingdom as a whole. This kingdom had a crucial function in the eyes of the Assyrian and Urartian Empires. In fact, Šubria probably owes its independence and prosperity to its buffer state role. The multiethnic population residing here—Hurrians, Arameans, Assyrians, and Urartians—confirms this status. Radner and Schachner (2001, 756–57) argue that Šubria and the Taurus piedmont area in general were probably among the last holdouts of the fallen Mitanni Empire. The Hurrian names of the Šubrian rulers (e.g., Hu-Tešup, Ik-Tešup) (Salvini 1967, 48, 50; Radner and Schachner 2001, 757) reported in Neo-Assyrian texts support this theory, as does the Hurrian name of 'Eli-Tešup in the nearby kingdom of Alzi, west of the Upper Tigris. Moreover, according to Kessler (1995, 55), the etymology of Šubria should be linked to the past political and geographical area of Šubarû, or Subartu, which in the thirteenth century BCE was still independent and not a part of the so-called Nairi lands. We know that the Hurrian polity of Subartu, or Šubarû, was first recorded under the reign of Assur-uballit I (1366–1330 BCE). Radner (2012, 244), in fact, claims that Šubria, along with the smaller polities of Kumme and Musasir, may "certainly be described as (linguistically and culturally) Hurrian states."

The ethnic admixture of Šubria also expanded its Hurrian base during the Middle Assyrian Period when a famine that struck the Upper Tigris and the Middle Assyrian city of Tuššum, the future Neo-Assyrian capital of Tušhan, whose inhabitants, according to the texts, moved to Šubria to survive (Grayson 1991, 202, 242–43). In addition to this scenario, letters from the northern provinces depict an extremely singular portrait of this kingdom. Deserters, traitors, murderers, and any kind of criminal fugitives unwanted in their homeland (including Urartu) fled to this area (Lanfranchi and Parpola 1990, e.g., letters nos. 32, 35, 52, 53, 54; Parker 2001, 245–46). Perhaps the most famous episode of all, also mentioned in the Bible (2 Kings 19:37; Isaiah 37:38), is that of the assassins of the Assyrian ruler Sennacherib (704–681 BCE), who sought asylum in Šubria after committing their crime (Parker 2001, 245, 246). Following these events, Sennacherib's brother and successor, Esarhaddon (680–669 BCE), moved toward Šubria in 673 BCE, claiming in his "Letter to the God" that his act was connected to the attempt to capture his brother's assassins (Borger 1956, Text 106, lines 23–269). He then conquered and transformed the kingdom into two provinces, Uppumu and Kullimeri, shifting the empire's borderland further to the north and greatly damping the local communities' presence and identity manifestations.

The main goal of the empire during the final phase of the NAP, therefore, was to acquire and maintain control over this strategically relevant area, not only for its resources, which appear to have been abundant considering the tribute (e.g., Grayson 1991, 262), but also as the main line of defense against the northern belligerent populations. First among them was Biainili, the Ur(u)atri (which the Assyrians called Urartu) that once was one of the tribal groups of Nairi (Salvini 1967; Chahin 2001, 55). Other groups also threatened the northern border, such as the Muški and the Cimmerians. This final phase of the empire reveals several details of administration and everyday life in the northern borderland, thanks to the discovery of the rich correspondence established between the court of Sargon II and the governors of Tušhan and Bīt-Zamāni (see Lanfranchi and Parpola 1990, nos. 1–40), which will not be explored here because of space restrictions.

Commodities

Commodity procurement and trade attracted Aššur from the early stages of the period under examination. In fact, in addition to the Old Assyrian trade colonies established in the early second millennium BCE in central Anatolia, during the MAP and even more intensively during the NAP, the empire harvested from the Upper Tigris Borderland and surrounding areas many of the most important types of commodities. These were necessary to keep the imperial machine active and productive because most of these commodities were completely absent in Mesopotamia. Copper, silver, semi-precious stones, and stone slabs, as well as cereal grains, straw, resins, textiles, and especially timber, were exploited and transported from southeastern Anatolia to the heartland.

The most effective solution the Assyrians adopted for acquiring these commodities was frequent military campaigns in which Assyrian troops forcibly confiscated goods from local cities and villages or subjected local governments to a levy. These practices greatly weakened local political opponents while keeping them under control, although they were less effective with mobile communities. The constant and abundant supply of raw wool, textile products, and leather, among others, furnished by the local populations of southeastern Anatolia, in particular those with a semi-nomadic lifestyle, contributed significantly to the northern Mesopotamian and imperial economic system. Recently, Porter (2012) stressed the importance of the role played by nomads and their wool production in the Near Eastern state formation process. A similar fabric production pattern, which was suitably adapted and perhaps in symbiosis with sedentary household manufacturing, can easily be traced within the Upper Tigris Assyrian–local interaction, since the southeast was one of the major areas of textile production in Anatolia starting in the Old Assyrian Period (Wisti Lassen 2010, 169). The control of commodities was strictly linked to extensive trading activities with the heartland or other provinces of the empire. Creating a trade network was, in fact, one of the main reasons to colonize this area and gain control over the small polities within it.

Symbolic Landscape

A number of symbolically charged elements of the Upper Tigris Borderland landscape had a major impact on its local and foreign societies and a direct role in their interaction. First, in the eyes of Mesopotamian civilizations, the highlands, traditionally the Zagros Mountain chain, were the end of the world and the access point to the underworld, the sacred kur^A ("mountain," "foreign land," also "netherworld") (Kramer 1972, 110; Black, Green, and Rickards 1992, 114). A second feature, among others, was even more important and ideologically completed the first. Northwest of the Upper Tigris River Valley rises the so-called source of the Tigris (Birkleyn Çay). Here, Assyrian sovereigns carved their images and inscribed their royal words as signs of their passage and greatness. Harmanşah (2007), in his study on the "source of the Tigris," has observed a few important points of contact with the local communities. He claims that "commemorative sites became event-places where state spectacles encountered and merged with local practices that were anchored to those places. By definition, commemorative practices are also ideological. Sites of commemoration, therefore, served as public spheres in which elite and local ideologies interacted in a set of material and discursive practices related to notions of kingship and servitude. They constituted *loci* for the display and its material embodiment, becoming places through which local histories were negotiated and written" (Harmanşah 2007, 180).

This perspective seems to be confirmed by the data gathered at Birkleyn by Schachner and his team (2009, 231–41). He argues that although we have the relief and inscription of Shalmaneser III, there is no Assyrian pottery belonging to that period, almost as if some kind of agreement or religious tolerance was kindled by this holy place and its significance for local communities. Moreover, this site had major symbolic significance for the Assyrians, since the greatest and purest gift of all, the Tigris, was the same river that flowed through their heartland.

AGRICULTURE

The agricultural sphere of interaction, perhaps the most relevant of all, was based on an extensive agricultural production system concerning mainly cereal grains, pulses, vineyards, olive groves, and orchards. Scholars (Parker 2003, 526, 2006, 85; Wilkinson et al. 2005, 41; Matney 2010, 136) and the Assyrian annals themselves (Postgate 1974, 237) have defined the Upper Tigris Neo-Assyrian colonization as "agricultural" because of the central role this production system played in the imperial expansion.

The Upper Tigris Borderland is located above the 400 mm isohyet, which in theory should guarantee self-sufficient agriculture without the aid of irrigation (see Van De Mieroop 2004, 7, map. 1.1). This type of farming, known as dry farming, was not possible in southern Mesopotamia where the annual rainfall did not meet the minimum 200 mm isohyet. The higher rainfall in the Upper Tigris contributed to the Assyrian interest in this fertile land. Nevertheless, to sustain such a large system and the occasional droughts that struck this area, the use of complex hydraulic technology was of paramount importance. Therefore, water channeling and other irrigation technologies such as cisterns, dams, and devices like the *shadouf* (a lever with a bucket and a rope to lift water above its level) were mastered by the Assyrians during the first millennium thanks to the Tigris River water source. Other sourcing strategies were adopted, such as the use of natural springs and *qanats* (artificial tunnels in proximity to mountain slopes to intercept and convey downstream the deepwater strata within). The Upper Tigris Borderland is in fact scattered with the remains of water procurement structures, such as channels, cisterns, checkdams, and wells. Although we cannot date all of these, it is highly probable that similar, if not identical, practices and devices were in part developed and used by the Assyrians. In addition, recent surveys and studies of the Upper Tigris (see Hammer 2014; Ur and Hammer 2009) seem to indicate that the pastoral nomads present in the region were also creating and adopting these devices extensively, in antiquity as well as today. These semi-nomadic groups, which formed a large portion of the local communities, played a major role in the demand for and creation of this kind of supply because of their constant need of water for their encampments and herds.

To develop and maintain this agricultural production system, a constant and large amount of labor was required. Although a small amount of land was probably outsourced through private contracts, as happened in the Balikh valley, the remainder was assigned to tenant farmers or directly organized by Assyrian officials. For this and other purposes tied to imperial land use and administration, Assyrians co-opted the necessary workforce mainly from the subdued villages and also through military campaigns (Wiggermann 2000, 174). Many local and foreign prisoners of war were employed in the fields. To satisfy the growing demand for labor, starting in the thirteenth century BCE and more frequently in the eighth century BCE, the Assyrians conducted mass deportations, in particular from the Levant but also from nearby regions, to the Upper Tigris and other areas of the empire. This practice also had the strategic side effect of weakening the local elite to achieve a higher degree of control over local ruling classes. For example, under Tiglath-pileser III we know that 83,000 people were deported from the area of Hamath to the Upper Tigris (Tadmor 1994, 63). As one example, Parker and colleagues (2001) suggest that the site of Boztepe might represent this kind of settlement because of the presence of pottery strictly connected to the Levant. Moreover, the cuneiform tablet discovered in 2009 at Ziyaret Tepe—the Assyrian capital of the Upper Tigris region known as Tušhan—which bears 144 female names,

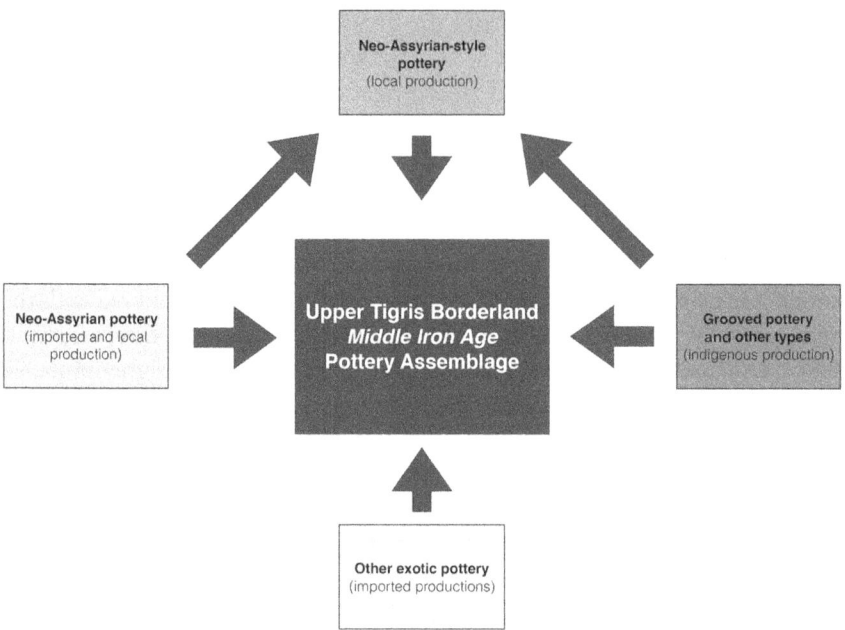

FIGURE 3.2. *Diagram of pottery productions and influence dynamics (arrows) within the Upper Tigris Borderland*

seems to confirm this practice. The etymology of the names on this tablet is of Assyrian, Hurrian, Luwian, and possibly Indo-Iranian origin, while most of them cannot be identified (MacGinnis 2012, 19). The displacement of groups of people by the Assyrians during their domination contributed significantly to the enlargement of the ethnic admixture of the Upper Tigris Borderland and the Nairi lands in general.

Material Culture

The material culture sphere of interaction, in our case, pottery, exposes more than others the overlapping of cultures and is of great importance for better understanding the dynamics of production and, where possible, the local-foreign relationship. The quantities of Middle Assyrian pottery retrieved in this area (at sites such as Giricano, Gre Dimse, Üçtepe, and Ziyaret Tepe) are modest, and its production was in most cases defined by and separated from indigenous production, which is why I will focus on the Neo-Assyrian Period. Nevertheless, it is important to mention the case of Hakemi Use, since it heralds a behavior that was standard during the NAP: the merging of foreign and indigenous characteristics in a single production. According to the excavators, the LBA stratum of Hakemi Use features local production of Middle Assyrian pottery. The morphology is Middle Assyrian, but the inclusions of ceramic temper are local (Tekin 2004, 455). This means that local imitations were produced within indigenous contexts, as attested also by other sherds at smaller sites like Kenan Tepe and Salat Tepe (Tenu 2009, 218, 223).

In the Neo-Assyrian Period (i.e., the Middle Iron Age [MIA]) it is difficult to identify the exact dynamics of production for each pottery typology because of the convergence and merging of local and foreign traits (figure 3.2), both of which are sometimes present in the same site. When one examines the Upper Tigris Borderland archaeological record of this period, it is possible to roughly subdivide the imported and local pottery assemblages into three main productions: (1) indigenous Grooved pottery and other types, (2) local or imported Neo-Assyrian pottery, and (3) local Neo-Assyrian-style pottery. These productions are in some cases accompanied by a fourth category of exotic imports, which will not be explored here because of its paucity and its low impact on the other productions.

Indigenous Grooved Pottery and Other Types

The presence of Middle Iron Age Grooved pottery, very similar to that of the Early Iron Age, is well attested in the neighboring regions of the Upper Tigris as it is, for example, in the Van Basin (Belli and Konyar 2003; Köroğlu and Konyar 2008), in the Erzurum-Kars region (Sagona 2012), and abundantly in the Upper Euphrates (Ökse 1988; Bartl 2001; Müller 2005). Although in the north and northwest we have numerous reliable contexts, within the Upper Tigris this production is difficult to frame,[5] perhaps because of the stronger and extensive Assyrian presence in the region during this period.

A clear indigenous MIA context was discovered at Gre Amer (Pulhan and Blaylock 2013, 402) in the nearby Garzan Valley. Gre Amer not only features Grooved pottery but also well-preserved architecture, in contrast with the semi-nomadic contexts of the Early Iron Age. Concerning the Upper Tigris Borderland, we have only a few clear contexts in which we find an interesting coexistence of indigenous Grooved pottery along with Neo-Assyrian pottery, local Neo-Assyrian-style pottery, or both. These include the Assyrian strata of the sites of Üçtepe (Köroğlu 1998, 51, figs. 21–22), Ziyaret Tepe (Matney et al. 2009, 54), Hakemi Use (Tekin 2011, 612), and perhaps Hirbemerdon Tepe (Guarducci 2011, 170, fig. 24b). East of the Upper Tigris River Valley were other examples of this association, such as at Zeviya Tivilki (Ökse et al. 2014, 117–26) and Kilokki Rabiseki (Ökse et al. 2014, 127–43).

Obviously, it is impossible to establish whether the Grooved pottery discovered in these sites belongs exclusively to an indigenous production and was therefore imported to the site or to an Assyrian local production that imitated this type of pottery. Another possibility is that local people produced Grooved pottery within Assyrian contexts, forcibly or collaboratively or perhaps diachronically (i.e., abandonment and immediate reoccupation by the opposite group). What appears clear is that the majority of the MIA local ceramic exemplars vary from those of the EIA by having a more refined temper, different types of clay hues, more accurate decorations (including grooves), better control of the firing process (including higher temperatures), and the use in most cases of a slow wheel, or *tournette*, in molding the vases. Although Grooved pottery remains the index fossil for the local Iron Age pottery assemblage, the indigenous production featured other types of pottery as well, which are often difficult to identify because of the lack of contexts. Although most of the information is made available through similar contexts outside the Upper Tigris, at Ziyaret Tepe, Matney was able to identify this production, defining it as a local Late Iron Age assemblage (ca. tenth–seventh centuries BCE) (1998, 13, fig. 8; Matney et al. 2009, 54).

Local or Imported Neo-Assyrian Pottery

The Neo-Assyrian pottery, imported from the heartland or locally produced, is found in much lower concentrations and is mainly retrieved from large settlements such as Ziyaret Tepe (Matney 1998, fig. 9; Matney et al. 2007, 45–47, fig. 19) and other large centers like Üçtepe (Sevin 1989; Köroğlu 1998) and Pornak (Köroğlu 1998, 105). Moreover, a few fragments of Palace Ware (eighth–seventh centuries BCE fine Assyrian pottery) were discovered in large sites like Ziyaret Tepe (Matney and Rainville 2005, 44, fig. 16) and Üçtepe (Köroğlu 1998, 39, 51, res. 9:1) but also in smaller sites like Hirbemerdon Tepe (Guarducci 2011, 114) and farther east at Zeviya Tevilki (Ökse et al. 2014, 137), demonstrating a circulation of this high-quality centralized production in the borderland's urban and small agricultural settlements.

Local Neo-Assyrian-Style Pottery

The local Neo-Assyrian-style pottery is the production that more than others embraces a full combination of the two source productions—the indigenous production and the local or imported Neo-Assyrian production—which merged at some point into a new trend that is abundant in the Neo-Assyrian sites of the Upper Tigris Borderland. This production features a variety of typical Neo-Assyrian-inspired shapes, fabrics, and surface treatments, along with local morphological and technological elements. The most evident characteristic is a marked presence of burnishing of the ceramic surface. This is a purely Anatolian feature, differing from the production of the Assyrian heartland (Matney et al. 2007, 46). The local Assyrian production is coarser in respect to the original Assyrian production of this period, mostly with a medium mineral temper. The ceramic hues range mainly within the Munsell pink, light brown, to reddish-brown color charts.

The surveys (Algaze et al. 1991; Parker 2001) and excavation projects in this area—such as Ziyaret Tepe (Matney et al. 2007, 2009), Hakemi Use (Tekin 2013), Kavušan Hoyuk (Kozbe 2008), Gre Dimse (Karg 2002), and Hirbemerdon Tepe (Guarducci 2011)—have broadly documented this production, its characteristics, and its contexts. Both Assyrian colonies and local communities produced and/or used this typology of pottery, since we find examples in both Assyrian and local contexts. For this reason it is difficult to establish in every site who produced/used what, since many indigenous sites were reutilized by the Assyrians, and vice versa, over the centuries. In other cases we have a coexistence of these two productions, as described above for the indigenous production, as well as cohabitation of foreign and local groups in the same settlement. Considering the similarities with the original Neo-Assyrian production and the fact that the MIA excavated sites of the Upper Tigris Borderland have yielded a higher number of Assyrian contexts than those of indigenous type, it is fair to think that this production was organized and used mainly by Assyrians. The exact Assyrian-local proportions of use and production, however, remain unknown.

THE UPPER TIGRIS BORDERLAND SOCIOECONOMIC LANDSCAPES

The main aspects of the Assyrian and local interaction and the relationship with the Upper Tigris Borderland territory were established in the previous section. In this section the interpretive models related to imperial expansion and exploitation systems are discussed. The combination of the interaction and model data sets allows the assessment of the Upper Tigris Borderland Middle and Late Assyrian socioeconomic landscapes according to land use and development strategies. By addressing these specific issues, we will gain a better understanding of the role and modus operandi of the Assyrians in the northern part of the empire as well as the local communities' involvement in and response to its foreign domination during the fluctuating periods of conflict and compromise.

The Middle Assyrian Period

The expansion strategy model of the Middle Assyrian Empire elaborated by Liverani (1988) for the Middle Euphrates appears to also be very suitable for the Upper Tigris Borderland. Liverani (1988) describes how the Assyrians tended to create fortified installations, garrisons in foreign lands that functioned as isolated lookouts. These garrisons were "islands of power" forming a "network-empire" (figure 3.3, top) that only subsequently would have been homogeneously connected to the rest of the dominion and fully occupied as a "territorial empire" (figure 3.3, bottom) (Liverani 1988, 86, 90–92; see also Parker 1997, 77; Brown 2013, 118–19). Postgate (1992, 255–56) added that this network was probably able to control the rest of the territory through local village authorities. This consideration is probably true for the Middle Euphrates but rather unlikely for the Upper Tigris, except perhaps during the NAP. The local communities, especially those north of the Tigris, certainly did not conform to the imperial system because of their mobile lifestyle, which was prevalent during this phase. Not even at the peak of its power was the Neo-Assyrian Empire able to have complete and constant control over the entire Upper Tigris region. In this perspective, what is lacking in the Assyrian presence in the Upper Tigris Borderland is chronological and territorial continuity, which is why many scholars have difficulty describing its dominance as an empire (see, e.g., Tenu 2009, 25–27; Liverani 2005). The territory was controlled and exploited sporadically and in a discontinuous manner through "islands of power." These "islands" had settlements at their cores, which acted as self-sufficient foci with a restricted range of organizational and administrative power.

During the MAP it is possible to regroup the Assyrian settlements in the Upper Tigris Borderland into three main types (figure 3.3, top). The first type (U) embraces large to medium-size residential and administrative settlements built, reconstructed (after Mitanni control), captured, or indirectly controlled by the Assyrians. A few examples are Ziyaret Tepe, Üçtepe, Pornak, and other minor sites (see Tenu 2009, 218). The second type (A) of Assyrian settlement we encounter in this area had a strong agricultural and administrative purpose. This group includes small settlements called *dunnu* (the Mitannian *dimtu*, "tower"), which helped organize and exploit large portions of arable land, like the site of Giricano. This is true especially if we consider the data from the

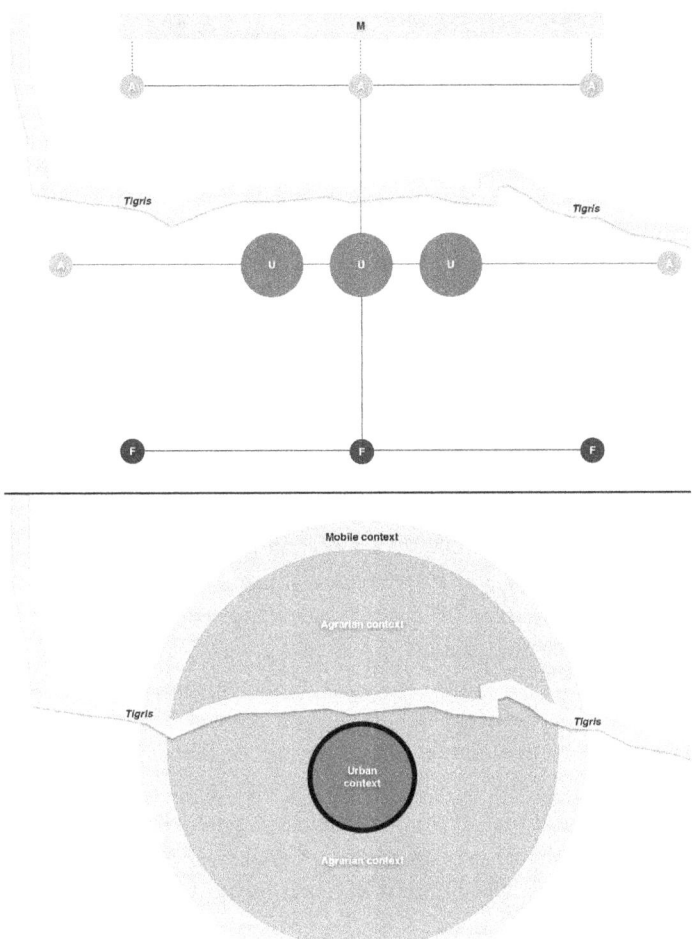

FIGURE 3.3. *The Middle Assyrian network-empire and its settlement types (top); the Neo-Assyrian territorial empire and its main contexts (bottom)*

most striking example of all, Tell Sabi Abyad in the Balikh Valley, a royal fortified type of *dunnu* for which Wiggermann (2000, 180–83) calculated 2,076 ha of cultivated land.

Regarding the Upper Tigris Borderland, Radner (2004, 71) is convinced that *dunnu* settlements regulated most of the agricultural land during this phase, calculating a total of over 6,100 ha of cultivated land distributed among Giricano (ca. 900 ha) and four other *dunnu* settlements just for the area around Ziyaret Tepe (Babahaki, 1,300 ha; Çayırlık Tepe, 1,200 ha; Çöltepe, 2,100 ha; Hakemi Use, 600 ha). This type of settlement was usually privately owned by families close to the king and was obtained as a grant or payment for their achievements. The farmers who worked in a *dunnu* were dependent employees of the *dunnu*-owning family (Szuchman 2009b, 536). The farmers must have also been of unfree status (*šiluḫlu*) or deported prisoners of war (Wiggermann 2000, 173; Fales 2014, 232), which in the MAP could have easily included members of the local communities. Wiggermann suggests that the involvement of indigenous people also included the "*ālajū*, free born dependent 'villagers' under *ilku* obligations originating in the tenure of a sustenance field" (2000, 174, citing Postgate 1971, 496–99, 1982). The *dunnu* was entrusted to an administrator who reported to the owner, who commonly had a residence in the city nearby (Wiggermann 2000, 173). Even if the *dunnu* estate may be defined as private, it had a political and public role—which is why we find official administrative texts within its contexts—and was one of the main instruments in gaining control over a certain area and making it productive at the same time. How and in what percentage the agricultural production reached the local capital and the heartland administration centers remains to be established (Fales 2014, 232).

The cuneiform tablets found at the site confirm that Giricano is a *dunnu* (Dunnu-sha-Uzibi, Radner 2004), although it does not appear to have any kind of external defensive structures, which instead are present during the Middle Bronze Age. This fact strengthens the hypothesis that there was extensive control over the area and hence a looser defensive system. Even though we could hypothesize a perishable type of defensive wall, it appears more plausible to interpret the site layout as focused on farming activities, to which the term *dunnu* mainly refers. Moreover, Giricano, along with neighboring sites, was probably benefiting from the protection offered by the presence of the nearby large Assyrian settlements like Tušhan and Tidu, which would explain why the site was not equipped with a defensive wall. Giricano appears to embody the statements by Koliński (2001, 109–10) and Wiggermann (2000, 174) in their studies of this type of settlement, in which they assert that *dunnu* settlements were exclusively agricultural enterprises. Schachner shares this view.[6]

This introduces our third type (F) of settlement: fortified sites that constituted a reinforced military network that garrisoned the frontier and supported the agricultural production and administrative system. As described by the Assyrian rulers in their annals, a good number of settlements along the Tigris were systematically fortified, rebuilt, or founded to create a more powerful defensive system. For example, Shalmaneser I reconstructed the fortifications of Sinabu and Tidu for this purpose (Radner and Schachner 2001, 758). We must bear in mind that the Upper Tigris Borderland was an area of strategic relevance, a station and a crossing point toward the north and the rich resources available in the northwest (see Radner 2006). In addition, I have mentioned that from the north, local communities, along with other external groups, frequently threatened this extensive border. For these reasons, adequate protection all along the upper course of the Tigris River was required. Nevertheless, this arrangement did not exclude the presence of local groups in the borderland and their interaction with the Assyrians, particularly beyond the natural border the Tigris River created. Szuchman (2009b, 537–38) underlines how the texts referring to the agricultural system, *dunnu* settlements in particular, in very few cases (7 of 138 documents) mention facts related to animal husbandry or pastoral products, which one would expect to be mentioned frequently in a rural production context. Therefore, he suggests that for the residents' meat, dairy, and textile needs, many products were acquired through trade with pastoral nomads, the larger segment of the local LBA-EIA population in the Upper Tigris Borderland, although we have no evidence to support this possibility. This symbiotic relationship is, in fact, strikingly similar to the one established in the Middle Euphrates in the Balikh valley between the Suteans, a pastoral nomad group, and the Assyrian community *dunnu* Tell Sabi Abyad (see Szuchman 2007, 100, 114; Wiggermann 2008, 380).

The Neo-Assyrian Period

After a hiatus recorded in the Early Iron Age stratigraphy, the late phase of Assyrian domination in northern Mesopotamia reached a different dimension compared with that of the earlier phase. In fact, the forerunning elements I have overviewed during the MAP were now fully developed and exploited, with more structured organization and territorial networking among the various elements of the borderland imperial system (see Düring, this volume, for further elements of continuity and disruption). A sense of the massive proportions and extension of the socioeconomic shift that took place in this region following the MAP is made available by the survey data collected, first by Algaze and his colleagues (1989; Algaze et al. 1991) and greatly expanded by Parker (2001, 2003). In fact, when comparing the data sets of the LBA-EIA with those of the MIA, inhabitation of the Upper Tigris River Valley increased by over 300 percent (figure 3.4). Parker (2003, 536) has also estimated that the total amount of occupied hectares increased from 32.54 in the EIA to 89.27 in the MIA. Moreover, several other areas of the empire underwent a

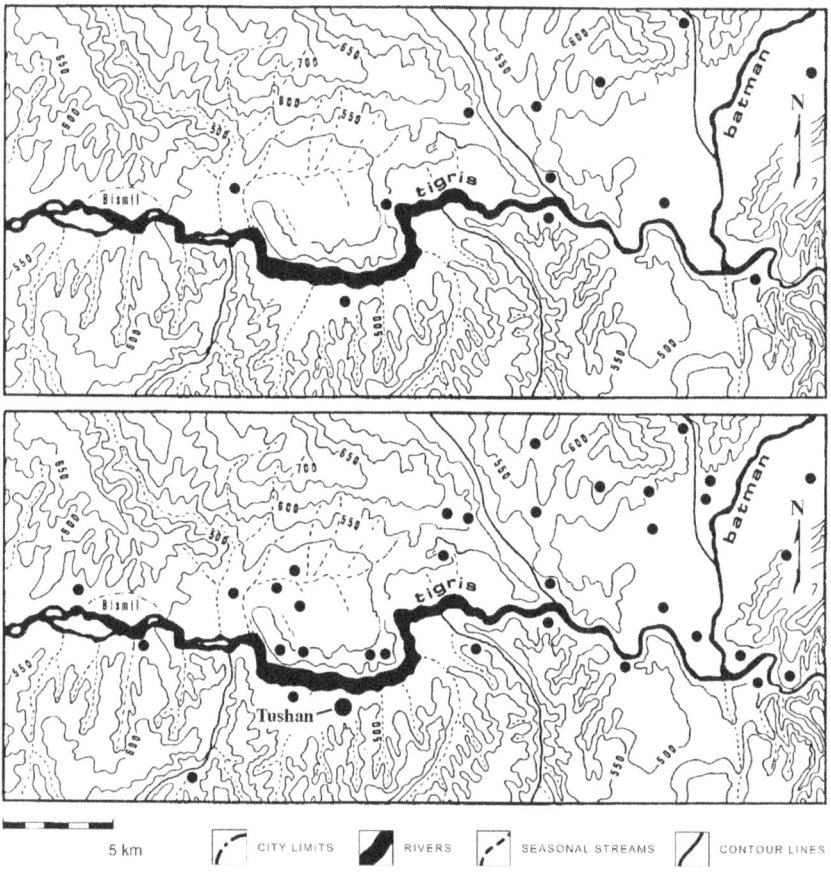

FIGURE 3.4. *Upper Tigris River Valley settlement increase from the Early Iron Age (top) to the Middle Iron Age (bottom) (after Parker 2003). Courtesy, Archaeological Institute of America and American Journal of Archaeology.*

similar rearrangement (figure 3.5), as recently underlined by Wilkinson and colleagues (2005), confirming the idea that in most cases this was standard procedure in gaining control over an area outside the heartland.

This new phase of Assyrian domination in the Upper Tigris Borderland began under the reign of Ashur-dan II in 934 BCE and was followed in 883 BCE by the aggressive policy of Ashurnasirpal II (883–859 BCE), who immediately dedicated his attention to this area by (re)founding the capital Tušhan and a number of strongholds along the Tigris (Parker 2003, 535). These first steps and the following centuries clearly show a strong colonial imprint in

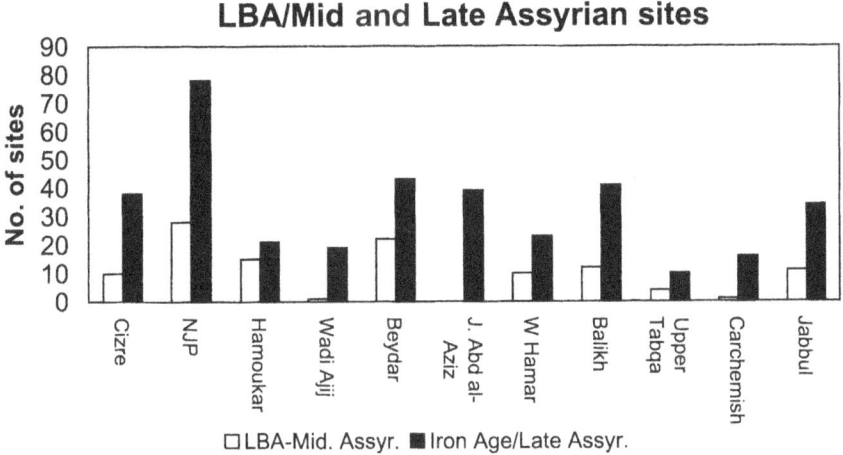

FIGURE 3.5. *Middle and Late Assyrian number of sites recorded from selected survey areas (after Wilkinson et al. 2005)*

the renewed approach to this area. The Assyrian state during this phase was determined to systematically exploit the Upper Tigris region as well as to consolidate its processes as a permanent mechanism of the imperial machine. A deep involvement with and intensive exploitation of the local and deported populations were crucial to achieve such results. According to Parker (2001, 82–83), the consolidation process started by reinforcing the forts and garrison towns of the frontier because of the growing threat exercised by northern groups, in particular the state of Urartu. The Assyrian network models recently proposed by Matney (2010) and Parker (2001), along with the more general models proposed by Postgate (1979) for the Assyrian rural economic structure and by Wilkinson and colleagues (2005) for the imperial landscape, help us understand the Upper Tigris Borderland socioeconomic structures and the engagement with local communities during this period.

The Upper Tigris Borderland during the NAP can be schematically organized into three main contexts connected to and in many cases overlapping one another: the urban context, the agrarian context, and the mobile context (figure 3.3, bottom). At the core of the Neo-Assyrian system of colonization, we find the three major urban sites of Tušhan, Sinabu, and Tidu. Tušhan is now the main administration center at 32 ha, the capital of the province, directly linked to the heartland and at the same time to the rest of the borderland rural settlement fabric. These centers represent the urban context and are the engines for the different rural areas of the borderland, including the processes of organization, coordination, product transformation, stocking, and redistribution with satellite sites as well as with Assyria proper.

The next context encompasses the main objective of this colonization: agricultural production. Therefore, the agrarian context implies the control of very large portions of land through a widespread network of hamlets, villages, and farmsteads[7]—such as Kavušan, Gre Dimse, and Hakemi Use—which finds its main representative in the *kapru* estate, a small agricultural holding linked to the area's urban center (Fales 1990, 102–5; Radner 2004, 118). The *kapru* network may be considered the evolution and at the same time the deconstruction of the Middle Assyrian *dunnu* system. In fact, we find continuity with the farmstead arrangement, the association of the original owner's name with the settlement, and a decentralization of the land-use organization in a plurality of sites connected with each other and with the area's main urban center.[8]

As Parker (2003, 536) noted, there are no middle-size settlements between the large urban centers and the small rural hamlets and villages, denoting an artificial settlement pattern created by the empire exclusively for colonization purposes. Moreover, this process of landscape infilling, as defined by Wilkinson and colleagues (2005, 25, 40–41), demanded a number of additional synergic elements, such as infrastructure, intermediate administration foci, and irrigation canals,[9] necessary to maintain such a complex apparatus. In contrast with the MAP, when the administrative work was mainly carried out by "Houses," the NAP featured a "civil service" (Postgate 1979, 202) because of the enlargement of the empire and therefore the necessity of a more structured sociopolitical organization—in other words, a provincial system with the heartland at its core.

The agrarian context appears to have been arranged in multiple types of communities. According to the available data and the Assyrian texts examined in the models mentioned above, it is possible to roughly subdivide the agrarian communities into two main types: the Assyrian-led communities and locally led communities. This subdivision takes into account those settlements that were in some way tied to the Assyrian system. Obviously, a multitude of local villages and hamlets, sedentary and semi-nomadic, were located outside the range of control of the empire; they were exclusively of indigenous character. The Assyrian-led communities represented the majority and were characterized by a strong presence of Assyrian personnel or by their direct control, along with a variable percentage of local and deported individuals. A predominance of Neo-Assyrian and/or local Neo-Assyrian-style pottery and Assyrian structures for production purposes characterizes this type of context, which in a few cases, as explored above, may be associated with indigenous types of pottery. Köroğlu (2015, 118–19) offers other data in this regard, considering the presence of cremation burials in Assyrian contexts, as in Ziyaret Tepe and Kavuşan, a marker of local semi-nomadic presence. This is an important element that confirms the co-presence of local and foreign groups in the same site.

Assyrian-led communities also incorporated a widespread type of arrangement—estates that belonged to state officials, who in many cases resided in the nearby cities (Matney 2010, 136). Slaves and prisoners of war were broadly employed in this type of estate (Postgate 1974, 231). The locally led communities were much lower in number and must be considered the result of negotiation between different degrees of indirect Assyrian control and the necessity to delegate power to local small or relatively distant communities. In these cases we can expect a preponderance of indigenous pottery and possibly a lower percentage of local Neo-Assyrian-style pottery, if any. Locally led communities were not necessarily autonomous, although it is highly possible that they were, as suggested by Postgate (1974, 230) and Wilkinson (2003, 133) in examining similar contexts. Neither can we exclude the presence of Assyrians in some form, even if they were not directly in charge. According to Matney's (2010, 140–44) model, the MIA strata of Giricano, possibly Talavaş Tepe, and Salat Tepe, appear to be good examples of this category because of the absence of Neo-Assyrian pottery and architecture and the proximity to large urban centers.

These two types of communities, along with those of the urban context, interacted with those of our third and last context, the mobile context (i.e., nomads and semi-nomads). As I have discussed elsewhere (Guarducci 2014), the archaeological record has demonstrated that pastoral nomad groups have been present in the area for a long time and still exist today (see Ur and Hammer 2009; Thevenin 2011). An indefinite percentage of these groups should probably be understood as agro-pastoralists, since their semi-nomadic behavior was primarily tied to basic forms of seasonal agricultural practices, as the archaeological record of Kenan Tepe and Boztepe seems to indicate (Parker 2006, 89). In other cases the mobile groups merged or became involved with the sedentary population for these and other production purposes in which they were skilled, for example, metalworking activities (Yakar 1985, 26). We must remember that the preceding Early Iron Age saw a newly increased presence of mobile groups in southeastern Anatolia who also came to encamp on the Upper Tigris with their flocks, especially for the winter period. While the majority of EIA local communities were semi-nomadic, a lower but considerable percentage of the Upper Tigris population still adopted this kind of lifestyle during the MIA, or Neo Assyrian Period (Köroğlu 2015, 117–19). Local sedentary communities were also rare, especially during the initial phase of the NAP, and for this reason scholars speak about a resettling process during this phase.[10] A sedentary and local presence is confirmed by the continuity of local material culture characteristics (Matney 2011, 453), as well as by the Assyrian texts. Based on the annals of Tukulti-Ninurta II (890–884 BCE) and Ashurnasirpal II, Postgate (1974, 237) concludes that "northern Mesopotamia was entirely deserted, except for nomadic tribes and enclaves of settlements along the rivers." This is probably an overstatement, but it is a fact that we have very little knowledge about the *local* sedentary contexts of the Upper Tigris Borderland during the Early and Middle Iron Ages.

It was during the second phase of the MIA, in which the imperial system was fully developed, that the pastoral nomad communities greatly decreased in number, for a few simple reasons. First, the socioeconomic landscape had been steered toward sedentary behavior, leading to the abandonment of that kind of lifestyle and means of subsistence. Second, the massive increase in agricultural land left very little space for the mobile communities' flocks, which were considered a threat to the crops. Lastly, despite interaction with the empire, nomadic communities were probably not welcome in large numbers in the Upper Tigris. This situation appears to be confirmed by the abundant presence of MIA Grooved pottery and architecture in contexts outside and around the Upper Tigris Borderland, more specifically within the Upper Euphrates and the Van Basin. A large part of the communities probably migrated to nearby areas outside the control of the Assyrians and in some cases settled permanently or was absorbed by local polities. In fact, we have a high percentage of Grooved pottery within Urartian contexts, especially tombs (see Köroğlu and Konyar 2008).

The mobile context did not disappear, however, and was certainly involved in the Upper Tigris local and imperial landscape. The presence of local communities and interaction with Assyrians are confirmed by textual and archaeological evidence (Matney et al. 2009, 54; Matney 2010, 137), which comprised a percentage of mobile groups—as in the earlier period—becauseof the important role they played in the area's economic development and networking. The mobile context was a key piece of the borderland imperial system. As highlighted by the scholarly models, mobile groups connected and interacted with the urban and agrarian contexts on a large scale. A specific range of products was implemented or possibly entirely supplied in certain time frames by local pastoral nomads, as happened during the MAP (Szuchman 2009b, 538).

FINAL CONSIDERATIONS

The Assyrian strategy of expansion and exploitation of the Upper Tigris Borderland in relation to local communities is marked by two distinct approaches, one of conflict and one of compromise. Roughly, we can consider the MAP and the beginning of the NAP to be a phase dominated by military conflicts because of the imperial expansion and the suppression of local power structures. The rest of the NAP is a phase of strategic compromise as a result of the urgency of organizing on a broad scale the various components of the imperial apparatus, also through the involvement of local communities.

During the MAP, the empire was focused on the northwest and the southeast of Mesopotamia. Surely the wealth of resources had always attracted Aššur to Anatolia ever since the period of its colonies in Cappadocia, as well as to the Upper Tigris region and its environs. Nevertheless, during the LBA, the aggressiveness of the Nairi lands' local communities, the limited extension of the Middle Assyrian Empire, the lack of manpower, and the encumbrance of other strong polities in northern Mesopotamia—especially Hatti and Mitanni—did not facilitate a territorially homogeneous domination but took the shape of a discontinuous and patchy structure. This discontinuous layout is described by Liverani (1988) as formed by "islands of power" that were much easier to control but at the same time almost devoid of any kind of backup or infrastructural system on which to rely. Consequently, the economic system was also rather weak without a large, organized urban center coordinating the smaller settlements and an extensive agricultural system.

It is no coincidence that the *dunnu* farmsteads—the settlement par excellence for this period—are in many cases defined as rural fortified estates, a combination of defensive and agricultural purposes in a single settlement, which was the result of the lack of a strong network or territorial domination. This is one of the major periods of conflict for the empire, which was struggling mightily to maintain its achievements and the high standards demanded by the heartland. Engagement with the local communities of the Upper Tigris Borderland was kept at its minimum. The local involvement in the production areas and administration sites must have been rather limited except for a discontinuous relationship with some of the pastoral nomads for trade purposes, as suggested by Szuchman (2009a). Texts and Assyrian reliefs belonging to this period report harsh repression of people of the Nairi lands. The fortification process of the settlements along the Assyrian northern *limes*, which followed approximately the upper course of the Tigris River, confirms this determination and the sense of insecurity aroused by the people from the north. When the large political organizations collapsed at the end of the Bronze Age and the pressure of the new tribal groups started to increase considerably, Assyria had to gradually contract its boundaries until the complete abandonment of the Upper Tigris Borderland. During this particular phase, the Early Iron Age, nomadic groups increased their presence in the area and merged with the remnants of the population of the Mitanni state. In the following period some of these same groups eventually settled and possibly evolved into organized polities, such as Šubria and Urartu, or into new national states based on their tribal origins, such as the Aramaean state of Bīt-Zamāni.

The subsequent period opened with another series of severe conflicts aimed at bringing the yoke of Aššur definitively over the Upper Tigris Borderland. The new enemies of the empire were coming from further north, especially from Urartu, which became the largest local political organization. Once it reestablished its predominance, the Neo-Assyrian Empire revolutionized its mechanics by systematically reorganizing its socioeconomic network to optimize its colonization process. The settlement of the Upper Tigris Borderland increased by over 300 percent compared with the Early Iron Age. Agricultural production was at the core of imperial priorities, demanding a substantial amount of manpower and resources. To fuel this massive machine, which grew larger and more structured every year through the incorporation of other regions, Assyrian rulers started local and international mass deportations to the Upper Tigris and other areas. With this newly restored order and highly productive arable land, the Neo-Assyrian Empire reached its apex, also thanks to the broad coercive but voluntary involvement of local elites of the sedentary and mobile communities. Part of these communities could have been left autonomous or under looser control, while the majority was most likely employed or enslaved within the new administrative framework embodied by the provincial system. More specifically, the interaction between urban centers and the rural landscape, ideally developed in the extensive *kapru* system, was both assisted by and networked in a symbiotic relationship by the pastoral nomad communities—in particular with their labor, pastoral products, trade enhancement, and metalworking skills.

As stated at the beginning of this chapter, it is impossible to neatly fit the Middle and Late Periods of the Assyrian Empire into a specific approach. The Assyrians of the Upper Tigris Borderland surely encountered greater difficulties there than in other areas of the empire. The episodes of conflict during the MAP were debilitating and impoverished the local population. The Neo-Assyrian Empire, once it reestablished its predominance, activated numerous solutions of compromise and integration, similar to those displayed by the Roman Empire in its provinces (Mann 1986, 250–59). The commodities, agricultural potential, strategic location, and functional role of this region as a frontier led a succession of Assyrian rulers to invest heavily in the area and to finally reach an equilibrium between the two sides of the border—in several cases adopting the use of force, but not exclusively. As I briefly explored above, the interaction between the two sides in terms of compromise was embodied by or can be observed through six main aspects: (1) acceptance of indirect control by the Assyrians to preserve a percentage of autonomy and identity (e.g., the Aramaeans and other smaller polities); (2) the signing of alliances or treaties between the local and Assyrian parties in place of military actions by the latter (e.g., Bīt-Zamāni); (3) the merging of local and Assyrian cults (e.g., "Source of the Tigris"); (4) authorization of local independence or semi-independence tied to agricultural production through private contracts, tribute payments, and the like; (5) the strong mutual influence and coexistence within the same contexts of local and Assyrian pottery as the result of an apparently unrestrained or moderately restrained interaction and cooperation; and (6) the symbiosis established between the sedentary Assyrian communities with the nomadic or semi-nomadic communities (i.e., agricultural products exchanged for pastoral and textile products, and so on).

These signs of compromise, also reflected in the correspondence texts, testify to the renovated approach of the empire toward local communities in negotiating a profitable balance by yielding a few privileges and a degree of autonomy in exchange for full territorial control. The participation of the local population was of paramount importance to the empire in exploiting this area fully and rapidly to maximize the effectiveness and growth of the imperial machine without a constant status of expensive and unproductive warfare. The effectiveness of this arrangement allowed the control of the entire borderland and the territories beyond, leading to the creation of new provinces (Uppumu and Kullimeri) and the full annexation of the area to the empire.

NOTES

1. Including the Batman, Garzan, Bitlis, and Bohtan River Valleys.

2. Between the thirteenth and ninth centuries BCE, the Assyrians designated by the Nairi toponym a very large area that encompassed the western part of the Urmia Basin in the southeast, probably the Black Sea or the Çoroh Valley in the northwest and the Tur Abdin in the southwest. Thus, the southern area of Nairi included the Upper Tigris River Valley (Salvini 1967, 23).

3. The "kings" mentioned in the texts were probably tribal chieftains of aristocratic tradition (Salvini 1967, 21), controlling little more than clusters of villages (Burney 1966, 60).

4. The primary meaning of the Sumerian term *kur* is "mountain." In fact, as Kramer (1972, 110) has underlined, the cuneiform sign used to write this word is a pictograph representing a mountain. Penglase (1994, 193) points out that in Mesopotamia, the mountain or mountains are associated with the netherworld in iconography and myth. For example, he mentions the fact that Inanna/Ishtar and Utu/Šamaš are often represented as seals on top of a mountain or mountains in relation to their voyage in the underworld. Moreover, in the text of the poem "Inanna's Descent to the Netherworld," the name used for netherworld is indeed *kur*.

5. Although scholars, including the author, tend to follow the EIA and MIA pottery distinction in the Upper Tigris based on empirical information (i.e. *comparanda*, context, strata, and techno-morphological differences), currently we do not have enough evidence to make similar distinctions for most of the sites. Multiple and reliable radiocarbon datings are required to properly frame the chronology of the pottery production of these two cultural phases because of the continuity of the main morphological characteristics.

6. Personal communication, April 16, 2017. Schachner is convinced that Giricano did not have a fortification wall or other defensive systems. This conclusion appears to be correct if we observe the extension and location of the excavated areas and the steepness of the mound. The idea of a fortified *dunnu*, continues Schachner, generates from the first excavated example, Tell Sabi Abyad, which was a royal *dunnu*.

7. For similar patterns in the Syrian Jazirah, see Morandi Bonacossi (2000); Wilkinson et al. (2005, 38).

8. For other types of facilities, see Fales (1990); Postgate (1979).

9. Because it receives more generous rainfall, the Upper Tigris Borderland does not feature massive hydraulic solutions like those erected by Sennacherib in the Nineveh region, but we can easily imagine a multitude of smaller and temporary devices like those adopted by the pastoral nomads (see Hammer 2014) and the people of Urartu up north (see Burney 1972; Belli 1997). See also Fales (1990, 131–32); Wilkinson (2003, 45–52, 71–99).

10. Sargon II defines the northern regions as "desolate steppe" in which he created furrows "in a barren land that had not known the plough" (Radner 2000, 238).

WORKS CITED

Algaze, Guillermo. 1989. "A New Frontier: First Results of the Tigris-Euphrates Archaeological Reconnaissance Project, 1988." *JNES* 48 (4): 241–81.

Algaze, Guillermo, Ray Breuninger, Chris Lightfoot, and Michael Rosenberg. 1991. "The Tigris-Euphrates Archaeological Reconnaissance Project: A Preliminary Report of the 1989–1990 Seasons." *Anatolica* 17: 175–240.

Bartl, Karin. 2001. "Eastern Anatolia in the Early Iron Age." In *Migration und Kulturtransfer: Der Wandel vorder- und zentralasiatischer Kulturen im Umbruch vom 2, zum 1: vorchristlichen Jahrtausend*, ed. Ricardo Eichmann and Hermann Parzinger, 383–410. Bonn: Habelt.

Belli, Oktay. 1997. "Dams, Reservoirs, and Irrigation Channels of the Van Plain in the Period of the Urartian Kingdom." *AnSt* 49: 11–26.

Belli, Oktay, and Erkan Konyar. 2003. *Early Iron Age Fortresses and Necropolises in East Anatolia*. Istanbul: Arkeoloji Sanat Yayınlari.

Black, A. Jeremy, Anthony Green, and Tessa Rickards. 1992. *Gods, Demons, and Symbols of Ancient Mesopotamia: An Illustrated Dictionary*. Austin: University of Texas Press.

Borger, Riekele. 1956. *Die Inschriften Asarhaddons Königs von Assyrien, Graz: E.* Osnabrück, Germany: Weidner.

Brown, Brian. 2013. "The Structure and Decline of the Middle Assyrian State: The Role of Autonomous and Nonstate Actors." *JCS* 65: 97–126.

Burney, Charles. 1966. "A First Season of Excavations at the Urartian Citadel of Kayıldere." *AnSt* 16: 55–63.

Burney, Charles. 1972. "Urartian Irrigation Works." *AnSt* 22: 179–86.

Chahin, Mack. 2001. *The Kingdom of Armenia*. London: Routledge.

Fales, Frederick M. 1990. "The Rural Landscape of the Neo-Assyrian Empire: A Survey." *SAAB* 4 (2): 81–142.

Fales, Frederick M. 2014. "Hamlets and Farmsteads in the Balīḫ River Valley: The Middle Assyrian and the Neo-Assyrian Evidence." In *Settlement Dynamics and Human Landscape Interaction in the Dry Steppe of Syria*, ed. Daniele Bonacossi Morandi, 227–41. Wiesbaden: Harrassowitz.

Finkelstein, Jacob J. 1953. "Cuneiform Texts from Tell Billa." *JCS* 7: 111–76.

Grayson, Albert K. 1987. *Assyrian Rulers of the Third and Second Millennia BC (to 1115 BC)*. Toronto: University of Toronto Press.

Grayson, Albert K. 1991. *Assyrian Rulers of the Early First Millennium BC I (1114–859 BC)*. Toronto: University of Toronto Press. https://doi.org/10.3138/9781442671089.

Guarducci, Guido. 2011. *Facing an Empire: Hirbemerdon Tepe and the Upper Tigris Region during the Early Iron Age and Neo-Assyrian Period*. Piscataway, NJ: Gorgias.

Guarducci, Guido. 2014. "Linking the Mountains to the Plains: The Material Culture and Lifestyle of the Local Communities in Southeastern Anatolia during the Iron Age." In *Proceedings of the 8th ICAANE*, vol. 1: *30 April–4 May 2012, University of Warsaw*, ed. Piotr Bieliński, Michał Gawlikowski, Rafał Koliński, Dorota Ławecka, Arkadiusz Sołtysiak, and Zuzanna Wygnańska, 61–77. Wiesbaden: Harrassowitz.

Hammer, Emily L. 2014. "Local Landscape Organization of Mobile Pastoralists in Southeastern Turkey." *JAA* 35: 269–88.

Harmanşah, Ömür. 2007. "Source of the Tigris: Event, Place, and Performance in the Assyrian Landscapes of the Early Iron Age." *AD* 14 (2): 179–204.

Karg, Norbert. 2002. "Sounding at Gre Dimse 2000." In *Salvage Project of the Archaeological Heritage of the Ilisu and Carchemish Dam Reservoirs: Activities in 2000*, ed. Nurman Tuna, Jean Öztürk, and Jâle Velibeyoğlu, 723–37. Ankara: Middle East Technical University.

Kessler, Karlheinz. 1995. "Šubria, Urartu, and Aššur: Topographical Questions around the Tigris Sources." In *Neo-Assyrian Geography*, ed. Mario Liverani, 55–67. Rome: Università di Roma La Sapienza.

Koliński, Rafal. 2001. *Mesopotamian Dimātu of the Second Millennium BC*. Oxford: Archaeopress.

Köroğlu, Kemalettin. 1998. *Üçtepe I: Yeni Kazı ve Yüzey Bulguları Işığında Diyarbakır/Üçtepe ve Çevresinin Yeni Assur Dönemi Tarihi Coğrafyası*. Ankara: Türk Tarih Kurumu.

Köroğlu, Kemalettin. 2015. "Conflict and Interaction in the Iron Age: The Origins of Urartian-Assyrian Relations." *EJA* 18 (1): 111–27. https://doi.org/10.1179/1461957114Y.0000000080.

Köroğlu, Kemalettin, and Erkan Konyar. 2008. "Comments on the Early/Middle Iron Age Chronology of Lake Van Basin." *ANES* 45: 123–46.

Kozbe, Gulriz. 2008. "The Transition from Late Bronze Age to Early Iron Age in the Upper Tigris Region, Southeastern Anatolia: Identifying Changes in Pottery." In *Ceramics in Transitions: Chalcolithic through Iron Age in the Highlands of the Southern Caucasus and Anatolia*, ed. Karen S. Rubinson and Antonio Sagona, 291–322. Leuven, Belgium: Peeters.

Kramer, Samuel N. 1972. *Sumerian Mythology: A Study of Spiritual and Literary Achievement in the Third Millennium BC*, rev. ed. Philadelphia: University of Pennsylvania Press.

Kühn, Dagmar. 2014. "II: Society, Institutions, Law, and Economy." In *The Aramaeans in Ancient Syria*, ed. Herbert Niehr, 37–70. Leiden: University of Tübingen. https://doi.org/10.1163/9789004229433_004.

Lanfranchi, Giovanni B., and Simo Parpola. 1990. *The Correspondence of Sargon II, Part II: Letters from the Northern and Northeastern Provinces*. Helsinki: Helsinki University Press.

Liverani, Mario. 1988. "The Growth of the Assyrian Empire in the Habur/Middle Euphrates Area: A New Paradigm." *SAAB* 2 (2): 81–98.

Liverani, Mario. 2005. "Imperialism." In *Archaeologies of the Middle East: Critical Perspectives*, ed. Susan Pollock and Reinherd Bernbeck, 223–43. Oxford: Blackwell.

MacGinnis, John D.A. 2012. "Evidence for a Peripheral Language in a Neo-Assyrian Tablet from the Governor's Palace in Tušhan." *JNES* 71 (1): 13–20.

Mann, Michael. 1986. *The Sources of Social Power: A History of Power from the Beginning to AD 1760*, vol. 1. Cambridge: Cambridge University Press.

Matney, Timothy. 1998. "The First Season of Excavation at Ziyaret Tepe in the Diyarbakır Province: Preliminary Report." *Anatolica* 24: 7–30. https://doi.org/10.2143/ANA.24.0.2015475.

Matney, Timothy. 2010. "Material Culture and Identity: Assyrians, Aramaeans, and the Indigenous Peoples of Iron Age Southeastern Anatolia." In *Agency and Identity in the Ancient Near East*, ed. Sharon R. Steadman and Jennifer C. Ross, 129–47. London: Equinox.

Matney, Timothy. 2011. "The Iron Age of Southeastern Anatolia." In *The Oxford Handbook of Ancient Anatolia (10000–323 BCE)*, ed. Sharon R. Steadman and Gregory McMahon, 443–63. Oxford: Oxford University Press.

Matney, Timothy, Tina Greenfield, Britt Hartenberger, Azer Keskin, Kamalettin Köroğlu, John MacGinnis, Willis M. Monroe, Lynn Rainville, Mary Shepperson, Tasha Vorderstrasse et al. 2009. "Excavation at Ziyaret Tepe 2007–2008." *Anatolica* 35: 37–84. https://doi.org/10.2143/ANA.35.0.2038072.

Matney, Timothy, and Lynn Rainville. 2005. "Archaeological Investigations at Ziyaret Tepe, 2003–2004." *Anatolica* 31: 19–68. https://doi.org/10.2143/ANA.31.0.2011751.

Matney, Timothy, Lynn Rainville, Kamalettin Köroğlu, Azer Keskin, Tasha Vorderstrasse, Nursen Özkul Fındık, and Ann Donkin. 2007. "Report on Excavations at Ziyaret Tepe, 2006 Season." *Anatolica* 33: 23–74. https://doi.org/10.2143/ANA.33.0.2021754.

Morandi Bonacossi, Daniele. 2000. "The Syrian Jezireh in the Late Assyrian Period: A View from the Countryside." In *Essays on Syria in the Iron Age*, ed. Guy Bunnens, 349–96. Leuven, Belgium: Peeters.

Müller, Uwe. 2005. "Norşun Tepe and Lidar Höyük, Two Examples for Cultural Change during the Early Iron Age." In *Anatolian Iron Ages 5, Proceedings of the Fifth Anatolian Iron Ages Colloquium Held at Van, 6–10 August 2001*, ed. Altan Çilingiroğlu and Gareth Darbyshire, 107–14. Ankara: British Institute.

Ökse, Tuba A. 1988. *Mitteleisenzeitliche Keramik Zentral-Ostanatoliens: Mit dem Schwerpunkt Karakaya-Stauseegebiet am Euphrat*. Berlin: Reimer.

Ökse, Tuba A., Nihat Erdoğan, Ahmet Görmüş, and Erkan Atay. 2014. *Salvage Project of the Construction Area of the Ilısu Dam I: The Iron Age*. Mardin, Turkey: Mardin Müze Müdürlüğü.

Parker, Bradley J. 1997. "Garrisoning the Empire: Aspects of the Construction and Maintenance of Forts on the Assyrian Frontier." *Iraq* 59: 77–87. https://doi.org/10.1017/S0021088900003363.

Parker, Bradley J. 2001. *The Mechanics of Empire: The Northern Frontier of Assyria as a Case Study in Imperial Dynamics*. Helsinki: Neo-Assyrian Text Corpus Project.

Parker, Bradley J. 2003. "Archaeological Manifestations of Empire: Assyria's Imprint on Southeastern Anatolia." *AJA* 107 (4): 525–57. https://doi.org/10.3764/aja.107.4.525.

Parker, Bradley J. 2006. "Toward an Understanding of Borderland Processes." *American Antiquity* 71 (1): 77–100. https://doi.org/10.2307/40035322.

Parker, Bradley J., Andrew Creekmore, and Charles Easton. 2001. "The Upper Tigris Archaeological Research Project (UTARP) Excavations and Survey at Boztepe and Intensive Survey at Talavaş Tepe, 1999: A Preliminary Report." In *Salvage Project of the Archaeological Heritage of the Ilısu and Carchemish Dam Reservoirs: Activities in 1999*, ed. Numan Tuna, Jean Öztürk, and Jean Velibeyoğlu, 565–91. Ankara: Middle Eastern Technical University.

Penglase, Charles. 1994. *Greek Myths and Mesopotamia: Parallels and Influence in the Homeric Hymns and Hesiod*. New York: Routledge. https://doi.org/10.4324/9780203443910.

Porter, Ann. 2012. *Mobile Pastoralism and the Formation of Near Eastern Civilizations: Weaving Together Society*. Cambridge: Cambridge University Press. https://doi.org/10.1017/CBO9780511895012.

Postgate, Nicholas J. 1971. "Land Tenure in the Middle Assyrian Period: A Reconstruction." *BSOAS* 34 (3): 496–520. https://doi.org/10.1017/S0041977X00128514.

Postgate, Nicholas J. 1974. "Some Remarks on Conditions in the Assyrian Countryside." *JSEHO* 17: 225–43.

Postgate, Nicholas J. 1979. "The Economic Structure of the Assyrian Empire." In *Power and Propaganda: A Symposium on Ancient Empires*, ed. Mogens T. Larsen, 193–221. Copenhagen: Akademisk Forlag.

Postgate, Nicholas J. 1982. "Ilku and Land Tenure in the Middle Assyrian Kingdom: A Second Attempt." In *Societies and Languages of the Ancient Near East: Studies in Honour of I. M. Diakonoff*, ed. Muhammad A. Dandameyev, Ilya Gershevitch, Horst Klengel, Géza Komoroczy, and Mogens T. Larsen, 304–13. Warminster, UK: Aris and Phillips.

Postgate, Nicholas J. 1992. "The Land of Assur and the Yoke of Assur." *WA* 23 (3): 247–63.

Pulhan, Gül, and Stewart R. Blaylock. 2013. "New Excavations at the Late Bronze Age and Iron Age Site of Gre Amer on the Garzan River, Batman Province." In *Across the Border: Late Bronze-Iron Age Relations between Syria and Anatolia*, ed. Aslihan Yener, 393–419. Leuven, Belgium: Peeters.

Radner, Karen. 2000. "How Did the Neo-Assyrian King Perceive His Land and Its Resources?" In *Rainfall and Agriculture in Northern Mesopotamia*, ed. Remko M. Jas, 233–45. Leiden: Nederlands Instituut voor het Nabije Oosten.

Radner, Karen. 2004. *Das mittelassyrische Tontafelarchiv von Giricano/Dunnu-sha-Uzibi.* Turnhout, Belgium: Brepols.

Radner, Karen. 2006. "How to Reach the Upper Tigris: The Route through the Tur Abdin." *SAAB* 15: 273–305.

Radner, Karen. 2012. "Between a Rock and a Hard Place: Musasir, Kumme, Ukku, and Šubria—The Buffer States between Assyria and Urartu." In *Biainili-Urartu: The Proceedings of the Symposium Held in Munich, 12–14 October 2007*, ed. Stephan Kroll, Claudia Gruber, Ursula Hellwag, Michael Roaf, and Paul Zimansky, 243–64. Leuven, Belgium: Peeters.

Radner, Karen, and Andreas Schachner. 2001. "From Tušhan to Amēdi: Topographical Questions Concerning the Upper Tigris Region in the Assyrian Period." In *Salvage Project of the Archaeological Heritage of the Ilisu and Carchemish Dam Reservoirs: Activities in 1999*, ed. Nurman Tuna, Jean Öztürk, and Jâle Velibeyoğlu, 729–76. Ankara: Middle Eastern Technical University.

Sagona, Antonio. 2012. "Some Remarks on the Iron Age of Eastern Anatolia." In *Anatolian Iron Ages 7: The Proceedings of the Seventh Anatolian Iron Ages Colloquium Held at Edirne, 19–24 April 2010*, ed. Altan Çilingiroğlu and Antonio Sagona, 253–67. Leuven, Belgium: Peeters.

Salvini, Mirio. 1967. *Nairi e Ur(u)atri: Contributo alla Storia della Formazione del Regno di Urartu.* Rome: Edizioni dell'Ateneo.

Schachner, Andreas. 2009. *Assyriens Könige an Einer der Quellen des Tigris, Archäologische Forschungen im Höhlensystem von Birkleyn und am sogenannten Tigris-Tunnel.* Tübingen, Germany: Wismut Verlag.

Sevin, Veli. 1989. *Excavations at Üçtepe.* Istanbul: Arkeoloji ve Sanat Yayınları.

Szuchman, Jeffrey. 2007. *Prelude to Empire: Middle Assyrian Hanigalbat and the Rise of the Aramaeans.* Los Angeles: University of California Press.

Szuchman, Jeffrey. 2009a. "Bit Zamani and Assyria." *Syria* 86 (86): 55–65. https://doi.org/10.4000/syria.511.

Szuchman, Jeffrey. 2009b. "Revisiting Hanigalbat: Settlement in the Western Provinces of the Middle Assyrian Kingdom." *SCCNH* 18: 531–44.

Tadmor, Hayim. 1994. *The Inscriptions of Tiglath-Pileser III, King of Assyria.* Jerusalem: Israel Academy of Sciences and Humanities.

Tekin, Halil. 2004. "Preliminary Results of the 2001 Excavations at Hakemi Use." In *Salvage Project of the Archaeological Heritage of the Ilısu and Carchemish Dam Reservoirs: Activities in 2001*, ed. Numan Tuna, Jean Greenhalgh, and Jâle Velibeyoğlu, 450–62. Ankara: Middle Eastern Technical University.

Tekin, Halil. 2011. "Preliminary Results of the 2002 Excavations at Hakemi Use." In *Salvage Project of the Arcaheological Heritage of the Ilısu and Carchemish Dam

Reservoirs: Activities in 2002, vol. 2, ed. Numan Tuna and Owen Doonan, 571–621. Ankara: Middle Eastern Technical University.

Tekin, Halil. 2013. "Hakemi Use Excavations." In *The Ilısu Dam and HEP Project Excavations Season 2004–2008*, 103–34. Diyarbakir, Turkey: Kultur ve Turizm Bakanligi Yayinlari.

Tenu, Aline. 2009. *L'Expansion Medio-assyrienne Approche Archéologique*. Oxford: Archaeopress.

Thevenin, Michael. 2011. "Kurdish Transhumance: Pastoral Practices in Southeast Turkey." *Pastoralism: Research, Policy, and Practice* 1 (1): 23. https://doi.org/10.1186/2041-7136-1-23.

Ur, Jason A., and Emily L. Hammer. 2009. "Pastoral Nomads of the Second and Third Millennia AD on the Upper Tigris River, Turkey: Archaeological Evidence from the Hirbemerdon Tepe Survey." *JFA* 34 (1): 37–56. https://doi.org/10.1179/009346909791071087.

Van De Mieroop, Marc. 2004. *A History of the Ancient Near East ca. 3000–323 BC*. Oxford: Blackwell.

White, Richard. 1991. *The Middle Ground: Indians, Empires, and Republics in the Great Lakes Region, 1650–1815*. Cambridge: Cambridge University Press. https://doi.org/10.1017/CBO9780511584671.

Wiggermann, Franciscus A.M. 2000. "Agriculture in the Northern Balikh Valley: The Case of Middle Assyrian Tell Sabi Abyad." In *Rainfall and Agriculture in Northern Mesopotamia*, ed. Remko M. Jas, 171–231. Leiden: Nederlands Instituut voor het Nabije Oosten.

Wiggermann, Franciscus A.M. 2008. "Cuneiform Texts from Tell Sabi Abyad Related to Pottery." In *The Pots and Potters of Assyria: Technology and Organisation of Production, Ceramic Sequence, and Vessel Function at Late Bronze Age Tell Sabi Abyad, Syria*, ed. Kim Duistermaat, 377–82. Leiden: Brepols.

Wilkinson, Tony J. 2003. *Archaeological Landscapes of the Near East*. Tucson: University of Arizona Press.

Wilkinson, Tony J., Jason A. Ur, Eleanor Wilkinson, and Mark Altaweel. 2005. "Landscape and Settlement in the Neo-Assyrian Empire." *BASOR* 340: 23–56.

Wisti Lassen, Agnete. 2010. "Wool Trade in Old Assyrian Anatolia." *JEOL* 42: 159–79.

Yakar, Jak. 1985. "Regional and Local Schools of Metalwork in Early Bronze Age Anatolia: Part II." *AnSt* 35: 25–38.

4

The Southern Levant under the Neo-Assyrian Empire

A Comparative Perspective

Avraham Faust
(Bar-Ilan University)

Following a little over a decade of Assyrian aggression (by Tiglath-pileser III, Shalmaneser V, and Sargon II), by 720 BCE most of the southern Levant had been conquered by the empire. The northern part of the region, including the territories of the kingdom of Israel and of the different Aramean states, was annexed by Assyria. The more southern kingdoms of Judah, Ammon, Moab, Edom, and the Philistine cities (as well as Phoenicia) were subordinated to Assyria but maintained some autonomy. Subsequent military campaigns to the region did not significantly alter this situation. The territories of the Aramean kingdoms and the kingdom of Israel were divided between local provinces—for example, Megiddo, Samaria, and the Gilead—and an Assyrian governor ruled each province. In the south, by contrast, local dynasties paid heavy tribute to Assyria but continued to rule (and so was the situation in Phoenicia).

The impact of the Neo-Assyrian Empire on the areas it conquered and dominated was substantial and is evidenced in practically every aspect of life. Many studies have therefore been devoted to this period, and various attempts have been made to reconstruct the empire's policies in its provinces and toward its vassals. Although studies of Assyrian hegemony and influence were conducted in various regions of the empire, some features make the southern Levant an extremely appropriate case study. First, this is a relatively small region, incorporating different geographical and ecological subregions, some with significant geopolitical importance

DOI: 10.5876/9781607328230.c004

and some remote and insignificant. In addition, the region includes both provinces—regions annexed by Assyria and directly controlled by it—and client kingdoms that maintained partial autonomy. Finally, the southern Levant is probably the most studied region in the world in terms of the number of excavations and surveys per area (mainly in Cisjordan). It is therefore the aim of this chapter to use the large archaeological data sets available to reconstruct the settlement, demography, and economic reality in the region during the time of Neo-Assyrian rule by comparing the various sub-regions according to their geographical and political significance in relation to each other and to Assyria—for example, client states versus provinces.

To identify geographical patterns and understand the demographic and economic systems in their entirety, the chapter will review the archaeological evidence in each sub-region, creating a detailed settlement picture of the Neo-Assyrian Period (late eighth–seventh centuries, hereafter referred to as the seventh century BCE). This will enable us to identify similarities and differences between sub-regions and political units and analyze them according to their geographical potential and political status. To have a better appreciation of the demographic and economic patterns identified, the data will also be compared to those of the eighth century BCE, prior to the Assyrian conquests. These comparisons will enable us to gain a better understanding of the impact of the Assyrian conquest on the region's settlement and economy. This bottom-up approach might allow us to gain some insights into Assyrian policies in the southern Levant, and this, in turn, might have implications for our understanding of the empire's policies in the west at large.

THE SOUTHERN LEVANT IN THE SEVENTH CENTURY BCE: SETTLEMENT AND DEMOGRAPHY

In this section I review the detailed settlement evidence within Cisjordan by sub-regions to enable a subtle analysis of the differences between them.[1] I begin with the southwest and will, generally speaking, move northward and eastward while distinguishing between the client kingdoms and the provinces. This will be followed by a brief summary of the (less detailed) evidence from Transjordan (which in a sense can serve as a control group) (figure 4.1).[2]

Client Kingdoms in the South
Philistine Cities in the Southern Coastal Plain

The southern Coastal Plain was of great geopolitical importance. This is the region through which the international highway, connecting Egypt with

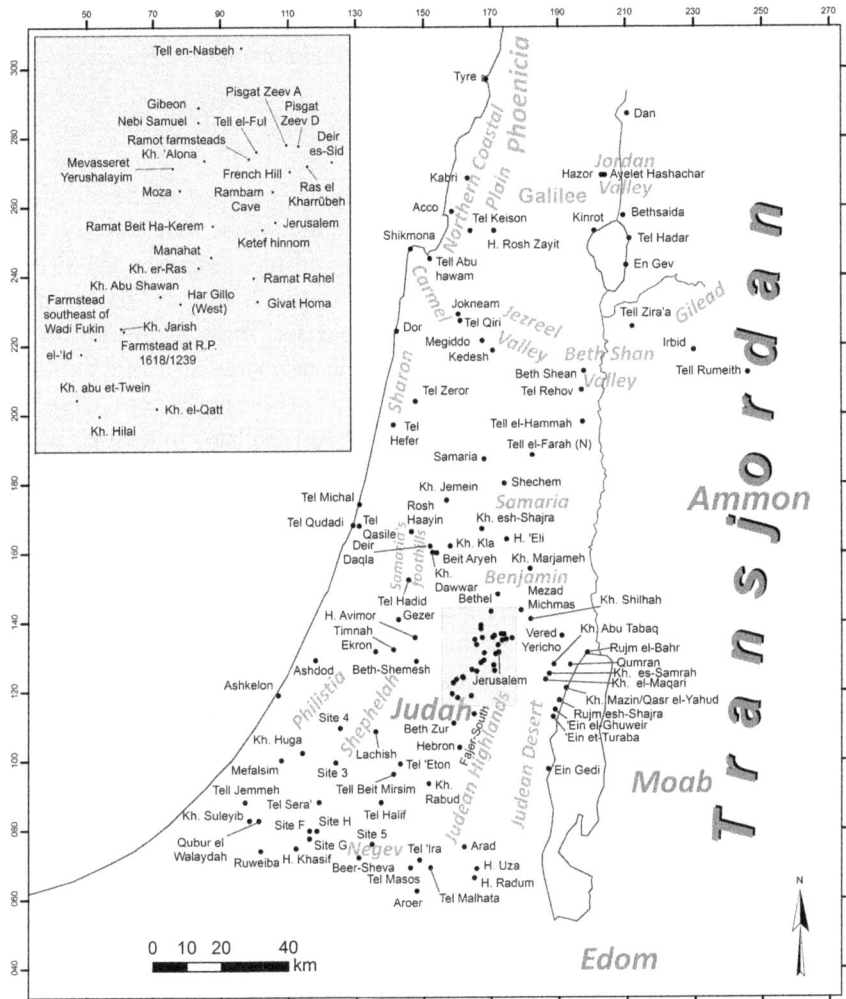

FIGURE 4.1. *Map of the sites mentioned in the text*

Syria and Mesopotamia, passed; as such, it also served (for Assyria) as the gate to Egypt. Its proximity to the Mediterranean also enhanced its importance when compared with other sub-regions. Settlement in Philistia prospered in the seventh century. The sites of Ashkelon and Ekron reached a peak at the time (600 and 300 *dunams*, respectively; Dothan and Gitin 1993; Stager 1996). Additional sites that existed include Timnah (Tel Batash; Mazar and Panitz-Cohen 2001), Tell Jemmeh (Ben-Shlomo 2014), Tel Sera' (Oren 1993), probably Ashdod (Ben-Shlomo 2003, 2005, although the dating is debated by some), and other sites, as well as many small sites known as the *haserim* (Faust 2012, 62–64 and references).

The Kingdom of Judah

The Negev: This is a semiarid region in the southern part of the kingdom of Judah, and settlement there was usually quite sparse. Surprisingly, this region prospered in the seventh century BCE, and most scholars believe the number of seventh-century sites in this region exceeds that of previous periods (Na'aman 1987; Finkelstein 1994, 1995; but see Thareani Sussely 2007). Excavated seventh-century sites include several new sites that were founded (or re-founded) at the time, including Tel Masos (Kempinski 1993, 989), Tel 'Ira (Beit Arieh 1999), Horvat Uza (both a fort and a village; Beit Arieh 2007), and Horvat Radum (a fort; Beit Arieh 2007). Other sites (e.g., Arad [Aharoni 1993], Aroer [Thareani 2011; contra Biran 1993], Tel Malhata [Kochavi 1998], and probably Beersheba near the old market of the modern city [Gophna and Yisraeli 1973, but see Panitz-Cohen 2005; Fabian and Gilead 2007]) continued to exist (see also Faust 2008, 2012, 156–58).

Shephelah: The hilly region to the west of Philistia had served in the past as a settlement hub of the kingdom of Judah but was in a great settlement decline at the time, probably as a result of Sennacherib's 701 BCE campaign. All of the eighth-century sites in the region—Tel 'Eton, Tell Beit Mirsim, Tel Halif, Beth-Shemesh, and others—were destroyed by the Assyrians (figure 4.2), and most were not resettled afterward. Seventh-century BCE settlement in the region was sparse (Faust 2008, 2012, 152–54 and references). Although not the only one, Lachish is notable among the sites that did exist at the time (Ussishkin 2004, 90–92; limited settlements probably also existed below other mounds).

Judean Highlands: The Judean highlands—the core of the kingdom of Judah—prospered. Most of the sites that were destroyed by Sennacherib recovered, many settlements actually expanded, and a large number of small sites were established at the time. Excavated sites from this period include Ramat Rahel (Lipschits et al. 2011), Beth Zur (Funk 1968, 8, 1993), Hebron (Eisenberg and Nagorski 2002), Kh. Rabud (Kochavi 1974), and many rural settlements such as Khirbet Abu Shawan, Kh. el-Qatt, Har Gillo (West), a farmstead southeast of Wadi Fukin, a farmstead at R.P. 1618/1239, the village at Kh. Jarish, Fajer-South (a wine press), the village at Kh. abu et-Twein, the village below the fort of el-'Id, as well as Kh. Hilal and Kh. Anim (for discussion and references, see Faust 2008, 2012, 50–56, 162–65).

FIGURE 4.2. *Assyrian destruction layer at Tel 'Eton. Courtesy, Tel 'Eton expedition.*

Jerusalem and Its Environs: Jerusalem—Judah's capital—expanded at this time, probably reaching an unprecedented peak of 900–1,000 settled *dunams* (including extramural neighborhoods; Faust 2014 and references; contra Na'aman 2009). The city's hinterland also reached an unparalleled peak, with hundreds of rural settlements, mainly farmsteads, dotting the landscape around the city. Among the excavated sites (for discussion and references, see Faust 2012, 38–48, 160–62) are Kh. er-Ras, Manahat, Nahal Zimri, the French Hill, Ketef Hinnom, Pisgat Zeev A, Pisgat Zeev D, Givat Homa, Kh. 'Alona, Mevasseret Yerushalayim, the Ramot farmsteads (five isolated buildings), the Ramat Beit Ha-Kerem farmstead, a settlement near the Rambam Cave, Kh. Abu Shawan, and more.

The Region of Benjamin: Settlement to the north of Jerusalem also reached a peak during the seventh century, and the settlements were larger and more numerous than ever before, including Tell en-Nasbeh (biblical Mizpah; Zorn 1993), Gibeon (Pritchard 1964), Tell el-Ful (Lapp 1978), Nebi Samuel (Magen and Dadon 1999, 62–63), Ras el Kharrûbeh (Biran 1985, 209–10), Deir es-Sid (Biran 1985, 211–13), Kh. Shilhah (Mazar, Amit, and Ilan 1996), Mezad Michmas (Riklin 1995), and some additional rural settlements nearer Jerusalem that were mentioned above with Jerusalem's northern hinterland (see also Faust 2012, 49–50).

Judean Desert: The entire region east of Jerusalem, through the arid Judean desert to the Dead Sea shore, was almost empty of settlement earlier in the Iron Age. During the seventh century, however, it witnessed an unparalleled wave of settlement that included Ein Gedi (Stern 2007), Rujm el-Bahr (Bar Adon 1989, 3–14), Qumran (de Vaux 1993, 1236), Khirbet Mazin/Qasr el-Yahud (Bar Adon 1989, 18–29), 'Ein el-Ghuweir (Bar Adon 1989, 33–40), 'Ein et-Turaba (Bar Adon 1989, 41–48), Rujm esh-Shajra (Bar Adon 1989, 86), and others. Several additional sites were excavated in the Boqe'ah valley, including Khirbet Abu Tabaq, Khirbet es-Samrah, and Khirbet el-Maqari (Cross and Milik 1956; Stager 1976). Other sites were discovered slightly to the north, such as the structure at Vered Yericho (Eitan 1983) and the large site near Jericho (on the bank of Wadi Qelt; Eitan 1983; also Stern 2001, 192) (for detailed discussion and references, see Stager 1976; Bar-Adon 1989; Stern 1994; Faust and Weiss 2005; Faust 2008, 2012, 50, 154–56).

The Provinces

Territories of the Former Kingdom of Israel

Samaria Foothills and the Gezer Region: This was the southeastern edge of the province of Samaria. The international highway crossed the topographically lower part of the region, but its hilly part (Samaria's foothills) was a waterless and rocky zone that had barely been settled before. Surprisingly, there was a surge in settlement activity in this area at this time (Faust 2006), and many farmsteads (and perhaps a few hamlets) were established in the ecologically inferior region on Samaria's foothills. About twenty of these sites were excavated (Faust 2012, 57–60; Faust forthcoming, references). At nearby Rosh Ha'ayin, the remains of a village that continued its existence from the Iron Age were excavated (Avner-Levy and Torge 1999), and it appears that a similar situation prevailed at Tel Hadid (Brand 1998). Gezer (Dever 1993, 505) also existed at the time and was probably of importance, even if it was smaller than its predecessor. Horbat Avimor is another small hamlet that was unearthed nearby (Golani 2005). Although insignificant demographically, this sub-region exhibits a relatively impressive process of settlement at the time (more below; see also Aster and Faust 2015).

Samaria (region): This hilly region formed the core of the province of Samaria. The city of Samaria, the former capital of the kingdom of Israel, existed at the time and served as provincial capital, but it is clear that the remains from the Assyrian center were limited—regardless of the question of the site's destruction—and that it had a much more limited role at this time (Master 2013). Many other sites were destroyed during the Assyrian conquest, and subsequent settlement was significantly smaller, in many cases much smaller, than its predecessor, for example, at Tell el-Farah (N) (Chambon 1993, 440), Shechem (Campbell 1993, 1353), and Bethel (Greener 2013). Other sites did not recover at all after the Assyrian conquest and were apparently abandoned, such as the town of Kh. Marjameh (Mazar 1993, 966) and the villages of Kh. Jemein (Yezerski 2013, 94), Kh. esh-Shajra (Yezerski 2013, 94), Beit Aryeh (Riklin 1997, 19), Kh. Dawwar (Har Even 2012), Deir Daqla (Har Even 2011), Kh. Kla (Eitam 1987, 24–26), and more. Horvat 'Eli (Hizmi 1996), a small site with just a few structures, seems to have been established at the time; while this is the only excavated exception, it is likely that there were more such sites. There were differences within this region, whereas in the south devastation was far more total than in the north (Tavgar 2012; Faust 2015). All in all, it is clear that the region was devastated by the Assyrians and did not recover.

Sharon Coastal Plain: Most of this region was a marshy marginal zone. Still, its access to the Mediterranean in the west and the international highway that passed along its eastern edge made these parts more important. The political status of the region is debated, and some have suggested that it formed an independent province (Gilboa 1996, references). Dor, the central city in this region, seems to have been fortified at the time (Gilboa 1996, 122, 131–32). Other sites declined significantly in size, but some Assyrian era remains were unearthed (sometimes very limited), for example, at Tel Zeror (Kochavi 1993). Other sites were apparently not settled at the time, such as Tel Hefer, where limited evidence for human activity in the eighth century was unearthed (Paley and Porath 1993), probably reflecting a small settlement that ceased to exist following the Assyrian conquest. It appears that the situation at Tel Michal (Herzog 1993) was similar.[3] Other sites, like Tel Qasile, do exhibit seventh-century remains, but they might postdate Assyrian rule (Mazar 1985, 128). Thus, the central Coastal Plain as a whole experienced decline in the Assyrian period, and practically every eighth-century excavated site was impacted by the campaigns.

Northern Valleys: This region formed the core of the Megiddo province. This was one of the most important sub-regions in the southern Levant, with large valleys with good, fertile soil and a good climate. The valleys also hosted a number of major roads, including the international highway. A relatively large number of sites were excavated in this region, and almost all experienced destruction and decline. Notably, while most sites were part of the kingdom of Israel, it appears that at least one site (and maybe more) was part of an Aramean kingdom (Bethsaida). However, the overall pattern of the sites that were located within the same geographical unit is similar, and it is justified to address them together. Some sites, although affected by the Assyrian conquest, still prospered afterward, including Dan (Biran 2008, 1688–89) and probably also Tell el-Hammah (Cahill and Tarler 1993, 561), while others turned into hamlets, such as Kinrot (Fritz 2008, 1685) and Jokneam (Ben-Tor 1993, 807). Some remains were also unearthed at Tel Qiri (Ben-Tor 1987, 103–5, 110, 116). Other sites were thoroughly devastated, and Assyrian era remains are very limited at best—as at Hazor (Ben-Tor 2008, 1775), Bethsaida (Arav 2009, 64–70, 114–15), Beth Shean (Mazar 2008a, 1621), and Tel Rehov (Mazar 2008b, 2018)—or even nonexistent, as at Tel Hadar (Yadin and Kochavi 2008, 1757), En Gev (Kochavi and Tsukimoto 2008, 1725), and probably also Kedesh (Stern 1993a, 860; the nature of the preceding Iron Age IIB settlement is not clear, however). Israelite Megiddo was destroyed by the Assyrians but rebuilt as an Assyrian administrative center—the only known city to be built by them in the region (Stern 2001, 48). All in all, the northern valleys were devastated, and the region suffered a major blow (see also Pakkala, Munger, and Zangenberg 2004, 25; Faust 2015).[4]

Galilee: This is a hilly and mountainous region on the fringe of the northern valleys. An examination of the excavated sites exposes a gloomy picture: the towns of Qarney Hittin (Gal 1992), Tel Gath Hefer (Alexandre, Covello-Paran, and Gal 2003, 168), Tel Yin'am (Liebowitz 2000, 17), and probably also the one at Karm er-Ras (Alexandre 2008), as well as the village at Horvat Rosh Zayit (Gal and Alexandre 2000) and the farmstead at Horvat Malta (Covello-Paran 2008), were all destroyed in the late eighth century.

Northern Coastal Plain (Phoenicia)

The political affiliation of many of the sites in this area is not clear, and it is likely that most of them belonged to the Phoenician city-state of Tyre, which was an autonomous polity. Overall, the decline in this area was much less severe than in other regions in the north, although damage was identified at practically every site. Some sites were destroyed but then restored, such as Acco (Dothan 1993, 21–22) and Tel Keison (Humbert 1993, 866). At Kabri there was a fort at the time (Lehmann 2002, 85–86), and an administrative building was unearthed at Akhziv (Yasur-Landau, Press, and Arie 2016). Tell Abu Hawam was probably abandoned (Balensi, Herrera, and Artzi 1993, 10), and Shiqmona apparently declined significantly (Elgavish 1994, 1375). Most sites were impacted by the Assyrian conquest, and many experienced decline. Still, perhaps because of its subordination to Tyre, the level of continuity and recovery in this region is larger than in other regions in the north.

Transjordan

Transjordan is less known archaeologically than Cisjordan and hence is discussed separately. The northern part of the region, which before the Assyrian conquests was part of the kingdom of Israel, was turned into the Assyrian province of Gilead. All the sites excavated in the Gilead—Tell Zira'a (Vieweger and Haser 2007, 165), Tell Rumeith (Barako 2015), and Irbid (e.g., Lenzen 1992, 456)—declined dramatically at the time. The Gilead was devastated (also Vieweger and Haser's 2007, 165; Herr and Najjar 2008, 323). The situation in central and southern Transjordan was different. Ammon, Moab, and Edom maintained their autonomy, and the late eighth and seventh centuries constituted a period of settlement growth. Ammon "reached its florescence in terms of both political power and material culture" in the Iron Age IIC (Younker 2014, 764, see also 766; Tyson 2014). In Moab, the Assyrian campaigns "did not seriously alter the organization of the state" (Steiner 2014, 779), and the region continued to flourish. Likewise, the settlement in the Edomite Plateau flourished at exactly this time (Bienkowski 2014, 785).

DISCUSSION

While the various sub-regions differed from one another as a result of their ecological potential and geopolitical importance, the overall picture makes these regional differences marginal. The very clear dichotomy that is revealed by the data presented above distinguished the provinces from the client kingdoms. In the client states in the south (in both Cisjordan and Transjordan)[5] the seventh century BCE is a settlement peak, exceeding the settlement of the eighth century, whereas in the provinces in the north (on both sides of the Jordan River), this is a period of severe decline. These settlement trends are striking because in the eighth century it was the north that was the center of settlement of the entire region, as it was in most periods. Thus, Broshi and

Finkelstein (1992, 53–54)[6] estimated that prior to the Assyrian conquests, the population of the kingdom of Israel (excluding the Gilead) was 222,500. The population of the kingdom of Judah, by contrast, was estimated as 110,000, less than half that of its northern neighbor (if the Gilead was included, the gap would have been much larger).[7]

This all changed after the Assyrian conquests, and it appears that following the processes that turned them into Assyrian provinces, the relevant regions declined dramatically. The situation in the south is the opposite, and the region grew in importance. Hence, the Neo-Assyrian era reveals the reversal of the typical role of the various regions: the south was far more central than the north. It is clear, however, that we are not just discussing a north versus south dichotomy but rather a differentiation between the Assyrian provinces (in the north) and the semi-autonomous regions of Philistia, Judah, Ammon, Moab, and Edom (in the south). It must be reiterated that the division between the reality in the provinces and the client states is sharp, and sub-regional differences based on ecology and the like are insignificant compared with this clear-cut distinction. Thus, while differences within the provinces and within the various client states can be identified, the striking feature is how different the two are from each other. In the south, even arid and semiarid regions seem to flourish (relatively), whereas in the north, the fertile valleys are only sparsely settled. The impact of the Assyrian conquests and annexations appears unambiguous.

Singer-Avitz's (2014) suggestion, published only after this chapter was completed, that sites with Iron Age IIC finds in the north should be subdivided into two phases has significant implications for the discussion. Singer-Avitz suggests that the majority of the Iron Age IIC sites she studied in the north were established only in the later part of this period, perhaps even after the Assyrian withdrawal near the end of the seventh century. Thus, in addition to the fact that not all the sites in the north coexisted—thereby reducing the number of sites attributed to any time period in the north even farther—only a minority of the sites listed above existed in the first generation or two after the Assyrian conquest. This means that the settlement reality was even "darker" than the (gloomy) picture presented above.

THE SOUTHERN LEVANT IN THE SEVENTH CENTURY BCE: ECONOMY

Not surprisingly, there is a high correlation between settlement and economic prosperity.

Economy in the Client Kingdoms in the South

Ekron (approximately 30 hectares) is probably the best-known example of prosperity in the south, with well over 100 installations for the production of olive oil, making it the largest center for the production of olive oil in the ancient world (Gitin 1995, 1997; Eitam 1996). Ashkelon (about 60 hectares) seems to have functioned as a major center of trade. Its port served as a gate to the Mediterranean, and various imports were found in the city, including from Phoenicia, Egypt, and Judah (Master 2003). The latter, for example, seems to have sent agricultural products, including wheat, to Ashkelon (Weiss and Kislev 2004; Faust and Weiss 2005). It appears that Ashkelon was also a center of production, as is indicated by the winery that was unearthed there (Stager 1996). Jerusalem also prospered at the time, and this megacity (at least in Levantine terms, probably 65 hectares within the city walls and 90–100 hectares including extramural neighborhoods) was surrounded by hundreds of farmsteads. It is likely that the major area of specialization in this region was wine, although there is evidence for grain surpluses as well (at Moza; Greenhut and De Groot 2009). Evidence for production of surpluses and for trade is also abundant in other sites throughout the south, such as at Timnah (Mazar 1997, 262–63). In the Beersheba Valley, about 10 percent of the wood unearthed in excavations (seventh-century levels) is cedar from Lebanon (Liphschitz and Biger 1991), indicating the significance of trade at the time.

While the evidence for manufacture and trade is extensive, Weiss and I presented in the past a scenario that combines all of the discreet lines of evidence into a larger economic picture (Faust and Weiss 2005, 2011). When the economic information is taken into account, along with ecological data on the various regions, we believe that all of the archaeological data become complementary. The archaeological evidence indicates that the economy of the desert and the highland (Judah), as well as the lowland (Shephelah) and the Coastal Plain (e.g., Ashkelon), was highly integrated in the seventh century, both within these regions and with the international maritime trade (figure 4.3). At the heart of the local system was Ashkelon (and perhaps also Gaza, of which we know practically nothing). As the major port of the south, it was the gate through which desired imports entered the region and through which commodities were exported. Ashkelon itself must have been a major consumer of commodities for export and food for consumption. Located on the coast in the midst of dunes, Ashkelon could not have supported itself agriculturally and must have imported most of its food. Forming the best location within the geographical/economical system of the south, Ashkelon

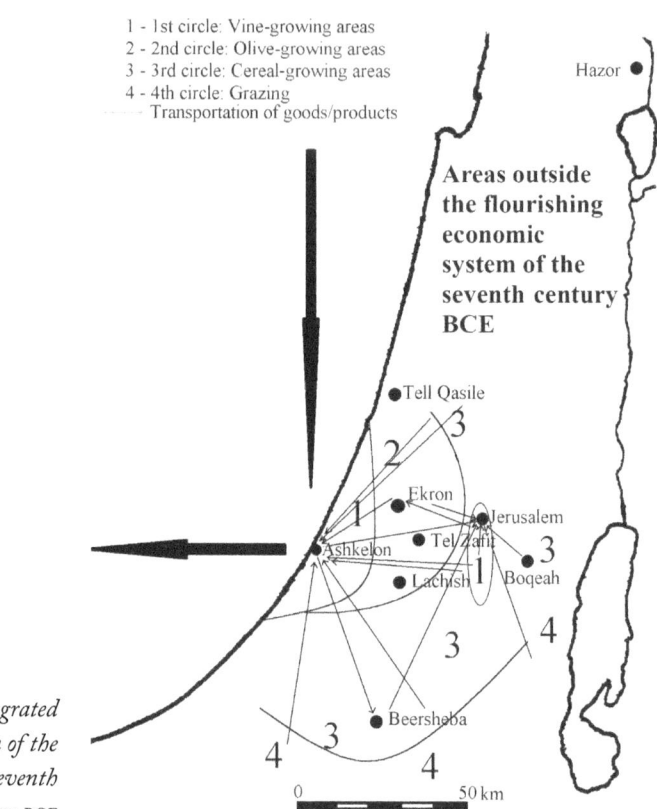

FIGURE 4.3. *Integrated economic system of the south in the seventh century* BCE

used its own hinterland mainly, though probably not solely, for the production of wine—the most "profitable" economic activity (Faust and Weiss 2005, 2011).

The second zone was in the Inner Coastal Plain and the Shephelah. Here the major product was olive oil, represented by the huge production center of Ekron. Olive oil, however, was produced at other sites such as Timnah (e.g., Mazar 1997, 211–18) and as far as Tel Hadid (Brand 1998). At the latter site a large industrial area with twenty-five oil presses was excavated, and it represents another center of production at the edge of this zone (at the edge of an Assyrian province; see also Aster and Faust 2015; also below). While the local population probably produced some wine and grain, olive oil was the primary product from the second zone. This also explains the somewhat awkward situation of Ekron in relation to the probable location of most of the olive groves. Ekron, as noted, for example, by Eitam and Shomroni (1987, 49; also Eitam 1996, 184), is situated on the edge of the olive-growing area and became the major production center not because of its central location as far as the olive-supplying area was concerned but because of its proximity to the coast and to Ashkelon.

The third zone was mostly in Judah. Apparently, Judah manufactured surpluses of what the other areas, especially Ashkelon, needed: grain (and herd products, see below). While it is clear that Judah also produced wine and olive oil, as the archaeological evidence clearly indicates (Faust and Weiss 2005, 80–82), the existence of secondary centers is expected. Still, its contribution to the overall system was mainly grain and herd products. Now we can understand why Judah had expanded into the inhospitable regions of the desert and the desert fringe. Following Finkelstein (1994), I believe this region probably produced grain surpluses (see also Beit Arieh 2015, 14; contra Master 2009); obviously, the very limited surpluses of the Judean desert did not go to Ashkelon. These surpluses supplied part of Jerusalem's needs, but this freed up other grain-producing areas to provide grain for Ashkelon. The fourth zone was grazing, mainly in the Judean desert and the Negev. It is more than likely that even southern Transjordan was part of this prosperity and that the expansion of settlement in Edom, for example, is related to the trade routes that crossed this region.

We can now understand why Ashkelon grew vines and imported grain, why Ekron produced so much olive oil, and why Judah expanded to the desert. This also explains why cedars were brought to the Negev, how Judah paid for its fish, and similar factors. All lines of evidence seem, therefore, to converge; and it appears that Phoenicia, Philistia, and even Judah were part of this flourishing economy, which was part of the Mediterranean economic system.[8] Thus, while one can identify differences between the various sub-regions in the south, they were all part of the same system.

ECONOMY IN THE PROVINCES

While the political climate under Assyrian rule no doubt enabled the above developments, it is interesting that the north of the country—which was under direct Assyrian control—did not participate in this prospering economic system. We have no evidence for the production of significance surpluses in the new provinces that were established in the territories of the former kingdom of Israel or for any significant trade there (more below). Settlement was limited and on a relatively subsistence level. The only settlement from this era in the territories of the former kingdom of Israel in which evidence for the production of surpluses was unearthed is Tel Hadid. Not surprisingly, this settlement is located in the southernmost part of those territories, on the border with Philistia and Judah. It is clear that this is just the northern edge of the prospering region in Philistia (Faust and Weiss 2005, 2011). The installations unearthed were very similar to the ones found at Ekron and Timnah, and thus Tel Hadid should be understood as a site in this second zone of production. It prospered because of its proximity to the south, although politically it was within an Assyrian province (for an expanded discussion of the importance of this region also from administrative and military perspectives, see Aster and Faust 2015).

In summary, the economic data match the data regarding settlement prosperity. The Assyrian provinces in the north were not part of any prosperity, while the semi-independent kingdoms of the south were, in contrast to the situation there earlier in the Iron Age. This was partially a result of the devastation of the north, which opened the way to the new peak in the south. This conclusion, which is based on a comparison of the settlement patterns and economic realities in both the south and the north, can be further supported by an examination of the temporal development of olive oil production in the region.

Assyria and Economic Prosperity: The Olive Oil Industry as a Temporal-Spatial Test Case

The best evidence for the economic backwardness of the territories of the new provinces can be seen when examining the role of olive oil in the Iron Age economy (following Faust 2011). During the eighth century, the kingdom of Israel boasted the largest centers for the production of olive oil in the region. Centers in which olive surpluses were produced included Horvat Rosh Zayit, Shiqmona, Beit Aryeh (figure 4.4), Kh. Kla, Deir Daqla, and many others (Faust 2011 references; see also Gal and Alexandre 2000; Gal and Frankel 1993). Not one of those centers survived the Assyrian campaigns, and no new centers emerged in those regions after the conquest. All subsequent centers for the production of significant olive oil surpluses were located in Judah (late eighth century BCE) and Philistia (seventh century BCE). Those include, among others, Tell Beit Mirsim, Beth-Shemesh (Judah), Ekron, and perhaps Timnah (Philistia) (figure 4.5).[9]

This temporal analysis across space shows that the north prospered while it was independent and ceased to prosper once it became part of the Assyrian provincial system. In tandem with the Assyrian conquest and the decline in the north, the south began to prosper, but prosperity seems to have always been just outside direct imperial control.

FIGURE 4.4. *One of the eighth-century BCE olive presses at Beit Aryeh*

INTERNATIONAL TRADE AND ASSYRIA: EAST GREEK POTTERY IN THE PROVINCES AND VASSAL KINGDOMS

The distribution of East Greek Pottery in the seventh century clearly shows that trade was concentrated in the south, and the north was not part of it.[10] While earlier in the Iron Age Greek pottery was found mainly in the north, with two sites in Philistia (Waldbaum 1994, 54–59; Fantalkin 2001, 2008, 196), it was rare during most of the seventh century (Waldbaum 1994, 59; Fantalkin 2006, 201–2, 2008). It reappeared, however, in even greater quantities in the late seventh century, but mainly in southern sites (Waldbaum 1994, 59–60; Fantalkin 2008, 236). While these imports to the south date mainly from the period after Assyrian rule, they still serve as evidence for the economic potential of the different regions. Whatever the cause for the rarity of Greek imports during most of the seventh century BCE (Waldbaum 1994, 59; Fantalkin 2006, 201–2), once this reason vanished and the area was integrated with the Mediterranean, the pottery reappeared. While scholars debate whether the main users of the Greek pottery were mercenaries (Waldbaum 1994, 1997; Fantalkin 2006, 2008), it is clear that not every sherd was used by

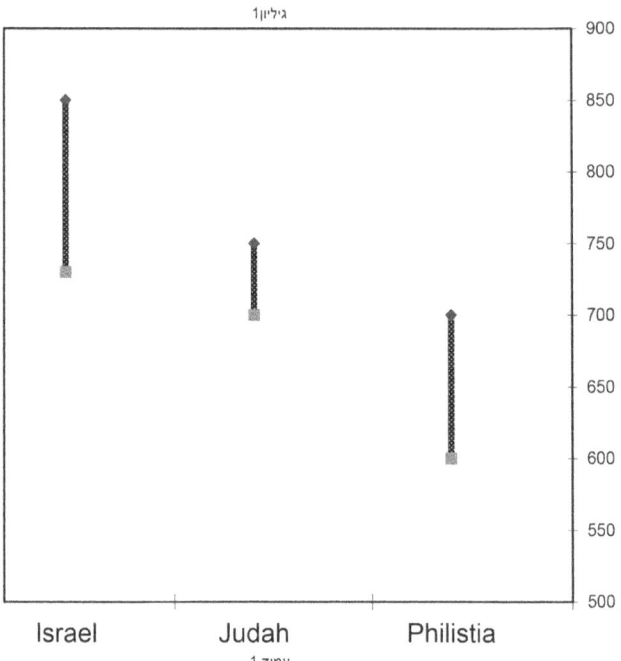

FIGURE 4.5. *Distribution of olive oil production centers in time and space (rounded dates)*

mercenaries and that the many scattered and isolated finds should be attributed to trade. Thus, areas that flourished and participated in long-distance trade revealed this pottery. Its concentration in the south indicates that this was the region that prospered, reversing the situation that existed in the earlier parts of the Iron Age. Earlier, the north was central and played a more central role in international trade, while the south was very peripheral. Now, it was the south where the imports were found, whereas their number in the north was much more limited (and the finds were concentrated almost solely in the northern Coastal Plain, which was probably part of Tyre's hinterland).

DISCUSSION: ASSYRIAN POLICY IN THE WEST

There is an intense debate regarding Assyrian policy in the west. In a series of insightful and highly influential articles, Gitin (1995, 1997) suggested that the flourit of Ekron was a result of Assyrian policy and ideology that promoted trade, profit, and urbanization. Many scholars followed suit, and this thesis influenced the overall understanding of the Assyrian Empire (e.g., Van De Mieroop 2007, 252, 259). This is not the place for an extensive discussion (Faust 2011, references), but it must be stressed that this view is not accepted by all. Grayson (1991, 216–17), for example, claimed that the "Assyrian view of the economy of the empire was simplistic: the ruled territories were there to supply the central state with as much wealth and labour as could be squeezed out of them, and no thought was given to long-range schemes and profits" (see also Grayson 1995, 963; Stager 1996; Schloen 2001, 146; Faust 2011; Faust and Weiss 2011).

When reviewing the settlement, demographic, and economic reality in the Land of Israel under Neo-Assyrian rule, it is clear that the prosperity was in the south, in the semi-independent kingdom of Judah and the Philistine cities, while the north was in a sharp decline (with the exception of Phoenicia). This is reflected by practically every parameter I examined—number of settlements, their sizes and density, and the existence of significant hinterland—as well as by the evidence for the production of surpluses and international trade. Whether a sub-region was located within the annexed territories or in client kingdoms seems to be the deciding factor, and this was far more influential than any ecological or regional advantages and disadvantages. As we have seen above, in the client states even marginal regions flourished; in the provinces even central areas were in decline. The internal variation within each area (i.e., within the provinces or within the client states) was marginal compared to the differences between them.

The prosperity in the south contrasts with the gloomy reality in the north, not only when comparing the reality in each region to the other but also when comparing it to the situation in the eighth century BCE, prior to the Assyrian conquests. During the eighth century the center of settlement was in the north—in the kingdom of Israel—which was also far more significant economically. The north was the center of production and trade, and the south was in its shadow. This was the "natural" order of things. The fact that it changed in the seventh century requires an explanation. It was not only that the north declined and the south prospered, but even in absolute terms the south was now far more central than the north. The only explanation for the peculiar reality in which the south prospered—more than ever before—while the north was devastated and marginal is the Assyrian campaigns and the destruction they brought about, along with the policy that followed. This is in line with other studies about Assyrian policies in the region (for references, see Faust 2011, 2018). The regions in the north were devastated during the Assyrian conquest, most cities were destroyed, agricultural hinterlands were laid waste and sacked (Faust 2015, references), and a significant percentage of the population died during the battles and in epidemics and starvation during the wars (for these mechanisms, although in a slightly different context, see Faust 2012, 140–43, references). Some were executed after the wars ended, and more died from subsequent epidemics and starvation. After all, the Assyrian army took all the food (there was no other form of supply for the military), leaving the local population in a horrible state, whereas epidemics continued to spread as a result of the many dead that were lying around and the weak state of the survivors. To this one should add exiles. The devastation was therefore severe, and the elite were especially devastated, which made recovery even more difficult. While the Assyrians brought some deportees to the region (and clearly enabled some livelihood and supported the settlers), this was on a comparatively minor scale (Oded 1979, 28; see also Faust 2015, 776–78). The evidence from the southern Levant indicates that the Assyrians devastated the regions they conquered, and recovery was very limited.

The independent regions in the south, in contrast, were able to take advantage of the economic opportunities offered by the international maritime trade (and also the long-distance overland trade), and they prospered. Those regions were greatly influenced by the Neo-Assyrian Empire in every possible way—culturally and religiously (both directly and, probably mainly, indirectly) and economically (mainly by the heavy tribute they paid)—but the prosperity was not a result of a calculated Assyrian policy aimed at maximizing production or trade. Rather, it was a result of the ability of local rulers to be integrated into the Mediterranean world, whose engine was the Phoenicians.

The local rulers paid tribute to Assyria, which greatly benefited from this practice, and the Assyrians made sure not to miss a single boat that entered any port so they could extract taxes. Nor did they want to miss a single caravan, for the same reason. But the Assyrians did not initiate this prosperity—not in terms of the number of settlements, their size and nature, and not even as far as the economic developments are concerned. The fact that they greatly benefited from the prosperity does not mean it was their doing, let alone that they planned it.

If the Assyrians "wanted" to benefit from the trade and economic prosperity, if it was part of their "policy," they would not have destroyed the territories that became theirs, or they would have made the recovery much more significant. After all, this area was part of Assyria, and they could extract a higher percentage from the surpluses that would have been grown there. The fact that they did not suggests that they did not have a master plan for recovery or urbanization. They came, conquered, and sacked. They enabled economic activity only to a very limited extent and did not change their taxation policies to enable growth in the longer term. But once their vassals made profits, they were there extracting taxes and imposing tribute.

TEXTUAL EVIDENCE FOR ASSYRIAN INVESTMENT?

Responding to some of my previous publications (Faust 2011; Faust and Weiss 2005), Younger (2015) recently addressed the Assyrian economic impact on the southern Levant on the basis of Assyrian administrative texts. Younger claimed that the texts show that the Assyrian Empire was interested in economic growth and development and invested in obtaining these goals. Younger's article was published only after this chapter was submitted, and here I would like to briefly address his important contribution (see also Faust 2018).

All of the texts Younger cited as exemplifying Assyrian "investment" relate to other regions, for example, to Tell Shioukh Fawqani (Bûr-marîna), located on the Euphrates (Younger 2015, 183); to canals on the Habur and the Euphrates, such as at Tell Šeh Hamad (ancient Dur-Katlimmu; Younger 2015, 183); and to the fort system along the Upper and Middle Euphrates (Younger 2015, 183). Assyrian policy, however, changed through time and space in accordance with the circumstances and the potential of each region, and it is inadmissible to extrapolate data relating to one region onto the situation in other regions, especially when they conflict with all of the archaeological (and textual) information available on this region. Among other things, the regions discussed by Younger were central to the empire, located much closer to its heart and along major waterways that enabled easy economic exploitation. The southern Levant was remote, and transportation of bulk commodities to Assyria was so expensive that it was practically impossible to transport them. The data from the Euphrates are therefore irrelevant for the present discussion.

Furthermore, Younger did not address the archaeological data on the region, presented here and elsewhere. The devastation of settlements and the cessation of the olive oil industry must be accounted for when reconstructing the Assyrian policy.

In addition, and perhaps even more significant, the texts on the southern Levant discussed by Younger do not suggest an Assyrian investment. Esarhaddon's treaty with Tyre (Parpola and Watanabe 1988, text no. 5), for example, only shows that the Phoenicians were in effective control of the Mediterranean trade, giving Assyria some nominal control over Tyrian trade and the ability to tax it. This text shows Assyrian involvement and interest in the region, but none of the Assyrian activities attested in this text can be termed "investment" (expenditure of resources). Tyre, which was outside Assyria proper, prospered (unlike the nearby provinces), and the Assyrians made sure that it paid its due. This text and practically all others relating to the southern Levant support the scenario presented here—the Assyrian Empire took whatever and whenever it could, and there was much more to take from the vassals than from the provinces. The relevant texts do not hint at any investment whatsoever (and many other texts show that the area was in a recession; Faust 2018).

Also of importance in this regard is the small number of texts (both those uncovered in Mesopotamia, which mention the region, and those unearthed in it) and the distribution of the few that were uncovered, which show that the provinces in the region were relatively insignificant economically for the empire (Aster and Faust 2015).

In summary, none of the documents mentioned by Younger say anything about Assyrian investment in the southern Levant—only that they were heavily involved in the ports, exercised political control, and imposed taxes, as can be expected from such an empire. The texts also show that the Assyrian imperial administration appears to have been more economically interested in the vassals than in its own provinces in the southern Levant (the reason was, as we have seen, that the latter had very limited economic potential at this time). Interestingly, in practice, Younger did differentiate between the southern Levant and the regions outside it, as he uses the words *invest* and *investment* only when he describes the action of the empire in other regions (four times in four separate cases; 2015, 183) but not once when addressing the southern Levant. For the latter, Younger chose to use the words *involved* and *interest* (2015, 192, 195n37, 197–98). To put these keywords in their proper place in relation to the southern Levant, we can say that the Assyrians were "interested" in anything that prospered (mainly outside the provinces), but their "involvement" included taxation or the like but not "investment."

Younger's article is of importance because it highlights the nature of Assyrian involvement and investment in other parts of the empire. These regions, however, were mostly annexed long before the kingdom of Israel was and were located much closer to Assyria's heartland, on riverine transportation routes. While both the location of these regions and the timing of their conquest mean they cannot be used to learn about the situation in the southern Levant (especially given the counter evidence), they do highlight the complex nature of Assyrian imperialism and administration and the fact that as a result of various considerations these varied across time and space.

CONCLUSION

The clear-cut dichotomy between the north (provinces) and the south (client kingdoms) demonstrates that the important factor in determining the fate of a sub-region was its status in relation to the Assyrian Empire, which overshadowed any local, regional, or ecological qualities. Thus, the finds presented in this chapter indicate that the prosperity in the south resulted from the fact that the region was outside direct Assyrian control rather than from a purposeful policy of the empire. The impact of the Assyrian Empire on the west was immense and was expressed in cultural and religious influences, political domination, and decisions of life and death (for more extensive discussion, see Faust 2011, 2018; Faust and Weiss 2011). It influenced settlement patterns and demography, for example, by devastating large areas. The empire influenced the economy in numerous ways: by destroying some areas and not destroying others, by extracting tribute, and by creating a more "relaxed" period, sometimes termed the "Assyrian Peace," or Pax Assyriaca. But its direct impact on the economy of the southern Levant was mainly in destroying, looting, and extracting wealth rather than a planned policy aiming to maximize the prosperity, with a view to more taxes and tribute in the future. Prosperity was a by-product of the development brought about by the semi-independent polities in the south and their incorporation into the expanding Mediterranean trade. The Assyrians greatly benefited from these developments that took place outside their border, but they did not initiate them or directly invest there.

Finally, the next step should be to compare the information obtained from the southern Levant with the known data on other regions in the Assyrian Empire. The above comparisons between the northern and southern parts of the country in the seventh century BCE and between the seventh and eighth centuries BCE in the same region were very fruitful. It is therefore likely that comparing the situation in the southern Levant to that in the northern Levant and other parts of the empire (even if the available archaeological information is far more limited) will contribute to a better understanding of the policies of the Assyrian Empire at large and might allow us to decipher possible changes in these policies over time.

NOTES

1. Because of the problems inherent in surveys, I rely mainly on the data from excavations. Given the hundreds of excavations carried out so far in the region, it appears that the data are representative and can be used to learn about settlement processes (Faust and Safrai 2005, 2015).

2. Because of space considerations, in the following section I attempted to limit the references to only one source per discussed site (in most cases, either a final report or a summarizing article). For similar reasons, when discussing rural settlements (e.g., the *haserim* phenomenon, or the countryside around Jerusalem and the Judean highlands), I sometimes only referred to summarizing works and did not supply a reference for each site. Broad works that summarize the data on the various regions are also mentioned throughout the discussion to direct readers to additional sources of information and references.

3. The situation at Tel Qudadi is more difficult to ascertain, and it appears that its fate differed (Fantalkin and Tal 2015; Faust 2018).

4. Some sites in the region were interpreted as Assyrian palaces or forts, but not only is this interpretation doubted (e.g., Stern 2001, references), the sites are small and demographically insignificant (also Faust 2018).

5. It is likely that the situation in Phoenicia was similar, but the evidence above pertained only to the fringe of this area, so I will not elaborate on it.

6. One can question the methods used by Broshi and Finkelstein, and while I have some reservations about our ability to count ancient populations, the trends produced by such studies are more reliable than the numbers and should be considered.

7. If Philistia and the northern coast had been included, the gap between north and south would have been smaller.

8. It is true that the complex system described above was reconstructed mainly on the basis of the finds in the destruction layers caused by Nebuchadnezzar's armies and in theory can be dated only to the period after Assyrian rule. Still, the probable dating of some components of the system to an earlier part of the seventh century (e.g., the finds at Tel Hadid), along with the understanding that such a system did not evolve overnight, support dating it—or at least parts of it—to the time of the Neo-Assyrian Empire (and some components are probably even earlier). Moreover, the distinct dichotomy between north and south (below) is clearly a result of Assyrian rule and not of later policies.

9. Olive oil for local and regional consumption was also produced in many sites earlier in the Iron Age, but here I refer to centers for the production of significant surpluses.

10. Avoidance of imports can result from cultural approaches, but this does seem to explain the phenomenon observed. Negative views of imports were prevalent in Judah and may account for the low number of ceramic imports there (Faust 2006), especially when compared with evidence for trade in timber, for example (Lipschitz and Biger 1991). We have no reason to suspect such an approach for the population in the north at this time, especially when the absence of imported pottery fits nicely with other indicators of economic activity.

WORKS CITED

Aharoni, Miriam. 1993. "Arad, the Israelite Citadels." In *The New Encyclopedia of Archaeological Excavations in the Holy Land*, 4 vols., ed. Ephraim Stern, 1:82–87. Jerusalem: Israel Exploration Society.

Alexandre, Yardena. 2008. "Karm er-Ras (Areas A, B)." *ESI* 120: 574–78.

Alexandre, Yardena, Keren Covello-Paran, and Zvi Gal. 2003. "Excavations at Tel Gat Hefer in the Lower Galilee." *Atiqot* 44: 143–70.

Arav, Rami. 2009. "Final Report on Area A, Stratum V: The City Gate." In *Bethsaida: A City by the North Shore of the Sea of Galilee*, ed. Rami Arav, 4:1–122. Kirksville, MO: Truman State University Press.

Aster, Shawn-Zelig, and Avraham Faust. 2015. "Administrative Texts, Royal Inscriptions, and Neo-Assyrian Administration in the Southern Levant: The View from the Aphek-Gezer Region." *Or* 84: 292–308.

Avner-Levy, Rina, and Hagit Torge. 1999. "Rosh Ha-'Ayin." *ESI* 19: 40*, 58–59.

Balensi, Jacqueline, Maria D. Herrera, and Michal Artzi. 1993. "Abu Hawam, Tel." In *The New Encyclopedia of Archaeological Excavations in the Holy Land*, 4 vols., ed. Ephraim Stern, 1:7–15. Jerusalem: Israel Exploration Society.

Bar-Adon, Pesach. 1989. *Excavations in the Judean Desert* (Hebrew). Jerusalem: Israel Antiquities Authority.

Barako, Tristan J. 2015. "Summary and Conclusions." In *Tell er-Rumeith: The Excavations of Paul W. Lapp, 1962 and 1967*, ed. Tristan J. Barako and Nancy L. Lapp, 189–95. Boston: American Schools of Oriental Research.

Beit Arieh, Itzhak. 1999. *Tel 'Ira, a Stronghold in the Biblical Negev*. Tel Aviv: Tel Aviv University.

Beit Arieh, Itzhak. 2007. *Horvat Uza and Horvat Radum: Two Fortresses in the Biblical Negev*. Tel Aviv: Tel Aviv University.

Beit Arieh, Itzhak. 2015. "Tel Malhata: The Site." In *Tel Malhata: A Central City in the Biblical Negev*, ed. Itzhak Beit Arieh and Liora Freud. 11–16. Winona Lake, IN: Eisenbrauns.

Ben-Shlomo, David. 2003. "The Iron Age Sequence of Tel Ashdod: A Rejoinder to 'Ashdod Revisited' by Israel Finkelstein and Lily Singer-Avitz." *TA* 30: 83–107.

Ben-Shlomo, David, 2005. "Introduction." In *Ashdod VI: The Excavations of Areas H and K (1968-1969)*, ed. Moshe Dothan and David Ben-Shlomo, 1–9. Jerusalem: Israel Antiquities Authority.

Ben-Shlomo, David, 2014. "Tell Jemmeh, Philistia, and the Assyrian Empire during the Iron Age." *Levant* 46: 58–88.

Ben-Tor, Amnon. 1987. "The Iron Age: Stratigraphy, Architecture, and Key Loci." In *Tel Qiri (Qedem, 24)*, ed. Amnon Ben-Tor and Yuval Portugali, 53–131. Jerusalem: Hebrew University of Jerusalem.

Ben-Tor, Amnon. 1993. "Joqneam." In *The New Encyclopedia of Archaeological Excavations in the Holy Land*, 4 vols., ed. Ephraim Stern, 3:805–11. Jerusalem: Israel Exploration Society.

Ben-Tor, Amnon. 2008. "Hazor." In *The New Encyclopedia of Archaeological Excavations in the Holy Land, Supplementary Volume*, vol. 5, ed. Ephraim Stern, 1769–1876. Jerusalem: Israel Exploration Society.

Bienkowski, Piotr. 2014. "Edom in the Iron Age II Period." In *Oxford Handbook of the Archaeology of the Levant, c. 8000–332 BCE*, ed. Margreet L. Steiner and Ann E. Killebrew, 782–94. Oxford: Oxford University Press.

Biran, Avraham. 1985. "On the Identification of Anathoth" (Hebrew). *ErIsr* 18: 209–14.

Biran, Avraham. 1993. "Aroer (in Judea)." In *The New Encyclopedia of Archaeological Excavations in the Holy Land*, 4 vols., ed. Ephraim Stern, 1:82–87. Jerusalem: Israel Exploration Society.

Biran, Avraham. 2008. "Dan." In *The New Encyclopedia of Archaeological Excavations in the Holy Land, Supplementary Volume*, vol. 5, ed. Ephraim Stern, 1864–69. Jerusalem: Israel Exploration Society.

Brand, Eti. 1998. *Salvage Excavations Near Tel Hadid—a Preliminary Report* (Hebrew). Tel Aviv: Institute of Archaeology, Tel Aviv Univ.

Broshi, Magen, and Israel Finkelstein. 1992. "The Population of Palestine in the Iron Age II." *BASOR* 287: 47–60.

Cahill, Jane M., and David Tarler. 1993. "Hammah, Tell el." In *The New Encyclopedia of Archaeological Excavations in the Holy Land*, 4 vols., ed. Ephraim Stern, 2:561–62. Jerusalem: Israel Exploration Society.

Campbell, Edward. 1993. "Shechem." In *The New Encyclopedia of Archaeological Excavations in the Holy Land*, 4 vols., ed. Ephraim Stern, 4:1345–54. Jerusalem: Israel Exploration Society.

Chambon, A. 1993. "Far'ah, Tell el-(North)." In *The New Encyclopedia of Archaeological Excavations in the Holy Land*, 4 vols., ed. Ephraim Stern, 433–40. Jerusalem: Israel Exploration Society.

Covello-Paran, Karen. 2008. "Excavations at Horbat Malta, Lower Galilee." *Atiqot* 59: 5–86.

Cross, Frank M., and J. T. Milik. 1956. "Explorations in the Judaean Buqeah." *BASOR* 142: 5–17.

de Vaux, Roland. 1993. "Qumran, Khirbet, and 'Ein Feshkha.'" In *The New Encyclopedia of Archaeological Excavations in the Holy Land*, 4 vols., ed. Ephraim Stern, 4:1235–41. Jerusalem: Israel Exploration Society.

Dever, William G. 1993. "Gezer." In *The New Encyclopedia of Archaeological Excavations in the Holy Land*, 4 vols., ed. Ephraim Stern, 2:496–506. Jerusalem: Israel Exploration Society.

Dothan, Moshe. 1993. "Acco." In *The New Encyclopedia of Archaeological Excavations in the Holy Land*, 4 vols., ed. Ephraim Stern, 1:17–23. Jerusalem: Israel Exploration Society.

Dothan, Trude, and Seymour Gitin. 1993. "Miqne, Tel (Ekron)." In *The New Encyclopedia of Archaeological Excavations in the Holy Land*, 4 vols., ed. Ephraim Stern, 3:1051–59. Jerusalem: Israel Exploration Society.

Eisenberg, Emanuel, and Alla Nagorski. 2002. "Tel Hevron (Er-Rumeidi)." *ESI* 114: 91*–92*.

Eitam, David. 1987. "Olive Oil Production during the Biblical Period." In *Olive Oil in Antiquity*, ed. Michael Heltzer and David Eitam, 16–36. Haifa: University of Haifa.

Eitam, David. 1996. "The Olive Oil Industry at Tel Miqne-Ekron in the Late Iron Age." In *Olive Oil in Antiquity: Israel and Neighbouring Countries from the Neolithic to the Early Arab Period*, ed. Michael Heltzer and David Eitam, 167–96. Padova, Italy: Sargon.

Eitam, David, and Amir Shomroni. 1987. "Research of the Oil Industry during the Iron Age at Tel Miqne." In *Olive Oil in Antiquity*, ed. Michael Heltzer and David Eitam, 37–56. Haifa: University of Haifa.

Eitan, Avi. 1983. "Vered Yeriho." *ESI* 2: 106–7.

Elgavish, Joseph. 1994. *Shikmona* (Hebrew). Jerusalem: Israel Exploration Society.

Fabian, Peter, and Itzhak Gilead. 2007. "The Iron Age Settlement within the Modern City of Beer-Sheva." In *New Studies on Beersheba, the Settlement in the Negev and the Edomites during the Iron Age* (abstract booklet, Hebrew), ed. Ya'akov Baumgarten and Sharon Gal, 3–4. Omer: Israel Antiquities Authority.

Fantalkin, Alexander. 2001. "Low Chronology and Greek Protogeometric and Geometric Pottery in the Southern Levant." *Levant* 33 (1): 117–25. https://doi.org/10.1179/lev.2001.33.1.117.

Fantalkin, Alexander. 2006. "Identity in the Making: Greeks in the Eastern Mediterranean during the Iron Age." In *Naukratis—Greek Diversity in Egypt: Studies on East Greek Pottery and Exchange in the Eastern Mediterranean*, ed. Alexandra Villing and Udo Schlotzhauer, 199–208. London: British Museum.

Fantalkin, Alexander. 2008. "Contacts between the Greek World and the Southern Levant during the Seventh-Sixth Centuries BCE." PhD dissertation, Tel Aviv University, Tel Aviv.

Fantalkin, Alexander, and Oren Tal. 2015. *Tell Qudadi: An Iron Age IIB Fortress on the Central Mediterranean Coast of Israel*. Leuven, Belgium: Peeters.

Faust, Avraham. 2006. "Farmsteads in Western Samaria's Foothills: A Reexamination." In *"I Will Speak the Riddles of Ancient Times (Aḥiḏoṯ minnî ḳeḏem—Ps 78:2b): Archaeological and Historical Studies in Honor of Amihai Mazar on the Occasion of His Sixtieth Birthday*, ed. Aren M. Maeir and Pierre De Miroschedji, 477–504. Winona Lake, IN: Eisenbrauns.

Faust, Avraham. 2008. "Settlement and Demography in Seventh Century Judah and the Extent and Intensity of Sennacherib's Campaign." *PEQ* 140 (3): 168–94. https://doi.org/10.1179/174313008X341528.

Faust, Avraham. 2011. "The Interests of the Assyrian Empire in the West: Olive Oil Production as a Test-Case." *JESHO* 54: 62–86.

Faust, Avraham. 2012. *Judah in the Neo-Babylonian Period: The Archaeology of Desolation*. Atlanta: Society of Biblical Literature. https://doi.org/10.2307/j.ctt5vjz28.

Faust, Avraham. 2014. "On Jerusalem's Expansion during the Iron Age II." In *Exploring the Narrative: Jerusalem and Jordan in the Bronze and Iron Ages*, ed. Eveline van der Steen, Jeannette Boertien, and Noor Mulder-Hymans, 256–85. London: Bloomsbury T&T Clark.

Faust, Avraham. 2015. "Settlement, Economy, and Demography under Assyrian Rule in the West: The Territories of the Former Kingdom of Israel as a Test-Case." *JAOS* 135: 765–89.

Faust, Avraham. 2018. "The Assyrian Century in the Southern Levant: An Overview of the Reality on the Ground." In *The Southern Levant under Assyrian Domination*, ed. Shawn Zelig Aster and Avraham Faust, 20–55. Winona Lake, IN: Eisenbrauns.

Faust, Avraham, and Zeev Safrai. 2005. "Salvage Excavations as a Source for Reconstructing Settlement History in Ancient Israel." *PEQ* 137 (2): 139–58. https://doi.org/10.1179/003103205x62981.

Faust, Avraham, and Zeev Safrai. 2015. *The Settlement History of Ancient Israel: A Quantitative Analysis*. Ramat Gan, Israel: Ingeborg Rennert Center for Jerusalem Studies.

Faust, Avraham, and Ehud Weiss. 2005. "Judah, Philistia, and the Mediterranean World: Reconstructing the Economic System of the Seventh Century BCE." *BASOR* 338: 71–92.

Faust, Avraham, and Ehud Weiss. 2011. "Between Assyria and the Mediterranean World: The Prosperity of Judah and Philistia in the Seventh Century BCE in Context." In *Interweaving Worlds: Systemic Interaction in Eurasia, 7th to 1st Millennia BC*, ed. Toby C. Wilkinson, Susan Sherratt, and John Bennet, 189–204. Oxford: Oxbow.

Finkelstein, Israel. 1994. "The Archaeology of the Days of Manasseh." In *Scripture and Other Artifacts: Essays on the Bible and Archaeology in Honor of Philip J. King*, ed. Michael D. Coogan, J. Cheryl Exum, and Lawrence E. Stager, 169–87. Louisville, KY: Westminster John Knox.

Finkelstein, Israel. 1995. *Living on the Fringe: The Archaeology and History of the Negev, Sinai, and Neighbouring Regions in the Bronze and Iron Ages*. Sheffield, GB: Sheffield Academic Press.

Fritz, Volkmar. 2008. "Chinnereth, Tell." In *The New Encyclopedia of Archaeological Excavations in the Holy Land, Supplementary Volume, vol. 5*, ed. Ephraim Stern, 1684–85. Jerusalem: Israel Exploration Society.

Funk, Robert B. 1968. "The History of Beth-zur with Reference to Its Defenses." In *The 1957 Excavations at Beth-Zur*, ed. Ovid R. Sellers, Robert B. Funk, John L. McKenzie, Paul Lapp, and Nancy Lapp, 4–17. Cambridge, MA: American Schools of Oriental Research.

Gal, Zvi. 1992. *Lower Galilee during the Iron Age*. Winona Lake, IN: Eisenbrauns.

Gal, Zvi, and Yardena Alexandre. 2000. *Horbat Rosh Zayit: An Iron Age Storage Fort and Village*. Jerusalem: Israel Antiquities Authority. https://doi.org/10.2307/j.ctt1fzhfg1.

Gal, Zvi, and Rafael Frankel. 1993. "An Olive Oil Press Complex at Hurvat Rosh Zayit." *ZDPV* 109: 128–40.

Gilboa, Ayelet. 1996. "Assyrian-Type Pottery at Dor and the Status of the Town during the Assyrian Occupation Period" (Hebrew). *ErIsr* 25: 122–35.

Gitin, Seymour. 1995. "Tel Miqne-Ekron in the 7th Century BCE: The Impact of Economic Innovation and Foreign Cultural Influences on a Neo-Assyrian Vassal City-State." In *Recent Excavations in Israel: A View to the West*, ed. Seymour Gitin, 61–79. Dubuque, IA: Kendall/Hunt.

Gitin, Seymour. 1997. "The Neo-Assyrian Empire and Its Western Periphery: The Levant, with a Focus on Philistine Ekron." In *Assyria 1995, Proceedings of the 10th Anniversary Symposium of the Neo-Assyrian Text Corpus Project*, ed. Simo Parpola and Robert M. Whiting, 77–103. Helsinki: Neo-Assyrian Text Corpus Project.

Golani, Amir. 2005. "Horvat Avimor." *Archaeological News: Excavations and Surveys in Israel* 117 (internet edition).

Gophna, Ram, and Yael Yisraeli. 1973. "Soundings at Beer Sheva (Bir es-Seba')." In *Beer-Sheba I, Excavations at Tel Beer-Sheba 1969–1971 Seasons*, ed. Yohanan Aharoni, 115–18. Tel Aviv: Tel Aviv University.

Grayson, Kirk A. 1991. "Assyria 668–635 BC: The Reign of Assurbanipal." In *Cambridge Ancient History*, ed. John A. Boardman, 3/2:194–228. Cambridge: Cambridge University Pres.

Grayson, Kirk A. 1995. "Assyrian Rule of Conquered Territory in Ancient Western Asia." In *Civilizations of the Ancient Near East*, ed. Jack M. Sasson, 1:959–68. New York: Scribner's.

Greener, Aaron. 2013. "Bethel." In *The Oxford Encyclopedia of Bible and Archaeology*, ed. Daniel M. Master, 98–104. New York: Oxford University Press.

Greenhut, Zvi, and Alon De Groot. 2009. *Salvage Excavations at Moza*. Jerusalem: Israel Antiquities Authority.

Har Even, Benaymin. 2011. "Khirbet Deir Daqla." Paper presented at the Second Annual Meeting on *In the Highland's Depth*, Hashmonaim, Israel, October 23.

Har Even, Benaymin. 2012. "Khirbet ed-Dawwar: A Rural Iron Age II Settlement on the Western Slopes of Samaria." Paper presented at the Twenty-second Annual Meeting on Judea and Samaria Research Studies, Ariel University, Israel, June 22.

Herr, Larry, and Mohammed Najjar. 2008. "The Iron Age." In *Jordan: An Archaeological Reader*, ed. Russell B. Adams, 311–34. London: Equinox.

Herzog, Zeev. 1993. "Michal, Tel." In *The New Encyclopedia of Archaeological Excavations in the Holy Land*, 4 vols., ed. Ephraim Stern, 3:1036–41. Jerusalem: Israel Exploration Society.

Hizmi, Hananya. 1996. "Horbat 'Eli." *ESI* 18: 51–52.

Humbert, Jean-Baptiste. 1993. "Keisan, Tell." In *The New Encyclopedia of Archaeological Excavations in the Holy Land*, 4 vols., ed. Ephraim Stern, 3:862–67. Jerusalem: Israel Exploration Society.

Kempinski, Aharon. 1993. "Masos, Tel." In *The New Encyclopedia of Archaeological Excavations in the Holy Land*, 4 vols., ed. Ephraim Stern, 3:988–89. Jerusalem: Israel Exploration Society.

Kochavi, Moshe. 1974. "Kh. Rabud = Debir." *TA* 1: 2–33.

Kochavi, Moshe. 1993. "Zeror, Tel." In *The New Encyclopedia of Archaeological Excavations in the Holy Land*, 4 vols., ed. Ephraim Stern, 4:1524–26. Jerusalem: Israel Exploration Society.

Kochavi, Moshe. 1998. "The Excavations at Tel Malhata: An Interim Report" (Hebrew). *Qad* 115: 30–39.

Kochavi, Moshe, and Akio Tsukimoto. 2008. "En Gev." In *The New Encyclopedia of Archaeological Excavations in the Holy Land, Supplementary Volume, vol. 5*, ed. Ephraim Stern, 1724–26. Jerusalem: Israel Exploration Society.

Lapp, Nancy L. 1978. "The 7th–6th-Century Occupation: Period III." In *The Third Campaign at Tell el-Ful: The Excavations of 1964*, ed. Nancy L. Lapp, 39–46. Cambridge, MA: BASOR.

Lehmann, Gunnar. 2002. "Area E." In *Tel Kabr: The 1986–1993 Excavation Seasons*, ed. Aharon Kempniski, 73–90. Tel Aviv: Tel Aviv University.

Lenzen, Cherie J. 1992. "Irbid, Tell." In *Anchor Bible Dictionary*, ed. David N. Freedman, 3:456–57. New York: Doubleday.

Liebowitz, Harold A. 2000. *Tel Yin'am I: The Late Bronze Age*. Austin: University of Texas Press.

Lipschits, Nili, and Gideon Biger. 1991. "Cedar of Lebanon (*Cedrus Libani*) in Israel during Antiquity." *IEJ* 41: 167–75.

Lipschits, Oded, Yuval Gadot, Benjamen Arubas, and Manfred Oeming. 2011. "Palace and Village, Paradise and Oblivion: Unraveling the Secrets of Ramat Rahel." *NEA* 74: 2–49.

Magen, Yitzhak, and Michael Dadon. 1999. "Nebi Samwil (Shmuel Hanavi–Har Hasimha)" (Hebrew). *Qad* 118: 62–77.

Master, Daniel M. 2003. "Trade and Politics: Ashkelon's Balancing Act in the Seventh Century BCE." *BASOR* 330: 47–64.

Master, Daniel M. 2009. "From the Baqê'ah to Ashkelon." In *Exploring the Longue Durée: Essays in Honor of Lawrence E. Stager*, ed. J. David Schloen, 305–17. Winona Lake, IN: Eisenbrauns.

Master, Daniel M. 2013. "Samaria." In *Oxford Encyclopedia of Bible and Archaeology*, ed. Daniel M. Master, 329–36. New York: Oxford University Press.

Mazar, Amihai. 1985. *Excavations at Tell Qasile, Part Two: The Philistine Sanctuary, Various Finds, the Pottery, Conclusions, Appendixes*. Jerusalem: Hebrew University.

Mazar, Amihai. 1993, "Marjameh, Khirbet." In *The New Encyclopedia of Archaeological Excavations in the Holy Land*, 4 vols., ed. Ephraim Stern, 3:965–66. Jerusalem: Israel Exploration Society.

Mazar, Amihai. 1997. *Tel Batash I (Qedem 37)*. Jerusalem: Hebrew University.

Mazar, Amihai. 2008a. "Beth-Shean." In *The New Encyclopedia of Archaeological Excavations in the Holy Land, Supplementary Volume, vol. 5*, ed. Ephraim Stern, 1616–22. Jerusalem: Israel Exploration Society.

Mazar, Amihai. 2008b. "Rehov." In *The New Encyclopedia of Archaeological Excavations in the Holy Land, Supplementary Volume, vol. 5.*, ed. Ephraim Stern, 2013–18. Jerusalem: Israel Exploration Society.

Mazar, Amihai, David Amit, and Zvi Ilan. 1996. "Hurvat Shihah: An Iron Age Site in the Judean Desert." In *Retrieving the Past: Essays on Archaeological Research and Methodology in Honor of Gus W. Beek*, ed. Joe D. Seger, 193–211. Winona Lake, IN: Eisenbrauns.

Mazar, Amihai, and Navah Panitz-Cohen. 2001. *Timnah (Tel Batash) II: The Finds from the First Millennium BCE (text)*. Jerusalem: Hebrew University.

Na'aman, Nadav. 1987. "The Negev in the Last Century of the Kingdom of Judah" (Hebrew). *Cathedra* 42: 3–15.

Na'aman, Nadav. 2009. "The Growth and Development of Judah and Jerusalem in the Eighth Century BCE: A Rejoinder." *RB* 116: 321–35.

Oded, Busteny. 1979. *Mass Deportation and Deportees in the Neo-Assyrian Empire*. Wiesbaden: Dr. Ludwig Reichert.

Oren, Eliezer, 1993. "Sera, Tel." In *The New Encyclopedia of Archaeological Excavations in the Holy Land*, 4 vols., ed. Ephraim Stern, 4:1329–35. Jerusalem: Israel Exploration Society.

Pakkala, Juha, Stefan Munger, and Jurgen Zangenberg. 2004. *Kinneret Regional Project: Tel Kinrot Excavations*. Vantaa: Finnish Institute of the Middle East Report.

Paley, Samuel M., and Yosef Porath. 1993. "Hefer, Tel." In *The New Encyclopedia of Archaeological Excavations in the Holy Land*, 4 vols., ed. Ephraim Stern, 2:609–14. Jerusalem: Israel Exploration Society.

Panitz-Cohen, Navah. 2005. "A Salvage Excavation in the New Market in Beersheba: New Light on Iron Age IIB Occupation at Beersheba." *IEJ* 55: 143–55.

Parpola, Simo, and Kazuko Watanabe. 1988. *Neo-Assyrian Treaties and Loyalty Oaths*. Helsinki: Helsinki University Press.

Pritchard, James B. 1964. *Winery, Defenses, and Soundings at Gibeon*. Philadelphia: University Museum.

Riklin, Shimon. 1995. "A Fortress at Michmas on the North-Eastern Border of Judean Desert." *Judea and Samaria Research Studies* 4: 69–73.

Riklin, Shimon. 1997. "Bet Arye" (Hebrew). *Atiqot* 32: 7–20.

Schloen, David. 2001. *The House of the Father as Fact and Symbol*. Winona Lake, IN: Eisenbrauns.

Singer-Avitz, Lily. 2014. "The Pottery of Megiddo Strata III-II and a Proposed Subdivision of the Iron IIC Period in Northern Israel." *BASOR* 372: 123–45.

Stager, Lawrence E. 1976. "Farming in the Judean Desert during the Iron Age." *BASOR* 221: 145–58.

Stager, Lawrence E. 1996. "Ashkelon and the Archaeology of Destruction: Kislev 604 BCE." *ErIsr* 25: 61*–74*.

Steiner, Margreet L. 2014. "Moab during the Iron Age II Period." In *Oxford Handbook of the Archaeology of the Levant, c. 8000–332 BCE*, ed. Margreet L. Steiner and Ann E. Killebrew, 770–81. Oxford: Oxford University Press.

Stern, Ephraim. 1993a. "Kedesh, Tel." In *The New Encyclopedia of Archaeological Excavations in the Holy Land*, 4 vols., ed. Ephraim Stern, 3:860. Jerusalem: Israel Exploration Society.

Stern, Ephraim, ed. 1993b. *The New Encyclopedia of Archaeological Excavations in the Holy Land*. 4 vols. Jerusalem: Israel Exploration Society.

Stern, Ephraim. 1994. "The Eastern Border of the Kingdom of Judah." In *Scripture and Other Artifacts: Essays on the Bible and Archaeology in Honor of Philip J. King*, ed. Michael D. Coogan, J. Cheryl Exum, and Lawrence E. Stager, 399–409. Louisville, KY: Westminster John Knox.

Stern, Ephraim. 2001. *Archaeology of the Land of the Bible: The Assyrian, Babylonian, and Persian Periods (732–332 BCE)*. New York: Doubleday.

Stern, Ephraim. 2007. *En-Gedi Excavations I: Final Report (1961–1965)*. Jerusalem: IES and Hebrew University.

Stern, Ephraim, ed. 2008. *The New Encyclopedia of Archaeological Excavations in the Holy Land, Supplementary Volume, vol. 5*. Jerusalem: Israel Exploration Society.

Tavgar, Aharon. 2012. "Settlement and Political Processes at Mount Ephraim in the Assyrian, Babylonian, and Persian Periods." MA dissertation, Bar-Ilan University, Ramat Gan, Israel.

Thareani, Yifat. 2011. *Tel 'Aroer: The Iron II Caravan Town and the Hellenistic–Early Roman Settlement*. Jerusalem: Hebrew Union College, Jewish Institute of Religion.

Thareani-Sussely, Yifat. 2007. "The 'Archaeology of the Days of Menasseh' Reconsidered in the Light of Evidence from the Beersheba Valley." *PEQ* 139 (2): 69–77. https://doi.org/10.1179/003103207X194091.

Tyson, Craig W. 2014. "Peripheral Elite as Imperial Collaborators." *JAR* 70: 481–509.

Ussishkin, David. 2004. "A Synopsis of the Stratigraphical, Chronological, and Historical Issues." In *The Renewed Archaeological Excavations at Lachish (1973–1994)*, ed. David Ussishkin, 50–119. Tel Aviv: Tel Aviv University.

Van De Mieroop, Marc. 2007. *A History of the Ancient Near East, ca. 3000–323 BC*. Oxford: Blackwell.

Vieweger, Dieter, and Jutta Haser. 2007. "Tall Zira'a: Five Thousand Years of Palestinian History on a Single-Settlement Mound." *NEA* 70: 147–67.

Waldbaum, Jane C. 1994. "Early Greek Contacts with the Levant, ca. 1000–600 BC: The Eastern Perspective." *BASOR* 293: 53–66.

Waldbaum, Jane C. 1997. "Greeks in the East or Greeks and the East: Problems in the Definition and Recognition of Presence." *BASOR* 305: 1–17.

Weiss, Ehud, and Mardechai E. Kislev. 2004. "Plant Remains as Indicators of Economic Activity: A Case Study." *JAS* 31: 1–13.

Yadin, Esther, and Moshe Kochavi. 2008. "Hadar, Tel." In *The New Encyclopedia of Archaeological Excavations in the Holy Land, Supplementary Volume, vol. 5*, ed. Ephraim Stern, 1756–57. Jerusalem: Israel Exploration Society.

Yasur-Landau, Assaf, Michael D. Press, and Eran Arie. 2016. "Rethinking Tel Achziv: An Iron II Architectonic and Ceramic Sequence from Southern Phoenicia." *TA* 43: 188–220.

Yezerski, Irit. 2013. "Iron Age Burial Customs in the Samaria Highlands." *TA* 40: 72–98.

Younger, K. Lawson. 2015. "The Assyrian Economic Impact on the Southern Levant in the Light of Recent Study." *IEJ* 65: 179–204.

Younker, Randall W. 2014. "Ammon during the Iron Age II Period." In *Oxford Handbook of the Archaeology of the Levant, c. 8000–332 BCE*, ed. Margreet L. Steiner and Ann E. Killebrew, 757–69. Oxford: Oxford University Press.

Zorn, Jeffrey R. 1993. "Nasbeh, Tell en-." In *The New Encyclopedia of Archaeological Excavations in the Holy Land*, 4 vols., ed. Ephraim Stern, 3:1098–1102. Jerusalem: Israel Exploration Society.

5

Reaction, Reliance, Resistance?

Judean Pillar Figurines in the Neo-Assyrian Levant

Erin Darby
(University of Tennessee)

DOI: 10.5876/9781607328230.c005

Judean pillar figurines (JPFs) have been the recipients of a great deal of attention over the past century, and much of that energy has focused on the iconography of the figurines and what figure they represent. Prominent among these interpretations are connections drawn with goddesses, such as Asherah (Kletter 1996, 10–17; Darby 2014, 34–46). Only relatively recently have scholars attempted to collate archaeological data that can be brought to bear on the interpretation of the figurines, but these approaches have emphasized their connection with domestic spaces and thus household religion (e.g., Holladay 1987; Kletter 1996; Schmitt 2012).

For the sake of clarification, JPFs are female figurines consisting of a solid hand-modeled pillar base, breasts, arms either holding or supporting the breasts, and two different styles of heads. One type consists of a separately molded face joined to the base by a clay tang (figure. 5.1). The molded faces have between one and six rows of horizontally arranged curls, smiling faces, eyes, and eyebrows. The other major type consists of a hand-pinched head made in tandem with the body (figure 5.2). Variations within this corpus include hollow and wheel-turned bases, figurines holding discs or children, and heads with applied features, such as a cap, turban, and side-locks (figure 5.3). The figurines are only attested in clay (rather than metal, stone, or faience). They were fired, whitewashed, and painted, although the whitewash and paint are

FIGURE 5.1. *Molded head figurine from the City of David. Courtesy, Hebrew University of Jerusalem.*

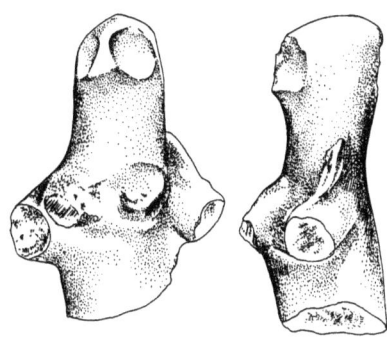

FIGURE 5.2. *Pinched head figurine from the City of David. Courtesy, Hebrew University of Jerusalem.*

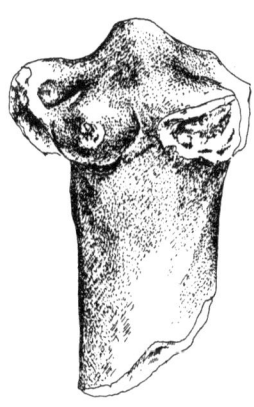

FIGURE 5.3. *JPF body from the City of David. Courtesy, Hebrew University of Jerusalem.*

usually poorly preserved. When present, the paint is found on the faces and the headdress and in stripes above the breasts, perhaps depicting a necklace or aegis (Kletter 1996; Darby 2014).

Pillar figurines with other stylistic characteristics (e.g., vertical braids, holding objects, hollow and wheel-formed pillar bases) were produced throughout the region in the eighth through sixth centuries BCE (Kletter 1996). Judean pillar figurines are so named because their distribution corresponds with the political boundaries of ancient Judah. Though outnumbered by the Judean variety, other styles of pillar figurines are occasionally found within the boundary of Judah as well.

Although data from archaeological excavations have not yet clarified who the figurines depict (see more below), they have shed light on their chronological range. Recent research suggests that these figurines arise in Judah at the end of the ninth through the beginning of the eighth centuries BCE and become more numerous in the eighth and seventh centuries BCE. Moreover, data from many sites indicate that the figurines cease in the first half of the sixth century, probably in coordination with the Babylonian destruction of Judah (Kletter 1996; Darby 2014, 213–58).

Thus, JPFs are used for a relatively short period of time—about 225 years. And this begs the question of what historical circumstances might account for their rise, dissemination, and denouement. Scholars who study figurines sometimes credit trade networks with the spread of images (Stern 1989, 22–29; Gubel 1991, 132–36; Press 2012). This may lead to the supposition that JPFs were adopted from foreign religion, an interpretation that already enjoys a long history in the scholarly record (e.g., Pritchard 1962, 120; Holland 1975, 174, 187; Holladay 1987, 274–80; Nadelman 1989, 123; Franken and Steiner 1990, 128; Miller 2000, 52–53; Dever 2005, 55).

In contrast with this theory, the evidence suggests that figurines were rarely traded. Iron II trade across the Neo-Assyrian Empire focused on elite goods, such as semi-precious stones, metals, wood, and cloth (Van de Mieroop 1987; Elat 1991, 23–29). Relatively few data about potters survive from any period of ancient Near Eastern history, including the ninth through sixth centuries, probably because it was impractical for states to control the production and distribution of such a non-elite material as clay (Heltzer 1979, 475, 488, 493, 495; 1987, 243; Moorey 1994, 17, 141; Steinkeller 1996, 233–34, 247, 249–50; 1996, 279; Postgate 1987, 259; Stein and Blackman 1993, 49–55; Duistermaat 2008, 347, 420–21). Meanwhile, iconographic analysis has shown that territories were not simply importing iconographic styles from neighboring regions (Kletter 1996; Ben-Shlomo 2010; Press 2012; Darby 2014). Rather, regional figurine styles were strongly developed by the end of the eighth century, as evidenced in Israel (Kletter 1996), Judah (Kletter 1996; Darby 2014), Philistia (Ben-Shlomo 2010; Press 2012), Cyprus (Karageorghis 1991), Syria (Pruß 2010), Ammon, Moab, Edom ('Amr 1980; Kletter 1996; Daviau 2001), Egypt (Waraksa 2009), and Mesopotamia (Woolley 1926; Van Buren 1930; Green 1983; Nakamura

2005). Finally, recent petrographic analysis has demonstrated that figurines found in Jerusalem seem to have been made locally and rarely traded outside of the settlement in which they were produced (Darby 2014, 183–212; Ben-Shlomo and Darby 2014). All of this information combines to suggest that trade cannot be the simple one-stop answer to why figurines arise and fall in this period of time.

Other scholars have noticed that the time period during which JPFs become popular also coincides with Assyrian domination of the region. Ryan Byrne (2004, 140–41, 145), Ian Douglas Wilson (2012, 275), and Cynthia R. Chapman (2012) have all commented on the confluence of JPFs and Assyrian hegemony, and they all suggest that JPFs were used to consolidate local identities against imperial power. Unfortunately, it is difficult to move beyond surface-level speculation about the motivations of people making and using figurines in the eighth and seventh centuries BCE. For example, what evidence might be wielded to suggest that Judeans understood JPFs as a means of identity consolidation or counter-hegemony?

Moreover, these authors do not account for other possibilities. It is equally plausible that the popularization of figurines signifies an acceptance of larger cultural forces set in motion by the expansion of the Neo-Assyrian Empire or that the figurine tradition was influenced by and reacting to the figurine styles of neighboring states (e.g., Ammon, Edom, Phoenicia, Philistia), brought into relief by the larger imperial system. Some combination of acceptance and resistance is also likely (cf. Johnston 1995, 371, 381). In an attempt to move beyond speculation based on the circumstantial confluence of JPFs and Assyrian control of Judah, this chapter investigates the rise of healing rituals and figurine rituals throughout the Mediterranean in the ninth through sixth centuries BCE.

FIGURINES ACROSS THE EMPIRE

The first step toward understanding the relationship between Judah's figurine tradition and its role in the Neo-Assyrian Empire is to acknowledge that Judah is not the only place with a developing figurine tradition in the ninth through eighth centuries. Rather, figurines are attested during this period in almost every region of the empire, including the imperial center. In most areas this period of production seems to be marked by a wide variety of stylistic and technological adaptations that may signify a diversity of opinions and practices. By the middle to the end of the eighth century, regional styles seem to have crystallized, perhaps also signifying an increasing codification of figurine rituals (Green 1983, 87n2; Ellis 1995, 164–65; Press 2012; Darby 2014, 355–57, 373–74).

While the iconography of figurines varies, in most regions the new figurine styles build on the traditions of previous periods and show a marked regional influence rather than an international iconographic homogeneity. For example, in Judah the JPF style reflects close iconographic ties with previous Levantine traditions, like Late Bronze naked female plaque figurines, Iron II female appliqués on cult stands, and even female images in monumental art (see below). At the same time, JPFs also represent a new domestic adaptation of images previously used in more official space, like the females on cult stands and boxes found in shrines in the preceding centuries (Darby 2014, 319–21, 330–34). In Mesopotamia, Iron II figurines draw from images in Assyrian and Babylonian mythology, such as *apkallū* and the bullman, and long-standing rituals, such as burying foundation deposits (Van Buren 1931, 75; Preusser 1954, 22, 58, taf. 15, 28–29; Mallowan 1966a, 226–27, 347n41, 1966b, 384, 387, fig. 312, 388–90; Nakamura 2005). Here, too, there is some relationship between the iconography of Iron II figurines and images previously found in the official space of palaces and temples (Green 1983, 88; Wiggermann 1992; Gane 2012, 16–20). Thus, in both Judah and Assyria, the imagery adopted by figurine makers reflects marked regional styles, but both also suggest the increased use of these images outside of "official" space.

That being the case, what historical scenario might account for this empire-wide turn toward miniature terracottas? This question depends in part on the function of figurines, which has been discussed at length elsewhere (Darby 2014). At present, it is sufficient to summarize as follows. Taking textual descriptions of figurines in the imperial center together with naked female imagery in the Levant suggests that figurines may have been used in rituals of protection and healing throughout the empire. This conclusion is supported by the myriad texts describing a wide variety of figurines in sympathetic, exorcistic, and apotropaic rituals in Mesopotamia, Anatolia, and Egypt from the Bronze and Iron Ages (Darby 2014, 59–97).[1]

Also in narrative form from the Levant, the epic of Kirtu describes El fashioning a clay female to banish Kirtu's sickness (Lewis 2013, 2014). In Egyptian magico-medical literature, breast milk was even used during some healing rituals (Robins 1993, 90; Allen 2005, 34).

The protective nature of Levantine female figurines is indicated by the variety of contexts and media in which the naked female trope appears during the Late Bronze through the Iron II (Darby 2014, 325–28, 330–33, 344–47), including cult stands and boxes found in shrine spaces,[2] monumental art

(Winter 2010, 275, fig. 3), metal and ivory horse trappings (Orchard 1967, 29, no. 144, pl. XXXI; Burkert 1992, 16, 18, fig. 2, 20; Gubel 2005, 126, fig. 14, 129, fig. 17, 130; Winter 2010, 340, 374, fig. 2), and seals whose inscriptions prove they were owned by males (Avigad 1977; Hübner 1993, 142–43; Sass 1993, 233, fig. 142, 236). The breadth of the tropes' application does not suggest a unique connection between images of naked females and actual women, as is often claimed for the figurines. However, the image may connote protection across these various formats.[3]

Moreover, when the figurines are considered in combination with the documentary evidence mentioned above, as well as the possible synergy between these texts and a variety of anthropomorphic vessels that depict either breasts (e.g., Weippert 1977; Winter 1983, 372–74) or a woman expressing breast milk into a cup (Allen 2005, 33, fig. 27–28), it seems that a connection between the naked female and healing cannot be easily dismissed. Even the archaeological context of JPFs provides some evidence to undergird this association, as will be presented below.

MAGICO-MEDICAL TRADITIONS ACROSS THE EMPIRE

At present, the question is whether the spread of magico-medical figurine rituals during the Iron Age can provide a plausible historical scenario for the rise of figurines in this period. In fact, healing rites were spreading across the empire in the Iron II.[4] It is not that local cultures were devoid of their own healing rituals, but it seems to have become palatable to canvas far and wide for extra-national deities and practices, particularly in regard to healing and sickness. The most obvious biblical examples are the Syrian general Na'aman in 2 Kings 5 and Ahazia consulting Baal-zebub of Ekron (2 Kings 1:2–16; Avalos 1995, 283; Smith 2010, 114).

In the eighth century, even the Neo-Assyrian Empire increasingly adopted images of Babylonian deities and guardians in palace construction (Reade 1979, 335, 341) and in figurine rituals (Darby 2014, 75–91). Simo Parpola (2007, 260–64) notes the presence of Egyptian dream interpreters, Hittite augurs, and Babylonian scholars as royal advisers in the Assyrian court. Private individuals may have hired Babylonian scholars to teach the arts of exorcism, astrology, and extispacy.[5]

While interactions prior to the Iron Age may have accounted for the spread of some rituals, the Iron II saw unique developments in Mesopotamian healing rites (Von Soden 1994, 163; Scurlock and Andersen 2005, 6–7). The diagnostic and prognostic handbook was in preparation between 1430 and 1050 BCE and was redacted under the patronage of Adad-apla-iddina (1068–1047 BCE). Ashurbanipal also preserved a large collection of these texts in his Nineveh library, and another collection was found in Aššur (Von Soden 1994, 155–56). Ashurbanipal's collection should be considered in light of the continuous sickness of his father, Esarhaddon, and Esarhaddon's consistent interest in religious matters in general and in medical rituals in particular (Nevling Porter 1993, 68–71; Melville 1999, 81).

Moreover, it seems that magico-medical and figurine rituals spread from the Near East at least as far as ancient Greece. Beginning with Tiglath-pileser III and continuing through the reigns of Shalmaneser V, Sargon II, Sennacherib, and Ashurbanipal, the Neo-Assyrian Empire was increasingly involved in Aegean matters in both trade and warfare (Burkert 1992, 11–14; Noegel 2007, 29; Smith 2009, 11). Thus, some scholars have hypothesized that foreign itinerant seers and purification priests in Greece spread "sacred," "magical," and "medical" traditions.[6] These traditions include the introduction of child-killing demons, the Gorgon masks, dog images, incense burning, purifactory rituals, hepatoscopy, and foundation deposits,[7] suggesting a "continuous and gradual infiltration of medical and herbal lore from the Near East and Egypt" (Scarborough 1991, 140, 162; Faraone 1992, 26–27; Noegel 2007, 30). Markham J. Geller (2004, 23–25, 59–60) likewise notes the possibility that NAM.BÚR.BI- and Šurpu-style rituals, which originated in Mesopotamia, were used in Greece for cure and protection from portended or actual disease,[8] going so far as to suggest that the Babylonian-style medicine was the one major system of medicine prior to the fifth century.

It seems that the spread of medicinal practices in the Iron II, including those associated with figurines, is best situated during the Neo-Assyrian Empire. Performing the medical rituals in the imperial center were the *asû*, a type of pharmacist or healer, and the *āšipu*, variously understood as conjurers, healers, exorcists, scribes, and priests (Cryer 1994, 205; Scurlock 1999, 69; Scurlock and Andersen 2005, 7, 10).[9] The extant ritual texts indicate that these professionals seem to have performed rituals in the domestic units where sick individuals were housed rather than in the temple (Cryer 1994, 207n4; Avalos 1995, 173–82). Furthermore, the *āšipu* performed a number of figurine rituals related to sympathetic, medical, exorcistic, and apotropaic ritual needs (Darby 2014, 71–72, 81–91). The patron goddess of medicine was Gula, a deity who often acted as an intermediary between the patient and the god or goddess responsible for the patient's illness (Avalos 1995, 100–110, 191, 227; Geller 2010, 9). In addition to deities, spirits were commonly attributed with the ability to inflict illness (Scurlock and Andersen 2005, 11–12). Even the selection of bricks for royal building projects may have been motivated by the stones' apotropaic and healing qualities (Russell 1997, 299–300).

MAGICO-MEDICAL RITUALS IN JUDAH

To return to Judah, recent scholarship has demonstrated the significant impact Judah's role in the empire had on Judean society in the Iron II (Smith 2010, 131–85; Darby 2014, 375–82). More specifically, Mesopotamian practice shares some important similarities with healing rituals mentioned in the Bible, the most important of which is that patients were to remain in the home rather than travel to the temple (Avalos 1995, 173–82, 249, 251–54, 258), so the locus of healing and protective rituals would have been the domestic compound.

As is well-known, JPFs predominate in domestic contexts, particularly in Jerusalem, the capital city of Judah (Kletter 1996; Darby 2014). While JPFs do appear on extramural city streets and occasionally in tombs surrounding the city, they are virtually absent in public buildings or shrine spaces (Darby 2014).[10] By far the most common contexts are related to domestic compounds, including floors, fills, walls, pits, or alleyways. Even outside Jerusalem, JPF fragments are rarely found in shrines or with cultic implements, such as altars and standing stones, and are far more numerous in domestic contexts (Kletter 1996; Darby 2014). While domestic contexts have sometimes been cited as evidence that JPFs were used primarily in fertility or lactation rituals (Darby 2014, 55–59), as yet, little data support the argument (see above). Clearly, other types of rituals were performed in the home as well, especially those relating to healing, exorcistic, and apotropaic rituals.

There remains the question of who might have been performing these rituals in ancient Judah. Unlike the *āšipu* of Mesopotamia, the Bible does not preserve a record of healing rituals performed by the priest, whose main concerns in the text relate to identifying purity and impurity (Avalos 1995, 365–67; Brown 1995, 96–97). This does not necessarily imply that healing rituals were not performed. The Bible preserves another set of texts that refer to "healers" (Avalos 1995, 286–87).[11] In fact, a bulla of a seal belonging to a "healer" was actually recovered in the City of David excavations from Area G, the elite quarter (Shoham 1994, 58). Incidentally, this quarter also produced scores of JPF fragments (Darby 2014, 151–60). Furthermore, if Hector Avalos (1995, 395) is correct to suggest that some postexilic authors considered healers problematic, this may help explain the relative absence of anthropomorphic figurines from Yehud in that period (Stern 1989).

In sum, a review of the Mediterranean in the ninth through seventh centuries BCE reveals that the spread of magico-medical, apotropaic, and exorcistic figurine rituals at exactly this time may account for the newfound popularity of miniature terracottas. This does not necessarily imply that Judean artisans or ritual experts borrowed Assyrian-style figurine rituals or that they did so in a simplistic way. Rather, iconographic evidence already discussed suggests that JPF style shared a relationship with a host of Levantine traditions. Texts from Egypt and Ugarit reveal that images of females, breasts, and breast milk may have been associated with healing and protection sometime prior to the Late Bronze collapse. However, one cannot escape the fact that free-standing female figurines did not become popular again until the period of Neo-Assyrian expansion and that this period was also marked by the rise of small clay figurines used for healing, exorcism, and apotropaism in Assyria as well as in the outer reaches of the imperial system.

Given the evidence at present, little more can be said about how such rituals might have spread or who was officiating such rituals in Levantine communities in this period. At best, it might be postulated that the interaction between various locales and their figurine traditions was facilitated by a learned class of healers. In Assyria, some of these professionals were also scribes who worked for the king and various temples, in addition to serving local inhabitants (Darby 2014, 73). Mark S. Smith (2010, 152–56) has suggested that Neo-Assyrian influence might have moved through scribal channels, even hypothesizing that Judean scribes participated in some type of cultural exchange.

It is also difficult to clarify what types of ritual adaptations might have been communicated across a scribal healing network. One possibility is the reassertion of the home as the locus for healing rituals. This development suggests a possible shift in ritual techniques from votive practice in shrine contexts to exorcistic and apotropaic practice in the home. New associations drawn among illness, the spiritual entities causing illness, and their access to domestic and neighborhood spaces may have been responsible for the new adaptations of the female image and its deposition.

One factor that may have catalyzed healing rituals in general and household rituals in particular was the rise of large-scale plagues in the late ninth through eighth centuries. It is not that sickness was unknown prior to this point, but the Neo-Assyrian center experienced a number of epidemics in this period (Martinez 1990; Gallagher 1999, 247).[12] As the empire became increasingly connected by population movements related to war, trade, and urbanization, epidemics may have become more common, as might the de facto practice of quarantining the diseased in the home and a general interest in healing, exorcistic, and apotropaic rituals. Thus, in each area, regional traditions may have been adapted in response to the developing public health landscape.

CONCLUSION

This chapter has problematized current scholarly treatments of "JPFs as resistance" and suggested some different historical scenarios that might account for the rise of JPFs in the eighth century. Above all, it must be kept in mind that Judah was not alone in producing figurines in this period; all of Judah's neighbors were producing clay female figurines at the same time. This suggests that if JPFs were popularized in resistance to Assyrian hegemony, a more supportable theory would include them as part of a regional, Levantine reassertion of long-standing female figurine traditions associated with protection and healing. In fact, the connection between JPFs and national style was never based on the iconographic subject matter of the figurines alone, since female pillar figurines occur in most of the Levantine polities. Rather, it is the unique stylistic features of JPFs—such as the arrangement of the hair or wig, the width of the face, the predominant gestures, the solid pillar—that are cited as evidence for their connection with national identity and that distinguish Judah from the small states that also produced female figurines with different stylistic features.

Mark Smith offers some explanation for this phenomenon. He argues that when equal and competing imperial powers are absent, as was the case when the Neo-Assyrian Empire ruled virtually unchallenged, a regional discourse emerges that focuses on cultural interactions between close neighbors (Smith 2010, 99–103, 128–29). This period of regional interactions also saw the rise of JPFs, perhaps in connection with other artisan traditions in Phoenicia or northern Israel (Darby 2014, 314–19, 343–47, 356–57). Thus, the distinctive style of JPFs might have crystallized as an important identity marker only after it had been in existence for some time. It would then serve to distinguish Judah from neighboring traditions.

This does not imply, however, that Assyrian influence was absent prior to the end of the Judean monarchy in the early sixth century BCE. Far from a relationship of mere opposition, the evidence suggests that Judah interacted with and benefited from its position in the empire. Nor can the cross-cultural interactions between Levantine neighbors be isolated from Assyrian expansion. In fact, the empire may have facilitated the further development of such polities as well as their interactions, whether in cooperation with or opposition to Assyrian power (Finkelstein 1999; Panitz-Cohen 2010, 129).[13] It is possible that figurine rituals arose in the ninth through sixth centuries BCE across the empire and that various regions were influenced by their neighbors, by the distant imperial center, or by a general cultural diffusion characterized less by a "sender-and-receiver" model and more by multiple network connections. Nor can it be ruled out that Assyrian interactions with the Levant might have undergirded the development of miniature apotropaic figurines in the Assyrian tradition.

Despite these hypotheses, scholars cannot know what figurine producers, ritual officiants, or the Judean population thought about figurines and thus whether they intended to use them to build national identity or to resist Assyrian hegemony. As no Assyrian-style figurines have been uncovered in Jerusalem or Judah, there can be no evidence that JPFs were created or popularized primarily to counteract an encroaching Assyrian iconographic tradition. While the emerging model in current scholarship implies that resistance was a central motive for figurine producers and users, it is difficult to identify the motivations behind the production of style groups. In actuality, a "style group" could simply indicate a long-standing tradition that marks how artisan communities of a particular area produced figurines. Furthermore, the motivations for preserving a style group could have varied between producers and could have changed over time.[14]

That having been said, JPFs may have contributed to national identity without either figurine producers or users intending them for that purpose. As Catherine Bell states, ritual agents often cannot articulate to themselves what ritual does. Regardless, when individuals participate in ritual activity, they are also structured by it (Bell 1992, 1997).[15] Thus, the repeated use of a symbol portrayed with unique Judean stylistic features, in contrast to the features of figurines in surrounding nations, may have reproduced in the ritual agents a sense of social and political identity. It may also have confirmed the power structures of the political entity that reinforced that identity, as well as the gender hierarchies encoded in that social and political organization. This distinctive image, when used in healing rites associated with liminal states between life and death, may have reaffirmed the individual's participation in a broader social network. Performed as a rite of transition, the ritual initiates the person healed not only into the community of the living but also into a particular social, political, and gendered version of that community. As implements in a rite of protection, the figurines remind the ritual agents of the dangers of liminality and reinforce positive regard for the forces responsible for physical, personal, and social order.

NOTES

1. Examples are well-documented in every area, especially in Neo-Assyrian literature, for example, ŠÀ.ZI.GA (Biggs 1967), *bît rimki* (Læssøe 1955), NAM.BUR.BI (Caplice 1974; Maul 1994), *Šumma Izbu* (Leichty 1970), *Šurpu* (Reiner 1958), *Maqlû* (Abusch 2002), Hand of Ghost (Scurlock 2006), and *šep lemutti ina bīt amēli parāsu* (Wiggermann 1992).

2. For example, Beck 2002, 185, figs. 1, 2, 3a, 209, fig. 10, 414; Tadmor 2006, 322; Kletter and Ziffer 2010, CAT84, 245, pls. 21:1; 43:1 bottom; 119; 120:1; CAT85, 246, pl. 41:1; 120:2–3; CAT86, 246, pl. 21:2; 121; CAT92, 248–49, pl. 23:2; 125:2–3; 126:1–2; CAT113, 257–58, pl. 26:1; 143:2; 144; CAT123, 261, pl. 150:2; CAT28, 220–21, pls. 9:2; 69; 70:1; CAT29, 221, pls. 47:3; 70:2–3; CAT57, 234, pls. 7:1; 17:2; 99–100; CAT90, 247–48, pl. 1:2–3; 40:1–2; 41; 123:3–4; CAT37, 224–25, pls. 11:1; 76–77; 78:1–2; CAT44, 227–28, pls. 13:1; 84–85; CAT49, 230, pls. 2:2, bottom; 14:2; 90:1, 3; 91:1 (claims ridges beneath figures represent legs but conjectural at best); CAT59, 236, pls. 33:1; 103:2–3.

3. Following Schroer (2007, 430–38) and her interpretation of frontally molded females on cult stands. In contrast with the present author, Schroer does not believe her interpretation applies to JPFs.

4. As for the inclusion of healing rites in religious ritual, Scurlock (1999, 69–80) has already argued that older scholastic models differentiating between secular medicine and sacred healing in Mesopotamia are highly problematic. Biggs (2005, 1, 10–15) agrees that any distinction is highly problematic, although he divides his article into separate functions for the *asû* and the *āšipu*. Maul (2004, 79–91) argues that the *āšipu* were entrusted with both magico-religious and medical treatments.

5. It is unclear how frequently private individuals hired ritual experts. In the present case, the individual was denounced to the king because these arts were considered a "royal prerogative." For more, see Parpola (1997, 315–23n18). For a more widespread set of examples, some of which date to the Bronze Age, see Burkert (1992, 42).

6. Burkert (1992, 55–64) expresses a note of caution on the purification priests. He admits that "suggestive possibilities" connect the Greek purification rituals to those of the *āšipu*, but there are no "inconvertible proofs." Rather, Burkert's evidence consists of similar ritual actions but performed for different purposes. He attempts to relate the use of rituals to combat illness in Mesopotamia to the use of similar rituals for social purity in Greece but admits the substantial challenges to the theory. On traveling craftsmen of many kinds in both the ancient Near East and Greece, see Burkert (1992, 24–25). On the inclusion of healing arts under the rubrics of "craftsmen" and "seers," see Burkert (1992, 41–42).

7. Faraone (1992, 26–27) is following Burkert rather than making a new argument. For the spread of hepatoscopy, there is evidence that its popularity arose in the Bronze Age rather than the Neo-Assyrian Period in the Near East, but Burkert (1992, 48–49) claims it spread to Greece ca. 700 BCE.

8. For more on the spread of Assyrian iconography to Crete, Cyprus, and Greece, see Braun-Holzinger and Matthaeus (2000). They discuss the spread of images of *apkallū* and demons.

9. For more on the debate over the functions of these two professionals, see Geller (2010, 50–52). While Geller (2010, 125, 162–63) believes these two occupations were distinct, he also recognizes that after the eighth century BCE their roles increasingly overlapped.

10. Although Kathleen Kenyon's Jerusalem excavations found JPF fragments in Cave I, often interpreted as a heterodox cult shrine, this interpretation remains problematic. For more on the archaeological data from Cave I and the common interpretations, see Darby (2014, 98–138); Kletter (1996, 63). In short, there are many problems with identifying Cave I as a cultic center. The archaeological evidence suggests instead that the figurines were part of a ceramic storage context and that many of the objects found in Cave I were originally housed in an adjacent room. The contents of that room (Room J) likely collapsed into Cave I after the building outside Cave I (and into which Cave I was incorporated) was abandoned.

11. Avalos believes the Hebrew Bible indicates that "healers" were frowned upon in the eighth through sixth centuries. See, for example, Jeremiah 8:22, 46:11, 51:8–9. Rather than passages demonstrating that a human healer is always ineffective, as Avalos (1995, 290) suggests, these passages actually rely on the common practice of going to healers and using materials such as balm for healing purposes. They do not work in these cases, however, because Judah's sin is so great. In the case of Asa in 2 Chronicles 16:12, by the postexilic period healers may have been considered problematic. This does not necessarily apply to conceptions in the Iron IIB–C. Antagonism toward healers would have complemented certain attitudes toward the sick and their exclusion from the temple that Avalos (1995, 375–76 for Qumran) describes. Furthermore, he shows that the healer actually receives a positive evaluation from Sirach (Avalos 1995, 294–95, citing Sirach 38). In direct contrast with the way Avalos interprets the prophetic metaphors, see Brown (1995, 44–46). On the 2 Chronicles text, Brown (1995, 51) interprets Asa's problem differently. It was not that he sought a healer but that he did not repent for his numerous sins (described in the first half of chapter 16), for which he was punished. He also argues that Asa makes an oracular consultation from the healer (Brown 1995, 51–52).

12. Gallagher notes the evidence for plagues in Assyria during the years 802, 765, 759, and 707 BCE. Both Gallagher and Martinez argue that plague may have been even more widespread than these dates suggest, based on the common six-year interval between plague outbreaks. Note also the circumstantial confluence of epidemics in the Late Bronze Age (Robertson 2007, 39) and Levantine figurines in domestic contexts. In comparison, Geller (2010, 68–70) suggests that epidemics circulating in the second

millennium may have increased the demand for exorcists. In particular, exorcists and lamentation priests were responsible for purifying the city after burials.

13. This is not to say that cultural interactions could not have taken place in the Iron I or early Iron II but that the period during which many of these interactions are attested was already marked by increasing Assyrian interaction with, if not outright control of, small polities in the Levant. In contrast, Smith (2010, 99–102) has suggested that Israel emerged in between two periods of international politics. Thus, in the absence of foreign imperial control, regional governments emerged. He further claims that this situation is reflected in the biblical text. Smith does not address the possibility that Assyrian trade and expansion might have affected the development of Levantine states in the Iron IIA–C. Further, many of his texts date to the monarchic–late monarchic period, placing them squarely in the period of Assyrian expansion (Smith 2010, 102–3).

14. Analyses of style have often been used to study regional variation and self-identity. See Wobst (1999); Winter (2010, 434). Winter (2010, 434) defines "style" as a "sense of shared characteristics of form and sometimes of content in a number of works, such that the group would constitute a recognizable typological unit distinct from other units." Furthermore, Winter argues that style and iconography are not two discrete categories and that style contributes to the meaning of an image. On this point, see Winter (2010, 407, 421–22). For Winter (2010, 407), style contributes to meaning by betraying "unconscious expressions of underlying cultural attitudes and patterns," or "it can be a consciously deployed strategic instrument with specific rhetorical ends." For an overview of stylistic analyses in anthropological archaeology, see Conkey (1989). Note, however, the difficulty identifying which variable elements indicate a regional style versus those that result from the preference of individual artisans. On this point, see Herrmann (2005, 11–20).

15. Bell has been criticized for this view. See Grimes (2004, 132, 134–35). Grimes argues that Bell maintains a privileged place for herself as the theorist who understands what the ritual actors themselves cannot see, tapping into a long-ranging debate over emic and etic approaches to the study of religion. While he concedes that ritual actors often do not understand the full implications of their actions, he claims to attribute them with more agency than he believes Bell allows. His critique is correct, in the sense that Bell does not discuss the privileged position she creates for the theorist (herself) who views and analyzes the cultural system. At times, however, Grimes's criticism approaches caricature, exaggerating the extremity of Bell's position and missing the nuance of the Foucaultian power analytics she incorporates into her work. Elsewhere, Bell is credited with emphasizing the role of the participant in ritual (Collins 1998, 4).

WORKS CITED

Abusch, Tzvi. 2002. *Mesopotamian Witchcraft: Toward a History and Understanding of Babylonian Witchcraft Beliefs and Literature.* Leiden: Brill.

Allen, James P. 2005. *The Art of Medicine in Ancient Egypt.* New Haven, CT: Yale University Press.

'Amr, Abdel-Jalil. 1980. "A Study of the Clay Figurines and Zoomorphic Vessels of Trans-Jordan during the Iron Age, with Special Reference to Their Symbolism and Function." PhD dissertation, University of London, London, England.

Avalos, Hector. 1995. *Illness and Health Care in the Ancient Near East: The Role of the Temple in Greece, Mesopotamia, and Israel.* Atlanta: Scholars Press.

Avigad, Nahman. 1977. "Two Ammonite Seals Depicting the Dea Nutrix." *BASOR* 225: 63–66.

Beck, Pirhiya. 2002. *Imagery and Representation: Studies in the Art and Iconography of Ancient Palestine: Collected Articles.* Tel Aviv: Institute of Archaeology, Tel Aviv University.

Bell, Catherine. 1992. *Ritual Theory, Ritual Practice.* New York: Oxford University Press.

Bell, Catherine. 1997. *Ritual: Perspectives and Dimensions.* New York: Oxford University Press.

Ben-Shlomo, David. 2010. *Philistine Iconography: A Wealth of Style and Symbolism.* Fribourg, Switzerland: Academic.

Ben-Shlomo, David and Erin Darby. 2014. "A Study of the Production of Iron Age Clay Figurines from Jerusalem." *TA* 41: 180–204.

Biggs, Robert D. 1967. *ŠÀ.ZI.GA: Ancient Mesopotamian Potency Incantations.* Locust Valley, NY: J. J. Augustin.

Biggs, Robert D. 2005. "Medicine, Surgery, and Public Health in Ancient Mesopotamia." *JAAS* 19: 1–19.

Braun-Holzinger, Eva Andrea, and Hartmut Matthaeus. 2000. "Schutgenien in Mesopotamien und in den angrenzenden Gebieten: Ihre Übernahme in Zypern, Kreta und Griechenland." In *Images as Media: Sources for the Cultural History of the Near East and the Eastern Mediterranean (1st Millennium BCE),* ed. Christoph Uehlinger, 283–314. Fribourg, Switzerland: University Press Fribourg.

Brown, Michael L. 1995. *Israel's Divine Healer: Studies in Old Testament Biblical Theology.* Grand Rapids, MI: Zondervan.

Burkert, Walter. 1992. *The Orientalizing Revolution: Near Eastern Influence on Greek Culture in the Early Archaic Age.* Trans. Margaret E. Pinder and Walter Burkert. Cambridge, MA: Harvard University Press.

Byrne, Ryan. 2004. "Lie Back and Think of Judah: The Reproductive Politics of Pillar Figurines." *NEA* 67: 137–151.

Caplice, Richard I. 1974. *The Akkadian Namburbi Texts: An Introduction*. Los Angeles: Undena.

Chapman, Cynthia R. 2012. "'Oh That You Were Like a Brother to Me, One Who Had Nursed at My Mother's Breasts': Breast Milk as Kinship-Forging Substance." *JHS* 12, article 7: 1–41. https://doi.org/10.5508/jhs.2012.v12.a7.

Collins, Elizabeth. 1998. "Reflections on Ritual and on Theorizing about Ritual." *JRitSt* 12: 1–7.

Conkey, Margaret W. 1989. "The Use of Diversity in Stylistic Analysis." In *Quantifying Diversity in Archaeology*, ed. Robert D. Leonard and George T. Jones, 118–29. Cambridge: Cambridge University Press.

Cryer, Frederick H. 1994. *Divination in Ancient Israel and Its Near Eastern Environment: A Socio-Historical Investigation*. Sheffield, England: Sheffield Academic Press.

Darby, Erin. 2014. *Interpreting Judean Pillar Figurines: Gender and Empire in Judean Apotropaic Ritual*. Tübingen, Germany: Mohr Siebeck.

Daviau, P. M. Michèle. 2001. "Family Religion: Evidence for the Paraphernalia of the Domestic Cult." In *The World of the Arameans 2: Studies in History and Archeology in Honor of Paul Eugene Dion*, ed. P. M. Michèle Daviau, John W. Wevers, and Michael Weigl, 199–229. Sheffield, England: Sheffield Academic Press.

Dever, William G. 2005. *Did God Have a Wife? Archaeology and Folk Religion in Ancient Israel*. Grand Rapids, MI: Eerdmans.

Duistermaat, Kim. 2008. *The Pots and Potters of Assyria: Technology and Organisation of Production, Ceramic Sequence, and Vessel Function at Late Bronze Age Tell Sabi Abyad, Syria*. Turnhout, Belgium: Brepols.

Elat, Moshe. 1991. "Phoenician Overland Trade within the Mesopotamian Empires." In *Ah, Assyria . . . : Studies in Assyrian History and Ancient Near Eastern Historiography Presented to Hayim Tadmor*, ed. Mordechai Cogan and Israel Eph'al, 21–35. Jerusalem: Magnes.

Ellis, Richard S. 1995. "The Trouble with 'Hairies.'" *Iraq* 57: 159–65.

Faraone, Christopher A. 1992. *Talismans and Trojan Horses: Guardian Statues in Ancient Greek Myth and Ritual*. New York: Oxford University Press.

Finkelstein, Israel. 1999. "State Formation in Israel and Judah: A Contrast in Context, a Contrast in Trajectory." *NEA* 62: 35–52.

Franken, Hendricus J., and Margreet L. Steiner. 1990. "Conclusions." In *Excavations in Jerusalem 1961–1967*, vol. 2: *The Iron Age Extramural Quarter on the South-East Hill*, ed. Hendricus J. Franken and Margreet L. Steiner, 123–32. Oxford: Oxford University Press.

Gallagher, William R. 1999. *Sennacherib's Campaign to Judah: New Studies*. Leiden: Brill.

Gane, Constance Ellen. 2012. "Composite Beings in Neo-Babylonian Art." PhD dissertation, University of California, Berkeley.

Geller, Markham J. 2004. "West Meets East: Early Greek and Babylonian Diagnosis." In *Magic and Rationality in Ancient Near Eastern and Graeco-Roman Medicine*, ed. H.F.J. Horstmanshoff and Marten Stol, 11–61. Leiden: Brill.

Geller, Markham J. 2010. *Ancient Babylonian Medicine: Theory and Practice*. Malden, MA: Wiley-Blackwell. https://doi.org/10.1002/9781444319996.

Green, Anthony. 1983. "Neo-Assyrian Apotropaic Figures: Figurines, Rituals, and Monumental Art with Special Reference to the Figurines from the Excavations of the British School of Archaeology in Iraq at Nimrud." *Iraq* 45 (1): 87–96. https://doi.org/10.2307/4200182.

Grimes, Ronald L. 2004. "Performance Theory and the Study of Ritual." In *New Approaches to the Study of Religion*, vol. 2: *Textual, Comparative, Sociological, and Cognitive Approaches*, ed. Peter Antes, Armin W. Geertz, and Randi R. Warne, 109–38. Berlin: Walter de Gruyter.

Gubel, Eric. 1991. "From Amathus to Zarephath and Back Again." In *Cypriote Terracottas: Proceedings of the First International Conference of Cypriote Studies, Brussels-Liège-Amsterdam, 29 May–1 June 1989*, ed. Frieda Vandenabeele and Robert Laffineur, 131–40. Brussels-Liège: A. G. Leventis Foundation, Vrije Universiteit Brussel–Université de Liège.

Gubel, Eric. 2005. "Phoenician and Aramean Bridle-Harness Decorations: Examples of Cultural Contact and Innovation in the Eastern Mediterranean." In *Crafts and Images in Contact: Studies on Eastern Mediterranean Art of the First Millennium* BCE, ed. Claudia E. Suter and Christoph Uehlinger, 111–47. Fribourg, Switzerland: Academic.

Heltzer, Michael. 1979. "Royal Economy in Ancient Ugarit." In *State and Temple Economy in the Ancient Near East 2: Proceedings of the International Conference Organized by the Katholieke Universiteit Leuven from the 10th to the 14th of April 1978*, ed. Edward Lipiński, 459–96. Leuven, Belgium: Department Oriëntalisktiek.

Heltzer, Michael. 1987. "Labour in Ugarit." In *Labor in the Ancient Near East*, ed. Marvin A. Powell, 237–50. New Haven, CT: American Oriental Society.

Heltzer, Michael. 1996. "Crafts in the West (Syria, Phoenicia, Palestine, ca. 1500–331 BCE)." *AoF* 23: 278–83.

Herrmann, Georgina. 2005. "Naming, Defining, Explaining: A View from Nimrud." In *Crafts and Images in Contact: Studies on Eastern Mediterranean Art of the First Millennium* BCE, ed. Claudia E. Suter and Christoph Uehlinger, 11–21. Fribourg, Switzerland: Academic Press Fribourg.

Holladay, John S., Jr. 1987. "Religion in Israel and Judah under the Monarchy: An Explicitly Archaeological Approach." In *Ancient Israelite Religion: Essays in Honor of Frank Moore Cross*, ed. Patrick D. Miller Jr., Paul D. Hanson, and S. Dean McBride, 249–99. Philadelphia: Fortress.

Holland, Tom A. 1975. "A Typological and Archaeological Study of Human and Animal Representations in the Plastic Art of Palestine." PhD dissertation, Oxford University, Oxford, England.

Hübner, Ulrich. 1993. "Das ikonographische Repertoire der ammonitischen Siegel und seine Entwicklung." In *Studies in the Iconography of Northwest Semitic Inscribed Seals: Proceedings of a Symposium Held in Fribourg on April 17–20, 1991*, ed. Benjamin Sass and Christoph Uehlinger, 130–60. Fribourg, Switzerland: University Press Fribourg.

Johnston, Sarah Iles. 1995. "Defining the Dreadful: Remarks on the Greek Child-Killing Demon." In *Ancient Magic and Ritual Power*, ed. Marvin Meyer and Paul Mirecki, 361–87. Leiden: Brill. https://doi.org/10.1163/9789004283817_019.

Karageorghis, Vassos. 1991. "The Coroplastic Art of Cyprus: An Introduction." In *Cypriote Terracottas: Proceedings of the First International Conference of Cypriote Studies, Brussels-Liège-Amsterdam, 29 May–1 June 1989*, ed. Frieda Vandenabeele and Robert Laffineur, 9–15. Brussels-Liège: A. G. Leventis Foundation, Vrije Universiteit Brussel–Université de Liège.

Kletter, Raz. 1996. *The Judean Pillar-Figurines and the Archaeology of Asherah*. Oxford: Tempus Reparatum.

Kletter, Raz, and Irit Ziffer. 2010. "Catalogue 1: The Cult Stands." In *Yavneh 1: The Excavation of the "Temple Hill" Repository Pit and the Cult Stands: With Contributions by David Ben-Shlomo, Amir Gorzalczany, Henk K. Mienis, Dvory Namdar, Ronny Neumann, Nava Panitz-Cohen, and Steve Weiner*, ed. Raz Kletter, Irit Ziffer, and Wolfgang Zwickel, 211–60. Fribourg, Switzerland: Academic.

Læssøe, Jørgen. 1955. *Studies on the Assyrian Ritual and Series bît rimki*. Copenhagen: Bianco Lunos Bogtrykkeri A/S.

Leichty, Erle. 1970. *The Omen Series Šumma Izbu*. Locust Valley, NY: J. J. Augustin.

Lewis, Theodore J. 2013. "The Sha'tiqatu Narrative from the Ugaritic Story about the Healing of King Kirta." *JANER* 13: 86–112.

Lewis, Theodore J. 2014. "The Identity and Function of Ugaritic Sha'tiqatu: A Divinely Made Apotropaic Figure." *JANER* 14: 1–28.

Mallowan, Max E.L. 1966a. *Nimrud and Its Remains: Volume I*. London: Collins, the British School of Archaeology in Iraq.

Mallowan, Max E.L. 1966b. *Nimrud and Its Remains: Volume II*. London: Collins, the British School of Archaeology in Iraq.

Martinez, Robert M. 1990. "Epidemic Disease, Ecology, and Culture in the Ancient Near East." In *Bible in the Light of Cuneiform Literature*, ed. William W. Hallo, Bruce William Jones, and Gerald L. Mattingly, 413–57. Lewiston, NY: Edwin Mellon.

Maul, Stefan M. 1994. *Zukunftsbewältigung: Eine Untersuchung altorientalischen Denkens anhand der babylonisch-assyrischen Löserituale (Namburbi)*. Mainz am Rhein: Philipp von Zabern.

Maul, Stefan M. 2004. "Die 'Lösung vom Bann': Überlegungen zu altorientalischen Konzeptio-nen von Krankheit und Heilkunst." In *Magic and Rationality in Ancient Near Eastern and Graeco-Roman Medicine*, ed. H.F.J. Horstmanshoff and Marten Stol, 79–95. Leiden: Brill.

Melville, Sarah Chamberlin. 1999. *The Role of Naqia/Zakutu in Sargonid Politics*. Helsinki: Neo-Assyrian Text Corpus Project.

Miller, Patrick D., Jr. 2000. *The Religion of Ancient Israel*. Louisville, KY: Westminster John Knox.

Moorey, Peter R.S. 1994. *Ancient Mesopotamian Materials and Industries: The Archaeological Evidence*. Oxford: Clarendon.

Nadelman, Yonatan. 1989. "Iron Age II Clay Figurine Fragments from the Excavations." In *Excavations in the South of the Temple Mount: The Ophel of Biblical Jerusalem*, ed. Eilat Mazar and Benjamin Mazar, 123–27. Jerusalem: Hebrew University of Jerusalem.

Nakamura, Carolyn. 2005. "Mastering Matters: Magical Sense and Apotropaic Figurine Worlds of Neo-Assyria." In *Archaeologies of Materiality*, ed. Lynn Meskel, 18–45. Oxford: Blackwell. https://doi.org/10.1002/9780470774052.ch2.

Nevling Porter, Barbara. 1993. *Images, Power, and Politics: Figurative Aspects of Esarhaddon's Babylonian Policy*. Philadelphia: American Philosophical Society.

Noegel, Scott B. 2007. "Greek Religion and the Ancient Near East." In *A Companion to Greek Religion*, ed. Daniel Ogden, 21–37. Malden, MA: Blackwell. https://doi.org/10.1002/9780470996911.ch2.

Orchard, J. J. 1967. *Equestrian Bridle Harness Ornaments, Catalogues and Plates: Ivories from Nimrud (1949–1963): Fascicule I, Part 2*. London: British School of Archaeology in Iraq.

Panitz-Cohen, Nava. 2010. "The Pottery Assemblage." In *Yavneh 1: The Excavation of the "Temple Hill" Repository Pit and the Cult Stands: With Contributions by David Ben-Shlomo, Amir Gorzalczany, Henk K. Mienis, Dvory Namdar, Ronny Neumann, Nava Panitz-Cohen, and Steve Weiner*, ed. Raz Kletter, Irit Ziffer, and Wolfgang Zwickel, 110–45. Fribourg, Switzerland: Academic.

Parpola, Simo. 1997. "The Man without a Scribe and the Question of Literacy in the Assyrian Empire." In *Ana šadê Labnāni lū allik: Festschrift für Wolfgang Röllig*, ed. Hartmut Kühne and Paolo X.B. Pongratz-Leisten, 315–24. Neukirchen-Vluyn, Germany: Neukirchener Verlag.

Parpola, Simo. 2007. "The Neo-Assyrian Ruling Class." In *Studies on Ritual and Society in the Ancient Near East, Tartuer Symposium 1998–2004*, ed. Thomas Richard, 257–74. Berlin: Walter de Gruyter.

Postgate, J. Nicholas. 1987. "Employer, Employee, and Employment in the Neo-Assyrian Empire." In *Labor in the Ancient Near East*, ed. Marvin A. Powell, 257–70. New Haven, CT: American Oriental Society.

Press, Michael David. 2012. *Ashkelon 4: The Iron Age Figurines of Ashkelon and Philistia*. Winona Lake, IN: Eisenbrauns.

Preusser, Conrad. 1954. *Die Wohnhäuser in Assur: Mit einem Stadtplan, 31 Lichtdrucktafeln und einer Abbildung im Text*. Berlin: Verlag Gebr. Mann.

Pritchard, James Bennett. 1962. *Gibeon, Where the Sun Stood Still: The Discovery of the Biblical City*. Princeton, NJ: Princeton University Press.

Pruß, Alexander. 2010. *Die Amuq-Terrakotten: Untersuchungen zu den Terrakotta-Figuren des 2, und 1, Jahrtausends v. Chr. aus den Grabungen des Oriental Institute Chicago in der Amuq-Ebene*. Turnhout, Belgium: Brepols.

Reade, Julian. 1979. "Ideology and Propaganda in Assyrian Art." In *Power and Propaganda: A Symposium on Ancient Empire (Mesopotamia)*, ed. Mogens T. Larsen, 29–43. Copenhagen: Akademisk.

Reiner, Erica. 1958. *Šurpu: A Collection of Sumerian and Akkadian Incantations*. Graz, Austria: Im Selbstverlage des Herausgebers.

Robertson, Warren C. 2007. "Drought, Famine, Plague, and Pestilence: Ancient Israel's Understandings of and Responses to Natural Catastrophes." PhD dissertation, Drew University, Madison, NJ.

Robins, Gay. 1993. *Women in Ancient Egypt*. Cambridge, MA: Harvard University Press.

Russell, John Malcolm. 1997. "Sennacherib's Palace without Rival Revisited: Excavations at Nineveh and in the British Museum Archives." In *Assyria 1995: Proceedings of the 10th Anniversary Symposium of the Neo-Assyrian Text Corpus Project, Helsinki, September 7–11, 1995*, ed. Simo Parpola and Robert M. Whiting, 295–306. Helsinki: Neo-Assyrian Text Corpus Project.

Sass, Benjamin. 1993. "The Pre-Exilic Hebrew Seals: Iconism vs. Aniconism." In *Studies in the Iconography of Northwest Semitic Inscribed Seals: Proceedings from a Symposium Held in Fribourg on April 17–20, 1991*, ed. Benjamin Sass and Christoph Uehlinger, 194–256. Fribourg, Switzerland: University Press Fribourg.

Scarborough, John. 1991. "The Pharmacology of Sacred Plants, Herbs, and Roots." In *Magika Hiera: Ancient Greek Magic and Religion*, ed. Christopher A. Faraone and Dirk Obbink, 138–74. Oxford: Oxford University Press.

Schmitt, Rüdiger. 2012. "Elements of Domestic Cult in Ancient Israel." In *Family and Household Religion in Ancient Israel and the Levant*, ed. Rainer Albertz and Rüdiger Schmitt, 57–219. Winona Lake, IN. Eisenbrauns.

Schroer, Silvia. 2007. "Frauenkörper als architektonische Elemente: Zum Hintergrund von Ps 144,12." In *Bilder als Quellen/Images as Sources: Studies on Ancient Near Eastern Artifacts and the Bible Inspired by the Work of Othmar Keel*, ed. Susanne

Bickel, Silvia Schroer, Renee Schurte, and Christoph Uehlinger, 425–50. Fribourg, Switzerland: Academic.

Scurlock, JoAnn. 1999. "Physician, Exorcist, Conjurer, Magician: A Tale of Two Healing Professionals." In *Mesopotamian Magic: Textual, Historical, and Interpretative Perpsectives*, ed. Tzvi Abusch and Karel van der Toorn, 69–80. Groningen, The Netherlands: Styx.

Scurlock, JoAnn. 2006. *Magico-Medical Means of Treating Ghost-Induced Illnesses in Ancient Mesopotamia*. Leiden: Brill.

Scurlock, JoAnn, and Burton R. Andersen. 2005. *Diagnoses in Assyrian and Babylonian Medicine: Ancient Sources, Translations, and Modern Medical Analyses*. Urbana: University of Illinois Press.

Shoham, Yair. 1994. "A Group of Hebrew Bullae from Yigal Shiloh's Excavations in the City of David." In *Ancient Jerusalem Revealed*, ed. Hillel Geva, 55–61. Jerusalem: Israel Exploration Society.

Smith, Joanna S. 2009. *Art and Society in Cyprus from the Bronze Age into the Iron Age*. Cambridge: Cambridge University Press.

Smith, Mark S. 2010. *God in Translation: Deities in Cross-Cultural Discourse in the Biblical World*. Grand Rapids, MI: Eerdmans.

Stein, Gil J., and M. James Blackman. 1993. "The Organizational Context of Specialized Craft Production in Early Mesopotamian States." *REA* 14: 29–59.

Steinkeller, Piotr. 1996. "The Organization of Crafts in Third Millennium Babylonia: The Case of Potters." *AoF* 23: 232–53.

Stern, Ephraim. 1989. "What Happened to the Cult Figurines? Israelite Religion Purified after the Exile." *BAR* 15: 22–29, 53–54.

Tadmor, Miriam. 2006. "Realism and Convention in the Depiction of Ancient Drummers." In *Essays on Ancient Israel in Its Near Eastern Context: A Tribute to Nadav Na'aman*, ed. Yairah Amit, Ehud Ben Zvi, Israel Finkelstein, and Oded Lipschits, 321–38. Winona Lake, IN: Eisenbrauns.

Van Buren, Elizabeth Douglas. 1930. *Clay Figurines of Babylonia and Assyria*. New Haven, CT: Yale University Press.

Van Buren, Elizabeth Douglas. 1931. *Foundation Figurines and Offerings*. Berlin: Hans Schoetz.

Van de Mieroop, Marc. 1987. *Crafts in the Early Isin Period: A Study of the Isin Craft Archive from the Reigns of Išbi-Erra and Šū-Ilišu*. Leuven, Belgium: Departement Oriënalistiek.

Von Soden, Wolfram. 1994. *The Ancient Orient: An Introduction to the Study of the Ancient Near East*. Trans. Donald G. Schley. Grand Rapids, MI: Eerdmans.

Waraksa, Elizabeth A. 2009. *Female Figurines from the Mut Precinct: Context and Ritual Function*. Fribourg, Switzerland: Academic.

Weippert, M. 1977. "Kanaanäische 'Gravidenflaschen': Zur Geschichte einer ägyptischen Gefäßgattung in der asiatischen 'Provinz.'" *ZDPV* 93: 268–82.

Wiggermann, Frans A.M. 1992. *Mesopotamian Protective Spirits: The Ritual Texts.* Groningen, The Netherlands: Styx.

Wilson, Ian Douglas. 2012. "Judean Pillar Figurines and Ethnic Identity in the Shadow of Assyria." *JSOT* 36 (3): 259–78.

Winter, Irene J. 2010. *Of the First Millennium* BCE, vol. 1: *On Art in the Ancient Near East.* Leiden: Brill.

Winter, Urs. 1983. *Frau und Göttin: Exegetische und ikonographische Studien zum weiblichen Gottesbild im alten Israel und in dessen Umwelt.* Freiburg, Switzerland: Universitätsverlag Freibourg Schweiz.

Wobst, Martin H. 1999. "Style in Archaeology or Archaeologists in Style." In *Material Meanings: Critical Approaches to the Interpretation of Material Culture*, ed. Elizabeth Chilton, 118–32. Salt Lake City: University of Utah Press.

Woolley, C. Leonard. 1926. "Babylonian Prophylactic Figures." *JRAS* 3: 689–713.

6

Dining under Assyrian Rule

Foodways in Iron Age Edom

Stephanie H. Brown
(University of California, Berkeley)

Theories of ancient empires have often asked top-down questions that assume historical agency lies at the imperial core and therefore generalize the periphery as an entity that passively reacted to the whims of imperial rule, without taking into account the agency and complexity of local communities (see Herrmann and Tyson, this volume). Often, this top-down approach is the unfortunate result of the distribution and preservation of historical evidence, which is often more prolific at an empire's core. By using foodways to lend a voice to the imperial periphery, this chapter works to correct this imbalance through its investigation of the relationship between the Neo-Assyrian Empire and the polity of Edom, located in southwest Jordan, over which the empire claimed political control. The chapter explores the degree to which the average inhabitants of Edom engaged with the Neo-Assyrian Empire, either directly or indirectly, through their attachment to (or detachment from) both local and imperial hegemonic powers as understood through their daily subsistence activities.

EDOM IN THE IRON AGE

A framework chronology for the settlement and occupation of southern Jordan during the Iron Age (figure 6.1) is possible largely as a result of Bienkowski's publications of Crystal Bennett's excavations at Tawilan (Bennett and Bienkowski 1995),

FIGURE 6.1. *Map of southern Jordan and the Negev in the Iron Age. Image created by Andrew T. Wilson.*

Busayra (Bienkowski 2002), and Umm al-Biyara (Bienkowski 2011), as well as ongoing excavation and survey to the west of the Edomite Plateau in the Wadi Faynan (Levy 2004, 2009a, 2009b; Levy et al. 2005; Smith and Levy

2008; Ben-Yosef 2010).¹ It is now clear that as early as the tenth century BCE there was large-scale economic intensification in the area within and surrounding the Wadi Faynan. This intensification was associated with several identified settlements or copper production centers, such as Khirbet en-Nahas and Khirbet al-Jariya (Ben-Yosef 2010; Ben-Yosef et al. 2010). The majority of the workers associated with this copper production, however, maintained a nomadic or semi-nomadic lifestyle (Levy, Adams, and Shafiq 1999, 306; Levy 2009b, 154).

Beginning in the late eighth century, southern Jordan experienced a dramatic shift in settlement, which saw the copper production centers in the Wadi Faynan largely abandoned and permanent settlements beginning to appear across the Edomite Plateau. Though scholars agree that this shift occurred, there has been much debate about its cause. The chronological correlation between the settlement shift in southern Jordan and Edom's first appearances in the Neo-Assyrian inscriptions of Adad-nirari III (810–783 BCE) and Tiglath-pileser III (744–727 BCE) (Millard 1992) has caused many archaeologists working in southwest Jordan to argue that this shift in settlement and subsistence strategy was an effect of either direct or indirect imperial pressure or influence, though the nature and degree of this involvement is debated (see Bennett 1982; Bartlett 1989; Hart 1989; Knauf 1992; Bienkowski and van der Steen 2001; Crowell 2004; Porter 2004).

Perhaps the strongest view of Neo-Assyrian involvement in Edom's political development is taken by Hart (1989, 131), who suggests that the Neo-Assyrian rulers, in their desire to protect the desert frontier, may have imported conquered peoples from elsewhere and forcibly settled them in Edom. Similarly, Knauf (1992, 53) asserts that "Edom can not only be described as a secondary state, but . . . can also be described as a secondary culture." He further argues that Busayra is the only true instance of an urban center, suggesting that its "architecture is as imported as is the institution which this architecture served" and that Busayra may not have even constituted an Edomite settlement in that it "may more adequately be called an (extended) castle, or citadel [belonging to Assyria]" (Knauf 1992, 52).

The positions of Hart and Knauf are considerably stronger than those taken by Bennett (1982) and some of her other contemporaries, who assumed that Assyrian agents directly occupied Edomite territory without assuming that these agents were directly responsible for every settlement and lifestyle change evident in Edom's archaeological record (Eph'al 1982; Oded 1970; Bienkowski 1992). Rather, these scholars saw in the material culture excavated in southwest Jordan several instances of specific objects or architecture that at the time found their closest parallels among the ruins of the Neo-Assyrian palaces of northern Mesopotamia. Excavations in Areas A and C at Busayra yielded an elite building program whose remains conspicuously exhibit Mesopotamian influences. Each of these areas is dominated by a monumental building, both of which are elevated on artificial, or built, podiums. This building practice is found throughout the core of Assyria, at its royal capitals Khorsabad, Nineveh, and Nimrud, but also throughout the Levant at sites such as Til Barsip, Zincirli, and Megiddo (Bienkowski 1995, 141). The podiums at Busayra consist of a network of walls built on bedrock that were then filled with debris and sediment. The walls vary in height based on the elevation of the bedrock to achieve level platforms on which the monumental buildings could be built.

The architectural plans of the Area A and C Buildings at Busayra also contain Mesopotamian architectural elements. The Area A Building, which has been interpreted as a temple (Bienkowski 2002, 95), is a large rectangular building within which sit two large courtyards surrounded by small rooms likely used for storage. In the northern courtyard is a possible cultic niche, the entrance to which is marked by a remarkable sandstone threshold. Just to the southeast of the niche is a room possibly used for some sort of ritual cleaning or ablution, suggested by the presence of a drain that leads from this room to a cistern in the middle of the courtyard. Large palatial and temple structures that feature central courtyards find many parallels in Assyrian architecture, both in the imperial core as well as at important sites in the Levant that underwent large-scale construction during the period of Assyrian political control (Bienkowski 2002, 94).

The Area C Building has been interpreted as a palace based on the similarities between its architectural plan and those of other buildings interpreted as palaces at the Iron II capitals of Dhiban and Amman. Furthermore, the sheer size of Building C and the presence of architectural features, such as the raised artificial platform on which the building sits, the reception room with its probable throne niche, and the bathroom located near the reception room, suggest that the building was heavily influenced by a specific building plan that finds parallels in Assyrian-Period palaces in both the Assyrian core and its peripheries. However, Building C is not by any means an exact copy of a typical Assyrian palace but rather a unique adaptation (Bienkowski 2002, 199).

In addition to Buildings A and C at Busayra, several objects excavated from Busayra and Tawilan are typically cited by scholars as belying Assyrian influence. These objects include an elaborately carved *tridacna squamosa* shell and two examples of stamped pottery depicting grazing stags from Busayra, as well as a carved ivory lion head and a scarab seal associated with the worship of Sîn (the chief god of Harran, in northwest Mesopotamia) from Tawilan. Scholars have argued that these objects have Assyrian stylistic origins based on parallels found in public buildings of the Assyrian capitals, especially Nimrud (Bennett 1982; Bienkowski 2000, 52; Crowell 2004, 248–53). I contend, however, that their presence in key Assyrian cities should be understood as the result of tribute payments or war booty from Levantine polities.[2] Recent work on these objects suggests that they were produced in the Levant and that they represent types of prestige objects which, based on their patterns of distribution, were popular throughout the Levant and in Assyria as well (Sedman 2002, 353–55; Stucky 2007, 223).

For most scholars the presence of this so-called Mesopotamian-inspired material has been evidence of direct Assyrian presence in Edom. Recent studies, however, suggest that these scholars may have overemphasized the role of the Neo-Assyrian rulers in Edom's social and political development. While their arguments are plausible, the available historical sources do not claim that Assyria physically occupied Edom; nor does the archaeological evidence demand such an interpretation. The historical evidence asserts that the Neo-Assyrian army traveled through Edom on its campaigns in the southern Levant and en route to Egypt, but there is no explicit evidence that suggests the Assyrians maintained a permanent presence in Edom (Millard 1992, 37).

More recently, scholars studying the relationship between Edom and the Neo-Assyrian Empire contend that it may have been local rulers or elites who encouraged political development and settlement as a means of extracting more labor from their populations (Bienkowski 2000; Crowell 2004; Porter 2004). Although this suggestion certainly places more agency with the inhabitants of Edom, albeit a specific class of inhabitants, it still cites direct imperial pressure as the impetus for political development in Edom during the eighth century (Crowell 2004, 1; Porter 2004, 378). This theory is satisfying on many levels: it explains the presence of Mesopotamian influence that is documented primarily from the excavations at Busayra but also from other sites on the Edomite Plateau, and it presents a history of Edom in which the Edomite elites were active actors.

That being said, two aspects of this explanation of Edom's political development remain dissatisfying. The first is that it does not take into account the political development that occurred to the west of the plateau in the area of the Wadi Faynan. Edom, as mentioned above, had a thriving and well-organized copper production industry based at Khirbet en-Nahas at least 100 years prior to the first Neo-Assyrian mention of Edom as a tribute-bearing polity (Levy et al. 2004). In addition, recent research conducted on ceramic evidence from the Wadi Faynan has identified continuity between some tenth- and ninth-century vessel types from Khirbet en-Nahas and the so-called Edomite pottery previously thought to have originated on the Jordanian Plateau in the eighth century (Smith and Levy 2008, 85). Whether the power structures established to manage the copper production in the Wadi Faynan were directly related to those observable on the southern Jordanian Plateau at the end of the eighth century remains to be seen. That being said, the evidence from the Wadi Faynan, at the very least, suggests that sociopolitical development and economic intensification in Iron Age southwest Jordan had begun long before the region felt any pressure from an imperial core and may have still been intact when the Neo-Assyrian Empire entered the region.

The second aspect of this theory that remains unsatisfactory is the fact that the non-elite inhabitants of Edom have yet to be considered as agents in Edom's political history. As is all too often the case, the elite members of a society are assumed to have wielded all of the power necessary to bring about large-scale change. It should go without saying, however, that for top-down change to occur, the consent of the populace is necessary. Without wading into the thorny issue of "individual choice" in the ancient world, it should suffice to say that regardless of whether an individual's consent was a conscious, explicit act, that individual either adapted to sweeping political change or resisted it. The necessity of elites to gain the consent of the populace actually gives the latter a tremendous amount of indirect power. How, though, can we as scholars understand that power? Perhaps even more challenging, how can we detect that power without historical documentation?

ENTANGLEMENT, TASTE, AND FOODWAYS

Dietler (1998, 2010) highlights the importance of a small-scale, local approach to understand the intricacies and complexities inherent within a contact situation in his exploration of the relationship between the indigenous societies of Iron Age France and the Etruscan, Greek, and Roman states that each attempted to colonize that region. He argues that essential to understanding contact situations and their consequences is the recognition that culture change is not the product of an abstract system or structure (Dietler 1998, 299). Though acknowledging that structuring sociopolitical and economic forces play a part in culture change, Dietler's work on the cultural interactions that occurred between empires and their peripheries emphasizes the role individual and group agency played in the selective adoption of specific cultural traits.

Dietler mobilizes the use of the term *entanglement* to describe the process through which the indigenous population of southern France adopted Greek cultural elements. Archaeological evidence from the region indicates that the native population did not just adopt these foreign cultural traits wholesale, as in earlier theories of diffusion and Hellenism. Rather, specific individuals and groups, working within local political and cultural structures, selected foreign cultural elements and combined them with existing cultural elements in strategic ways, transforming them into types of material culture and local practices that were altogether new. This type of selective adoption and consumption has broader consequences for the development of a colonial encounter, and it is this process of entanglement that Dietler (1998, 303–8; 2010, 55–74) argues links societies together in a variety of new sociopolitical, cultural, and economic ways.

Households are often sites of societal innovation and change at its most fundamental level as a result of the constant activity and decision-making that occur there. A factor frequently implicit in innovation and change in daily life is the flexible element of "taste." Taste is an embodied preference that often manifests itself in the material world as the driving force behind the choices agents make in both the production and consumption of material products (Bourdieu 1984). Taste, as a form of practical knowledge, has been used successfully to investigate cultural entanglements within colonial encounters (Stahl 2002). Because taste has the ability to express cultural meaning without relying on linguistic communication, it is a particularly useful entry point into the difficult task of elucidating the preferences of a culture group from whom scant written records survive, such as the Edomite populace. Taste can be discerned from any artifact class that is intentionally produced or modified by human agents, and within the context of this chapter it will be used to explore variations in ceramics and their associated foodways practices in Iron Age Edom.

Foodways refers to the sum total of the materials and practices necessary for the production of food by a particular group. The production and consumption of the quotidian meal constitutes a *habitus* practice in that its production produces regularities inherent in what Bourdieu (1977, 72–95) terms the "objective structures" of a particular culture group (such as gender roles or class distinction) while adjusting to the cognitive and motivating structures of the agents involved. The preparation of food, therefore, presents for archaeologists a practice wherein a dialectal relationship between tradition and innovation may be observed. From within the nexus of this relationship emerges the individual agent, who through the action of producing and consuming the

FIGURE 6.2. *Excavated areas at Busayra, Image created by Stephanie H. Brown. Courtesy, APAAME; image: APAAME_20141019_RHB-0257.*

quotidian meal is capable of both reproducing traditional elements inherent in her society as well as challenging them through innovation and change. The remainder of this chapter will explore Edomite foodways through a discussion and analysis of "Edomite" ceramic traditions found in southern Jordan and the Negev, with a particular focus on a new assemblage of ceramic evidence excavated from Busayra.

BUSAYRA

The Iron Age site of Busayra lies on a long spur of land bounded on three sides by deep valleys (figure 6.2). The site, widely believed to be the ancient site of Bozrah, has an "upper" and "lower" city, which occupy 2.6 hectares and 2.9 hectares, respectively. The complete expanse of the walled settlement's southern portion has been obscured by the construction of a modern school (which cuts into the site's acropolis or citadel) as well as a modern village. Busayra was first excavated under the direction of Crystal M. Bennett over the course of five seasons between the years 1971 and 1980, and these excavations established Busayra's importance as a regional Iron Age administrative center.

In addition to the monumental Buildings A and C (discussed above), Bennett's project also excavated two areas that yielded domestic architecture. To the southwest of Building A is Bennett's Area B, where a series of regular rectangular structures were excavated. Associated with these structures were a series of plaster floors, a possible courtyard in which a pit and *tabun* (oven) were uncovered, and a series of "shelves" or "benches" constructed against the building's walls (Bienkowski 2002, 128–34).

On the northeast side of Building A is Bennett's Area D, in which domestic architecture was also identified. Area D is the smallest of the five main areas associated with Bennett's excavations, consisting of only two small trenches. Within these trenches Bennett's team excavated a few small rectangular rooms that were oriented along the same line as the domestic structures in Area B. These rooms were associated with two phases of plaster floors; and the layers of collapsed stone rubble, ash, mudbrick, and plaster fragments above these floors suggest that the building in Area D was ultimately destroyed by a large fire (Bienkowski 2002, 207–23).

CERAMIC EVIDENCE FROM SOUTHWEST JORDAN AND THE NEGEV

The ceramic evidence from Busayra has been exceedingly relevant to discussions of political development in Edom and has therefore received a great deal of scholarly attention. This is largely a result of the fact that the standard ceramic typology for so-called Edomite pottery was developed by Oakeshott (1978, 1983) from the ceramic remains excavated by Bennett at Busayra, thus linking the defining characteristics of "Edomite" pottery in general with the ceramic evidence from Busayra. Although Oakeshott's typology provides an excellent catalog of ceramic forms from southwest Jordan, the typology is problematic in two major ways. First, because Busayra's archaeological stratigraphy is relatively flat and lacks chronological depth beyond the Iron II Period, this typology has not been particularly useful as a tool for refining an Edomite chronology. Second, further research has demonstrated that the pottery excavated from Busayra is somewhat atypical of pottery from other sites in southwest Jordan. Although the more utilitarian ceramic types from Busayra are found at sites such as Tawilan and Umm al-Biyara, the presence of fine wares and painted pottery is markedly higher at Busayra.

Although it may not come as a surprise that there was a higher quantity of decorated and finely made ceramics at the Edomite capital, it is perhaps problematic that the decorated and painted pottery found at a number of sites in the Negev is referred to as "Edomite" despite the fact that it is rarely found in southwest Jordan outside of Busayra. This is especially relevant when we start to consider the foodways of the Edomite populace, as it begs the question: if fine ware and highly decorative pottery is uncommon outside of Busayra, is Busayra an appropriate place to study the foodways of the Edomite populace? Although the initial answer might seem to be "no," this question is further complicated by the presence of this highly decorated "Edomite" pottery at sites in the Negev, mostly clustered around the Beersheba Valley that leads from the Wadi Arabah to Gaza.

Until recently, the dominant scholarly consensus was that at some point during the late seventh or early sixth centuries, large numbers of Edomites migrated from the Jordanian Plateau and forcibly conquered many of the Judean sites in the Negev. This theory was supported in large part by two *ostraca* found at the site of Arad, one that references the "evil" done by Edom (Ostracon 40; Aharoni 1970) and another dating to 598–597 BCE that orders troops to move to Ramat-negeb "lest Edom should come there" (Ostracon 24; Aharoni 1970, 16–28). Although this theory may seem to make sense based on the large amount of so-called Edomite pottery found at sites in the Negev, the earliest attestations of this pottery in strata such as Arad Stratum X, Tel Beersheba Strata III-II, and Tel 'Ira Stratum VII (the latter two strata were destroyed in 701 BCE by Sennacherib) suggest that already by the late eighth century, contemporary with the settlement of Busayra, a number of Edomites were residing west of the Wadi Arabah (Tebes 2011, 70).

For Tebes, this deeply complicates the designation of this pottery as "Edomite," and he instead refers to the assemblage as Southern Transjordan-Negev Pottery (STNP). The distribution of "Edomite" pottery, or STNP, inherently complicates a practice all too common in the Iron Age southern Levant, in which scholars determine political and ethnic territorial borders by drawing lines around cultural assemblages. If this practice were to be applied to the painted wares of the STNP assemblage, Busayra might begin to look like the capital of a polity that ran east-west across the Wadi Arabah to Gaza rather than one that ran north-south along the Jordanian Plateau. Therefore, it seems that although certain aspects of food production and consumption at Busayra may be unique among the sites of the Jordanian Plateau, they were much more common among the sites along the Beersheba Valley, where painted and decorated pottery was found in a variety of non-elite and domestic contexts. Thus, it seems appropriate that the domestic contexts from Busayra may be used to remark on broader foodways practices among sites that share a cultural connection to Busayra.

Recently, two scholars working on material from Edom have considered the utility of exploring foodways as a cultural phenomenon, and both have approached foodways through an analysis of "Edomite," or STNP, vessel types found throughout southwest Jordan and the Negev (Whiting 2007; Tebes 2011). Whiting's (2007) work moves beyond the culture-historical paradigm often used in the southern Levant to conflate ethnicity, geography, and material culture by employing an archaeology of practice. Her comparative analysis of Edomite vessels found in southwest Jordan versus those found in southern Israel indicates that the people living in southern Israel selected specific types of Edomite-style pottery whose functions were linked to cooking and serving (Whiting 2007, 108). Whiting uses these data to complicate the scholarly idea of a seventh–sixth century "Edomite invasion" of the Negev. Rather than suggesting the presence of Edomite population groups in the Negev, she argues that the presence of Edomite cooking and serving vessels simply suggests the adoption of alternative cooking and serving practices by those living in the Negev (Whiting 2007, 133).

Although Whiting's methodological and theoretical contributions to the study of "Edomite" ceramics should not be understated, an important aspect of her interpretation bears reconsideration. Whiting (2007, 110) suggests that the presence of "Edomite" vessels in southern Israel should not be understood as an indication of Edomite presence, arguing that if Edomites were living in the Negev, there would be more parallels between the ceramic assemblages found there and those found in southern Jordan. Although this may be a logical argument, recent foodways-centered research has demonstrated that it is not uncommon in multiethnic societies for individual households to use ceramic assemblages made up of vessel types from different cultural or ethnic traditions. For example, the same household might use storage vessels associated with Culture A and cooking vessels associated with Culture B. Furthermore, this research illustrates that vessels that would affect the taste or cooking style of the food can be used to help identify the cook's cultural affiliation or ethnic identity (Smith 2003; Stein 2012).

Tebes's (2011) work clearly accepts the idea that foodways can be used as a signifier of ethnic identity. It further suggests the ways social practice involving the production and consumption of food can be used to establish and strengthen social boundaries that may exist among individuals of different social strata, genders, or ethnic groups. Tebes builds on the statistical analyses done by Whiting to discuss the culinary differences that could be affected by the choice between "Edomite" cooking pots versus those more common in Judah. He explains two of the major differences: first, the Edomite cooking pots are almost always open forms, while both open and closed forms are found among Judean cooking pots, and second, the material used to produce Edomite cooking pots is made from a type of Nubian sandstone, which is most prolific east of the Arabah Valley in the area around the Nabataean site of Petra but is also found in smaller quantities in the Negev. Tebes (2011, 88) goes on to explain that these differences would have had quite an effect on the taste of the food, likely culminating in a drier meal than would have been produced in a typical Judean cooking pot, especially in a more closed form. The general tendency of cooking practices to be conservative in nature helps explain why ethnically or culturally Edomite individuals living in the Negev would have considered factors that account for taste and cooking style to be important enough to warrant the desire for a specialized type of cooking vessel similar to those used in the region typically associated with the Edomite homeland.

As Whiting's analyses indicated, in addition to Edomite cooking pots, Edomite serving vessels were also common in the Negev, and these vessels were often relatively flat, decorated bowls. Unlike the cooking pots, however, serving vessels were made of local clays from the Negev, although their shape and painted decoration clearly fit into the Edomite ceramic tradition. The liberal use of painted decoration suggests a manipulation of the consumption experience, perhaps by drawing attention to the quality of the food served. This decoration is often associated with, and is even an indication of, finer wares. As such, the use of decorated serving vessels is likely an indication of a type of conspicuous consumption that results from a desire to set the consumer of the product apart from the masses. The food served at a meal—especially one at which guests are present—as well as the vessels used to present the food can be an important indication of the host's status and wealth. Furthermore, the choice of individuals living within the geographic realm of the Judean state to use ceramic serving vessels that were culturally linked with Edom was likely a powerful way of differentiating themselves from their neighbors.

Among the high-quality Edomite serving vessels found at Busayra and in the Negev is the presence of so-called Imitation Assyrian Palace Ware. Beginning with Bennett's work, this pottery type almost always appears in discussions of Assyrian influence in southern Jordan. The presence of this pottery type is generally taken together with Busayra's monumental architecture and the above-mentioned items that have parallels at sites in northern

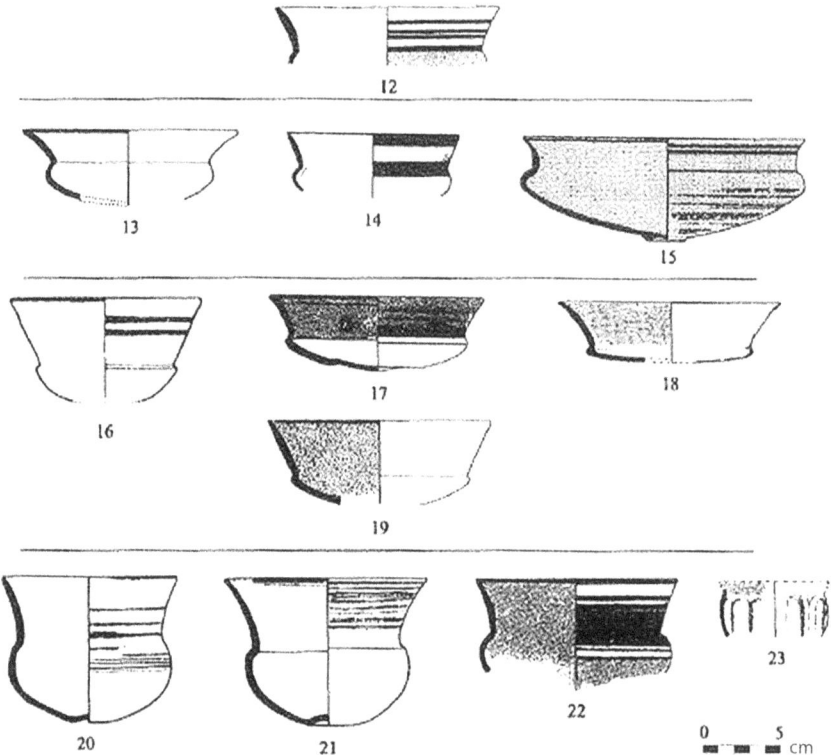

FIGURE 6.3. *Oakeshott's Bowl K. Image used with permission of Piotr Bienkowski.*

Mesopotamia to demonstrate the presence of either Assyrian elites living in Edom or of Edomite elites attempting to emulate practices associated with the imperial core (Bennett 1982; Bienkowski 1992, 2000; Crowell 2004; Tebes 2011). As I have mentioned, however, scholars differ in their opinions about the extent to which Assyrian influence penetrated Edom, both politically and socially. The Imitation Assyrian Palace Ware bowls found among Edomite assemblages are classified as Oakeshott's Bowl K (figure 6.3). The characteristic feature of this bowl type is its long everted rim, which juts out sharply from the vessel's shoulder and sits above a rounded base. The vessels are very often decorated with a polychrome slip and are highly burnished (Bienkowski, Oakeshott, and Berlin 2002, 282).

Bowl K closely imitates a type of carinated bowl made of high-quality ceramic fabric that was produced during the Iron Age in northern Mesopotamia and is referred to by scholars as "Assyrian Palace Ware." The ware of Bowl K is among the finest found in southern Jordan, but the decoration and style of manufacture suggest that these bowls are locally made. Although a recent neutron activation analysis of one example of Bowl K from Busayra indicated that the bowl's fabric was made from clay for which the provenance was unknown, it should still be assumed that Bowl K was a local imitation rather than an import until further data are collected to refute this assumption (Bienkowski, Oakeshott, and Berlin 2002, 282).

The assumption that Bowl K was made locally may also be supported by its parallels throughout the southern Levant, all of which date from the late eighth century BCE into the Persian Period (Gitin 1990, 197–98). Imported Assyrian Palace Ware has possibly been found in the southern Levant, but only at sites such as Tell Jemmeh and Tel Sera'—where there was a documented Assyrian presence and where Assyrian building projects occurred (van Beek 1993; Oren 1993)—and never east of the Jordan Rift Valley. Imitations of the Assyrian carinated bowls and beakers, however, are found throughout the southern Levant; although they are documented at most of the major Iron Age sites in southern Jordan, their number and quality is greatest at Busayra.

The production choices apparent in this Imitation Assyrian Palace Ware illuminate the discussion of Assyrian stylistic influence in southern Jordan and the Negev. Although Bowl K clearly resembles the general shape and quality of Assyrian Palace Ware, it is obvious that the bowl was adapted to fit local tastes and preferences. For example, the polychrome painted decoration often found on examples of Bowl K is not found on actual examples of Assyrian Palace Ware (Tebes 2011, 89). The presence of these bowls adds much to the discussion of elite emulation of imperial style throughout southwest Jordan and the Negev, as it is assumed that the presence of the bowls speaks to a strong Assyrian influence.

NEW CERAMIC EVIDENCE FROM BUSAYRA

Beginning in 2013, the Busayra Cultural Heritage Project (BCHP) renewed archaeological investigation at the site of Busayra.[3] One of the major aims of this renewed attention was to investigate the archaeological remains associated with domestic architecture at Busayra more closely. This prompted the BCHP to excavate four new trenches in a new area, designated Area DD. Area DD is an expansion of Bennett's Area D to the south, in which she excavated a portion of a building that belongs to a domestic structure that has now been designated Building DD001 by the BCHP.

FIGURE 6.4. *Buildings DD001 and DD002. Image created by Rachel Regelein.*

The BCHP's excavation in Area DD exposed the southeastern continuation of Building DD001 (figure 6.4) and identified a second structure to the northeast, called Building DD002. The architectural layout of Building DD001 is rectangular in nature and measures approximately 15 m × 2 m. Typical of Iron II domestic architecture in southern Jordan, the interior space of the building is subdivided by shorter walls, and thus far four of these subdivisions, or rooms, have been excavated. Although Bennett's team identified two occupation phases associated with Building DD001, the BCHP has thus far only excavated the later phase, including its associated plaster surface. Within the southernmost excavated room, two hearths were excavated, both of which were bounded by rings of stone and were filled with ash. The presence of these hearths seems to further confirm Bennett's designation of this building as a domestic space.

Building DD002 was discovered directly to the northeast of Building DD001. At present, not enough of Building DD002's architecture has been excavated to speculate as to the layout of the building. However, based on the orientation of the walls that have been excavated, Building DD002 seems to be oriented along the same lines as Building DD001, which is common in domestic complexes in southwest Jordan. The excavators were able to reach a plaster surface associated with the most recent occupation of Building DD002, which they believe to be contemporaneous with the second occupation phase of Building DD001.

Area DD at Busayra provides an opportunity to explore foodways in Edom. Because the excavated context is domestic in nature, the evidence has the potential to inform many foodways elements, including storage and cooking as well as dining. A functional ceramic analysis will suggest how the food products were stored, cooked, and served and the ways in which the practices show continuity with or divergence from general regional practices discussed above.

The ceramic data from the BCHP's excavation of domestic buildings DD001 and DD002 provide the best corpus of Late Iron Age ceramics from southwest Jordan, from which statistical conclusions may be drawn. Unlike the excavations carried out under Bennett's direction in the 1960s and 1970s, each piece of pottery excavated from Busayra's Area DD was collected and counted, making it possible to provide accurate information regarding form frequency and distribution that was impossible to ascertain using data from the earlier excavations. In total, 21,589 sherds were excavated from Area DD during the 2014 season, 2,800 of which were diagnostic sherds from which vessel form could be determined.

To address vessel form function, the forms are divided into four general categories: storage vessels, processing vessels, cooking vessels, and serving vessels. Storage vessels are understood as vessels that would store either dry or wet food products and in this assemblage are referred to as jars and jugs, whose mostly closed forms would facilitate storage (figure 6.5). Processing vessels are those with high vessel walls and relatively wide openings that would allow stirring and mixing, here referred to as kraters, as well as perforated vessels ideal for straining liquids. Cooking vessels are those designed to withstand high amounts of heat. Their openings were more closed than those of processing or serving vessels to prevent excess evaporation but not so closed as to cause the contents to boil over (figure 6.6). The final vessel category is serving vessels, which includes the largest number of vessel types. These vessel forms are, in general, the most open to allow for ease of consumption. The serving category includes bowls, platters, and cups (figure 6.7).

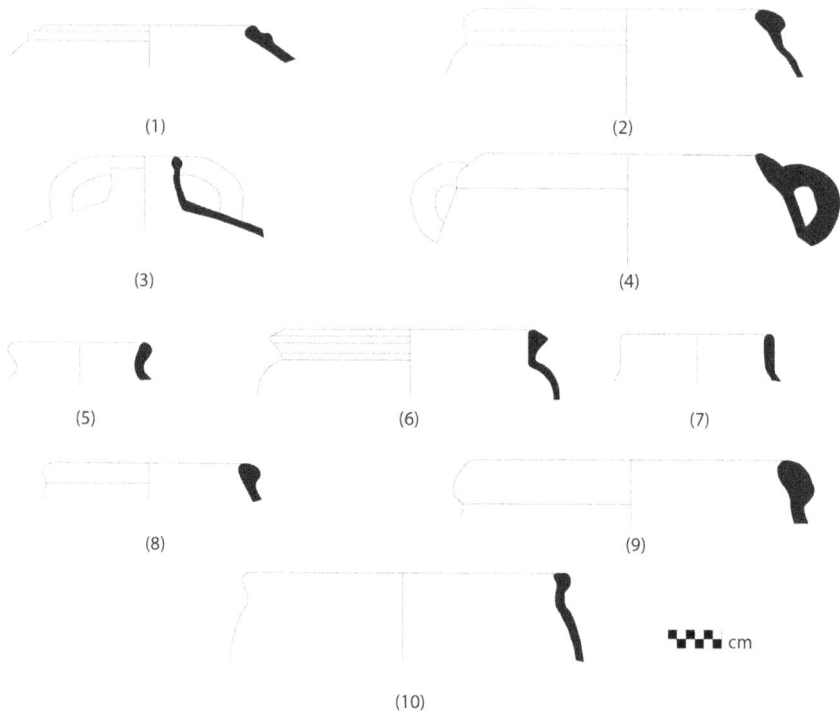

FIGURE 6.5. *Storage vessels from Busayra. Image created by Rachel Regelein.*

Among the 2,800 diagnostic sherds from Area DD, 608 belonged to storage vessels, making up 22 percent of the total assemblage. Sherds belonging to processing vessels accounted for just about 1 percent of the total assemblage, with 41 sherds; and cooking vessels made up about 4 percent of the total assemblage, with 100 sherds. Serving vessels occurred with the most frequency within the assemblage, in total 2,051 sherds, making up 73 percent of the total assemblage (figure 6.8). Despite the limited corpus available to Whiting for analysis, these trends are in general complementary to her findings. Her analyses indicate that from sites in southern Jordan, storage vessels made up about 29 percent of the total assemblage, while cooking vessels accounted for about 9 percent, and serving vessels (which include kraters) constituted about 62 percent (Whiting 2007, fig. 31).

Although storage and cooking practices can say a great deal about an individual's or a household's identity, the practices around serving and consuming a meal, especially in the presence of guests, capture an important place where

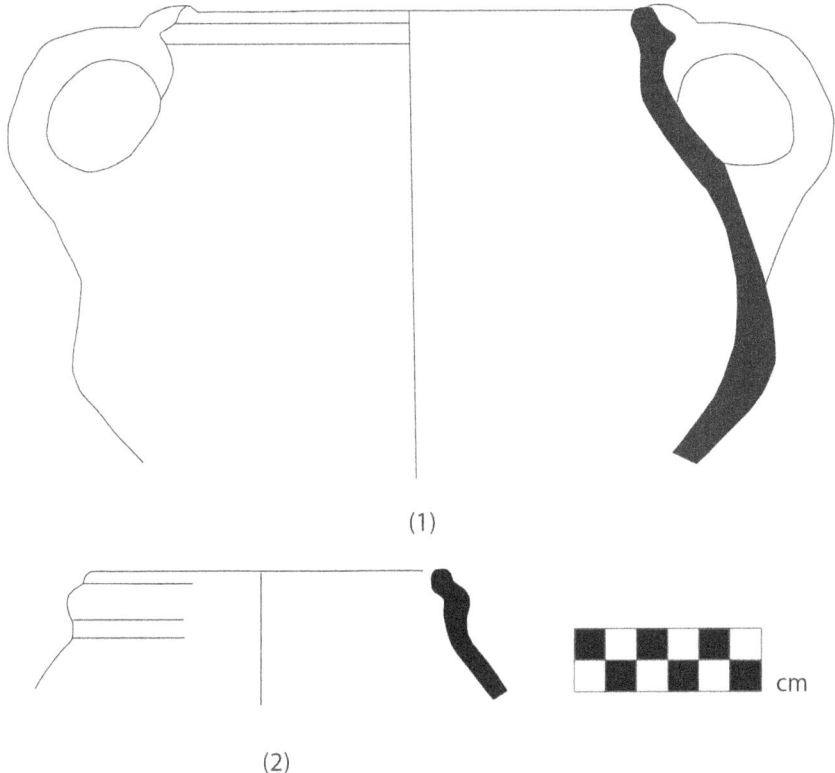

FIGURE 6.6. *Cooking vessels from Busayra. Image created by Rachel Regelein.*

individual or household identity meets with broader social practices and traditions. As discussed above, this conversation can be seen in the pottery from Busayra and the Negev, as personal taste is expressed through the use of painted or decorated serving vessels. I have mentioned the unusually large number of painted or decorated vessels from Busayra, and this holds true among the data collected from DD001 and DD002, where the 232 painted sherds account for about 1 percent of total sherds and about 8 percent of diagnostic sherds. In addition to sherds that exhibit painted decoration there were also 161 fine-ware sherds,[4] which account for about 6 percent of the diagnostic sherds (figure 6.9).

The final aspect of the ceramic data from Busayra I would like to discuss is the presence of Imitation Assyrian Palace Ware. As mentioned, much has been inferred about the scope of Assyrian influence in Edom from the use of this pottery at Busayra. The data from Buildings DD001 and DD002, however,

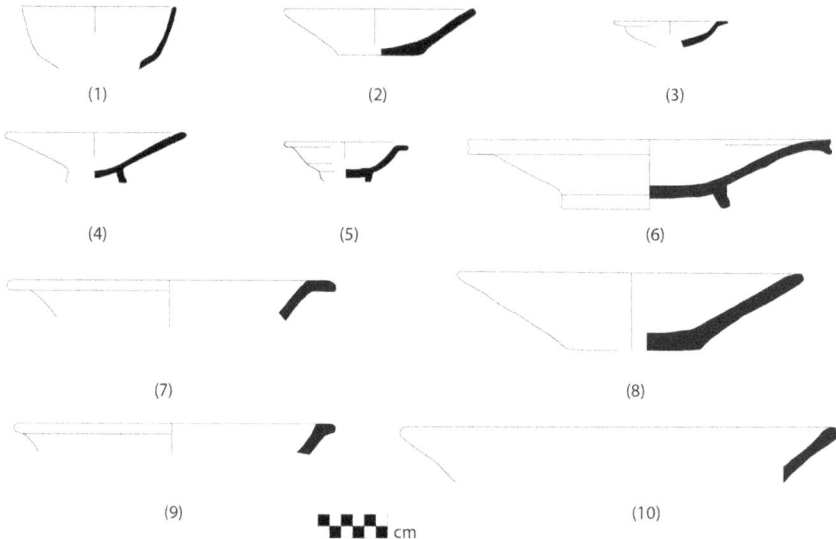

FIGURE 6.7. *Serving vessels from Busayra. Image created by Rachel Regelein.*

suggest that the importance of this form may have been overstated by past scholars. During the BCHP's 2014 excavation of Area DD, only 16 sherds of Imitation Assyrian Palace Ware were documented, making up just 0.6% of the diagnostic sherds[5] (figure 6.10). This small number of sherds does not seem to warrant the scholarly attention and weight given to the presence of this vessel form at Busayra. Unfortunately, because similar quantitative studies of this form do not exist from other sites in southwest Jordan, it is not possible to say whether this low percentage is the result of the domestic context from which the sherds were excavated or the quality and preservation of the diagnostic sherds or whether it is actually representative of the form's presence across the site. Whatever the case, at this time the data suggest that imitation Assyrian vessel forms were present in Buildings DD001 and DD002, but in very small quantities.

CONCLUSION

In conclusion, the newly excavated ceramic data from Buildings DD001 and DD002 confirm many earlier analyses and generalizations about foodways in southern Jordan. The size and architectural layout of Buildings DD001 and DD002 is clearly domestic and finds many parallels throughout Iron Age

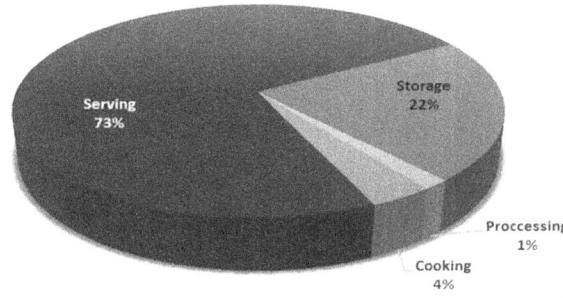

FIGURE 6.8. *Percentage of vessel types from Buildings DD001 and DD002 by function. Image created by Rachel Regelein.*

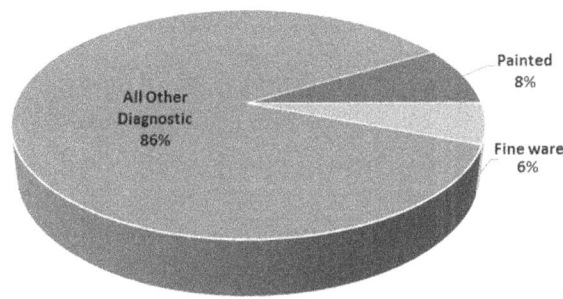

FIGURE 6.9. *Frequency of painted and fine-ware sherds from Buildings DD001 and DD002. Image created by Rachel Regelein.*

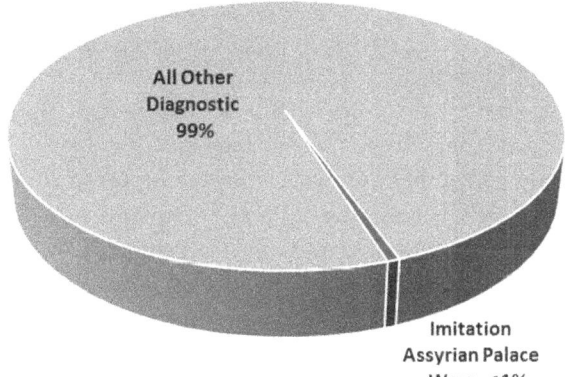

FIGURE 6.10. *Frequency of Imitation Assyrian Palace Ware. Image created by Rachel Regelein.*

southern Jordan, especially at Umm al-Biyara and Tawilan. In addition, the full range of ceramic vessel forms found within the buildings and their associated functions, such as storage, processing, cooking, and serving, fit well into

Whiting's functional analysis of pottery from sites in southern Jordan, most of which are associated with domestic architecture.

Certain aspects of the data, however, seem to suggest that the function of Buildings DD001 and DD002 was not exactly like that of other domestic structures in southwest Jordan. For example, there is a complete absence of small finds associated with the buildings, as well as a paucity of both faunal and botanical remains. In addition, the ceramic data demonstrated a relatively high number of painted and fine-ware sherds when compared to assemblages from other domestic structures in southwest Jordan (outside of Busayra).

The most likely explanation for these trends is found in the structures' proximity adjacent to the Building A temple, atop Busayra's "upper city." Although natural and anthropogenic taphonomic processes prevent a clear understanding of the stratigraphic relationship between Building A and Buildings DD001 and DD002, their proximity may suggest that Buildings DD001 and DD002 were a part of the extended Building A complex and were therefore inhabited by individuals associated with the temple. The structures themselves were not extraordinary, and because of the ordinary nature of the buildings, it does not seem likely that priests or high-level temple officials would have lived there. Perhaps, then, it is most logical to assume that low-ranking officials inhabited Buildings DD001 and DD002, perhaps individuals associated with aspects of the temples' maintenance or administration. The paucity of small finds, as well as of botanical and faunal remains, may suggest that the individuals living in Buildings DD001 and DD002 were not responsible for many of the primary processing practices associated with foodways in the Iron Age southern Levant, as these individuals would have likely had access to the products produced in Building A. The high number of decorated and fine-ware ceramic remains further suggests that these individuals were benefiting from the economic prosperity associated with Building A.

It should be emphasized, however, that of the decorated and fine-ware pottery excavated from Buildings DD001 and DD002, only a very small amount seems to fall into the category of Imitation Assyrian Palace Ware. Rather, the decorative choices associated with the many other types of serving vessels that were excavated, such as painted polychrome bands, seem to be Levantine, specifically Transjordanian, in nature. These and other fine-ware vessels were clearly part of a regional conversation about power and prestige, in which such vessels were accorded great value. The fact that these vessels are not uncommon in domestic structures both in the Negev and at Busayra suggests that this power and prestige was likely used to promote the status of the individuals living in those structures. On the other hand, this conversation about power and prestige does not seem to engage directly with Assyrian practice but remains uniquely Levantine in both its nature and scale.

The evidence examined in this chapter suggests that the domestic economy associated with Buildings DD001 and DD002 at Busayra was intimately tied to the local administration. This study did not identify any objects from these buildings that belied Mesopotamian influence, aside from the very small number of possible Assyrian Imitation Palace Ware fragments. It is clear from the evidence from Buildings DD001 and DD002 that the inhabitants were engaging in foodways practices that were above subsistence level and were more on par with what we would associate with elites. These elite practices and preferences seem tied to local power structures, and although the success of these local power structures may have resulted from their relationship to the Mesopotamian empires, the evidence does not suggest that imperial power structures played a driving force in the daily lives of the individuals living in Buildings DD001 and DD002 at Busayra.

In many ways, this seems to complement the other evidence from southwest Jordan. For example, the objects traditionally used by scholars to underscore Assyrian influence in Edom have been found to be much more in line with Levantine artistic tradition and influence. It seems that the only substantial evidence of Assyrian influence in Edom lies in the architectural designs of Buildings A and C at Busayra. Perhaps, then, these two most public buildings at Edom's capital were constructed as political acts of conspicuous consumption by Edomite elites and as such do not reflect a deep penetration of Assyrian influence into social life in Edom.

In summation, the direct archaeological evidence of Assyrian intervention in Edom, which was first highlighted by Bennett and some of her contemporaries, is becoming harder and harder to see. Crowell and Porter made important steps in positioning the Edomite elite as the intermediaries between the local populace and the Assyrian Empire who appropriated imperial influence to sustain and grow their power, but that, too, seems to be overreaching at this point. Undoubtedly, the Edomites were attempting to distinguish themselves among their peers, but the material language with which they "spoke" seems to have been one grounded in Levantine, rather than Assyrian, traditions and value regimes.

NOTES

1. Largely because of the important role of copper production in the area, the Wadi Faynan has been the site of intense archaeological attention since the late 1990s.

Under the direction of Thomas Levy, excavations have been conducted at the important copper production site of Khirbet en-Nahas (Levy et al. 2004; Smith and Levy 2008) and a unique tenth-century cemetery at Wadi Fidan 40 Cemetery (Levy, Adams, and Shafiq 1999). These excavations and others have contributed significantly to our archaeological understanding of some of the earliest Iron Age evidence of occupation and economic intensification in southern Jordan. The evidence collected from the Wadi Faynan confirms that as early as the tenth century there was a highly developed and centralized copper production industry in southern Jordan, one whose establishment and maintenance would have required strong sociopolitical organization (Levy 2009; Ben-Yosef 2010).

2. Stylistically, the scarab associated with Sîn would be an exception to this. The seal depicts a podium or altar that sits between two stylized trees. On the podium is a staff, the top of which bears an upturned crescent with an eight-point star inside. Although scarab stamp seals are associated with the Levant rather than with northern Mesopotamia, the worship of Sîn is much more closely connected to northern Levantine and Assyrian cultic practice than to that of the southern Levant (although seals depicting imagery related to Sîn are relatively common in the Assyrian provinces of Megiddo, Samaria, and Dor [Stern 2001, 32]). Therefore, although the seal itself was very likely produced in the Levant, it was obviously influenced by Assyrian themes.

3. The ceramic evidence presented in this chapter is a subset of a larger foodways data set collected as part of my dissertation research. The current chapter serves as a preliminary report on some of the findings from that research. In addition to ceramic evidence, the larger foodways data set includes zooarchaeological and paleoethnobotanical evidence that was undergoing analysis at the time this chapter was written. For the results of those analyses, please see Brown 2018.

4. While the designation of a particular sherd as "fine ware" can be somewhat arbitrary and subjective, I used relative comparability to the other sherds excavated from Buildings DD001 and DD002. Those sherds designed as fine ware had almost no visible mineral inclusions and were generally very thin and well burnished.

5. Because of the tendency of vessels with a sharp carination to break along that carination, it was impossible to judge in all cases whether a vessel may have belonged to the Bowl K type. The low count recorded here represents a liberal estimate that accounted for the possibility that a sherd may have been part of an Imitation Assyrian Palace Ware rim.

WORKS CITED

Aharoni, Yohanan. 1970. "Three Hebrew Ostraca from Arad." *BASOR* 197: 16–42.

Bartlett, John. 1989. *Edom and the Edomites*. Sheffield: Sheffield Academic Press.

Bennett, Crystal M. 1982. "Neo-Assyrian Influence in Transjordan." *SHAJ* 1: 181–87.
Bennett, Crystal M., and Piotr Bienkowski, eds. 1995. *Excavations at Tawilan in Southern Jordan*. Oxford: Oxford University Press.
Ben-Yosef, Erez. 2010. "Technology and Social Process: Oscillations in Iron Age Copper Production and Power in Southern Jordan." PhD dissertation, University of California, San Diego.
Ben-Yosef, Erez, Thomas E. Levy, Thomas Higham, Mohammad Najjar, and Lisa Tauxe. 2010. "The Beginning of Iron Age Copper Production in the Southern Levant: New Evidence from Khirbat al-Jariya, Faynan, Jordan." *Antiquity* 84 (325): 724–46. https://doi.org/10.1017/S0003598X00100195.
Bienkowski, Piotr. 1992. "The Beginning of the Iron Age in Southern Jordan: A Framework." In *Early Edom and Moab: The Beginning of the Iron Age in Southern Jordan*, ed. Piotr Bienkowski, 1–12. Sheffield, England: J. R. Collis.
Bienkowski, Piotr. 1995. "The Architecture of Edom." *SHAJ* 5: 135–43.
Bienkowski, Piotr. 2000. "Transjordan and Assyria." In *The Archaeology of Jordan and Beyond: Essays in Honor of James A. Sauer*, ed. Lawrence E. Stager, Joseph A. Greene, and Michael D. Coogan, 44–58. Winona Lake, IN: Eisenbrauns.
Bienkowski, Piotr, ed. 2002. *Busayra: Excavations by Crystal M. Bennett 1971–1980*. Oxford: Oxford University Press.
Bienkowski, Piotr. 2011. Umm al-Biyara: Excavations by Crystal-M. Bennett in Petra 1960–1965. Oxford: Oxbow.
Bienkowski, Piotr, Marion Oakeshott, and Andrea Berlin. 2002. "The Pottery." In *Busayra: Excavations by Crystal M. Bennett 1971–1980*, ed. Piotr Bienkowski, 233–351. Oxford: Oxford University Press.
Bienkowski, Piotr, and Eveline van der Steen. 2001. "Tribes, Trades, and Towns: A New Framework for the Late Iron Age in Southern Jordan and the Negev." BASOR 323: 21–47.
Bourdieu, Pierre. 1977. *Outline of a Theory of Practice*. Cambridge: Cambridge University Press. https://doi.org/10.1017/CBO9780511812507.
Bourdieu, Pierre. 1984. *Distinction: A Social Critique of the Judgment of Taste*. Cambridge: Cambridge University Press.
Brown, Stephanie H. 2018. "Living on the Edge of Empire: Edomite Households in the First Millennium BCE." PhD dissertation, University of California, Berkeley.
Crowell, Bradley L. 2004. "On the Margins of History: Social Change and Political Development in Iron Age Edom. PhD dissertation, University of Michigan, Ann Arbor.
Dietler, Michael. 1998. "Consumption, Agency, and Cultural Entanglement: Theoretical Implications of a Mediterranean Colonial Encounter." In *Studies in Cultural*

Contact: Interaction, Culture Change, and Archaeology, ed. James G. Cusick, 288–315. Carbondale: Southern Illinois University.

Dietler, Michael. 2010. *Archaeologies of Colonialism: Consumption, Entanglement, and Violence in Ancient Mediterranean France*. Berkeley: University of California Press. https://doi.org/10.1525/california/9780520265516.003.0002.

Eph'al, Israel. 1982. *The Ancient Arabs: Nomads on the Borders of the Fertile Crescent 9th–5th Centuries BC*. Jerusalem: Magnes.

Gitin, Seymour. 1990. *Gezer III: A Ceramic Typology of the Late Iron II, Persian, and Hellenistic Periods at Tell Gezer*. Jerusalem: Hebrew Union College.

Hart. Stephen. 1989. "The Archaeology of the Land of Edom." PhD dissertation, Macquarie University, Sydney, Australia.

Knauf, Ernst Axel. 1992. "The Cultural Impact of Secondary State Formation: The Cases of the Edomites and the Moabites." In *Early Edom and Moab: The Beginning of the Iron Age in Southern Jordan*, ed. Piotr Bienkowski, 47–54. Sheffield, England: J. R. Collis.

Levy, Thomas E. 2004. "Some Theoretical Issues Concerning the Rise of the Edomite Kingdom—Searching for 'Pre-Modern Identities.'" *SHAJ* 8: 253–61.

Levy, Thomas E. 2009a. "Pastoral Nomads and Iron Age Metal Production in Ancient Edom." In *Nomads, Tribes, and the State in the Ancient Near East: Cross-Disciplinary Perspectives*, ed. Jeffrey Szuchman, 147–77. Chicago: University of Chicago Press.

Levy, Thomas E. 2009b. "Ethnic Identity in Biblical Edom, Israel, and Midian: Some Insights from Mortuary Contexts in the Lowlands of Edom." In *Exploring the Longue Durée: Essays in Honor of Lawrence E. Stager*, ed. J. David Schloen, 251–61. Winona Lake, IN: Eisenbrauns.

Levy, Thomas E., Russell B. Adams, Mohammad Najjar, Andreas Hauptmann, James D. Anderson, Baruch Brandl, Mark A. Robinson, and Thomas Hingham. 2004. "Reassessing the Chronology of Biblical Edom: New Excavation and C14 Dates from Khirbat en-Nahas (Jordan)." *Antiquity* 78: 865–79.

Levy, Thomas E., Russell B. Adams, and Rula Shafiq. 1999. "The Jabal Hamrat Fidan Project: Excavations at the Wadi Fidan 40 Cemetery, Jordan (1997)." *Levant* 31 (1): 293–308. https://doi.org/10.1179/lev.1999.31.1.293.

Levy, Thomas E., Mohammad Najjar, Johannes van der Plicht, Thomas Higham, and Hendrik J. Bruins. 2005. "Lowland Edom and the High and Low Chronologies: Edomite State Formation, the Bible, and Recent Archaeological Research in Southern Jordan." In *The Bible and Radiocarbon Dating: Archaeology, Text, and Science*, ed. Thomas E. Levy and Thomas Higham, 129–63. London: Equinox.

Millard, Alan R. 1992. "Assyrian Involvement in Edom." In *Early Edom and Moab: The Beginning of the Iron Age in Southern Jordan*, ed. Piotr Bienkowski, 35–39. Sheffield, England: J. R. Collis.

Oakeshott, Marion F. 1978. "A Study of the Iron II Pottery of East Jordan with Special Reference to Unpublished Material from Edom." PhD dissertation, University of London, London, England.

Oakeshott, Marion F. 1983. "The Edomite Pottery." In *Midian, Moab, and Edom: The History and Archaeology of Late Bronze and Iron Age Jordan and North-West Arabia*, ed. John F. Sawyer and David J.A. Clines, 53–63. Sheffield, England: JSOT.

Oded, Bustenay. 1970. "Observations on Methods of Assyrian Rule in Transjordania after the Palestinian Campaign of Tiglath-Pileser III." *JNES* 29: 177–86.

Oren, Eliezer D. 1993. "Sera' Tel." In *The New Encyclopedia of Archaeological Excavations in the Holy Land*, ed. Ephraim Stern, 4:1329–35. Jerusalem: Carta.

Porter, Benjamin W. 2004. "Authority, Polity, and Tenuous Elites in Iron Age Edom (Jordan)." *Oxford Journal of Archaeology* 23 (4): 373–95. https://doi.org/10.1111/j.1468-0092.2004.00216.x.

Sedman, Leonie. 2002. "The Small Finds." In *Busayra: Excavations by Crystal M. Bennett 1971–1980*, ed. Piotr Bienkowski, 353–428. Oxford: Oxford University Press.

Smith, Neil G., and Thomas E. Levy. 2008. "The Iron Age Pottery from Khirbat en-Nahas, Jordan: A Preliminary Study." *BASOR* 352: 41–91.

Smith, Stuart T. 2003. "Pharaohs, Feasts, and Foreigners: Cooking, Foodways, and Agency on Ancient Egypt's Southern Frontier." In *The Archaeology and Politics of Food and Feasting in Early States and Empires*, ed. Tamara Bray, 39–64. New York: Kluwer Academic/Plenum. https://doi.org/10.1007/978-0-306-48246-5_3.

Stahl, Ann Brower. 2002. "Colonial Entanglements and the Practices of Taste: An Alternative to Logocentric Approaches." *AA* 104 (3): 827–45.

Stein, Gil. 2012. "Food Preparation, Social Context, and Ethnicity in a Prehistoric Mesopotamian Colony." In *The Menial Art of Cooking: Archaeological Studies of Cooking and Food Preparation*, ed. Sarah R. Graff and Enrique Rodríguez-Alegría, 19–63. Boulder: University Press of Colorado.

Stern, Ephraim. 2001. *Archaeology of the Land of the Bible*, vol. 2: *The Assyrian, Babylonian, and Persian Periods (732–332 BCE)*. New York: Doubleday.

Stucky, Rolf A. 2007. "Les tridacnes à décor gravé." In *La Méditerranéen des Phéniciens: De Tyr à Carthage: Catalogue de l'Exposition de l'Institut du Monde Arabe Paris, Novembre 2007—Avril 2008*, ed. Elisabeth Fontan and Hélène Le Meaux, 218–23. Paris: Institut du monde arabe.

Tebes, Juan M. 2011. "The Potter's Will: Spheres of Production, Distribution, and Consumption of the Late Iron Age Southern Transjordan-Negev Pottery." *BAIAS* 29: 61–101.

van Beek, Gus W. 1993. "Jemmeh, Tell." In *The New Encyclopedia of Archaeological Excavations in the Holy Land*, ed. Ephraim Stern, 2:667–74. Jerusalem: Carta.

Whiting, Charlotte M. 2007. *Complexity and Diversity in the Late Iron Age Southern Levant: The Investigations of 'Edomite' Archaeology and Scholarly Discourse*. Oxford: Archaeopress.

7

Peripheral Elite as Imperial Collaborators*

Craig W. Tyson
(D'Youville College)

Between the late eighth and sixth centuries BCE, a small, tribally organized society (LaBianca and Younker 1995; Younker 1997; LaBianca 1999)[1] located in and around what is now Amman, Jordan, underwent significant sociopolitical and economic growth and change. Although this society, known as the "sons of Ammon," "the Ammonites," or simply "Ammon," had existed before the late eighth century BCE, this was its most significant period of change. The changes and growth among the Ammonites began at roughly the same time the Neo-Assyrian Empire came to its classic form under the leadership of Tiglath-pileser III (744–727 BCE).

Tiglath-pileser III and his successors launched a series of campaigns that would bring the entire ancient Near East under their control, either as provinces or as vassals (Kuhrt 1995, 493–501; Van De Mieroop 2007b, 247–58). Among those who submitted to Assyrian power were the Ammonites, who appear alongside other small societies in Tiglath-pileser III's royal inscriptions as acknowledging his greatness and paying tribute (Tadmor and Yamada 2011, 122–23, no. 47: rev. 10'). For the next 150 years or so, the Ammonites remained as vassals, first to the Neo-Assyrian Empire and then to its successor, the Neo-Babylonian Empire (612–539 BCE). At some point during Neo-Babylonian

---

* This chapter is a slightly modified version of an article originally published under the same title in the *Journal of Anthropological Research* 70: 481–509.

DOI: 10.5876/9781607328230.c007

rule, the Ammonites rebelled and were subsequently conquered and converted into a province (Herr 1999, 232–34; Lipschits 2004, 39–41; Tyson 2013), a status that continued into the following Persian Period (538–331 BCE).

What is striking about the Ammonite case is the co-occurrence of sociopolitical and economic changes with a period of imperial rule. Did imperial rule in some way cause the changes in Ammon? If so, what were the processes and factors that brought them about? If not, what accounts for this striking coincidence? This chapter investigates this relationship and ultimately argues that the changes were stimulated by empire. It is thus justifiable to speak of these changes as secondary, as stimulated by exogenous forces. And yet, while empire—and the political, economic, military, and ideological worlds it creates—stimulated these responses, it was the local elite who brought many of them about. The Ammonite elite did not passively receive imperial influence; rather, they actively pursued their own agenda to the extent possible within the imperial framework. In this regard the sociopolitical and economic changes are the result of synergy between imperial concerns and the local elite.

In what follows, I track this synergy in the archaeological and textual records, explaining the relatively meager evidence with comparative data from the growing body of literature on empires and the societies that interacted with them. As the title of the chapter suggests, I argue that the Ammonite elite were really imperial collaborators, actively pursuing their own gain while fulfilling imperial expectations.[2] While the relationship was certainly uneasy and probably viewed with suspicion from both sides, each side benefited from the presence of the other—at least until the time was right for rebellion and the ruling Neo-Babylonian Empire no longer found collaborators among the Ammonites (figure 7.1).

EMPIRES AND IMPERIAL PRACTICE

The study of empires and the ways they exercise power over and affect smaller societies surrounding them has emerged as an important area of research in Old and New World anthropology and archaeology (D'Altroy 1992; Sinopoli 1994, 2001a, 2001b; Alcock et al. 2001; D'Altroy and Hastorf 2001; Parker 2001; Smith and Montiel 2001; Dietler 2010). The relatively large amount of archaeological and textual remains left by empires has been a boon in reconstructing their practices of control and management (D'Altroy 1992; Parker 2001). On the other side of the equation are the peripheral societies that are subject to imperial control and intrusions.[3] These societies' experience of empire varies depending on their sociopolitical organization and their geographic, economic,

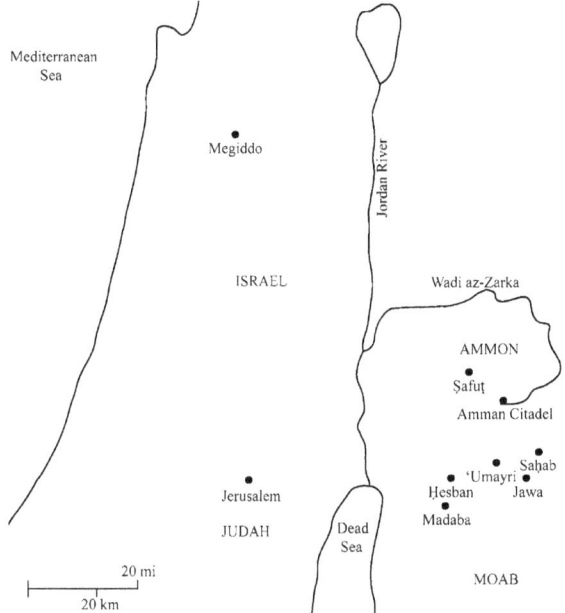

FIGURE 7.1. *Map of Ammon*

and military value to the empire. Their experience is also dependent on the approach the empire takes to control or exploit the region.

Typically, empires are interested in the extraction of wealth in various forms, the achievement of military security and, in some cases, the effecting of cultural transformation such as religious conversion in Arab empires (Sinopoli 2001a, 444). Because of the heterogeneous nature of imperial lands and the extractive goals, empires are organized "to administer and exploit diversity" (Barfield 2001, 29) in ways that reflect a cost-benefit analysis (D'Altroy 1992, 19; Parker 2001, 252). Depending on the circumstances, empires may incorporate different lands along a continuum of control from direct rule (provincialization) to little or no rule (buffer states/zones; Parker 2001, 249–50), what Terence D'Altroy calls the "Territorial-Hegemonic Model" (D'Altroy 1992, 19–24). On this continuum, vassalage falls under "hegemonic control," a form of control that uses indigenous political structures rather than imperial personnel and governmental structures to govern the area for the empire (D'Altroy 1992, 19; Parker 2001, 250–51). Hegemonic control uses a variety of economic, military, social, ritual, and ideological methods—both positive and negative—to control the vassal (D'Altroy 1992, 209; Morkot 2001, 239; Sinopoli 2001a, 454). Such an approach to controlling subjugated areas is cost-effective because it entails very little investment on the part of the empire (Sinopoli 2001a, 445; cf. Van De Mieroop 2007a, 112–19).

NEO-ASSYRIAN AND NEO-BABYLONIAN IMPERIAL PRACTICE

The Neo-Assyrian Empire into which the Ammonites were incorporated used a full complement of hegemonic tactics to coerce and control their vassals. I will not detail these here, as they have been discussed in the introductory chapter to this volume. However, a brief overview of Neo-Babylonian imperial practice will help round out the discussion before moving on to the case of the Ammonites.

The Neo-Babylonian Empire followed a similar pattern of imperial practice. Neo-Babylonian kings did not shy away from the use of force, especially when Nebuchadnezzar II (604–562 BCE) was consolidating the empire and made almost yearly campaigns to the west in an attempt to put down rebellions and gain control of Egypt (Kuhrt 1995, 589–93). On occasion, the kings used conscripts from subject areas, as indicated in Nabonidus's Harran Stele II (Schaudig 2001, 491, I II 6–10) and also the biblical text 2 Kings 24:2 (Liverani 2005, 185; Miller and Hayes 2006, 467). The Babylonians also practiced deportation, usually bringing deportees to the Babylonian heartland, perhaps aimed at rebuilding the region following the destructive wars with Assyria (Eph'al 1978, 81–82; ; Vanderhooft 1999, 110–12; Liverani 2005, 194–95).

The Neo-Babylonian Empire seems to have had provinces, although the evidence is slim (Vanderhooft 1999, 90–110; 2003, 237–48). However, Neo-Babylonian royal inscriptions make it clear that the Babylonians maintained relationships with vassal kings (Unger 1931, 286, no. 26 v:23–27; Grayson 1975, 100, chron. 5 obv. 17; Vanderhooft 1999, 38–39). There is a small amount of evidence of Babylonian treaties with these vassals (Vanderhooft 1999, 165n162), to which we can add a handful of biblical texts that imply treaties and oaths (Ezekiel 17; 2 Chronicles 36:13; 2 Kings 24:1; Jeremiah 27, 40:10).

The Babylonian Chronicles record the delivery of tribute, at least when the Babylonians traveled to vassal lands (e.g., Grayson 1975, 100, chron. 5 obv. 17). The Etemenanki Cylinder and the Istanbul Prism indicate that vassal kings and governors from the Levant were responsible for coordinating and sending supplies and laborers to Babylon to help with building projects (Unger 1931, 286, no. 26 v:23–27; Wetzel and Weissbach 1938, 46, cols. 3–4). The failure of a vassal to meet his obligations frequently resulted in punitive campaigns but did not always lead to the dissolution of the local political infrastructure (e.g., Grayson 1975, 102, chron. 5 rev. 11–13; 2 Kings 24:10–17; 2 Chronicles 36:9–10;

see also the sequence of rulers in Tyre; Josephus 1926, 1.20.143, 1.21.156–59; Zawadzki 2003, 278–79).

The Neo-Babylonian Empire also used officials in the administration of the western part of the empire. In particular, we hear of *šakkanakku* (Wetzel and Weissbach 1938, 46, 4:22–25; Schaudig 2001, 509) and (*bēl*) *pīḫatu* officials (Porten 1981, 36, line 9; Joannès 1994; Vanderhooft 1999, 38–39). Their titles suggest that they were governors of some type, even though their role cannot be easily specified (Frame 1992, 225–27). The biblical stories about Gedaliah (2 Kings 25:22–26; Jeremiah 40–41) suggest that in certain cases Babylon appointed indigenous leaders over territories even after they had rebelled (cf. Josephus 1926, 1.156–58).

The Neo-Babylonian ideological system is not as well attested as its Assyrian counterpart, and thus our main source for understanding it is the royal titulary, which tends to emphasize the king's piety, justice, and care for the land and temples (Vanderhooft 1999, 16–23). Nebuchadnezzar II's inscriptions, for example, portray him as a benefactor, protector, just ruler, one who gathers the peoples for good, and one whose movement of tribute to Babylon is appropriate given that Babylon is perceived as the center of the world (Vanderhooft 1999, 41–46). The later Neo-Babylonian king Nabonidus (555–539 BCE) reintroduced a more overtly militaristic ideology, perhaps in part to regularize relations with the periphery (Vanderhooft 1999, 51–59).

THE AMMONITES IN IRON AGE I–EARLY IRON AGE IIB

The economic and social disruptions that brought the Late Bronze Age (ca. 1550–1200 BCE) to an end around the beginning of the twelfth century BCE (Van De Mieroop 2007b, 190–206) left the Amman Plateau and other inland areas of the Levant relatively isolated. Perhaps to fill the economic void created by the collapse of trade networks, because of the diminished threat of Egyptian intrusions that had been more common during the Late Bronze Age, or for other reasons beyond the limits of the available evidence, a slow process of settlement of the Amman Plateau began during Iron Age I (figure 7.2). During this period, fifty-four small sites were added to the fifteen known from the Late Bronze Age–Iron Age I transition (table 7.1). The trend appears to have continued in Iron Age IIA, but we do not have precise numbers because at present there is no way to distinguish between Iron Age IIA and Iron Age IIB sites based on surface survey alone. Several of the larger sites (Amman Citadel, Saḥab, and Ṣafuṭ) probably functioned as local centers of power.

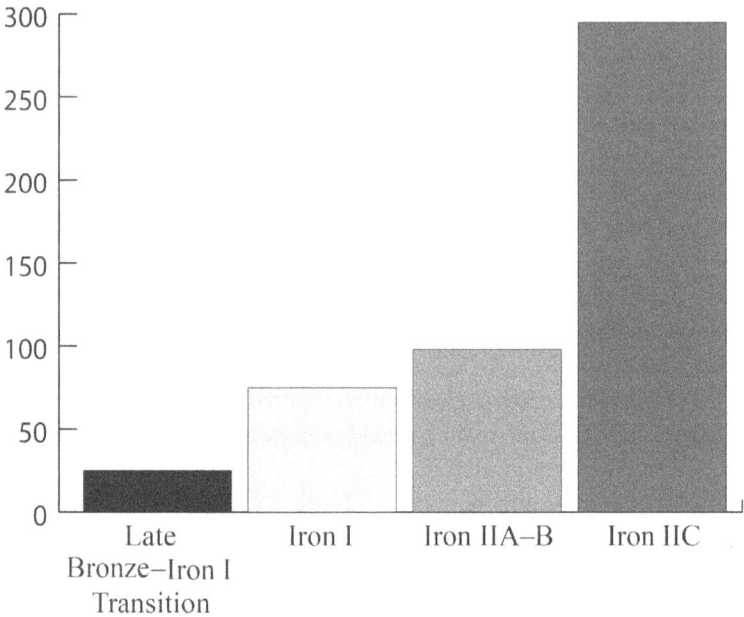

FIGURE 7.2. *Increase in number of identified sites from the Late Bronze Age–Iron Age I transition through Iron Age IIC (compiled from Ray 2001:151–54; Younker 2003:154–58).*

The almost complete lack of imported items during Iron Age I and IIA suggests that there were few long-distance trade connections. The most striking finds from Iron Age IIA are two anthropoid coffins from the Raghdan Royal Palace Tomb and an anthropoid coffin lid from Saḥab Tomb A, which, if correctly dated, may reveal elite burial traditions from the tenth century that used Egyptian artistic conventions (Albright 1932; ; Yassine 1975, 58–62; Dornemann 1983, 146–49). In addition to the archaeological evidence, several texts from the Hebrew Bible, which were written or compiled in the seventh or sixth century BCE, present encounters between the Israelite Kings David and Solomon and the Ammonites (2 Samuel 10–12; 1 Kings 11). The literary context of these stories suggests they may be literary creations; nevertheless, if they do reliably report historical data, no great social stratification or political complexity is implied.

The small quantity and unexceptional nature of the information on the Amman Plateau from Iron Age I through IIA fits comfortably within the broader context. In Iron Age IIA, Egypt was experiencing an insular period, in part because of political fragmentation (Taylor 2000, 330–31). Assyria regained

TABLE 7.1. Transjordanian chronology (following Herr and Najjar 2001)

Archaeological Period	Dates (BCE)
Late Bronze Age–Iron Age I transition	Late thirteenth–early twelfth centuries
Iron Age I	1200–1000
Iron Age IIA	1000–900
Iron Age IIB	900–700
Iron Age IIC	700–500

its strength and subsequently its hold over Upper Mesopotamia under Assurdan II (934–912 BCE) and his successors, Adad-nirari II (911–891 BCE) and Tukulti-Ninurta II (890–884 BCE), but it did not establish a foothold west of the Euphrates (Kuhrt 1995, 478–83). Thus, the Levant remained relatively insulated, permitting local groups to continue their lives undisturbed by imperial endeavors.

Although data are still limited, the early part of Iron Age IIB (ca. 900–750 BCE) evidences greater change and complexity than the preceding periods. Settlement probably increased modestly, but, as stated above, Iron Age IIB sites cannot be distinguished from Iron Age IIA sites based on survey data alone. Nevertheless, markers of wealth and power become visible in a small set of elite products, including a royal inscription generally referred to as the Amman Citadel Inscription (Horn 1969; Cross 2003b), volute capitals (Drinkard 2003),[4] several sculptures carved in stone (Abou Assaf 1980, 76; Zayadine 1989, pl. LI), and a few imports, including alabaster (Daviau 2002, 122; possibly Harding 1951, 40, pl. XIV:44) and marine shells used as beads or pendants (Reese 2002, 282–84, table 4A; possibly Dajani 1966, pl. 3, fig. 5:49–52; Harding 1948, 94, 1951, 40, pl. XIV:46). Likewise, monumental structures become more common. These include a possible gate and water system at the Amman Citadel (Dornemann 1983, 89–90, 170–72), a ramp and gate complex at Jalul (Younker 2007), and a fortified town at Tall Jawa Stratum IX, complete with a solid wall with offsets and insets, a retaining wall and possible glacis, passageways, a tower, and a guardroom (Daviau 2003, 49–57). Together, these items suggest new ways of representing power, new desires for exotic goods, the development of local artisanship in stone carving, and the use of writing for purposes of display. At about this time, the earliest reference to an Ammonite ruler appears in the annals of the Neo-Assyrian king Shalmaneser III, who describes a Levantine coalition he faced at Qarqar in 853 BCE (Yamada 2000, 159–61). Although an Ammonite military ruler may already have existed in response to pressure from regional powers such as Israel and Damascus, this reference confirms that the Ammonites had coalesced under a military ruler to defend themselves against imperial encroachment.

PERIPHERAL ELITE AS IMPERIAL COLLABORATORS

Areas incorporated into an empire by territorial or hegemonic means may experience a variety of interconnected changes depending on an array of contextual factors. These changes can be economic, technological, social, political, religious, dietary, and material cultural, to name a few. Some may result directly from imperial practices, while others may be the by-products of two-way interactions between local and "global" or imperial traditions (Sinopoli 2001a, 445; cf. LaBianca 2006, 2007; LaBianca and Walker 2007).

In the late eighth century BCE, the Ammonites became vassals of the Neo-Assyrian Empire as a result of Tiglath-pileser III's vigorous territorial expansion. The Ammonite rulers were now obliged to promote and protect Assyrian interests while also securing their authority over the local population. It was in this period, the last part of Iron Age IIB and Iron Age IIC (ca. 750–500 BCE), that the Ammonites, as vassals, reached the height of their sociopolitical complexity and economic growth. The growth and change is visible in both the volume and the quality of material available. There are more towns, more tombs, more small outlying sites (towers, forts, farmsteads), more examples of domestic architecture, more examples of elite and public architecture, more sculptures and decorative architectural objects, more imported and elite items, a greater use of writing, and a growing number of items that reflect influence from imperial or international styles. In what follows, I consider the changes the Ammonites experienced during this period in four major areas: settlement intensity and complexity, economic changes, sociopolitical complexity, and religious changes (following D'Altroy 1992; Crowell 2004, 266). Each area is prefaced by comparative material from the study of empires that orients the presentation and explanation of the Ammonite evidence.

Settlement Intensity and Complexity

Incorporation into an empire is often associated with changes in settlement patterns that are dependent on local factors and imperial interest in the area (Smith and Montiel 2001, 247, 249; Matthews 2003, 143–45). These may include changes in settlement intensification related to agricultural production, creation of regional centers, changes in the types of crops cultivated, land management and reclamation practices, land tenure, storage practices, and specialization (Matthews 2003, 143–45). Where specialization is present, subsequent dependence on exchange to acquire necessary food and supplies may ensue (Morrison 2001, 273). The imperial or local elite may encourage concentration of sedentary population because, as Schortman and Urban (1994, 405) write, it "reduces costs of supervising 'dependents,' collecting tribute, distributing goods and services, and exacting sanctions. Population concentration also undercuts the ability of subordinate elites to compete effectively with paramounts for commoner labor and surpluses" (see also Köksal 2006). Examples of such settlement changes are visible along the Upper Tigris River in southeastern Turkey between the ninth and seventh centuries BCE and for much of the upper region of Mesopotamia under direct Neo-Assyrian control (Parker 2001, 266–70, 2003, 529–48; Wilkinson et al. 2005). Similar types of settlement and cultural changes are apparent in areas under the rule of the Inka Empire (D'Altroy 1992; Hastorf and D'Altroy 2001, 5).

On the Amman Plateau, significant settlement changes occurred from Iron Age IIB to Iron Age IIC. Excavated tells (settlement mounds; also "talls") that show occupation in Iron Age IIB (Amman Citadel, Jalul, Tall Jawa, Ṣafuṭ, Saḥab, 'Umayri, and possibly Ḥesban) continued to be occupied in Iron Age IIC, with some showing evidence for expansion (e.g., Ḥesban, Ṣafuṭ) and others providing evidence of better planning (e.g., Saḥab, 'Umayri). The number of tells known from surveys increased by one from Iron Age IIB to Iron Age IIC (Ibach 1987, site nos. 7, 29, 100, 102, 103, 143). Most of the extant Iron Age tombs from the Amman Plateau have remains from Iron Age IIC.[5] Nearly all of them cluster around the central site of the Amman Citadel and contain a variety of elite grave goods, such as seals, bronze and iron objects, and various imported items. Equally important is the growth in small farmsteads and associated agricultural facilities (terraces, cisterns, presses) during Iron Age IIC. The total number of sites increased from about 100 in Iron Age IIA–Iron Age IIB to about 300 in Iron Age IIC (Ray 2001, 151–54; see figure 7.2 above), with the vast majority being small farmsteads or other agriculturally oriented sites. The shift represents a greater emphasis on agricultural pursuits, moving even into marginally productive ecological niches (Ray 2001, 153). It likewise included an investment in physical capital, such as terraces and presses, which improved the long-term productive use of the land and its products.[6]

It is likely that several forces were working together to produce the new settlement picture. The Neo-Assyrian Empire had an interest in increasing the productivity of lands under its control. This is apparent for the core areas around the capital cities as well as for provinces extending to the Euphrates (Wilkinson et al. 2005, 40–44). As Karen Radner (2000, 235–41) shows, efforts to make the land productive through canal projects and the redistribution of human populations were very important to Neo-Assyrian kings. What shape this interest took for the inland polities of the southern Levant is not clear, given that bulky agricultural goods were not typically shipped long-distance across land from the southern Levant to the Assyrian heartland. Certainly, however, the Assyrians needed supplies for their armies when on campaign and so would have been interested in their vassals' agricultural capacity. It was also in the interests of the Ammonite elite to encourage or coerce increased settlement to ensure a steady supply of food for their own use. Beyond food supplies, the empire and local elites had an interest in a more sedentary population because such populations are generally easier to control (Schortman and Urban 1994, 405; Köksal 2006). Given what the local and imperial elites had to gain, their active involvement in promoting increased settlement is highly likely, even if it does not fully explain the change in settlement patterns.

Economic Changes

Incorporation into an empire is often attended by economic changes, which may be related to the demand for tribute and other material support by the empire (Sinopoli 2001a, 456). In areas that are dependent on agricultural products and animal husbandry for subsistence, the demand for tribute may entail the development of markets and "monetization" (D'Altroy and Earle 1985, 188; Sinopoli 2001a, 456). Such developments may result from the need to pay tribute in high-value items, such as metals, linked with a productive base focused on agriculture and pastoralism. Local production may thus be intensified to create the surplus necessary for obtaining items suitable for payment as tribute (Morrison 2001, 267; Sinopoli 2001a, 456; Matthews 2003, 144).

The most obvious change related to the economy of the Amman Plateau is that of the settlement intensification mentioned above. The increased number of small, agriculturally oriented sites means there was a greater capacity for agricultural output. It is unlikely, however, that agricultural goods from Ammon were used to pay tribute or traded as exports because grain—and even wine and oil—are not typically valuable enough to be profitable for long-distance overland trade (Clark and Haswell 1970, 196–97, table XLVII, 274; Holladay 2006). Agricultural goods might have played a role in supplying camel caravans passing through the area, but such a role probably did not necessitate the kind of settlement growth documented on the Amman Plateau. The economic aspects of this settlement were likely connected more to the needs of the local elites than to imperial demands.

The number of imported items in excavated sites is the next-most-obvious aspect of change in the economy, and it shows that the expanding trade networks of the Neo-Assyrian and Neo-Babylonian Empires reached well into the marginal areas of the southern Levant. Imports included alabaster, ivory, marine shells, glass, semi-precious stones, metals (chiefly bronze and iron), and pottery (Tyson 2014, 58–63). Similarly, the textual evidence shows that the Ammonites had access to silver and gold and in some cases measured it in small pieces (e.g., *CAI* no. 80:6),[7] which points to at least some level of monetization. The evidence for weights (Platt 1991, 253, fig. 10.36; Daviau 2002, 90; Herr and Platt 2002, 368, fig. 16.12; possibly *CAI* no. 54c), measures (*CAI* nos. 65, 80, 137, 243), and management practices is likewise rare (e.g., the Ammonite ostraca, *CAI* nos. 47, 65, 76, 80, 94, 137, 144–47, 211, 238, 243), but it does indicate modest increases from the previous periods.

Neo-Assyrian texts mention various kinds of wool and textiles they received from their vassals as tribute. The Ammonites are not singled out as a source of textiles in any of these texts, but they do appear in lists of polities sending tribute that included metals and textiles (Tadmor and Yamada 2011, 123, no. 47: rev. 12'–13'). The prominence in these lists of wool alongside metals and other high-value goods shows that textiles were worth the attention of the empire and valuable enough to warrant long-distance overland trade.[8] Given the lack of any significant sources of metal in the Amman Plateau and the long history of sheep pastoralism in Jordan, the production of wool for export seems likely.

Sheep and goats represent 88.43 percent of the faunal assemblage at Ḥesban during this period (Ray 2001, 149, table 6.2, appendix C) and 84 percent at Tall Jawa (Popkin 2016, 325); other sites may have similar percentages, but their faunal assemblages have not been tabulated. The technologies necessary for textile production were readily available, as indicated by finds of loom weights at Ḥesban, Tall Jawa, and ʿUmayri, as well as spindle whorls, which are found regularly in excavations (Ibrahim 1975, 73; Geraty, Herr, and LaBianca 1988, 226; Lawlor 1997, 51). Peter R.W. Popkin's (2016, 445) recent contribution demonstrates that culling strategies of sheep and goats left sheep alive longer, pointing to their use for wool and not simply milk or meat. The overall evidence suggests domestic-level production of textiles; no industrial production areas have been found. Nonetheless, domestic-level production of textiles is common in the ancient world because it allowed women to multitask while caring for young children (Barber 1994, 29–33).

Although specialization and industrial production of textiles can produce substantial quantities of textiles (Barber 1994, 207–31), domestic production also has the potential to yield relatively large quantities. In the Aztec Empire, for example, part of the tribute the Triple Alliance required from its subjects was paid in textiles. The quantities were fairly large, and as far as is known, the textiles were produced domestically rather than in specialized workshops (Berdan 1987; Brumfiel 1991, 228–36). Inferring from the Aztec example, it is possible that the Ammonites produced wool textiles for export or tribute without specialized workshops.[9]

The evidence for economic changes linked specifically to imperial domination is minimal, given that the increased agricultural capacity is most likely not related to the production of exports. However, the increased capacity may be a by-product of the stability created by the Mesopotamian empires and the needs of the local elite. The visible changes are focused among the elite who had access to imports and probably gained from taxes and tolls on caravans moving through the region. The likely use of wool as an export adds to the picture of elite interest in international exchange, but the nature of the evidence means this cannot yet be documented archaeologically. Thus, rather than a massive reorganization of the economy to meet imperial demands, the local economy seems to have catered to the interests of the local elite. In this regard, one of the most important influences of the Neo-Assyrian and Neo-Babylonian Empires on Ammon's economy was the way they stimulated long-distance trade networks through which the local elite could acquire exotic goods.[10]

Sociopolitical Complexity

The kinds of economic changes visible on the Amman Plateau are often associated with increased social ranking and the creation or expansion of a local elite (Hastorf and D'Altroy 2001, 13; Sinopoli 2001a, 454, 2001b, 197–98). Likewise, interaction between empires and peripheral regions can create or cause changes in political groups (Tapper 1990, 52; Matthews 2003, 147). The creation or intensification of elites and political change may become visible in the material culture through the appearance of imported elite goods or of objects that emulate elite imperial styles (Matthews 2003, 143–44).

Elite Appropriations of Symbols of Status, Power, and Authority

The Ammonite elite were already making use of visible representations with which to legitimate and perpetuate their increasing power. These included monumental inscriptions, volute capitals, statuary, and the like that appear in the archaeological record from the preceding Early Iron Age IIB. That set of items had broad currency throughout the small polities of the Levant. However, the onset of imperial rule brought an imperial set of material representations

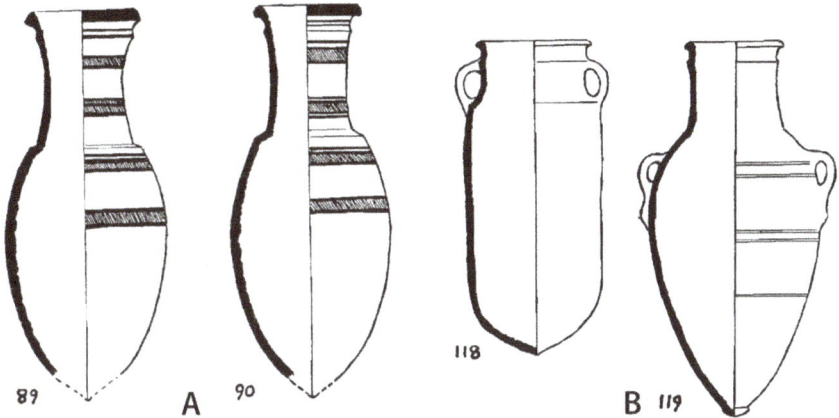

FIGURE 7.3. *Assyrian-style pottery from Ammon: (A) handle-less jars (from Harding 1953, fig. 22:89–90) and (B) pointed jars (from Harding 1953, fig. 23:118–19). Courtesy, Palestine Exploration Fund.*

of power, status, and authority that the Ammonite elite could appropriate for their own ends.

Studies of elite incorporation of foreign or imperial items into a local culture emphasize the agency of the local elite in choosing which items to adopt or adapt and the value of these items for articulating and advancing their own status and advantage (Marcus 1989, 55, 62, 1996, 43–53, 76–77; Routledge 1997, 38–39; Woolf 1997; Dietler 1998, 2010, 55–74; Schortman and Urban 1998, III; Hunter 2001 for a critical consideration of this issue, see Cifarelli, this volume). While it is not always possible to be certain that a particular cultural borrowing reflects the projection of status or legitimation of power, the aggregation of different categories of items in closely related contexts argues in favor of such an interpretation. The main categories for which the prestige of foreign-inspired items seems clear in the Ammonite context are architecture, drinking vessels made of pottery and metal, and iconography.

The main example for architecture is the open-court plan seen in buildings at Tall Jawa (Daviau 2001, 218–22) and on the Amman Citadel (Zayadine, Humbert, and Najjar 1989, 362; Humbert and Zayadine 1992, 249). Given its elite use in Assyria, the appropriation of the architectural plan at the Amman Citadel and in wealthy houses at Tall Jawa is not surprising.[11] Also noteworthy is the use of Assyrian fine-ware styles and metal bowls from the Neo-Assyrian, Neo-Babylonian, and Persian Periods (figure 7.3). The quality of the artifacts bespeaks their elite nature, as do their find spots in wealthy tombs

(Dornemann 1983, 51, figs. 33:9–10, 29–30, 55–56; figs. 40:1–6, 14, 15, 17) and large domestic complexes, such as at Tall Jawa (Daviau 2001, 225, figs. 5.1–2, 6.1–2). These artifacts represent specific social practices of drinking and feasting that can be converted into prestige and power (Dietler 1998; Dietler and Hayden 2001; Hunter 2001).

In the realm of iconography, Mesopotamian stylistic features appear on local stamp seals (figure 7.4)[12] and possibly on the reliefs found at Rujm al-Kursi (figure 7.5; Hübner 2009), reflecting the interest of local elites in the religious symbols and culture of their overlords.[13] Similarly, a number of sculptures from the area show broad international artistic influences from Syria, Phoenicia, and Egypt (figure 7.6; Abou Assaf 1980, 58; Dornemann 1983, 154–60; Prag 1987; ʿAmr 1990, 116–17; Zayadine 1991, 49–51). Although these influences do not point directly to Assyrian or Babylonian influence, they highlight the international connections empires foster.

Each of these items, while forging links to the imperial regime or the broader international elite style, also reflects local adaptation. The examples of open-court architecture are constrained by locally available materials and space. The Assyrian-style fine wares are, as far as is known, made of local clays (cf. Engstrom 2004) and do not always replicate the dimensions of their Assyrian counterparts. The iconography of the seals, while using some Mesopotamian motifs, appears on scarab-shaped stamp seals common to the southern Levant rather than on cylinder seals common to the Mesopotamian tradition. The sculptures contain mixed influences that go beyond that of Assyrian art, and the reliefs on the Rujm al-Kursi building replicate the standard of the Assyrian god Sîn of Harran but lack the tassels that are typical of his iconography from the Assyrian heartland. These appropriations underscore the creative use of these items in ways that resonate with existing local practices rather than replacing them.

What does not appear in the archaeological record is also revealing. The archaeology of the Amman Plateau preserves only a select group of artifacts that fit within already meaningful practices, such as drinking (cf. Hunter 2001, 298–303). The Ammonite elite did not adopt all of the accoutrements of the imperial elite. They had to legitimate their power to their own population, so they adapted the imperial representations of status and power in ways that communicated meaningfully within their local context.

Consumption of Luxury Goods

Similar to the appropriation of imperial symbols of status and power that visibly mark the elite, the increasing number of imported items found in Iron

FIGURE 7.4. *Seal illustrating Mesopotamian-style iconography with an Ammonite inscription: "Belonging to Shubʾel" (from Eggler and Keel 2006: ʿAmman 6).*

FIGURE 7.5. *Relief from Rujm al-Kursi showing local adaptation of the standard of Sin of Harran. Courtesy, the author.*

FIGURE 7.6. *Statue of Yaraḥʿazar illustrating a mix of iconographic styles. Drawing by Thomas Norman.*

Age IIC contexts, mentioned in the section on economic changes, indicates an interest in these items and the means to procure them through international trade. The concentration of these items along with other markers of status and power in wealthy tombs suggests socially limited access. Moreover, it strengthens the impression of the elite nature of a few families and individuals situated largely near the Amman Citadel.

King and Administration

The evidence for social stratification found in elite goods parallels evidence in the domain of political organization, with the appearance of at least the skeleton of an administrative apparatus. The extent of the Ammonite king's administrative apparatus is not clear, but he did have a small cadre of officials who served in different capacities. The best examples are two seals from secure archaeological contexts that are inscribed with the title ʿ*ebed*, "servant" (*CAI* nos. 40, 129), a term that typically designates royal officials.[14] Other titles possibly linked with an Ammonite governmental apparatus are *hmzkr*, "the herald" (*CAI* no. 124a); *hnss*, "the standard bearer" (*CAI* no. 68); *nʿr*, "young man," "steward" (*CAI* nos. 53, 54); and (*h*)*spr*, "(the) scribe" (*CAI* nos. 139, 209). Unfortunately, it is not known whether these titled men were attached specifically to the king or to other wealthy individuals. The seals thus provide limited evidence for people with specialized skills or positions, some of whom may have served in a small governmental apparatus.[15]

A few Ammonite ostraca (*CAI* nos. 65, 76, 80, 94, 137, 144–47, 211, 238, 243) provide late (ca. 600–500 BCE) and limited data on administrative practices. They demonstrate an interest in keeping track of disbursements and highlight the relatively consistent use and development of a regional script. What is difficult to extrapolate is whether they indicate anything about the exercise or centralization of political power. Nearly all of them come from the small towns of the Amman Plateau rather than the Amman Citadel. Furthermore, as a corpus, they provide few indications of connection to a central authority. The main exceptions are a reference to the king in Ḥesban AI (*CAI* no. 80:1) and the possible mention of a king in ʿUmayri Ostracon II (*CAI* no. 211:1). More broadly speaking, the development of a standardized Ammonite script in the late ninth through mid-sixth centuries indicates that elites were harnessing writing for their own administrative and ideological purposes (Sanders 2004; Rollston 2006, 68; cf. Carr 2008; Sanders 2009).[16] When the Ammonite ostraca found scattered throughout the region's towns are considered in the context of standardization of the script, they suggest the interest of the central authority in managing outlying sites.

Even given these data, it is difficult to conclude that there was more than a loose administrative integration of the Amman Plateau. Papyrus probably played a role in written communication and thus might have provided further evidence for centralized administration if it had survived. Given the weak indications for centralization, however, finds of papyrus would not likely alter this impression significantly. Finally, the earliest of the ostraca found in the area date to the end of the seventh century,[17] 100 years or more after the inception of Neo-Assyrian domination. Thus, whatever centralization the ostraca might suggest is late in Ammonite sociopolitical development.

RELIGIOUS CHANGES

As with the areas discussed above, incorporation into an empire can stimulate changes in local religion. In some cases religious change is an explicit part of the imperial agenda (Sinopoli 2001a, 444; Jennings 2003). For example, an empire might target specific aspects of the local religion in an effort to dismantle resistance while leaving other aspects of the local religion alone (Jennings 2003). In other cases, even when religion figures into the exercise of domination, the empire does not actively promote religious change. In such cases local populations sometimes adapt aspects of imperial religion, resulting in hybrid representations, practices, or beliefs (Evans 1998, 345–48; Wells 1998, 324–26; Webster 2001). Likewise, religion is a prime sphere in which local elites can ground their status and authority by associating themselves with elite symbols and by controlling certain aspects of divine-human relations (Schortman and Urban 1994, 410–11; Grijalvo 2005).

Assyrian state religion had a place for foreign gods within its symbolic system as lesser counterparts to the god Aššur. Cult statues from foreign lands could be removed when vassals rebelled as a sign that the vassals' god had abandoned their people. The cult statues could also be repatriated when the Assyrians were willing to do so. Whether the Assyrians actively meddled with local religious traditions is debated (Cogan 1974, 1993; cf. Spieckermann 1982); they certainly had motive for it. Even if the empire left religious traditions alone, the local elites may have used those traditions for their own ends.

Religious change can be seen in the Mesopotamian-inspired elements in the iconography of stamp seals and in the modified representation of Sîn of Harran found on the Rujm al-Kursi building (Hübner 2009; figure 7.5). The key is recognizing the social location of these borrowings on elite personal items (seals) and in elite architecture (Rujm al-Kursi building). What these borrowings represent in the realm of belief is not easy to determine. For example, the moon crescent of Sîn (*CAI* nos. 1, 17; Hübner 1993, 159, fig. 21; the Rujm al-Kursi building) could be understood to represent the Assyrian god Sîn of Harran, or it might have been adapted to represent the local moon god Yareaḥ. Either way, these borrowings could represent another attempt by the local elite to connect themselves with symbols of status and power. Beyond iconography, the Ammonite onomasticon contains occurrences of the Mesopotamian gods Nanay (*CAI*, no. 65:5) and 'Inurta (*CAI*, no. 55), and the Egyptian god Bes (*CAI*, no. 44), but the bearers of these names could be foreigners, so this is not clear evidence of local changes.

Also significant is the impact Mesopotamian imperialism may have had on local religion. In neighboring Judah the assertion of Assyrian might—including the preeminence of the Assyrian state god Aššur—was countered by the local elevation of the Judean patron or royal dynastic god Yahweh to a higher status, something approaching monotheism (Smith 2001, 157–66). Were similar processes operative among the Ammonites?

The Hebrew Bible portrays each of the peoples surrounding Judah as having a particular deity that occupies a roughly parallel position to that of the Judean god Yahweh. In the case of the Ammonites, it is the god Milkom (2 Kings 23:13). The archaeologically attested onomastic and iconographic evidence also points to Milkom being the patron or royal dynastic god of the Ammonites (Burnett 2009). What is difficult to determine on present evidence is whether Milkom was the object of a universalizing theology used to resist imperial pressure. In contrast to the Judeans, who rebelled on multiple occasions, the Ammonites were obedient vassals of both the Neo-Assyrian Empire and, at least for a time, the Neo-Babylonian Empire. The different political and military trajectory might indicate a weaker ideological response to Mesopotamian imperial ideology in Ammon, but there is insufficient evidence for a firm conclusion. What we *can* say is that Ammonite religion probably played a role in elite identity formation, manipulating local sociopolitical factions, and negotiating resistance or capitulation to the Neo-Assyrian and Neo-Babylonian Empires. As a powerful piece of the human ideological landscape, the elite surely would have taken advantage of local religious traditions, but a clearer understanding of how they used those traditions must await further discoveries.

Scale of Change

The preceding discussion of changes underscores items in the archaeological and textual records that indicate important sociopolitical and economic changes among the Ammonites during the Neo-Assyrian and Neo-Babylonian Periods. However, although these changes are meaningful, the analysis should be cognizant of the scale of change. The Ammonites inhabited a marginal ecological niche and a relatively marginal geographic space within the Neo-Assyrian and Neo-Babylonian Empires. Not surprisingly, the changes surveyed here pale in quantity and scale when compared with those in the cities of the imperial core. Moreover, the changes that took place in the late eighth through sixth centuries BCE do not indicate a radical break with earlier forms of sociopolitical organization. The Ammonites, literally "the sons of Ammon," continued to be referred to by kinship metaphors, and the available evidence does not suggest that the elite were dis-embedded from such kinship structures. This comports well with recent discussions of political change in Iron Age Transjordan that highlight the flexible role of tribalism in fluctuations between small social groups and larger supra-tribal polities. These studies highlight the fact that the movement toward a supra-tribal polity often comes in response to military pressures, economic opportunities, or both (Knauf 1992, 49–51; Knauf-Belleri 1995, 108–9; LaBianca and Younker 1995, 405–11; Younker 1997, 246; 1999, 206–9, 2003, 169–70 Steen and Smelik 2007, 152–53; Bienkowski 2009, 18) and is facilitated by the metaphors and mechanisms a kinship system provides (LaBianca and Younker 1995, 403; LaBianca 1999, 20; cf. Steen 2004, 126–29; 2006, 28, 2009, 105; Steen and Smelik 2007, 150; Bienkowski 2009, 17). The movement toward a supra-tribal polity among the Ammonites attracted multiple ways of articulating power and prestige, including architecture, iconography, and drinking vessels inspired by imperial and international prototypes; the control of imports; and the technology of writing. It did not, as far as we can tell, destroy the kinship metaphors or organization that antedated the changes.

CONCLUSION

At the beginning of this chapter, I asked how the co-occurrence of imperial rule and the changes visible in the archaeological and textual records of the Ammonites might be explained. The ensuing discussion has brought to the fore a number of issues that are important for answering that question. First and foremost is *to establish the co-occurrence through a diachronic analysis of change that leads to converging lines of evidence across multiple categories of the archaeological and textual records*. In the case of the Ammonites, a clear trend of change and increased complexity (settlement, wealthy tombs, imports, sculpture, inscriptions) began roughly around the time the Neo-Assyrian Empire gained control of the area and continued into the Neo-Babylonian and Persian Periods. If the diachronic analysis had turned up only one area of change, the explanation would of necessity be much more limited in scope and strength. It is the converging lines of evidence from different sources that establish the pattern as more than a coincidence or an isolated phenomenon unrelated to empire.

Second is *to determine the social location of the changes*. In the case considered here, the social location of many of the changes is concentrated among the elite and associated with specific practices, including eating, drinking, writing, and displaying prestige. Other changes, such as the intensity and complexity of settlement and the concomitant increase in agricultural productive capacity, are more difficult to link directly to the elite. Rulers almost universally have a keen interest in the productive capacity of their region, but it is impossible in this case to demonstrate an explicit policy of agricultural development directed by the elite. Explanations of such changes must therefore remain tentative.

Third is *to analyze the potential synergies created by hegemonic power*. The investigation of the ancient Near Eastern imperial context and comparison with other empires highlight the flexible approach empires took toward administering their vassals. Of particular importance is the way hegemonic power involved the empire's dependence on vassal elites. From what we can tell, the Neo-Assyrian and Neo-Babylonian Empires made some fundamental demands of their vassals: tribute, taxes, and military and political cooperation. What is needed to fulfill these obligations? A stable sociopolitical context in which economic exchange can be managed effectively to pay tribute and tax obligations. Local stability was created and enforced by the vassals, and the resultant products were used to pay tribute and taxes. For the Ammonites, as for most of the southern Levant, tribute and taxes were taken in metals and special fabrics, primarily wool. Wool was certainly produced locally, but there are no significant sources of metal in the Amman Plateau, so metals must have been acquired through exchange or taxes on caravan trade moving through the region.

The management of economic exchange to fulfill tribute obligations also provides an opportunity for the local elite to take advantage of the sociopolitical and economic context they manage. A well-managed society and economy can generate more than is needed to pay tribute and taxes, and the elite are in a position to claim it. In this regard the changes outlined here comport with the method of hegemonic rule and the local agents of that rule: the Ammonite elite. It does not, of course, prove that all the changes were the direct result of the Ammonite elite's management. Nonetheless, the imported raw materials and finished goods, as well as locally produced goods and architecture appropriating international and imperial styles, point in the direction of the elite. On the other hand, settlement complexity and intensity, while plausibly linked to elite interests, can also be related to factors beyond elite control.

Moving from the Ammonites to broader application, the key is to understand that hegemonic rule creates a dynamic relationship between ruler and ruled that varies depending on geography, natural resources, and other strategic interests. For this relationship to be productive in the long term, the empire needs ways of articulating its "rights" as the ruler while also providing the ruled with a real stake in the relationship. This relationship is a balancing act for both sides, constantly negotiated under varying political and economic circumstances. When the balance is lost and vassals can no longer tolerate the conditions of their vassalage, they may rebel. Likewise, when the benefits of retaining vassals are lost, empires are likely to turn vassal lands into provinces or destroy them and turn them into buffer zones. But if we focus too much on these extremes of imbalance, we will miss the productive middle ground. For the Ammonites at least, there was a period of about 130 years of loyalty to the Neo-Assyrian Empire. Although the weight of Neo-Assyrian obligations on the Ammonites was considerable, those demands were not so great as to induce rebellion and seem to have left significant room for the Ammonite elite to weave their own interests into the mechanisms necessary to fulfill their obligations. It is in this regard that the Ammonite elite are imperial collaborators.

The subjugation and subsequent provincialization of the Ammonites at some point during the Neo-Babylonian Period provide a clear break in the synergy between the Ammonite elite and the empire. The transformation into a province did not, however, immediately undo the sociopolitical and economic changes that had developed during the preceding era. The system of settlements and flow of imports continued into the early part of the Persian Period in the Persian province of Ammon, suggesting that the local elite maintained their role as collaborators under different political arrangements.

NOTES

The following individuals deserve thanks for the time and expertise they gave that have shaped the research for this project. My dissertation adviser at the University of Michigan, Brian Schmidt, and the members of my dissertation committee who pushed me to think in a broad and comparative way: Norman Yoffee, Carla Sinopoli, Gary Beckman, and J. P. Dessel. I would also like to thank Walter Aufrecht, Larry Herr, and Douglas Clark for sharing their expertise on all things Ammonite.

Michèle Daviau offered valuable thoughts on the chapter and timely bibliographic advice. Bradley Parker also deserves thanks for his comments and encouragement as I finalized this chapter. I extend my thanks to several anonymous reviewers whose comments significantly improved the focus and presentation of several parts of this chapter. The University of Michigan Rackham School of Graduate Studies, the University of Michigan Department of Near Eastern Studies, and the D'Youville College Faculty Research Council are to be thanked for funding that defrayed the cost of travel to Jordan in 2007 and 2012 and thus enabled me to complete this research successfully.

1. Although the Tribal Model of sociopolitical structure in the Transjordan is not above criticism (Routledge 2004:116–19), it is used in this chapter because it makes sense of the kinship metaphors used by the Ammonites and others to refer to them, namely, "the sons of Ammon" or "the house of Ammon."

2. I owe the formulation of the Ammonites being "collaborators" to J. P. Dessel.

3. I use the word *periphery* and its related term *core* to designate the spatial relationship between the Ammonites and the Neo-Assyrian and Neo-Babylonian Empires, as well as the differences between them in political, military, economic, and cultural power. Thus, the Ammonites are peripheral because they are on the far edge of the empires geographically and because the empires dominate the relationship politically, militarily, economically, and culturally. This aspect of domination in core/periphery relations is what Chase-Dunn and Hall (1997, 36) call "core/periphery hierarchy."

4. Lipschits's (2011, 217–22) study suggests that these capitals date to the subsequent Iron Age IIC period, the result of the Assyrians adopting the volute capital tradition from Israel and then encouraging its use among the vassals after Israel was destroyed in 722 BCE.

5. Amman Tombs A and B (Harding 1945; Henschel-Simon 1945); Amman Tomb C (Harding 1951); Amman Tomb E (Ma'ayeh 1960; Dajani 1966); Amman Tomb F (Dornemann 1983, 47n3, 132–42); Adoni-nur Tomb (Harding 1953; Tufnell 1953); Abu Nseir (Abu Ghanimeh 1984); Khilda Tombs 1 and 2 (Yassine 1988); Meqabelein (Harding 1950); Saḥab Tomb B (Harding 1948); and Umm Udayna (Abu Taleb 1985; Khalil 1986; Hadidi 1987).

6. Lipschits (2004) argues for one stage of site expansion radiating outward from the Amman Citadel during the Neo-Assyrian domination (Kletter 1991; Lipschits 2004), with a second stage of expansion under Neo-Babylonian domination radiating outward from the ʿUmayri-Ḥesban region (Herr 1995, 1999; Lipschits 2004).

7. CAI is A Corpus of Ammonite Inscriptions (Aufrecht 1989). Numbers 1–148 are in the original edition; numbers 149–214 are summarized in Aufrecht (1999, 177–81). Numbers 214 and up will be in the forthcoming second edition of *CAI*.

8. Comparative evidence from the nineteenth and twentieth centuries CE confirms the high value of wool relative to grain, wine, and oil (Clark and Haswell 1970, 274).

9. The site of Khirbat al-Mudayna ath-Thamad, which is south of Ammon in Moabite lands (Daviau 1997), has a building that seems to have been used for textile manufacture, dyeing operations, or both (Daviau and Dion 2002, 32–38, 46; Daviau et al. 2006, 257–59).

10. It is common to speak of the Pax Assyriaca as the general cause for settlement and prosperity in provincial and vassal lands of the Neo-Assyrian Empire. The economic, political, and military stability created by the Neo-Assyrian Empire was certainly a contributing factor to such changes, but it remains a very general explanation. Here I am suggesting something more specific—that in addition to relative stability, the economic networks stimulated by the Neo-Assyrian Empire and its successor empires created opportunities for acquiring wealth and luxury goods that otherwise would not have been as available to a landlocked polity in a semiarid ecological niche. A similar conclusion seems likely for other inland polities of the southern Levant, though the particular circumstances and evidence should be assessed independently. More generally, it would behoove scholars to replace references to the Pax Assyriaca—and the Pax of any other empire—as a general cause of change, with discussion of more specific causal mechanisms where the evidence allows.

11. Compare its use at Busayra in Edom (Bienkowski 2002, 162–67, 199).

12. Provenanced seals include Eggler and Keel (2006): ʿAmman 3, 5, 6, Safut 5. Non-provenanced seals that might be Ammonite are *CAI* nos. 1, 17, 84, 85, 108, 132. Cf. Hübner (1993).

13. Originally, I cited the use of Neo-Assyrian-style cylinder seals at Hasanlu as a model for the adoption of imperial iconography into a local context, following the work of Marcus (1989, 62, 1996, 49–50). Cifarelli's contribution to this volume, however, makes a compelling case that scholars have been much too Assyro-centric in their interpretation of the Hasanlu material. While this undercuts the use of the Hasanlu material as a model for processes in Ammon, Assyrian stylistic influences remain visible in Ammon. Note that the Assyrian stylistic influences in Ammon exist alongside and mixed with a broader international set of styles visible in Ammonite iconography.

14. Two other non-provenanced seals contain the ʿ*ebed* title and are likely Ammonite, given the onomastics and paleography (*CAI* nos. 13, 17).

15. General confirmation of royal officials can be found in the biblical prophet Amos's oracle against the Ammonite king and *śārāyw*, "his officials" (Amos 1:15).

16. The precise classification of the script found in Ammon is debated (Herr 1978, 55–57; Naveh 1987, 107–10; Cross 2003a).

17. Excluding the Nimrud Ostracon (*CAI* no. 47) that was found in Assyria and might be earlier.

WORKS CITED

Abou Assaf, Ali. 1980. "Untersuchungen zur ammonitischen Rundbildkunst." *UF* 12: 7–102.

Abu Ghanimeh, Khaled. 1984. "Abu Nseir Excavation." *ADAJ* 28: 305–10.

Abu Taleb, Mahmud. 1985. "The Seal of *plṭy bn m'š* the *mazkīr*." *ZDPV* 101: 21–29.

Albright, William F. 1932. "An Anthropoid Clay Coffin from Saḥâb in Transjordan." *AJA* 36 (3): 295–306. https://doi.org/10.2307/498391.

Alcock, Susan E., Terence N. D'Altroy, Kathleen D. Morrison, and Carla M. Sinopoli, eds. 2001. *Empires: Perspectives from Archaeology and History*. Cambridge: Cambridge University Press.

'Amr, Abdel-Jalil. 1990. "Four Ammonite Sculptures from Jordan." *ZDPV* 106: 114–18, Tafeln 7–8.

Aufrecht, Walter E. 1989. *A Corpus of Ammonite Inscriptions*. Lewiston, NY: Edwin Mellen.

Aufrecht, Walter E. 1999. "Ammonite Texts and Language." In *Ancient Ammon*, ed. Burton MacDonald and Randall W. Younker, 163–88. Leiden: Brill.

Barber, Elizabeth Wayland. 1994. *Women's Work, the First 20,000 Years: Women, Cloth, and Society in Early Times*. New York: W. W. Norton.

Barfield, Thomas J. 2001. "The Shadow Empires: Imperial State Formation along the Chinese-Nomad Frontier." In *Empires: Perspectives from Archaeology and History*, ed. Susan E. Alcock, Terence N. D'Altroy, Kathleen D. Morrison, and Carla M. Sinopoli, 10–41. Cambridge: Cambridge University Press.

Berdan, Frances F. 1987. "Cotton in Aztec Mexico: Production, Distribution, and Uses." *Mexican Studies/Estudios Mexicanos* 3 (2): 235–62. https://doi.org/10.2307/1051808.

Bienkowski, Piotr. 2002. *Busayra Excavations by Crystal-M. Bennet, 1971–1980*. Oxford: Oxford University Press.

Bienkowski, Piotr. 2009. "'Tribalism' and 'Segmentary Society' in Iron Age Transjordan." In *Studies on Iron Age Moab and Neighbouring Areas in Honour of Michèle Daviau*, ed. Piotr Bienkowski, 7–26. Leuven, Belgium: Peeters.

Brumfiel, Elizabeth M. 1991. "Weaving and Cooking: Women's Production in Aztec Mexico." In *Engendering Archaeology: Women and Prehistory*, ed. Joan M. Gero and Margaret W. Conkey, 224–51. Oxford: Blackwell.

Burnett, Joel S. 2009. "Iron Age Deities in Word, Image, and Name: Correlating Epigraphic, Iconographic, and Onomastic Evidence for the Ammonite God." *SHAJ* 10: 153–64.

Carr, David M. 2008. "The Tel Zayit Abecedary in (Social) Context." In *Literate Culture and Tenth-Century Canaan: The Tel Zayit Abecedary in Context*, ed. Ron E. Tappy and P. Kyle McCarter, 113–29. Winona Lake, IN: Eisenbrauns.

Chase-Dunn, Christopher, and Thomas D. Hall. 1997. *Rise and Demise: Comparing World Systems*. Boulder: Westview.

Clark, Colin, and Margaret Haswell. 1970. *The Economics of Subsistence Agriculture*, 4th ed. London: Macmillan. https://doi.org/10.1007/978-1-349-15390-9.

Cogan, Mordechai. 1974. *Imperialism and Religion: Assyria, Judah, and Israel in the Eighth and Seventh Centuries* BCE. Missoula, MT: Society of Biblical Literature.

Cogan, Mordechai. 1993. "Judah under Assyrian Hegemony: A Reexamination of Imperialism and Religion." *JBL* 112: 403–14.

Cross, Frank M. 2003a. "Ammonite Ostraca from Tell Ḥisbān." In *Leaves from an Epigrapher's Notebook: Collected Papers in Hebrew and West Semitic Palaeography and Epigraphy*, 70–94. Winona Lake, IN: Eisenbrauns.

Cross, Frank M. 2003b. "Epigraphic Notes on the ʿAmmān Citadel Inscription." In *Leaves from an Epigrapher's Notebook: Collected Papers in Hebrew and West Semitic Palaeography and Epigraphy*, 95–99. Winona Lake, IN: Eisenbrauns. (Originally published in 1969 in *BASOR* 193: 13–19.)

Crowell, Bradley L. 2004. "On the Margins of History: Social Change and Political Developments in Iron Age Edom." PhD dissertation, University of Michigan, Ann Arbor.

D'Altroy, Terence N. 1992. *Provincial Power in the Inka Empire*. Washington, DC: Smithsonian Institution Press.

D'Altroy, Terence N., and Timothy K. Earle. 1985. "Staple Finance, Wealth Finance, and Storage in the Inka Political Economy." *CA* 26: 187–206.

D'Altroy, Terence N., and Christine A. Hastorf, eds. 2001. *Empire and Domestic Economy*. New York: Kluwer Academic.

Dajani, Rafik W. 1966. "An Iron Age Tomb from Amman." *ADAJ* 11: 41–47.

Daviau, P. M. Michèle. 1997. "Moab's Northern Border: Khirbat al-Mudayna on the Wadi ath-Thamad." *BA* 60 (4): 222–28.

Daviau, P. M. Michèle. 2001. "Assyrian Influence and Changing Technologies at Tall Jawa, Jordan." In *The Land That I Will Show You: Essays on the History and Archaeology of the Ancient Near East in Honour of J. Maxwell Miller*, ed. J. Andrew Dearman and M. Patrick Graham, 214–38. Sheffield, England: Sheffield Academic Press.

Daviau, P. M. Michèle. 2002. *Excavations at Tall Jawa, Jordan*, vol. 2: *The Iron Age Artefacts*. Leiden: Brill.

Daviau, P. M. Michèle. 2003. *Excavations at Tall Jawa, Jordan*, vol. 1: *The Iron Age Town*. Leiden: Brill.

Daviau, P. M. Michèle, Robert Chadwick, Margreet Steiner, Michael Weigl, Annlee Dolan, Zoë Mcquinn, Noor Mulder-Hijmans, Margaret A. Judd, and Jonathan Ferguson. 2006. "Excavation and Survey at Khirbat al-Mudayna and Its

Surroundings: Preliminary Report of the 2001, 2004, and 2005 Seasons." *ADAJ* 50: 249–83.

Daviau, P. M. Michèle, and Paul-Eugène Dion. 2002. "Economy-Related Finds from Khirbat al-Mudayna (Wadi ath-Thamad, Jordan)." *BASOR* 328: 31–48.

Dietler, Michael. 1998. "Consumption, Agency, and Cultural Entanglement: Theoretical Implications of a Mediterranean Colonial Encounter." In *Studies in Culture Contact: Interaction, Culture Change, and Archaeology*, ed. James G. Cusick, 288–315. Carbondale: Southern Illinois University Press.

Dietler, Michael. 2010. *Archaeologies of Colonialism: Consumption, Entanglement, and Violence in Ancient Mediterranean France*. Berkeley: University of California Press. https://doi.org/10.1525/california/9780520265516.003.0002.

Dietler, Michael, and Brian Hayden. 2001. *Feasts: Archaeological and Ethnographic Perspectives on Food, Politics, and Power*. Washington, DC: Smithsonian Institution Press.

Dornemann, Rudolph H. 1983. *The Archaeology of the Transjordan in the Bronze and Iron Ages*. Milwaukee: Milwaukee Public Museum.

Drinkard, Joel, Jr. 2003. *The Volute Capitals of Israel and Jordan: A New Look at an Ancient Architectural Feature*. Virtual Karak Resources Project and Appalachian College Association. http://www.vkrp.org/studies/historical/capitals/.

Eggler, Jürg, and Othmar Keel. 2006. *Corpus der Siegel-Amulette aus Jordanien: Vom Neolithikum bis zur Perserzeit*. Fribourg, Switzerland: Academic.

Engstrom, Christin M.A. 2004. "The Neo-Assyrians at Tell el-Hesi: A Petrographic Study of Imitation Assyrian Palace Ware." *BASOR* 333: 69–81.

Eph'al. Israel. 1978. "The Western Minorities in Babylonia in the 6th–5th Centuries BC: Maintenance and Cohesion." *Or* 47: 74–90.

Evans, Susan Toby. 1998. "Toltec Invaders and Spanish Conquistadores: Culture Contact in the Postclassic Teotihuacán Valley, Mexico." In *Studies in Culture Contact: Interaction, Culture Change, and Archaeology*, ed. James G. Cusick, 335–57. Carbondale: Southern Illinois University Press.

Frame, Grant. 1992. *Babylonia 689–627 BC: A Political History*. Leiden: Nederlands Historisch-Archaeologisch Instituut te Istanbul.

Geraty, Lawrence T., Larry G. Herr, and Øystein S. LaBianca. 1988. "The Joint Madaba Plains Project: A Preliminary Report on the Second Season at Tell el-'Umeiri and Vicinity (June 18 to August 6, 1987)." *Andrews University Seminary Studies* 26: 217–52.

Grayson, A. Kirk. 1975. *Assyrian and Babylonian Chronicles*. Locust Valley, NY: J. J. Augustin.

Grijalvo, Elena Muñiz. 2005. "Elites and Religious Change in Roman Athens." *Numen* 52 (2): 255–82. https://doi.org/10.1163/1568527054024713.

Hadidi, Adnan. 1987. "An Ammonite Tomb at Amman." *Levant* 19 (1): 101–20. https://doi.org/10.1179/lev.1987.19.1.101.

Harding, G. Lankester. 1945. "Two Iron Age Tombs from ʿAmman." *QDAP* 11: 67–74.

Harding, G. Lankester. 1948. "An Iron-Age Tomb at Sahab." *QDAP* 13: 92–102.

Harding, G. Lankester. 1950. "An Iron-Age Tomb at Meqabelein." *QDAP* 14: 44–48.

Harding, G. Lankester. 1951. "Two Iron-Age Tombs in Amman." *ADAJ* 1: 37–40.

Harding, G. Lankester. 1953. "The Tomb of Adoni-Nur in Amman." *PEFA* 6: 48–65.

Hastorf, Christine A., and Terence N. D'Altroy. 2001. "The Domestic Economy, Households, and Imperial Transformation." In *Empire and Domestic Economy*, ed. Terence N. D'Altroy and Christine A. Hastorf, 3–25. New York: Kluwer Academic/Plenum.

Henschel-Simon, E. 1945. "Note on the Pottery of the ʿAmman Tombs." *QDAP* 11: 75–80.

Herr, Larry G. 1978. *The Scripts of Ancient Northwest Semitic Seals*. Missoula, MT: Scholars Press.

Herr, Larry G. 1995. "Wine Production in the Hills of Southern Ammon and the Founding of Tall Al-ʿUmayrī in the Sixth Century BC." *ADAJ* 39: 121–25.

Herr, Larry G. 1999. "The Ammonites in the Late Iron Age and Persian Period." In *Ancient Ammon*, ed. Burton MacDonald and Randall W. Younker, 219–37. Leiden: Brill.

Herr, Larry G., and Mohammed Najjar. 2001. "The Iron Age." In *The Archaeology of Jordan*, ed. Burton MacDonald, Russell Adams, and Piotr Bienkowski, 323–45. Sheffield, England: Sheffield Academic Press.

Herr, Larry G., and Elizabeth E. Platt. 2002. "The Objects from the 1989 Season." In *Madaba Plains Project 5: The 1994 Season at Tall al-ʿUmayri and Subsequent Studies*, ed. Larry G. Herr, Douglas R. Clark, Lawrence T. Geraty, Randall W. Younker, and Øystein S. LaBianca, 358–99. Berrein Springs, MI: Andrews University Press.

Holladay, John S., Jr. 2006. "Hezekiah's Tribute, Long-Distance Trade, and the Wealth of Nations ca. 1000–600 BC: A New Perspective." In *Confronting the Past: Archaeological and Historical Essays on Ancient Israel in Honor of William G. Dever*, ed. Sy Gitin, J. Edward Wright, and J. P. Dessel, 309–31. Winona Lake, IN: Eisenbrauns.

Horn, Siegfried H. 1969. "The Amman Citadel Inscription." *BASOR* 193: 2–13.

Hübner, Ulrich. 1993. "Das ikonographische Repertoire der ammonitischen Siegel und seine Entwicklung." In *Studies in the Iconography of Northwest Semitic Inscribed Seals: Proceedings of a Symposium Held in Fribourg on April 17–20, 1991*, ed. Benjamin Sass and Christoph Uehlinger, 130–60. Fribourg, Switzerland: University Press Fribourg.

Hübner, Ulrich. 2009. "Der Mondtempel auf Rugm al-Kursi in der Ammonitis." In *Israel zwischen den Mächten: Festschrift für Stefan Timm zum 65, Geburtstag*, ed. Michael Pietsch and Friedhelm Hartenstein, 145–53. Münster, Germany: Ugarit-Verlag.

Humbert, Jean-Baptiste, and Fawzi Zayadine. 1992. "Trois campagnes de fouilles à Ammân (1988–1991): Troisième terrasse de la Citadelle (Mission Franco-Jordanienne)." *RB* 1992: 214–60.

Hunter, Fraser. 2001. "Roman and Native in Scotland: New Approaches." *JRA* 14: 289–309.

Ibach, Robert D., Jr. 1987. *Archaeological Survey of the Hesban Region: Catalogue of Sites and Characterization of Periods, Hesban 5*. Berrein Springs, MI: Andrews University Press.

Ibrahim, Moawiyah M. 1975. "Third Season of Excavations at Sahab, 1975." *ADAJ* 20: 69–82, 169–78.

Jennings, Justin. 2003. "Inca Imperialism, Ritual Change, and Cosmological Continuity in the Cotahuasi Valley of Peru." *JAR* 59 (4): 433–62.

Joannès, Francis. 1994. "Une visite du gouverneur d'Arpad." *NABU* 1: 21–22.

Josephus, Flavius. 1926. *Against Apion*. Trans. H.S.J. Thackeray. *Josephus* 1:162–411. Loeb Classical Library 186. Cambridge, MA: Harvard University Press.

Khalil, Lufti A. 1986. "A Bronze Caryatid Censer from Amman." *Levant* 18 (1): 103–10. https://doi.org/10.1179/lev.1986.18.1.103.

Kletter, Raz. 1991. "The Rujm El-Malfuf Buildings and the Assyrian Vassal State of Ammon." *BASOR* 284: 33–50.

Knauf, Ernst Axel. 1992. "The Cultural Impact of Secondary State Formation: The Cases of the Edomites and Moabites." In *Early Edom and Moab: The Beginnings of the Iron Age in Southern Jordan*, ed. Piotr Bienkowski, 47–54. Sheffield, England: J. R. Collis.

Knauf-Belleri, Ernst Axel. 1995. "Edom: The Social and Economic History." In *"You Shall Not Abhor an Edomite for He Is Your Brother": Edom and Seir in History and Tradition*, ed. Diana V. Edelman, 93–117. Atlanta: Scholars Press.

Köksal, Yonca. 2006. "Coercion and Mediation: Centralization and Sedentarization of Tribes in the Ottoman Empire." *Middle Eastern Studies* 42 (3): 469–91. https://doi.org/10.1080/00263200600601171.

Kuhrt, Amélie. 1995. *The Ancient Near East c. 3000–330 BC*. 2 vols. London: Routledge.

LaBianca, Øystein S. 1999. "Excursus: Salient Features of Iron Age Tribal Kingdoms." In *Ancient Ammon*, ed. Burton MacDonald and Randall W. Younker, 19–23. Leiden: Brill.

LaBianca, Øystein S. 2006. "Tells, Empires, and Civilizations: Investigating Historical Landscapes in the Ancient Near East." *NEA* 69 (1): 4–11.

LaBianca, Øystein S. 2007. "Thinking Globally and Also Locally: Anthropology, History, and Archaeology in the Study of Jordan's Past." In *Crossing Jordan: North American Contributions to the Archaeology of Jordan*, ed. Thomas E. Levy, P. M. Michèle Daviau, Randall W. Younker, and May Shaer, 3–11. London: Equinox.

LaBianca, Øystein S., and Bethany Walker. 2007. "Tall Hisban: Palimpsest of Great and Little Traditions of Transjordan and the Ancient Near East." In *Crossing Jordan: North American Contributions to the Archaeology of Jordan*, ed. Thomas E. Levy, P. M. Michèle Daviau, Randall W. Younker, and May Shaer, 111–20. London: Equinox.

LaBianca, Øystein S., and Randall W. Younker. 1995. "The Kingdoms of Ammon, Moab, and Edom: The Archaeology of Society in the Late Bronze/Iron Age Transjordan (ca. 1400–500 BCE)." In *The Archaeology of Society in the Holy Land*, ed. Thomas E. Levy, 399–415. New York: Facts on File.

Lawlor, John I. 1997. "Field A: The Ammonite Citadel." In *Madaba Plains Project 3: The 1989 Season at Tell el-'Umeiri and Vicinity and Subsequent Studies*, ed. Larry G. Herr, Lawrence T. Geraty, Øystein S. LaBianca, and Randall W. Younker, 21–52. Berrein Springs, MI: Andrews University Press.

Lipschits, Oded. 2004. "Ammon in Transition from Vassal Kingdom to Babylonian Province." *BASOR* 335: 37–52.

Lipschits, Oded. 2011. "The Origin and Date of the Volute Capitals from the Levant." In *The Fire Signals of Lachish: Studies in the Archaeology and History of Israel in the Late Bronze Age, Iron Age, and Persian Period in Honor of David Ussishkin*, ed. Israel Finkelstein and Nadav Na'aman, 203–25. Winona Lake, IN: Eisenbrauns.

Liverani, Mario. 2005. *Israel's History and the History of Israel*. London: Equinox.

Ma'ayeh, Farah S. 1960. "Recent Archaeological Discoveries in Jordan." *ADAJ* 4–5: 114–16.

Marcus, Michelle I. 1989. "Emblems of Authority: The Seals and Sealings from Hasanlu IVB." *Expedition* 31 (2–3): 53–63.

Marcus, Michelle I. 1996. *Emblems of Identity and Prestige: The Seals and Sealings from Hasanlu, Iran. Commentary and Catalog*. Philadelphia: University Museum.

Matthews, Roger. 2003. *The Archaeology of Mesopotamia: Theories and Approaches*. London: Routledge.

Miller, J. Maxwell, and John H. Hayes. 2006. *A History of Ancient Israel and Judah*, 2nd ed. Louisville, KY: Westminster John Knox Press.

Morkot, Robert. 2001. "Egypt and Nubia." In *Empires: Perspectives from Archaeology and History*, ed. Susan E. Alcock, Terence N. D'Altroy, Kathleen D. Morrison, and Carla M. Sinopoli, 227–51. Cambridge: Cambridge University Press.

Morrison, Kathleen D. 2001. "Coercion, Resistance, and Hierarchy: Local Processes and Imperial Strategies in the Vijayanagara Empire." In *Empires: Perspectives from*

Archaeology and History, ed. Susan E. Alcock, Terence N. D'Altroy, Kathleen D. Morrison, and Carla M. Sinopoli, 252–78. Cambridge: Cambridge University Press.

Naveh, Joseph. 1987. *Early History of the Alphabet: An Introduction to West Semitic Epigraphy and Paleography*, 2nd ed. Jerusalem: Magnes.

Parker, Bradley J. 2001. *The Mechanics of Empire*. Helsinki: Neo-Assyrian Text Corpus Project.

Parker, Bradley J. 2003. "Archaeological Manifestations of Empire: Assyria's Imprint on Southeastern Anatolia." *AJA* 107 (4): 525–57. https://doi.org/10.3764/aja.107.4.525.

Platt, Elizabeth E. 1991. "The Objects." In *Madaba Plains Project 2: The 1987 Season at Tell el-'Umeiri and Vicinity and Subsequent Studies*, ed. Larry G. Herr, Lawrence T. Geraty, Øystein S. LaBianca, and Randall W. Younker, 246–65. Berrein Springs, MI: Andrews University Press.

Popkin, Peter R.W. 2016. "Iron Age Animal Management at Tall Jawa." In *Excavations at Tall Jawa, Jordan*, vol. 5: *Survey, Zooarchaeology, and Ethnoarchaeology*, ed. P. M. Michèle Daviau, 307–461. Leiden: Brill. https://doi.org/10.1163/9789004316201_009.

Porten, Bezalel. 1981. "The Identity of King Adon" *BA* 44 (1): 36–52.

Prag, Kay. 1987. "Decorative Architecture in Ammon, Moab, and Judah." *Levant* 19 (1): 121–27. https://doi.org/10.1179/lev.1987.19.1.121.

Radner, Karen. 2000. "How Did the Neo-Assyrian King Perceive His Land and Its Resources?" In *Rainfall and Agriculture in Northern Mesopotamia*, ed. R. M. Jas, 233–46. Leiden: Nederlands Instituut voor het Nabije Oosten.

Ray, Paul J., Jr. 2001. *Tell Hesban and Vicinity in the Iron Age, Hesban 6*. Berrein Springs, MI: Andrews University Press.

Reese, David S. 2002. "Shells and Fossils from Tall Jawa, Jordan." In *Excavations at Tall Jawa, Jordan*, vol. 2: *The Iron Age Artefacts*, ed. P. M. Michèle Daviau, 276–91. Leiden: Brill.

Rollston, Christopher A. 2006. "Scribal Education in Ancient Israel: The Old Hebrew Epigraphic Evidence." *BASOR* 344: 47–74.

Routledge, Bruce. 1997. "Mesopotamian 'Influence' in Iron Age Jordan: Issues of Power, Identity, and Value." *BCSMS* 32: 33–41.

Routledge, Bruce. 2004. *Moab in the Iron Age: Hegemony, Polity, Archaeology*. Philadelphia: University of Pennsylvania Press.

Sanders, Seth L. 2004. "What Was the Alphabet For? The Rise of Written Vernaculars and the Making of Israelite National Literature." *Maarav* 11: 25–56.

Sanders, Seth L. 2009. *The Invention of Hebrew*. Urbana: University of Illinois Press.

Schaudig, Hanspeter. 2001. *Die Inschriften Nabonids von Babylon und Kyros' des Großen samt den ihrem Umfeld entstandenen Tendenzschriften: Textausgabe und Grammatik*. Münster: Ugarit-Verlag.

Schortman, Edward M., and Patricia A. Urban. 1994. "Living on the Edge: Core/Periphery Relations in Ancient Southeastern Mesoamerica." *CA* 35: 401–30.

Schortman, Edward M., and Patricia A. Urban. 1998. "Culture Contact Structure and Process." In *Studies in Culture Contact: Interaction, Culture Change, and Archaeology*, ed. James G. Cusick, 102–25. Carbondale: Southern Illinois University Press.

Sinopoli, Carla M. 1994. "The Archaeology of Empires." *ARA* 23: 159–80.

Sinopoli, Carla M. 2001a. "Empires." In *Archaeology at the Millennium: A Sourcebook*, ed. Gary M. Feinman and T. Douglas Price, 439–71. New York: Kluwer Academic. https://doi.org/10.1007/978-0-387-72611-3_13.

Sinopoli, Carla M. 2001b. "Imperial Integration and Imperial Subjects." In *Empires: Perspectives from Archaeology and History*, ed. Susan E. Alcock, Terence N. D'Altroy, Kathleen D. Morrison, and Carla M. Sinopoli, 195–200. Cambridge: Cambridge University Press.

Smith, Mark S. 2001. *The Origins of Biblical Monotheism: Israel's Polytheistic Background and the Ugaritic Texts*. Oxford: Oxford University Press. https://doi.org/10.1093/019513480X.001.0001.

Smith, Michael E., and Lisa Montiel. 2001. "The Archaeological Study of Empires and Imperialism in Pre-Hispanic Central Mexico." *JAA* 20: 245–84.

Spieckermann, Hermann. 1982. *Juda unter Assur in der Sargonidzeit*. Göttingen: Vandenhoeck and Ruprecht. https://doi.org/10.13109/9783666538001.

Steen, Eveline J. van der. 2004. *Tribes and Territories in Transition: The Central East Jordan Valley and Surrounding Regions in the Late Bronze and Early Iron Ages: A Study of the Sources*. Groningen, The Netherlands: Rijksuniversiteit Groningen.

Steen, Eveline J. van der. 2006. "Tribes and Power Structures in Palestine and the Transjordan." *NEA* 69 (1): 27–36.

Steen, Eveline J. van der. 2009. "Tribal Societies in the Nineteenth Century: A Model." In *Nomads, Tribes, and the State in the Ancient Near East: Cross-Disciplinary Perspectives*, ed. Jeffrey Szuchman, 105–17. Chicago: University of Chicago Press.

Steen, Eveline J. van der, and Klaas A.D. Smelik. 2007. "King Mesha and the Tribe of Dibon." *JSOT* 32: 139–62.

Tadmor, Hayim, and Shigeo Yamada. 2011. *The Royal Inscriptions of Tiglath-Pileser III (744–727 BC) and Shalmaneser V (726–722 BC), Kings of Assyria*. Winona Lake, IN: Eisenbrauns.

Tapper, Richard. 1990. "Anthropologists, Historians, and Tribespeople on Tribe and State Formation in the Middle East." In *Tribes and State Formation in the Middle East*, ed. Philip S. Khoury and Joseph Kostiner, 48–73. Berkeley: University of California Press.

Taylor, John. 2000. "The Third Intermediate Period (1069–664 BC)." In *The Oxford History of Ancient Egypt*, ed. Ian Shaw, 330–68. Oxford: Oxford University Press.

Tufnell, Olga. 1953. "The Tomb of Adoni Nur in Amman: Notes and Comparisons." *PEFA* 6: 66–72.

Tyson, Craig W. 2013. "Josephus, *Antiquities* 10.180–182, Jeremiah, and Nebuchadnezzar." *JHS*, article 7: 13. https://doi.org/10.5508/jhs.2013.v13.a7.

Tyson, Craig W. 2014. *The Ammonites: Elites, Empires, and Sociopolitical Change (1000–500 BCE)*. London: Bloomsbury T&T Clark.

Unger, Eckhard. 1931. *Babylon: Die heilige Stadt nach der Beschreibung de Babylonier*. Berlin: de Gruyter. https://doi.org/10.1515/9783111653440.

Van De Mieroop, Marc. 2007a. *The Eastern Mediterranean in the Age of Ramesses II*. Malden, MA: Blackwell. https://doi.org/10.1002/9780470696644.

Van De Mieroop, Marc. 2007b. *A History of the Ancient Near East ca. 3000–323 BC*, 2nd ed. Malden, MA: Blackwell.

Vanderhooft, David Stephen. 1999. *The Neo-Babylonian Empire and Babylon in the Latter Prophets*. Atlanta: Scholars Press.

Vanderhooft, David Stephen. 2003. "Babylonian Strategies of Imperial Control in the West: Royal Practice and Rhetoric." In *Judah and the Judeans in the Neo-Babylonian Period*, ed. Oded Lipschits and Joseph Blenkinsopp, 235–62. Winona Lake, IN: Eisenbrauns.

Webster, Jane. 2001. "Creolizing the Roman Provinces." *AJA* 105 (2): 209–25. https://doi.org/10.2307/507271.

Wells, Peter S. 1998. "Culture Contact, Identity, and Change in the European Provinces of the Roman Empire." In *Studies in Culture Contact: Interaction, Culture Change, and Archaeology*, ed. James G. Cusick, 316–34. Carbondale: Southern Illinois University Press.

Wetzel, Friedrich, and Franz H. Weissbach. 1938. *Das Hauptheiligtum des Marduk in Babylon, Esagila und Etemenanki*. Leipzig: J. C. Hinrichs.

Wilkinson, T. J., Jason Ur, Eleanor Barbanes Wilkinson, and Mark Altaweel. 2005. "Landscape and Settlement in the Neo-Assyrian Empire." *BASOR* 340: 23–56.

Woolf, Greg. 1997. "Beyond Romans and Natives." *WA* 28: 339–50.

Yamada, Shigeo. 2000. *The Construction of the Assyrian Empire: A Historical Study of the Inscriptions of Shalmaneser III (859–824 BC) Relating to His Campaigns to the West*. Leiden: Brill.

Yassine, Khair. 1975. "Anthropoid Coffins from Raghdan Royal Palace Tomb in Amman." *ADAJ* 20: 57–68.

Yassine, Khair. 1988. *Archaeology of Jordan: Essays and Reports*. Amman: University of Jordan.

Younker, Randall W. 1997. "Moabite Social Structure." *BA* 60 (4): 237–48.

Younker, Randall W. 1999. "The Emergence of the Ammonites." In *Ancient Ammon*, ed. Burton MacDonald and Randall W. Younker, 189–218. Leiden: Brill.

Younker, Randall W. 2003. "The Emergence of Ammon: A View of the Rise of Iron Age Polities from the Other Side of the Jordan." In *The Near East in the Southwest: Essays in Honor of William G. Dever*, ed. B. A. Nakhai, 153–76. Boston: American Schools of Oriental Research.

Younker, Randall W. 2007. "Highlights from the Heights of Jalul." In *Crossing Jordan: North American Contributions to the Archaeology of Jordan*, ed. Thomas E. Levy, P. M. Michèle Daviau, Randall W. Younker, and Mae Shaer, 129–35. London: Equinox.

Zawadzki, Stefan. 2003. "Nebuchadnezzar and Tyre in Light of New Texts from the Ebabbar Archives in Sippar." *ErIsr* 27: 276*–81*.

Zayadine, Fawzi. 1989. "The 1988 Excavations on the Citadel of Amman: Lower Terrace, Area A." *ADAJ* 33: 357–63.

Zayadine, Fawzi. 1991. "Sculpture in Ancient Jordan." In *Treasures from an Ancient Land: The Art of Jordan*, ed. Piotr Bienkowski, 31–61. Phoenix Mill, UK: Alan Suttone.

Zayadine, Fawzi, Jean-Baptiste Humbert, and Mohammed Najjar. 1989. "The 1988 Excavations of the Citadel of Amman, Lower Terrace, Area A." *ADAJ* 33: 357–63.

8

East of Assyria?

Hasanlu and the Problem of Assyrianization

MEGAN CIFARELLI
(MANHATTANVILLE COLLEGE)

DOI: 10.5876/9781607328230.c008

Nearly forty years have elapsed since the Hasanlu Expedition ended its excavations at Hasanlu in the Ushnu-Solduz Valley of northwestern Iran.[1] The site is perhaps best known for the archaeological record of its grisly destruction at the end of Hasanlu Period IVb (1050–800 BCE) and artifacts found in the destruction level (Danti 2013a, 2013b, 2014) (figure 8.1). Speculation about the dependence of the material culture of Hasanlu on that of the Neo-Assyrian Empire has garnered far more attention than any other aspect of the site.[2] This chapter outlines a critique of the manner in which Hasanlu is treated in the literature as inevitably subject to the acculturating forces of Assyria. In preliminary reports excavators divided the material culture of Hasanlu into two categories: "Local" and Assyrian or Assyrian-influenced.[3] This "fact" about Hasanlu, which I will argue is itself an artifact of the era in which the excavations were conducted, soon became the basis for assertions that the elite at Hasanlu were in direct contact with Assyria, that they were in the thrall of Assyrian visual culture, and that they used Assyrian and Assyrianizing material culture to enhance their status locally. This Assyro-centric bias emerged early in the course of excavations, was developed in subsequent research, and was fully crystallized by 1989 when the volume of *Expedition Magazine* dedicated to Hasanlu was titled *East of Assyria* (Dyson and Voigt 1989). The centrality of Assyrian culture to that

FIGURE 8.1. *Excavation photograph of Period IVb destruction in Temple BBII. Courtesy, Penn Museum.*

of Hasanlu has been argued so persuasively and repeated so often that it has become canonical, establishing Hasanlu as an exemplar of "Assyrianization" at the frontier of the great hegemonic empire.

This chapter challenges these assertions, both the evidence for Assyrian and Assyrianizing objects on which they are based and the a priori assumption that Hasanlu played the role of "periphery" to Assyria's "center," which buttresses the inference that the elite residents of Hasanlu chose to emulate "superior" Assyrian material culture (see Faust, Brown, and Cannavò, this volume, for challenges to received wisdom on Assyrian impact in the western "periphery," the southern Levant, Iron Age Edom, and Cyprus, respectively). It is far beyond the scope of this brief chapter to marshal every relevant data point, particularly as the final excavation reports are still in preparation.[4] Instead, I consider this essay a thought experiment in which I evaluate existing data for the Assyrian impact at Hasanlu in the absence of the foundational assumption, articulated most clearly by Irene Winter (1977, 381), that "the embrace of Assyrian elements and the widespread presence of Assyrian goods was meaningful within the culture at Hasanlu."[5]

ASSYRIAN MATERIAL CULTURE AT HASANLU: A MYTHOLOGY OF ABUNDANCE AND MEANING

A brief look at the history of archaeology in the Ancient Near East can help explain why excavators initially categorized objects found at Hasanlu as either "Local" or "Assyrian/Assyrianizing" and why this notion has persisted in the literature, particularly those studies published between the beginning of the project in 1956 and the publication of *East of Assyria* in 1989. When the Hasanlu Expedition began its work in the 1950s, perhaps the most important and newsworthy excavation in the Near East was that of Nimrud, begun in 1949 by Sir Max Mallowan and the British School of Archaeology in Iraq. The extraordinary finds at Nimrud, which included hundreds of luxury objects made in Assyria, North Syria, and the Levant, supplemented and clarified the Assyrian archaeological discoveries of the nineteenth century. The Nimrud excavations were detailed in scholarly publications and heralded in the British popular press.[6] The participation of the Metropolitan Museum of Art at Nimrud and its 1955 exhibition of "treasure" obtained by the Met in partage brought a great deal of attention in the United States to the excavations and to Assyria itself.[7] By the time excavations began at Hasanlu in 1956, Assyrian and North Syrian material culture were well-published, extensively researched, and of great interest to scholarly and popular audiences alike. It is not surprising, then, that the excavators of Hasanlu used Assyrian objects as comparanda for their discoveries and Assyrian royal inscriptions when probing the identity of the citizens of Hasanlu. Strongly disposed toward Assyrian material culture, excavators determined that Hasanlu was "full of" Assyrian and Assyrianizing objects and, to a lesser extent, North Syrian objects (Dyson and Muscarella 1989, 3).

Excavators initially characterized the objects not immediately recognizable as Assyrian, North Syrian, or Assyrianizing as "Local," as if no other cultural attribution were possible (Dyson 1965).[8] Indeed, at the time of the Hasanlu excavations, the Late Bronze and Early Iron Age cultures to the north and east of Hasanlu, in Transcaucasia and the Talesh, were less well-known to the excavators than those in Mesopotamia. For much of the twentieth century, Transcaucasian regions now encompassed by Armenia, Georgia, and Azerbaijan were part of the USSR. Excavations were published predominantly in Russian, and exchange of archaeological information between the USSR and the West was limited. While the Russian excavations at Karmir Blur in Armenia ignited interest in Urartian archaeology (Barnett and Watson 1952; Barnett 1959),[9] the materials discovered there provided excavators with few useful parallels.[10] Non-Urartian indigenous material cultures in Transcaucasia and related areas in the Talesh remained less well-known to the Hasanlu

Expedition, resulting in the failure to recognize that many objects in the "Local" category were in fact imported from, or created in emulation of, the material culture of Transcaucasia.[11] The far greater volume and accessibility of published materials about Assyria ensured that those studying Hasanlu would do so through an Assyro-centric lens, one that led to assertions that not only were Assyrian and Assyrianizing objects common at the site, but they were employed by the local elite to enhance status by emulating Assyria.[12]

This ontological bias, combined with a publication strategy that focused on selected objects before contexts were well understood, led to a disproportionate emphasis on Assyrian material culture at the site (Danti and Cifarelli 2016). Recent evaluation of the original excavation records shows that only a very small proportion of the tens of thousands of objects found in the Period IVb citadel destruction and perhaps two objects from the cemetery can be attributed to Assyrian manufacture with any certainty, based on comparisons to objects excavated in the Assyrian heartland (Magee 2008; Danti and Cifarelli 2016).[13] Chief among these finds are fourteen ivories (Muscarella 1980, 280–93), six "Central Assyrian" and fifteen "Provincial Assyrian" cylinder seals (Marcus 1996, 57–77), and thirty-nine glazed vessels (Danti and Cifarelli 2016). In addition, scholars have identified six bone or ivory fly-whisk handles and whetstones, as well as a single shortsword, as Assyrian (Thornton and Pigott 2011, 166), based on their resemblance to items depicted on Assyrian reliefs—a questionable methodology for cultural attribution (Danti and Cifarelli 2016).

Finally, half of a broken stone macehead inscribed in cuneiform with "Palace of Ashur-uballit," found in the debris of a second-floor storeroom in Temple Burned Building (BB) V on the citadel at Hasanlu, is unquestionably Assyrian in origin but is hundreds of years older than the context in which it was deposited (Dyson and Pigott 1975, 183) (figure 8.2). While further analysis of unpublished objects from Hasanlu may reveal additional objects of Assyrian origin, this brief survey demonstrates that Hasanlu was far from "full of" Assyrian goods.

Assessing the local significance of imported objects and the way material culture impacts and is impacted by interaction between societies is no simple matter, as is evidenced by the volume of literature problematizing this issue. In his discussion of the archaeology of interregional interaction, Gil Stein (2002) suggests that the interpretation of the local significance of "foreign material culture," in this case Assyrian objects at Hasanlu, should entail comparison of the manner in which those "foreign" objects *are* and *are not* used at a given site. The archaeological record can certainly be brought to bear on the use of Assyrian goods at Hasanlu, the majority of which were found among dense clusters of exotic and high-value votive objects, both locally made

FIGURE 8.2. *Hasanlu citadel, Period IVb. Courtesy, Penn Museum.*

and imported, stored in the treasuries of the citadel temples. These contexts yielded all of the Central Assyrian and most of the Provincial Assyrian seals, nearly 98 percent of the Assyrian ivories, and 80 percent of the glazed vessels (Danti and Cifarelli 2016). Stored in largely cultic contexts, it appears that these objects were used as votives or cultic equipment.[14]

The objects found in the Period IVb destruction of the temples of Hasanlu, as well as similar collections in monumental elite residences on the Period IVb citadel, were amassed over generations and safeguarded.[15] Their broad geographical and chronological range is illustrated in part by a small number of inscribed objects. In addition to the Middle Assyrian macehead described above, excavators found in the treasuries of Temple BBII a stone bowl inscribed with the name of the Kassite ruler Kadashman-Enlil (ca. fourteenth–thirteenth centuries BCE) and two stone maceheads belonging to the king of Susa, Tan-Ruhuarater (ca. 2100 BCE) (Dyson 1989). Older un-inscribed luxury objects in Period IVb contexts include Kassite glass beakers from BBII (Marcus 1991) and in the elite residence Hasanlu BBIW, a sword of a type known from second millennium BCE Hittite eastern Anatolia (Thornton and Pigott 2011, 143) and the famous Hasanlu Gold Bowl (in fact, a beaker), believed to have been made three centuries before its deposition (Porada 1967; Winter 1989; Muscarella 2006). These objects survived an earlier destruction of the citadel at the end of Period IVc (1250-1050 BCE), a period for which interregional interaction is evidenced in the burials, as well as in fragments of ivories and glazed ceramics deposited under the floors of the Period IVb Temple BBII (Danti and Cifarelli 2016).[16] While we cannot know if these objects were true heirlooms, passed down from individual to individual over generations, they were undoubtedly links to the past. Their ownership and display were a means of negotiating rank (Lillios 1999, 241), and there may have been an understanding that their age enhanced their cultic potency and reified collective memory (Roßberger 2016).

The range of objects found on the citadel is clearly broader than can be described with the terms *Assyrian*, *Assyrianizing*, or *Local*. They also include seals, ivories, and "lion bowls" attributed to manufacture in North Syria, the northern Levant, and Iran (Muscarella 1974, 1980; Marcus 1996). Fragments of more than seventy copper alloy belts, a form of armor well-known from Transcaucasia and the Talesh, were found in a treasury of Temple BBII, and more than twenty of these belts are of a repoussé decorated type almost certainly imported from the north.[17] The complex geographic network represented by these objects, which includes Iran, Mesopotamia, Syria and the Levant, Transcaucasia, and the Talesh, is nearly identical to that evidenced in earlier burials at the site, demonstrating the persistence of patterns of long-distance and local interaction over the *longue durée* (Cifarelli 2013).

Collecting as a cultural phenomenon is not unique to Hasanlu, of course. A well-known strategy for signaling legitimacy, wealth, and power, it is characteristic of politically dominant groups in hierarchical societies (Appadurai 1994) and is well attested, for example, in Mesopotamian royal (Thomason 2005) and cultic (Roßberger 2016) contexts. At Hasanlu, we can conclude that the objects imported from Assyria were used within the framework of an established local elite tradition of acquiring and enclaving rare, beautiful objects, old and new, both local and imported from a wide geographic range.

According to Stein's formulation, the determination of how a foreign material culture is not used, the types of contexts in which it is not found, is an essential component of the interpretation of its social value. To further investigate the oft-repeated claims that local elites used Assyrian materials to bolster their status, I will briefly examine three settings in which one might expect to see residue of the construction and negotiation of elite identity and status: local administrative contexts, monumental elite residences on the citadel likely associated with secular authority, and burials.

The first of these is fairly straightforward. There is no evidence for the administrative practice of sealing at the site until Period IVb, where excavators found clusters of door and jar sealings indicating the presence of sealed second-floor treasuries in Temples BBII and BBV (Marcus 1996, 77).[18] None of these sealings were made with Central Assyrian–style seals. The majority were made with "Local-Style" seals (Marcus 1996, 5–22),[19] suggesting that while the practice of sealing itself was likely undertaken in emulation of more complex polities, the seals used to mark and control access to valuable goods emphasized local rather than Assyrian identity.

Excavators identified BBIW in the south portion of the citadel and BBIII in its northwest as elite residences (Dyson 1989; Danti 2013a, 2013b). The hundreds of objects found in the Period IVb destruction of BBIII have not been exhaustively analyzed, but field records show that the storerooms in the building contained many high-value objects such as furniture elaborately decorated in the Local Style (De Schauensee 2011), metal vessels, armor, weapons, beads, personal ornaments in copper alloy and gold, and cylinder seals (Marcus 1996). Among these elite objects, only two cylinder seals can be linked to Assyria (Marcus 1996, 65, 70). BBIW also contained thousands of valuable finds in storerooms and in contexts indicating that they were looted by Urartian soldiers as the building collapsed (Danti 2014). In addition to elite metal vessels such as the Silver Beaker (Porada 1959), excavators found two glazed Assyrian-style vessels in the storerooms. An Assyrian-style fly whisk was found among objects looted by the Gold Bowl group—three Urartian soldiers attempting to flee with valuable objects including the Gold Bowl, decorated sheet metal belts, and a gold dagger (Danti and Cifarelli 2016). A single Provincial Assyrian cylinder seal was found in an unstratified context in BBIW (Marcus 1996, no. 71; Danti and Cifarelli 2016). All told, Assyrian objects constitute an infinitesimally small proportion of the finds in

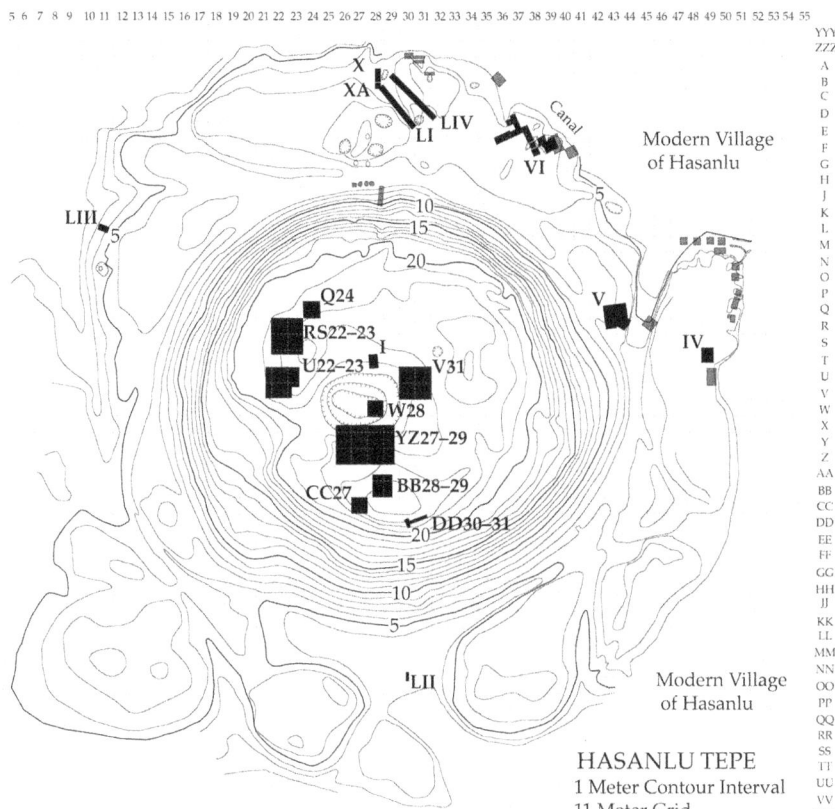

FIGURE 8.3. *Contour plan of Hasanlu, Iran, with burial excavations in the northeast quadrant. Courtesy, Penn Museum.*

buildings related to secular authority, suggesting that they played a minimal role in the visual construction of power.

Turning to the Hasanlu graves, excavators found approximately 100 Period IVb burials in the northern portion of the Low Mound, the area where graves were placed continuously from the Early Bronze Age forward (Danti 2013b; Cifarelli 2013; Danti and Cifarelli 2016) (figure 8.3). Burials, the rituals that attend them, and their associated assemblages are opportunities for the living to negotiate status and identity. If emulation of Assyrian material culture were an essential component of elite identity at Hasanlu, one would expect to find residue of emulatory behavior in the graves. At Kul Tarike, near Ziwiyeh in Iranian Kurdistan, for example, some burials contained

EAST OF ASSYRIA? 217

Neo-Assyrian cylinder seals and glazed vessels (Azarnoush and Helwing 2005, 220–21). At Ziyaret Tepe in the Upper Tigris region, cremation burials of local elites under the courtyard of the Bronze Palace included elite-quality Assyrian goods, such as pottery, stone and metal vessels, ivories, and personal ornaments (Wicke and Greenfield 2013, 69). With the exception of two potentially Assyrian-style glazed vessels (Danti and Cifarelli 2016), the burials at Hasanlu do not contain Assyrian or Assyrianizing material culture. It is interesting that the best-furnished burials of both men and women from Period IVb contain personal ornaments, belts, or weapons of types well-known from Transcaucasia and the Talesh (figure 8.4). The presence of these selected "imports" on and around the bodies of Hasanlu's wealthiest residents may suggest that adoption and emulation of northern, perhaps proto-Urartian, material cultures played a more significant role in the establishment of elite identity as manifest in burials at Hasanlu (Rubinson 2012; Danti and Cifarelli 2016).

In sum, Assyrian materials are not well represented in elite residences or integrated into local administrative practices, and there is no evidence either from burials or accompanying the bodies of those killed in the collapse of the citadel buildings that they participated in the construction and communication of a local elite identity. The role of Assyrian material culture is not readily distinguishable from that of other imported objects on the citadel, suggesting that the social value of Assyrian material culture was linked to its role in an established tradition of gathering and safeguarding exotic and valuable goods and dedicating these goods in the temples.

It is not surprising that overestimations of the volume of Assyrian material at Hasanlu, coupled with the assumption that Assyrian goods had a particularly high social value at the site, led to assertions of direct, high-level contact between Assyria and Hasanlu, even what Parker in this volume refers to as imperial "control." Combing assiduously through Assyrian royal inscriptions, scholars sought points of intersection between Assyria and Hasanlu to support the contention that these objects were Assyrian royal or diplomatic gifts to Hasanlu elites (Dyson and Pigott 1975, 183; Winter 1977, 378; Muscarella 1980; Dyson 1989; Marcus 1996; Collins 2006; Gunter 2009). While scenarios involving high-level contact are possible, the little that we know about the relationship between Assyria and Hasanlu, detailed below, renders such assertions unlikely. It is, moreover, important to remember that the artifacts listed above are portable luxury objects of types in broad circulation in the Late Bronze and Early Iron Ages (Danti and Cifarelli 2016). Their journey from the heartland of Assyria to the highlands of northwestern Iran could have

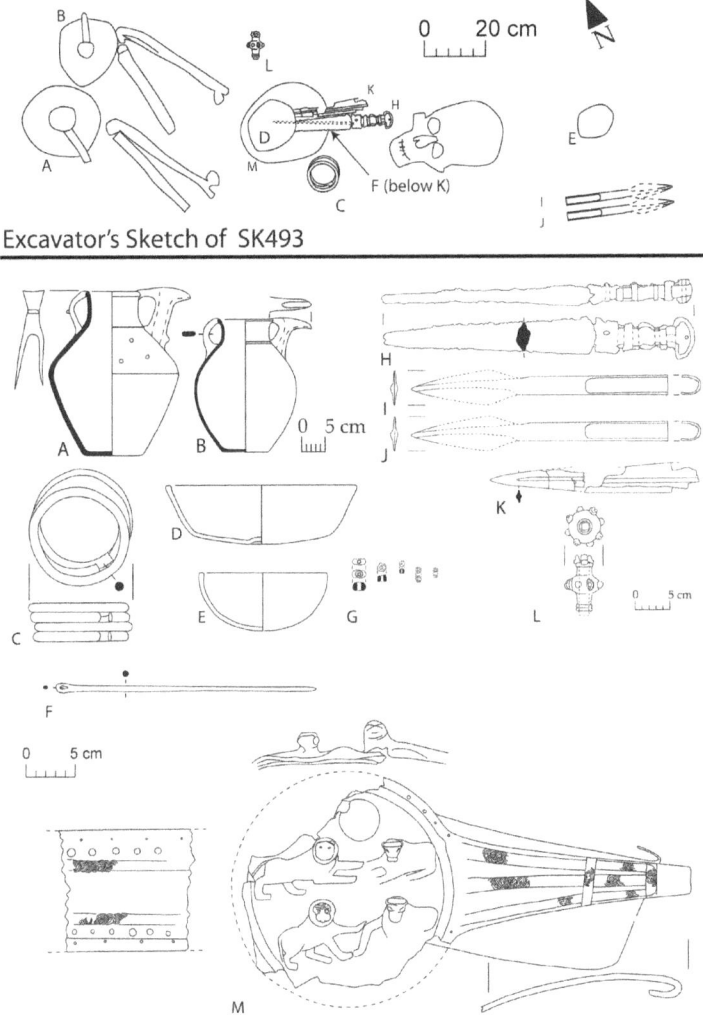

FIGURE 8.4. *Excavation drawing Burial SK493a, young male. Courtesy, Penn Museum.*

involved countless intermediaries, and their accumulation at Hasanlu, rather than necessarily demonstrating Assyrian interest in Hasanlu, is in keeping with long-established local cultural processes. On their own these objects are hardly sufficient to support the notion of direct contact between Assyria and Hasanlu (see also Potts 2014).

ASSYRIANIZING OBJECTS AT HASANLU: EMULATION OR SHARED HERITAGE?

Far more numerous at Hasanlu than objects believed to be imported from Assyria are those that have been characterized as "Assyrianizing"—objects created at Hasanlu in "selective and knowledgeable emulation" (Gunter 2009) of object types, styles, or subject matter characteristic of Neo-Assyrian imperial material culture. As was the case for Assyrian objects, the extent of "Assyrianization" was overemphasized because of Assyro-centric biases. An illustrative example is provided by the practice of decorating walls with terracotta wall tiles and knobs at Hasanlu, evidenced by the many examples found in situ in the collapse of BBII and elsewhere on the citadel. This practice was long considered the strongest evidence for the use of locally made objects in emulation of Assyrian palace decoration (e.g., Winter 1977; Nunn 1988; Marcus 1989, 1996). Edith Porada (1965, 123–24), however, noted that similar glazed wall tiles and knobs were found at the Elamite sites of Choga Zanbil and Tal-i Malyan in temples and on ziggurat platforms. While some of these wall decorations at Hasanlu do feature motifs that resemble Assyrian examples, the use of such architectural decorations in a cultic rather than palatial context has been shown to cleave more closely to patterns of use for such objects in the decoration of temples in Elam and Urartu (Basello 2012; Tourtet 2011; Dan 2012; Danti and Cifarelli 2016, 360).

The notion of purposeful emulation of Neo-Assyrian features in Local-Style craft production at Hasanlu, as first postulated by Edith Porada (1967, 2974–77) and Oscar W. Muscarella (1966, 129) and most persuasively presented by Irene Winter (1977), has become codified in the literature in the field and represents an important corrective to passive constructions of cultural influence. According to this proposal, the local crafts found in the destruction of Hasanlu Period IVb—including metalwork, ivories, and seals—integrated visual elements from Neo-Assyrian monumental relief sculptures of Ashurnasirpal II's Northwest Palace at Nimrud, as well as the bronze gate bands of Ashurnasirpal II and Shalmaneser III at Balawat. This integration involves the use of scenes of "Neo-Assyrian-inspired" battle, siege, hunting, and presentations in the decoration of locally produced objects and the presence of remarkable points of similarity in the rendering of certain iconographic details. According to this school of thought, artisans and elites at Hasanlu consciously emulated the visual culture of a "superior" polity in an effort to aggrandize themselves (Muscarella 1966, 129, 1980; Porada 1967, 2974–77; Winter 1977; Marcus 1989, 1996; Gunter 2009). For decades this position has been unassailable, given the "facts" that Assyrian objects were readily available at Hasanlu, that they were valued for their specifically Assyrian identity, and that Hasanlu was in close contact with Assyrian centers.

An essential, often unarticulated theoretical perspective that underpins these assertions is that the relationship between Assyria and Hasanlu could be described using the center/core-periphery paradigm—which is to say that Hasanlu was a less developed, dependent, and possibly exploited entity that existed in the periphery or at the frontier of the economically, militarily, and culturally dominant Assyrian Empire (e.g., Marcus 1990). The corollary of this proposed relationship is the inevitability of the subjection of Hasanlu to the acculturating forces of Assyria, that there was a one-way flow of culture from the center that altered the periphery, whether through diffuse and passive notions of "influence" or more actively through intentional emulation.

There are problems with the center-periphery paradigm itself, including assumptions about the relationship between political domination and material culture[20] and the Eurocentric, colonialist notions that bolster the idea that a "less developed" polity would wish to acquire the trappings of its "superior" neighbors.[21] How might "Assyria" as a concept have existed in the mind of Hasanlu? As an inherently superior, eminently sophisticated culture ripe for imitation? As brutally opportunistic marauders? As one of many far-flung locales whose flotsam made its way into the temple treasuries?

Thus far I have attempted to detach the materiality of Hasanlu from some of the foundational assumptions that fortify the application of this paradigm of cultural and political inequality and dependence: Hasanlu was not, in fact, replete with Assyrian materials valued for their specifically Assyrian identity and used to construct secular authority. I will further argue that Hasanlu was not, in terms of historical geography, in the Assyrian periphery or on the Assyrian "frontier" (figure 8.5). Finally, in terms of relative chronology, there is insufficient evidence that the emergence of the "Assyrianizing" characteristics of the Hasanlu Local Style postdates the Neo-Assyrian monuments they are purported to emulate.

The political relationship between Assyria and Hasanlu during Period IVb is difficult to assess. With no indigenous writing at the site, the only historical accounts of the region in this period are found in Assyrian and Urartian royal inscriptions. These sources must be treated with caution because it is difficult to identify Hasanlu with cities mentioned in those sources with any certainty,[22] and the "hazards of reading literally the ideological productions of distant hegemonic powers" (Khatchadourian 2011, 476) are well known. The suggestion that the place referred to as Gilzanu in Assyrian texts is in the region southwest of Lake Urmia is generally accepted, and if correct, then it appears that Assyrian interest in the region was limited to claims of the receipt of tribute in the

FIGURE 8.5. *Map of the region.*

eleventh century BCE and later to relatively infrequent opportunistic raids in the ninth century BCE, the most intensive period of contact being in the reign of Shalmaneser III (858–823 BCE) (Reade 1979; Radner 2011, 739).

These raids were discontinued after 820 BCE, when the army of Shamshi-Adad encountered unified Urartian resistance under King Ushpinu, and Assyrians stayed out of the region until well after the 800 BCE destruction of Hasanlu (Radner 2011). Whatever information Assyria's rulers gleaned through contact did not encourage them to attempt to integrate this region and its polities into the empire, as they did, for example, with the land of Zamua further south in the Zagros (Grayson 1991, AO101.17 iii 110, 136–37). During the ninth century BCE, there are no Assyrian records or physical evidence for the establishment of direct or indirect control of the region through governors, provincial centers, vassal states, or royal delegates.

In contrast, textual and archaeological evidence demonstrates that the region to the west and south of Lake Urmia was critically important to, and well on the way to being integrated into, the burgeoning state of Urartu in the late ninth century. There can be little doubt that by 800 BCE the region around Hasanlu was firmly in the power of the kingdom of Urartu, as evidenced by the inscriptions and archaeological evidence documenting the development of local fortresses along strategic corridors (Biscione 2003; Fuchs 2004, 2012; Magee 2008; Piller 2010; Kroll 2011 Salvini 2011, 87; Zimansky 2011, 556). The extent to which Hasanlu itself was under Urartian control or even the criteria by which that could be determined, given the lack of coherence of "Urartian" material culture outside the major fortress settlements (Zimansky 1995), are unknown. The "Urartian" material at Hasanlu was certainly minimized by the excavators, whether because it went unrecognized or because it failed to align with the narrative arc whereby Hasanlu was "Assyrianized"[23] (Dyson and Muscarella 1989; Magee 2008). In addition to the few Urartian finds in the citadel mentioned above,[24] the wealthiest male burials from Period IVb at Hasanlu contain some of the weapons, copper alloy belts, and personal ornaments of types best known from Transcaucasian and Urartian sites, suggesting that the material culture of the north—or possibly individual migrants from the north—played a role in the construction and communication of relative power at Hasanlu in this period (Rubinson 2012; Danti and Cifarelli 2015; Cifarelli 2017).

This rough sketch of the historical geography of the region encompassing Hasanlu during the ninth century BCE sheds some light on the potential interaction in this zone among the Neo-Assyrian Empire, the expanding kingdom of Urartu, and local entities like Hasanlu. Bradley J. Parker's (2006) examination of the nature and intensity of interactions between the Assyrian Empire and other polities in "contact zones" is more nuanced than center-periphery theory and more useful in the effort to describe the relationship between Hasanlu and Assyria. Parker's (2006) continuum ranges from the positive imperial control exerted by the empire in "Provinces" to the negative imperial control exerted by the empire against "Enemy States." With the advance of Urartu into the region southwest of Lake Urmia in the course of the ninth century BCE, Hasanlu shifted from an "autonomous state" subject to raids to an "enemy state" that was not attacked. As such, it can in no way be considered part of the "periphery" of Assyrian imperial control; nor can it be considered part of Assyria's frontier.[25]

Just as a review of the region's historical geography renders less likely the assumption of Hasanlu's political and cultural dependence on Assyria, chronology also poses a problem. A local elite class, with monumental architecture and differentiated material culture in the burials, emerged at Hasanlu in the Late Bronze Age (fourteenth–thirteenth centuries BCE) and developed steadily through the Period IVb destruction (Danti 2013b). The excavations on the citadel, however, focused primarily on Period IVb, with few objects found stratified in earlier levels.[26] All of the Local-Style objects at Hasanlu—including those whose imagery features battles, hunts, and iconographic details that resemble the art of ninth-century Assyrian centers—were found in Period IVb contexts, but there is no way to determine archaeologically whether they were made in that period, particularly given the presence of "heirlooms" in the same contexts. To accept the notion of "selective and knowledgeable emulation" (Gunter 2009, 49), however, one must accept that all of the "Assyrianizing" Local-Style production, which constitutes the great majority of the ivories, seals, and metalwork excavated in the destruction level, took place in a period of a few decades between the construction of Assyrian capitals in the early to mid-ninth century and Hasanlu's destruction around 800 BCE. While such rapid artistic development and lopsided production could have taken place under sufficiently strong cultural motivation, there is little evidence for factors that would have motivated the conscious and rapid incorporation of Neo-Assyrian iconography in the last decades of the ninth century BCE.[27]

If the significant and undeniable points of resemblance between the monumental artistic production of the Neo-Assyrian Empire in the ninth century BCE and the Local-Style artistic production of Hasanlu do not emerge from emulation, how can they be explained? In her magisterial art historical analysis of the Gold Bowl and the Silver Beaker, Porada (1967) suggested that the origins of the Local Style and the Gold Bowl itself dated to the second millennium BCE. Porada's (1959) second millennium date for the Gold Bowl was initially based on its perceived lack of Neo-Assyrian features, such as rigidity of composition and scenes of warfare (figures 8.6 and 8.7). The fact that this vessel considerably predates the destruction of Hasanlu is reinforced by Winter's (1989) identification of Hurrian mythological elements in its iconography and Karen Rubinson's (2003) discussion relating its imagery to that of Middle Bronze Age silver cups from Trialeti and Karashamb in the Caucasus. It is difficult to imagine that this object made of inherently valuable material, with such fine craftsmanship and complex iconography, represents an early point in the development of the Local Style rather than a well-developed stage. As manifest on the Gold Bowl, then, the Hasanlu Local Style emerged in the Late Bronze Age and is, according to Diana Stein (1989, 84), related to "the same cultural milieu in which Hurrians also participated."

There are many points of correlation between the decoration of the Gold Bowl and that of the Local-Style ivories, seals, and metalwork of Period IVb (Porada 1967; Winter 1977; Muscarella 1980; Marcus 1996), suggesting stylistic continuity over time. At some point between the middle of the second millennium and the destruction of Hasanlu, a choice was made at the site to incorporate into local artistic production the very types of imagery—scenes

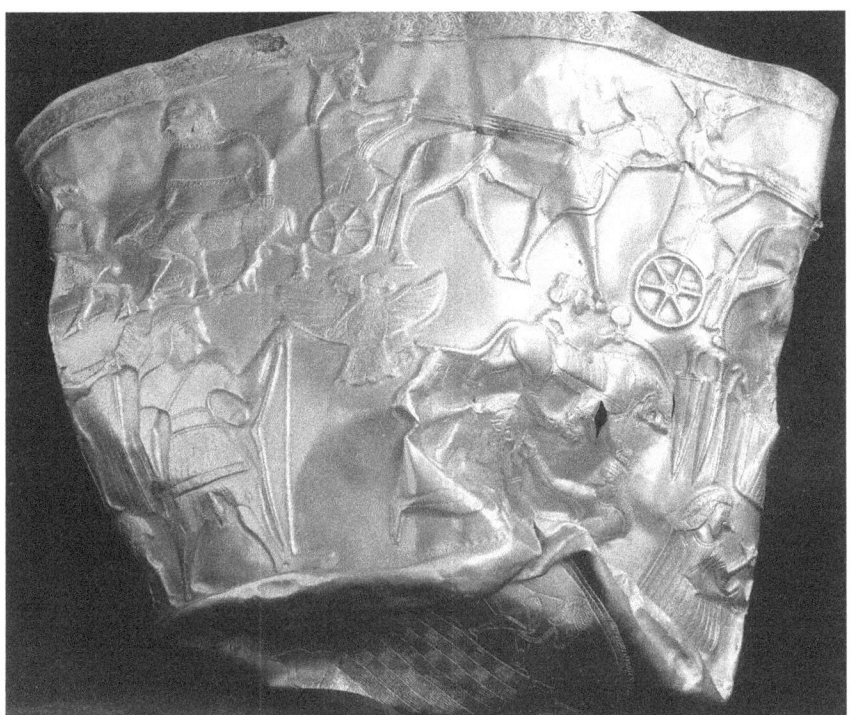

FIGURE 8.6. *Excavation photograph of the Gold Bowl. Courtesy, Penn Museum.*

of battle, hunting, and presentations—that would appear on monumental wall reliefs and bronze gate bands that decorated Neo-Assyrian palaces. This iconographic repertoire, however, is not limited to Neo-Assyrian art. These scenes are well represented in ancient Near Eastern art throughout the second millennium BCE and occur as well on monumental architectural reliefs at tenth-century BCE sites in North Syria and the northern Levant, including Carchemish, Malatya, Tell Halaf, and Zincirli (Muscarella 1980, 167–70). Moreover, details such as the "awkward" rendering of chariot horses with four feet on the ground in Local-Style ivories link the art of Hasanlu to that of North Syrian monumental reliefs (Muscarella 1966, 130–31).

Points of resemblance between objects created in Hasanlu and North Syria, although reinforced by the presence of North Syrian artifacts and architectural forms at the site, are not indications that the artisans at Hasanlu were directly emulating North Syrian monumental art any more than was the case for Assyrian art.[28] Choices made at Hasanlu cannot be reduced to a unilateral

FIGURE 8.7. *Excavation photograph of the Silver Beaker. Courtesy, Penn Museum.*

flow of "culture" between regions separated by hundreds of miles. According to Marian H. Feldman's (2014, 26) recent discussion of the study of luxury objects in the ancient Near East, when conclusions about ancient social behavior are based on visual attributes, "the social relations thus inferred are perhaps as much a product of our analytical apparatus as an . . . entity from the past." The art historical impulse to link stylistic elements directly to specific geopolitical entities and to underpin those links with colonialist assumptions about the dominance of "more developed" entities over those "less developed" cultures oversimplifies the artistic and cultural forces at play.

Nearly a century ago, Anton Moortgat (1930) cautioned against suppositions that the similarities between battle scenes in Assyrian and North Syrian reliefs result from "influence" traveling from one polity to another, arguing instead that these points of resemblance are a natural outgrowth of a shared artistic Mitanni-Hurrian heritage that was transmitted in the Late Bronze Age through portable objects (glyptic). Archaeological evidence suggests that Hasanlu participated, perhaps tangentially, in the broad, multivalent network of interaction by which the elements of this Bronze Age koine was transmitted.

The elite architectural core of the Hasanlu citadel, which has been related to northern Mesopotamia, takes shape in the Late Bronze Age; and the ceramic assemblage of that period "exhibits a significant degree of linkage to northeastern Mesopotamia," particularly the "Hurro-Mitanni" world (Danti 2013b, 182, 324). As discussed above, elites at Hasanlu seem to have deliberately collected and cared for high-value, portable objects over the centuries. Furthermore, the contents of storerooms on the citadel demonstrate links to cultures that were active participants in the artistic internationalism of the Late Bronze Age, including the Middle Assyrians and Kassites in Mesopotamia and Hittites in Anatolia. The ivory fragments and glazed ceramics stratified in the Period IVc destruction levels below the floors of Temple BBII (Danti and Cifarelli 2016) provide a tantalizing glimpse of Hasanlu's pre–Period IVb consumption of precious materials or finished goods of western origin and hint at the materials that could have been lost in the IVc destruction. Further indications of the awareness at Hasanlu of elements of "Late Bronze Age artistic internationalism" (Feldman 2015) are provided by the numerous Mitanni and Middle Assyrian elements that have been identified in the Local-Style ivories and seals of Hasanlu (Muscarella 1980; Marcus 1996).

The fact that "Local-Style" artisans demonstrate such remarkable syncretism of subject matter and hybridity of style and technique is well-known (e.g., Winter 1980). For example, a copper alloy belt from Hasanlu, discovered in the exceptionally well-furnished Period IVb burial of a young man, is an example of the use at the site of a Transcaucasian object type (Rubinson 2012) (figure 8.8). This belt, however, does not bear embossed decoration typical of Transcaucasian examples but is meticulously incised with a repeating, fluidly drawn scene of animals flanking stylized palmettes that has links to Middle Assyrian glyptic. The guilloche borders and surface decoration of these animals, however, mirror those seen in Elamite and other Iranian metalwork, including the Hasanlu Gold Bowl. The medallion "buckle" of the belt presents both incised guilloche and in high relief a contest scene with lions grasping couchant bulls, a Mesopotamian theme (Danti and Cifarelli 2015). It is one of the finest objects found at Hasanlu, found in the wealthiest burial at the site on the body of a heavily armed young man. This belt draws from an astonishing array of Bronze and Iron Age material culture, deftly amalgamated into an entirely local product.

The Hasanlu Local Style, then, need not emulate Neo-Assyrian models. There is ample evidence at Hasanlu—in the burials, the heirloom objects found in the destruction of the Period IVb citadel, and the ivory fragments associated with Period IVc—for its participation in interregional networks of interaction during the Late Bronze Age prior to the rise of the Neo-Assyrian Empire

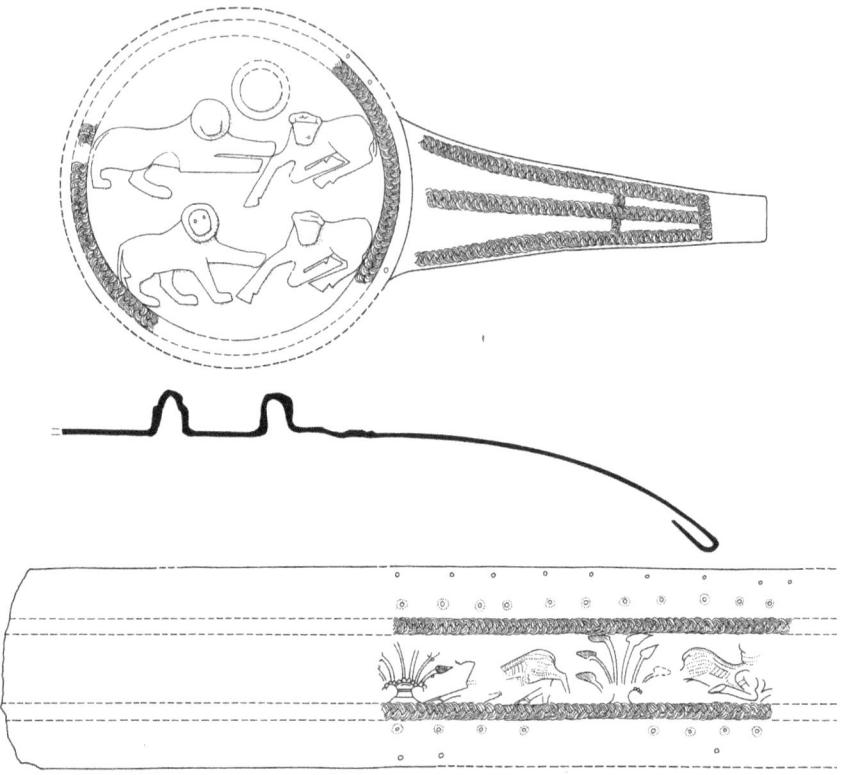

FIGURE 8.8. *Copper alloy belt from Burial SK493. Drawing by Denise L. Hoffmann. Courtesy, Penn Museum.*

(Danti and Cifarelli 2016, 368). In addition, traces of second millennium elements in the Local-Style objects demonstrate access of artisans to these older motifs, despite the lack of precise Bronze Age models for the scenes of hunting, warfare, sieges, and presentations among the objects found in the Period IVb destruction. The persistence of Bronze Age imagery over hundreds of years is not surprising, given the lack of impact in this region of the Late Bronze Age "collapse" and the reverence for the past manifested in the collecting practices.

Once assumptions about the nature of interaction between the Neo-Assyrian Empire and Hasanlu and about the volume and significance of Assyrian objects at Hasanlu are stripped away, we can view the decision to incorporate broadly available, particularly militaristic and hierarchical scenes into Hasanlu's visual culture through a decidedly local lens. The site of Hasanlu suffered two catastrophic, destructive events resulting from military activity. The first took place at the hands of unknown aggressors toward the end of Period IVc. The second attack took place at the hands of the Urartian state and resulted in the total destruction and a substantial abandonment of the site at the end of Period IVb (1050–800 BCE). Such dire occurrences were certainly not unusual in this region of ancient Iran between the eleventh and ninth centuries BCE and are documented in the archaeological records of numerous sites in the region (Danti 2013b, 367–68).

The threat of destruction at the hands of a marauding army left traces at Hasanlu, which are detectable in numerous ways in the archaeological record. Changes to the built environment in Periods IVc and IVb (Danti 2013a, 2013b) provide evidence for "crisis architecture" (Driessen 1995), with enhancements to the architectural control of access to elite buildings on the citadel, augmentation of internal citadel fortifications (Danti 2013a, Danti 2013b), and significant alterations to the functions of some monumental buildings (Cifarelli 2017). The sequestration of elite goods in temple storerooms and in elite residences on the citadel mirrors changes in the patterns of distribution of "prestige" goods in the cemetery, which show an increase in social stratification and gender differentiation in Periods IVc and IVb. The Period IVb burials in particular feature the conspicuous display and disposal of militaristic personal ornaments, the inclusion of weapons in the wealthiest male burials, and the militarization of male and female dress (Danti and Cifarelli 2015; Cifarelli 2017, 2018). The belief that the material culture by which the "haves" are distinguished from the "have-nots" is northern (perhaps Hurro-Urartian) in origin and inspiration provides an indication of whose authority the residents of Hasanlu might have been emulating.

In the context of the local cultural processes at the site, the choice by artisans and elites to integrate militarized and hierarchical imagery into their local artistic production can be viewed as part of a site-wide response to external threats and internal changes. Rather than consciously emulating a distant, hegemonic empire, the elites at Hasanlu, drawing on the visual vocabulary of the storied Bronze Age past, may have attempted to increase the social distance between themselves and their dependents—constructing a clearer hierarchy using imagery that signaled their military prowess, hunting skills, and rich banquets. This proposition is affirmed by the fact that Local-Style cylinder seals used to seal boxes, baskets, jars, and doorways in the treasuries of Temple BBII featured precisely such scenes (Marcus 1996, 86–94), indicating that these images were associated with those in control of access to the most elite areas and objects at the site.

CONCLUSION

The goal of this thought experiment was to remove the Assyro-centric lens through which the material culture of the site has been viewed since the earliest days of the Hasanlu Expedition and to attempt to view the site through the materiality of its local archaeological record. The Period IVb destruction level contained far fewer Assyrian objects than excavators initially believed. Careful analysis of the archaeological contexts for these Assyrian objects demonstrates that they constituted a small subset of massive collections of imported and locally made elite votive objects. Their social value at the site presumably derived from their role in those collections, not from their specifically "Assyrian" identity, which may not have been as obvious to the residents of Hasanlu as it was to the excavators. Consequently, if the materiality of the site does not support the conclusion that Assyrian material culture was predominant and played an exceptionally significant role at Hasanlu and that Assyria played the role of "center" and Hasanlu was in its "periphery," it is very difficult to sustain the notion that Hasanlu's elite and artisans deliberately emulated the art of palaces and temples in the Assyrian heartland in the decoration of Local-Style objects.

Rather than exemplify the privileged role of Assyria in the material culture of Hasanlu, the Local Style is a natural development of a local material culture that sought out, collected, and curated an eclectic array of elite objects, linking the present to the past and honoring the gods. As an alternative to emulation, we can emphasize the remarkable syncretism of the Hasanlu Local Style, ascribing any similarities to the art of Assyria or North Syria to their shared heritage of a Bronze Age visual culture featuring scenes of warfare, hunting, and presentations. And perhaps if we can move past characterizing Hasanlu, its people, and its material culture as an appendage of Assyria and a paradigm of the processes of "Assyrianization," we can more deeply appreciate the astonishing hybridity of the artistic traditions that developed in an era when one moment of destruction had underscored the precarious nature of life at Hasanlu and another would signal its end.

NOTES

The seed of this chapter was planted when Michael Danti and I presented at the conference "The Provincial Archaeology of the Assyrian Empire," hosted by the McDonald Institute for Archaeological Research at the University of Cambridge in December 2012, now published as Danti and Cifarelli (2016). In the intervening years, my views on the relationship between Hasanlu and the material culture of the Neo-Assyrian

Empire have evolved, the results of which you can read here. Thanks to the University of Pennsylvania Museum for permission to work on the Hasanlu materials and archives, particularly Michael Danti, Richard Zettler, and Holly Pittman, and to Katherine Blanchard, Fowler/Van Santvoord Keeper of Collections. None of my efforts would be possible without the pioneering work of Michelle Marcus. Thanks to Karen Rubinson, Paul Sanchez, and Michael Danti for reading drafts. Their comments have improved this chapter immeasurably. The mistakes remain my own.

1. Excavations were directed by Robert H. Dyson Jr. and supported by the University of Pennsylvania Museum, the Metropolitan Museum of Art, and the Archaeological Service of Iran. The project to complete the final excavation reports is well under way under the direction of Michael Danti (2004, 2013a, 2013b).

2. All Assyrian and "Assyrianizing" material at Hasanlu is found in the Period IVb destruction levels. The date of Hasanlu's destruction is unresolved, but this chapter agrees with the excavators who asserted that Hasanlu was destroyed by the Urartian army in about 800 BCE. Arguing for the 800 BCE destruction are Dyson and Muscarella (1989); Muscarella (2006, 75); Danti (2013a, 2013b, 2014). Contra are Medvedskaya (1988, 1991), as well as Magee (2008). A comprehensive reevaluation of this date and the radiocarbon and archaeological evidence on which it is based is under way as part of the Hasanlu publication project.

3. For example, Robert Dyson (1965, 199) wrote: "The objects found . . . form two distinct groups. One, imports or copies of Assyrian goods; the other, objects made according to local tradition."

4. Work on the excavation report for the Period IVb cemetery is well under way.

5. An extensive bibliography for Hasanlu can be found in Muscarella (2006). Some more recent publications continue to present these assumptions as if they were established conclusions (e.g., Gunter 2009).

6. Between 1949 and 1959, for example, the Nimrud excavations were featured in the *Illustrated London News* twenty-five times.

7. Sanka Knox, "Museum Showing an Ancient Hoard: Assyrian and Persian Ivory, Gold, and Silver on Public View for the First Time," *New York Times*, March 24, 1955, 28.

8. By 1989, Dyson had amended this characterization to include objects from Elam.

9. Richard D. Barnett's publication of English summaries of the reports of the excavations at Karmir Blur in Armenia by Boris Piotrovskii in *Iraq* (Barnett and Watson 1952; Barnett 1959), as well as Charles Burney's work in eastern Turkey, brought far wider attention to the kingdom of Urartu in the West and inspired further archaeological investigations at Urartian fortresses in Turkey and northern Iran (see Burney and Lang 1972; Kroll et al. 2012).

10. As is well-known, in 1995 Paul Zimansky characterized the material culture of the Urartian fortresses as a "state assemblage," an "official" artistic production that is found in Urartian fortresses and largely postdates the destruction of Hasanlu. The material culture of the lands between the fortresses and nominally under Urartian control is far more heterogeneous, and it is not surprising that the excavators of Hasanlu (Dyson and Muscarella 1989) identified only two object classes—helmets and maces—with Urartu and correlated those objects to the invasion forces. In more recent years investigators have identified Urartian pottery and the type of trident that would later appear as an Urartian royal symbol in the citadel (Kroll 2010, 2013), as well as personal ornaments (Danti and Cifarelli 2015) and possibly copper alloy belts (Rubinson 2012; Danti and Cifarelli 2015) in the citadel and burials.

11. Not surprisingly, the earliest account of potential interaction between Hasanlu and the Caucasus was published by researchers working primarily in Russian (Pogrebova 1977; Medvedskaya 1982). The excavators of Hasanlu were aware of these interactions in the 1970s (Karen Rubinson, personal communication, 2016), and in recent years these connections have become well established (Muscarella 1994; Biscione 2003; Rubinson and Marcus 2005; Thornton and Pigott 2011; Cifarelli 2013, 2016; Danti and Cifarelli 2015; Rubinson 2003, 2012, 2015).

12. As a crude metric of the relatively greater presence of Assyria in the literature with respect to Urartu and Transcaucasia, a quick search of peer-reviewed publications on the EBSCOhost database shows that during the period 1949–89, 1,701 articles included the word "Assyria," 239 included "Urartu," and 91 had "Transcaucasia," along with "archaeology."

13. As Muscarella (2006) has pointed out, the precise number of objects excavated at Hasanlu has been a moving target. While the latest publication by the excavators (Dyson 2003) states that 7,000 objects were discovered, this number seems to apply to the quantity of object numbers assigned in the field, many of which refer to multiple objects. My observations of objects at the University Museum indicate that, because of fragmentation and deterioration, some objects are, in fact, uncountable. Tens of thousands represents my conservative estimate of the quantity of individual objects found at Hasanlu.

14. Elise Roßberger (2016, 420) has recently argued that the distinction between temple inventory and gifts to deities is artificial. A previous study, based on the assignment of specific Assyrian-style seals to the bodies of individuals killed in the collapse of citadel buildings, concluded that Assyrian-style seals were worn by local elites to borrow prestige from the visual culture of their powerful neighbors so they could create powerful markers of status (Marcus 1989, 1990, 1996). For the most part, the original excavation records are neither sufficiently detailed nor sufficiently reliable, particularly in the earlier seasons when Temple BBII was poorly excavated and

recorded, to support such a fine-grained analysis. Often, the information we do have controverts Marcus's assertions; for a detailed analysis see Danti and Cifarelli (2016).

15. The point in time at which these "heirloom" objects came to Hasanlu is a subject of debate. While some have speculated that they are the product of ninth-century BCE diplomacy (Winter 1977, 378; Dyson 1989, 123), direct parallels between goods found in Middle Bronze Age burials at Hasanlu and those found in Period IVb temple treasuries suggest that at least some of the older objects had been at Hasanlu for generations (Cifarelli 2013).

16. The Period IVc levels were relatively unexplored on the citadel (Danti 2013a, 2013b).

17. Karen Rubinson (2012) relates the repoussé decorated sheet metal belt found in Period IVb Burial SK107 at Hasanlu to a South Caucasus tradition that would subsequently be adopted by the kingdom of Urartu. The dozens of fragments of belts of the same type found in a BBII treasury are unpublished but are recorded in field notebooks 13 (1960), 39 (1962), and 50 (1964).

18. The possibility that sealing was practiced earlier cannot be ruled out, as Period IVc levels under many buildings on the citadel were not excavated.

19. The extent to which the Hasanlu Local Style is "Assyrianizing" will be evaluated below.

20. As raised by Peter Magee (2008, 95) in his discussion of the relationship of Hasanlu's destruction, in which he asks "whether or not foreign artistic traditions can exist under potentially hostile political hegemony."

21. For a thoughtful assessment of the applicability of world-systems and acculturation models to the ancient Near East, see Stein (2002, 904), who argues for the "need to decolonize the archaeology of interregional interaction in order to free ourselves from the Eurocentric assumptions of traditional approaches to culture contact."

22. Assyriologists identify it as Gilzanu, a site appearing in Assyrian royal inscriptions (Reade 1979; Kroll et al. 2012, 164), and those who study Urartu identify it as the Urartian city of Meshta (Salvini 2011). Both identifications are in question, as they are founded on the belief that Hasanlu is the largest and most important site in the region, a notion for which there is much evidence to the contrary; see Danti (2013b); Magee (2008).

23. See note 9, above.

24. See note 12, above.

25. For the concept of a frontier, the word used frequently to describe the relationship of Hasanlu to the Assyrian Empire (e.g., Gunter 2009; Aruz, Graff, and Rakic 2014), see Parker (2006).

26. Among these few finds are fragments of ivories and glazed vessels found under the floor of Level IVb Temple BBII, indicating that objects of these types were present at Hasanlu in Period IVc (Danti and Cifarelli 2016).

27. Once we let go of the notion of emulation, we no longer have the burden of explaining why or how the "Assyrianizing" Local-Style imagery appears to draw upon material that is not present in the Assyrian objects at Hasanlu but rather is found miles away in the Assyrian capitals (Winter 1977).

28. This is the case despite the extensive evidence for interaction between North Syria and Hasanlu. Muscarella (1980), for example, identifies nearly four times as many carved fragments as "North Syrian" in manufacture as those he designates "Assyrian," and Danti and Cifarelli (2016) argue that features of the religious architecture at Hasanlu established in the Late Bronze Age—the use of large aniconic stone stelae at the entrance of the temple—show a clear relationship to the archaeological and textual record of Syria.

WORKS CITED

Appadurai, Arjun. 1994. "Commodities and the Politics of Value." In *Interpreting Objects and Collections*, ed. Susan M. Pearce, 76–91. London: Routledge.

Aruz, Joan, Sarah B. Graff, and Yelena Rakic. 2014. *Assyria to Iberia at the Dawn of the Classical Age*. New York: Metropolitan Museum of Art.

Azarnoush, Massoud, and Barbara Helwing. 2005. "Recent Archaeological Research in Iran: Prehistory to Iron Age." *AMIT* 37: 189–246.

Barnett, Richard D. 1959. "Further Russian Excavations in Armenia (1949–1953)." *Iraq* 21 (1): 1–19. https://doi.org/10.2307/4199644.

Barnett, Richard D., and William Watson. 1952. "Russian Excavations in Armenia." *Iraq* 14 (2): 132–47. https://doi.org/10.2307/4199560.

Basello, Gianpietro. 2012. "Doorknobs, Nails, or Pegs? The Function(s) of the Elamite and Achaemenid Inscribed Knobs." In *Dariosh Studies II: Persepolis and Its Settlements: Territorial System and Ideology in the Achaemenid State*, ed. Gianpietro Basello and Adriano V. Rossi, 1–66. Napoli: Università à degli Studi di Napoli "L'Orientale."

Biscione, Raffaele. 2003. "Pre Urartian and Urartian Settlement Patterns in the Caucasus." In *Archaeology in the Borderlands: Investigations in the Caucasus and Beyond*, ed. Adam Smith and Karen Rubinson, 167–84. Los Angeles: Cotsen Institute of Archaeology.

Burney, Charles, and David M. Lang. 1972. *The Peoples of the Hills: Ancient Ararat and Caucasus*. New York: Praeger.

Cifarelli, Megan. 2013. "The Personal Ornaments of Hasanlu VIb–IVc." In *Hasanlu V: The Late Bronze and Iron I Periods*, ed. Michael Danti, 313–23. Philadelphia: University of Pennsylvania Museum Press.

Cifarelli, Megan. 2016. "Masculinities and 'Militarization' at Hasanlu, Iran: A View from the Burials." In "Gender Archaeology," ed. Stephanie Budin and Jennifer Webb, special issue, *NEA* 79 (3): 196–204. https://doi.org/10.5615/neareastarch.79.3.0196.

Cifarelli, Megan. 2017. "Archaeological Evidence for Small Scale Crisis: Hasanlu between Destructions." In *From Crisis to Collapse: Archaeology and the Breakdown of Social Order*, ed. Timothy Cunningham and Jan Driessen. Louvain le Neuve, Belgium: Aegis.

Cifarelli, Megan. 2018. "Gender, Personal Adornment, and Costly Signaling in the Iron Age Burials of Hasanlu, Iran." In *Gender, Methodology, and the Ancient Near East*, ed. Agnès Garcia-Ventura and Saana Svärd, 77–112. Winona Lake, IL: Eisenbrauns.

Collins, Paul. 2006. "An Assyrian-Style Ivory Plaque from Hasanlu, Iran." *Metropolitan Museum Journal* 41: 19–31.

Dan, Roberto. 2012. "Nails in the Wall" In *Studies II: Persepolis and Its Settlements: Territorial System and Ideology in the Achaemenid State*, ed. Gianpietro Basello and Adriano V. Rossi, 301–12. Napoli: Università à degli Studi di Napoli "L'Orientale."

Danti, Michael. 2004. *The Ilkhanid Heartland: Hasanlu Tepe (Iran) Period I, Hasanlu Excavation Reports II*. Philadelphia: University of Pennsylvania Museum Press.

Danti, Michael. 2013a. "The Late Bronze and Early Iron Age in Northwestern Iran." In *The Oxford Handbook of Ancient Iran*, ed. Daniel T. Potts, 327–76. Oxford: Oxford University Press. https://doi.org/10.1093/oxfordhb/9780199733309.013.0006.

Danti, Michael. 2013b. *Hasanlu V: The Late Bronze and Iron I Periods*. Philadelphia: University of Pennsylvania Museum Press.

Danti, Michael. 2014. "The Hasanlu (Iran) Gold Bowl in Context: All That Glitters." *Antiquity* 88 (341): 791–804. https://doi.org/10.1017/S0003598X00050699.

Danti, Michael, and Megan Cifarelli. 2015. "Iron II Warrior Burials at Hasanlu, Iran." *IrAnt* 50: 61–157.

Danti, Michael, and Megan Cifarelli. 2016. "'Assyrianizing' Contexts at Hasanlu Tepe IVb? Materiality and Identity in Northwest Iran." In *The Provincial Archaeology of the Assyrian Empire*, ed. John MacGinnis and Dirke Wicke, 357–69. Cambridge: McDonald Institute for Archaeological Research.

de Schauensee, Maude, ed. 2011. *Peoples and Crafts in Period IVB at Hasanlu Tepe, Iran*. Philadelphia: University of Pennsylvania Museum Press.

Driessen, Jan. 1995. "'Crisis Architecture'? Some Observations on Architectural Adaptations as Immediate Responses to Changing Socio-cultural Conditions." *Topoi* 5 (1): 63–88. https://doi.org/10.3406/topoi.1995.1558.

Dyson, Robert H., Jr. 1965. "Problems of Protohistoric Iran as Seen from Hasanlu." *JNES* 24: 193–217.

Dyson, Robert H., Jr. 1989. "The Iron Age Architecture of Hasanlu, an Essay." *Expedition* 31: 107–28.

Dyson, Robert H., Jr. 2003. "Hasanlu Teppe." In *Encyclopaedia Iranica*, vol. 12, ed. Eshan Yarshater, 41–46. Boston: Routledge and Kegan Paul.

Dyson, Robert H., Jr., and Oscar W. Muscarella. 1989. "Constructing the Chronology and Historical Implications of Hasanlu IV." *Iran* 27: 1–27.

Dyson, Robert H., Jr., and Vincent C. Pigott. 1975 "Hasanlu." *Iran* 13: 182–85.

Dyson, Robert H., Jr., and Mary M. Voigt, eds. 1989. *East of Assyria: The Highland Settlement of Hasanlu*. Special issue of *Expedition* 31 (2–3).

Feldman, Marian H. 2014. *Communities of Style: Portable Luxury Arts, Identity, and Collective Memory in the Iron Age Levant*. Chicago: University of Chicago Press. https://doi.org/10.7208/chicago/9780226164427.001.0001.

Feldman, Marian H. 2015. "Qatna and Artistic Internationalism during the Late Bronze Age." In *Qatna and the Networks of Bronze Age Globalism*, ed. Peter Pfälzner and Michel Al-Maqdissi, 33–41. Wiesbaden: Harrassowitz.

Fuchs, Andreas. 2004. *Bis hin zum Berg Bikni: Zur Topographie und Geschichte des Zagrosraumes in altorientalischer Zeit*. Tübingen: Unpublished Habilitation.

Fuchs, Andreas. 2012. "Urartu in der Zeit." In *Biainili-Urartu, Acta Iranica 51*, ed. Stephan Kroll, Claudia Gruber, Ursula Hellwag, Michael Roaf, and Paul Zimansky, 135–61. Leuven: Peeters.

Grayson, A. Kirk. 1991. *Assyrian Rulers of the First Millennium BC II*. Toronto: University of Toronto Press. https://doi.org/10.3138/9781442671089.

Gunter, Ann. 2009. *Greek Art and the Orient*. Cambridge: Cambridge University Press.

Khatchadourian, Lori. 2011. "The Iron Age in Eastern Anatolia." In *The Oxford Handbook of Ancient Anatolia*, ed. Sharon R. Steadman and Gregory McMahon, 464–89. Oxford: Oxford University Press.

Kroll, Stephan. 2010. "Urartu and Hasanlu." In *Urartu and Its Neighbors*, ed. Aram Kosyan, Armen Petrosyan, and Yervand Grekyan, 21–35. Yerevan, Armenia: Association for Near Eastern and Caucasian Studies.

Kroll, Stephan. 2011. "Urartian Cities in Iran." In *Urartu: Transformation in the East*, ed. Kemalettin Köroğlu and Erkan Konyar, 150–71. Istanbul: Yapı Kredi Yayınları.

Kroll, Stephan. 2013. "Hasanlu Period III—Annotations and Corrections." *IrAnt* 48: 175–92.

Kroll, Stephan, Claudia Gruber, Ursula Hellwag, Michael Roaf, and Paul Zimansky, eds. 2012. *Biainili-Urartu, Acta Iranica 51*. Leuven: Peeters.

Lillios, Katina T. 1999. "Objects of Memory: The Ethnography and Archaeology of Heirlooms." *Journal of Archaeological Method and Theory* 6 (3): 235–62.

Magee, Peter. 2008. "Deconstructing the Destruction of Hasanlu: Archaeology, Imperialism, and the Chronology of the Iranian Iron Age." *IrAnt* 43: 89–106.

Marcus, Michelle I. 1989. "Emblems of Authority: The Seals and Sealings from Hasanlu IVB." *Expedition* 31 (2–3): 53–63.

Marcus, Michelle I. 1990. "Centre, Province, and Periphery: A New Paradigm from Iron-Age Iran." *Art History* 13 (2): 129–50. https://doi.org/10.1111/j.1467-8365.1990.tb00385.x.

Marcus, Michelle I. 1991. "The Mosaic Glass Vessels from Hasanlu, Iran: A Study in Large-Scale Stylistic Trait Distribution." *ABull* 73 (4): 536–60.

Marcus, Michelle I. 1996. *Emblems of Identity and Prestige: The Seals and Sealings from Hasanlu, Iran; Commentary and Catalog.* Philadelphia: University Museum, University of Pennsylvania.

Medvedskaya, Inna N. 1982. *Iran: Iron Age I.* BAR International Series, vol. 126. Oxford: British Archaeological Reports.

Medvedskaya, Inna N. 1988. "Who Destroyed Hasanlu IV?" *Iran* 26: 1–15. https://doi.org/10.2307/4299797.

Medvedskaya, Inna N. 1991. "Once More on the Destruction of Hasanlu IV: Problems of Dating." *IrAnt* 26: 149–61.

Moortgat, Anton. 1930. "Der Kampf zu Wagen in der Kunst des alten Orients." *OLZ* 33: 841–54.

Muscarella, Oscar W. 1966. "Hasanlu 1964." *BMM* 25 (3): 121–35.

Muscarella, Oscar W. 1974. "A Third Lion Bowl from Hasanlu." *Expedition* 16 (2): 25–59.

Muscarella, Oscar W. 1980. *The Catalogue of Ivories from Hasanlu, Iran: University Museum Monograph 40.* Hasanlu Special Studies 2. Philadelphia: University Museum, University of Pennsylvania.

Muscarella, Oscar W. 1994. "North-Western Iran: Bronze Age to Iron Age." In *Anatolian Iron Ages 3: The Proceedings of the Third Anatolian Iron Ages Colloquium Held at Van, 6–12 August 1990*, ed. Altan Cilingiroğlu and David H. French, 139–55. London: British Institute at Ankara.

Muscarella, Oscar W. 2006. "The Excavations of Hasanlu: An Archaeological Evaluation." *BASOR* 342: 69–94.

Nunn, Astrid. 1988. *Handbuch der Orientalistik: Die Wandmalerei und der glasierte Wandschmuck im Alten Orient.* Leiden: Brill.

Parker, Bradley J. 2006. "Toward an Understanding of Borderland Processes." *Antiquity* 71 (1): 77–100. https://doi.org/10.2307/40035322.

Piller, Christian. 2010. "Northern Iran in the Iron Age II and III: A Neighbor of Urartu?" In *Urartu and Its Neighbors*, ed. Aram Kosyan, Armand Petrosyan, and Yervand Grekyan, 53–75. Yerevan, Armenia: Association for Near Eastern and Caucasian Studies.

Pogrebova, Maria I. 1977. *Iran and the Caucasus in the Early Iron Age* [in Russian]. Moscow: Nauka.

Porada, Edith. 1959. "The Hasanlu Bowl." *Expedition* 1: 18–22.
Porada, Edith. 1967. "Notes on the Gold Bowl and Silver Beaker from Hasanlu." In *A Survey of Persian Art, 14*, ed. Arthur Pope, 2971–78. New York: Oxford University Press.
Potts, Daniel T. 2014. "Assyria's Eastern Frontier." In *Assyria to Iberia at the Dawn of the Classical Age*, ed. Joan Aruz, Sarah Graff, and Yelena Rakic, 75–78. New York: Metropolitan Museum of Art.
Radner, Karen. 2011. "Assyrians and Urartians." In *The Oxford Handbook of Ancient Anatolia*, ed. Sharon R. Steadman and Gregory McMahon, 734–51. Oxford: Oxford University Press.
Reade, Julian. E. 1979. "Hasanlu, Gilzanu, and Related Considerations." *AMI* 12: 175–72.
Roßberger, Elise. 2016. "Dedicated Objects and Memory Construction at the Ištar-Kitītum Temple at Iščāli." In *Proceedings, 9th ICAANE Basel 2014, vol. 1*, ed. Rolf Stucky, Oscar Kaelin, and Hans-Peter Mathys, 419–30. Wiesbaden: Harrasowitz.
Rubinson, Karen S. 2003. "The Hasanlu Gold 'Bowl': A View from Transcaucasia." In *Yeki Bud, Yeki Napud: Essays on the Archaeology of Iran in Honor of William M. Sumner*, ed. Naomi Miller and Kamyar Abdi, 237–42. Los Angeles: Cotsen Institute of Archaeology at UCLA.
Rubinson, Karen S. 2012. "Urartian (?) Belts and Some Antecedents." In *Biainili-Urartu: The Proceedings of the Symposium Held in Munch 12–14 October 2007*, ed. Stephan Kroll, Claudia Gruber, and Ursula Hellwag, 391–96. Leuven: Peeters.
Rubinson, Karen S. 2015. "Revisiting South Caucasus–Iranian Azerbaijan Connections." In *International Symposium on East Anatolia South Caucasus Cultures Proceedings I*, ed. Mehmet Isiki and Birol Can, 145–47. Newcastle, GB: Cambridge Scholars Publishers.
Rubinson, Karen, and Michelle I. Marcus. 2005. "Hasanlu IVB and Caucasia: Explorations and Implications of Context." In *Anatolian Iron Ages 5: Proceedings of the Fifth Anatolian Iron Ages Colloquium*, ed. Altan Cilingiroğlu and Gareth Darbyshire, 131–38. London: British Institute at Ankara.
Salvini, Mirjo. 2011. "An Overview of Urartian History." In *Urartu: Transformation in the East*, ed. Kemalettin Köroğlu and Erkan Konyar, 76–101. Istanbul: Yapı Kredi Yayınları.
Stein, Diana. 1989. "Art and Architecture." In *The Hurrians*, ed. Gernot Wilhelm, 80–90. Warminster: Aris and Phillips.
Stein, Gil J. 2002. "From Passive Periphery to Active Agents: Emerging Perspectives in the Archaeology of Interregional Interaction." *AA* 104 (3): 903–16.
Thomason, Allison Karmel. 2005. *Luxury and Legitimation: Royal Collecting in Ancient Mesopotamia*. Burlington, VT: Ashgate.

Thornton, Christopher, and Vincent Pigott. 2011. "Blade-Type Weaponry of Hasanlu Period IVB." In *Peoples and Crafts in Period IVB at Hasanlu, Iran*, ed. Maude de Schauensee, 135–82. Philadelphia: University of Pennsylvania Press.

Tourtet, Francelin. 2011. "Distribution, Materials, and Functions of the 'Wall Knobs' in the Near Eastern Late Bronze Age: From South-Western Iran to the Middle Euphrates in Susa and Elam." In *Archaeological, Philological, Historical, and Geographical Perspectives: Proceedings of the International Congress Held at Ghent University, Belgium, December 14–17, 2009*, ed. Katrin de Graef and Jan Tavernier, 173–90. Leiden: Brill.

Wicke, Dirke, and Tina Greenfield. 2013. "The 'Bronze Palace' at Ziyaret Tepe: Preliminary Remarks on the Architecture and Faunal Analysis." In *New Research on Late Assyrian Palaces: Conference at Heidelberg, January 22, 2011*, ed. David Kertai and Peter Miglus, 63–82. Heidelberg: Heidelberger Orientverlag.

Winter, Irene J. 1977. "Perspective on the 'Local Style' of Hasanlu IVB: A Study in Receptivity." In *Mountains and Lowlands: Essays in the Archaeology of Greater Mesopotamia*, ed. Louis D. Levine, 371–86. Malibu, CA: Undena.

Winter, Irene J. 1980. *A Decorated Breastplate from Hasanlu, Iran*. Philadelphia: University of Pennsylvania Museum Press.

Winter, Irene J. 1989. "The Hasanlu Gold Bowl: Thirty Years Later." *Expedition* 31 (2–3): 87–105.

Zimansky, Paul. 1995. "Urartian Material Culture as State Assemblage: An Anomaly in the Archaeology of Empire." *BASOR* 299–300: 103–15.

Zimansky, Paul. 2011. "Urartia and the Urartians." In *The Oxford Handbook of Ancient Anatolia*, ed. Sharon R. Steadman and Gregory McMahon, 548–59. Oxford: Oxford University Press.

9

In the Middle of the Sea of the Setting Sun

The Neo-Assyrian Empire and Cyprus—Economic and Political Perspectives

Anna Cannavò
(CNRS, UMR 5189 HiSoMA, MOM, Lyon)

Situated beyond the western borders of the Levant, for a long time Cyprus remained a distant, unknown, and possibly unreachable land, at least for a continental empire such as Assyria that did not have its own fleet. The memory of second millennium Cyprus (called Alashiya) had possibly vanished—at least in the Akkadian-speaking chancellery of the empire[1]—by the late eighth century BCE when the Assyrians started campaigning in the Levant and the Cilician plain and occasionally (as is recorded in the Annals of Sargon) "fished" some Ionian and Anatolian pirates who ravaged the coasts of the Gulf of Iskendurun (Brinkman 1989; Haider 1996; Mayer 1996; Casabonne and De Vos 2005; Rollinger 2007). It was during that time that the Assyrians (re)discovered Cyprus (then called Iadnana). While the Assyrians do not appear to have established any lasting territorial control over Cyprus, economic and political connections with the Phoenicians contributed to important societal changes on the island (table 9.1).

THE GREAT KING AND HIS VASSALS: THE EMPIRE FACING IADNANA

The origin of the name the Neo-Assyrian Empire gave to the new land located in the middle of the sea, Iadnana, is not clear. The best interpretation to date is that of Daniel D. Luckenbill (1914), recently elaborated by James D. Muhly (2009). According to

DOI: 10.5876/9781607328230.c009

TABLE 9.1. Cypriot chronology

Cypriot Chronology	Absolute Chronology (BCE)	Neo-Assyrian Chronology	
Late Bronze Age III	1200–1050		
Cypro-Geometric I	1050–950		
II	950–900		
III	900–750		
Cypro-Archaic I	750–600	Sargon II	721–705
		Sennacherib	704–681
		Esarhaddon	680–669
		Ashurbanipal	668–627
II	600–475		
Cypro-Classic	475–310		

Luckenbill and Muhly, Iadnana has to be analyzed as the juxtaposition of two West Semitic words, *'y*, "island," and *dnnym*, "Danunians," the inhabitants of the Neo-Hittite state of Cilicia around the town of Adana, which was known to the Assyrians as Quwe. Even if the Danunians can be placed in relation with Ahhiyawa (a second millennium west Anatolian political entity, possibly part of the Mycenaean world) and the Homeric Danaoi (one of the names used in the *Iliad* to name the Greek coalition against Troy), we can hardly define them as Greeks (Desideri and Jasink 1990, 111–63; Tekoğlu et al. 2000; Kaufman 2007; Lanfranchi 2009). In any case, whatever complex relationship existed among the Anatolian and Luwian peoples, the Greek mythological and historical tradition relating to them, and the Aegean peoples (merchants and pirates) who frequented southeastern Anatolia and Syria at the time, fine distinctions between them were hardly significant for the Assyrians. As Muhly (2009, 28) clearly stated, "For the Assyrians, who had no great interest in lands 'in the midst of the sea,' all these peoples of the archipelago of the eastern Mediterranean could be classified as Danunians because, as far as they were concerned, the 'Land of Danuna' was the most important political power in the region." We should thus consider the Assyrian name for Cyprus, Iadnana, a purely geographic rather than ethnic or political designation, meaning the "island of the Danunians" (i.e., the island off the coast of the Danunians' land).

Since no West Semitic document known to us calls Cyprus "Iadnana," we do not have any definitive proof for the hypothesis that the name, before being adopted by the Assyrian chancellery, originated in the West Semitic linguistic milieu. Nevertheless, the biblical Table of Nations (Genesis 10), which maps cultural relations through genealogy, seems to confirm Cyprus's connection with the Cilician area on the one hand and the Phoenician world on the other. In the Table of Nations, the sons of Yawan, the third generation of the western offspring of Noah, are Kittîm, Elishah, Dodanîm (possibly to be corrected to Rhodanîm, according to some scholars), and Tarshish. Cyprus, represented by the Phoenician Kition (Kittîm) and perhaps by Elishah as well, is thus connected to the Danunians (or to the Rhodians, if we accept the correction) and, through Tarshish, to the Phoenician world (Lipiński 1990; Vermeylen 1992; Liverani 2003, 264–66; Cannavò 2010, 182–83). When we consider all of these elements together, the following aspects appear characteristic of the Assyrian view of Cyprus at the time of the first contacts between the Neo-Assyrian Empire and the island, during the fifteenth year of Sargon II (708/707 BCE): its geographical isolation in the middle of the sea off the Cilician coast, its links with Anatolia (particularly Cilicia) and Phoenicia, and the connection with the Greek, especially the eastern Aegean, world.

The only explicit tradition attested in the Assyrian sources presents the submission of the island as a voluntary act, dictated by the Cypriot kings' fear when informed for the first time of the heroic deeds of the Assyrian king. This is how the events are related on the only Assyrian document discovered thus far in Cyprus, a gray basalt stele of Sargon II, today at the Vorderasiatisches Museum in Berlin (figure 9.1) and found at Larnaca in 1845 (Yon 2004, 345–54, no. 4001).[2] The Assyrian king and the symbols of the gods are represented in low relief on the front, and a long inscription describing the king's deeds up to the conquest of Iadnana covers the lower part of the front and the right and left sides. Even if the inscription is incomplete (the rear side of the stone was cut so it could be transferred to Berlin in 1846), the stereotypical text can easily be restored. According to the text, "A seven-day journey away [in the middle] of the Sea of the Setting Sun [the Cypriot kings have residence]—their seats (are so) far away (that) [since the] far-off days of taking possession of the land of Assur . . . the gods my fathers who [came] before (me) [they did not he]ar the name of their land" (left side, lines 29–35, author's translation). According to the "heroic priority" formula (Gelio 1981), the Assyrian king is the first to establish contact with the land far away and gain knowledge of its existence. Nevertheless, no military action by or concrete expedition of Sargon II to Cyprus is alluded to in the text; the Cypriot kings (unnamed in the stele), seized by the fear of Assyrian military power, took "gold, silver, [objects made of] ebony, and box wood, treasures of their land, [to B]abylon; in front of me

FIGURE 9.1. *Sargon II stele from Larnaca, 707 BCE, with a detail of the left side, lines 26–65. Courtesy, Vorderasiatisches Museum, Berlin, VA968 (© the author).*

[they brought the items and] kissed my feet" (left side, lines 39–42, author's translation). Thus, another formulaic motif, the offering of tribute, is used to describe the establishment of the first contacts (Cannavò 2015a). There is no doubt in any case that the stele—certainly an object of Assyrian type, even if possibly made locally by Assyrian workers (Radner 2010, 432)—was erected in Cyprus, somewhere in ancient Kition, modern Larnaca (Merrillees 2016).

The episode documented by the stele has been considered too standardized to be reliable. According to Nadav Na'aman (1998, 2001), the stereotypical version of the events presented on the monument hides a military campaign conducted in the name of Aššur by a certain Shilṭa of Tyre, who controlled the Cypriot kingdoms in the preceding years and had recourse to Assyrian help to put down a local revolt. But this interpretation depends largely on hypothetical or unattested elements—the existence of a presumed king of Tyre, Shilṭa; the alleged Tyrian control of Cyprus; the highly hypothetical reading of a greatly damaged and incomplete passage of the Annals of Sargon II (Annals, lines 393–98: Fuchs 1993, 175–77, 337)—and is therefore not entirely satisfying.[3] Its most significant point consists of underlining the importance of Tyrian agency for the establishment of Cypro-Assyrian contacts. If the Assyrians ever reached Cyprus—and they possibly did, just once, for the erection of the Larnaca stele—it was certainly on Phoenician boats (Briquel-Chatonnet 1992, 185). The choice of Kition as the designated location for the monument is not fortuitous. Kition was probably under the control of Tyre, which was acting as an agent of Assyrian power at the time of Sargon II (Menander of Ephesus cited by Flavius Josephus, *Jewish Antiquities*, 9, 28; Cannavò 2015a).

Things changed dramatically a few years later, in 701 BCE, when King Lulî of Tyre rebelled against Assyria.[4] While the Assyrian King Sennacherib laid siege to Tyre, Lulî was able to escape to Cyprus by sea (figure 9.2). Without the Tyrian fleet, the Assyrians did not (or could not) pursue him by sea, and so "from Tyre to Cyprus, which [is] in the middle of the sea, he fled and disappeared" (Grayson and Novotny 2014, 79, no. 46, 18–19, author's translation).[5] There is no record of Assyria asking Cyprus to return the fugitive king, probably because Assyria was unable to impose its power on Cyprus without Tyre's maritime expertise.

The next known contacts between Assyria and Cyprus took place at the time of Esarhaddon (680–669 BCE), on the occasion of the construction of the new royal palace in Nineveh. Cypriot kings are listed together with their homologues of the Levant as "the kings of the land of Hatti and over the sea," offering and carrying building material such as stones and wood to the Assyrian king's residence (Leichty 2011, 23–24, no. 1, V. 54–VI. 1).[6] As in the case of the first tribute Cypriot kings offered to Sargon II, one wonders if the contributions of the Cypriot and Levantine kings to the building activities at Esarhaddon should be considered "tribute" in a proper sense and thus a sign of formal dependency. An episode from more recent history offers an interesting parallel. In 1792 the British statesman Lord Macartney led an embassy to Beijing and presented products from his country to the Chinese emperor Ch'ien-lung. In the well-known reports on this embassy, the British offerings are described as "diplomatic gifts" intended to establish commercial exchanges between the

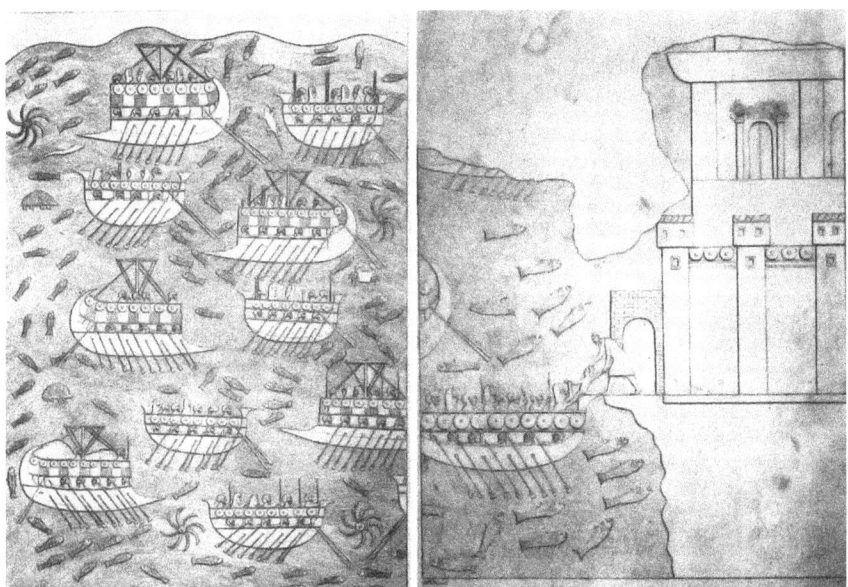

Figure 9.2. *Luli of Tyre escaping the Assyrians, 701 BCE. Low relief from Nineveh. Drawings by Austen H. Layard (after Barnett 1956, 93, fig. 9).*

two empires, but according to the Chinese reports on the same events, they are "tribute" offered as a sign of obeisance and respect to the Celestial Emperor. This example should inspire caution when considering similar claims in the Assyrian sources (Sahlins 1988; Cannavò 2015a).

The Cypriot contribution to the construction of the new royal palace—either as tribute or as a diplomatic gift—however, cannot be questioned. The Assyrian chancellery learned at that time the names of all the Cypriot kings and kingdoms, thus providing an invaluable list that constitutes our main source of knowledge about Archaic Cypriot history (Masson 1992; Bagg 2007) (figure 9.3; table 9.2). The same list of kings and kingdoms appears years later in Ashurbanipal's report of his war against Egypt in 664 BCE. This is the last recorded instance of Assyria claiming to have Cypriot kings as vassals. In this case they provided military aid and logistics and are also mentioned as offering generic "gifts," *tāmartu* (Borger 1996, 18–20, 212, C §14; on the *tāmartu*, see Cannavò 2007, 186). Even if the names of Cypriot kings are identical in both Esarhaddon's and Ashurbanipal's lists, the names of "the kings of the land of Hatti" with which the Cypriot kings are mentioned vary from one instance to another (at least some of them), suggesting that Ashurbanipal's list is not a mere copy of Esarhaddon's list.

FIGURE 9.3. *The Esarhaddon prism from Nineveh, 673 BCE. Courtesy, British Museum, London, 121.005 (© British Museum).*

These few documents are the main sources for understanding the Assyrian view of Cyprus during the decades of claimed political control on the island. It is evident that for the imperial core, Cyprus was nothing more than a far western appendage, a source of precious materials and useful technical skills[7] but in no way characterized by the essential logistical and geographical significance of the Levantine lands. Hanging among Cilicia of the Danunians, the western land of Yawan[8] and Hatti, and peopled by a varying number of kings (seven in Sargon's texts, which do not mention them individually; ten in the lists of Esarhaddon and Ashurbanipal, which seem more reliable since they specify their names), Cyprus appeared as a remote land, access to which was gained through the skills of Tyrian sailors and merchants. As soon as Assyria lost control of Tyre, it lost Cyprus as well.

TABLE 9.2. Cypriot kings named in the parallel lists of Esarhaddon (673–672 BCE) and Ashurbanipal (after 664 BCE)

Ekištura, king of Edi'il	Akestor (?), king of Idalion
Pilagura, king of Kitrusi	Philagoras, king of Chytroi
Kisu, king of Sillua	Kisu (unknown), king of Salamis (?)
Ituandar, king of Pappa	Etewandros, king of Paphos
Eresu, king of Silli	Eresu (unknown), king of Soloi (?)
Damasu, king of Kuri	Damasos, king of Kourion
Gir/Admesu, king of Tamesi	Admesu (unknown), king of Tamassos
Damusi, king of Qartihadasti	Damusi (unknown), king of Qarthadasht
Unasagusu, king of Lidir	Onasagoras, king of Ledra
P/Bušusu, king of Nuria	P/Bušusu (unknown), king of Nuria (unknown)

CYPRIOT KINGS AND THE ASSYRIAN MARKET: POLITICAL IMPLICATIONS OF ECONOMIC STRATEGIES

When looking for a Cypriot perspective on the same period and events, it is clear that Assyria appeared no less distant from Cyprus than Cyprus appeared to the Assyrians. As stated above, with the notable exception of the Sargon II stele, no other object of certain Assyrian origin has been found in Cyprus, and it would be difficult to claim a direct visible Assyrian impact on Cypriot civilization and material culture of the eighth–seventh centuries BCE (Reyes 1994, 49–68). At the same time, Cypriot kingdoms never produced the rich archival and literary documentation that facilitates (and orients as well) scholarly perception of Assyrian history and civilization. It is, then, an issue both of evidence and perspective that affects any evaluation of Cypriot history during the Neo-Assyrian Period.

Since we have up to now only minimal evidence of direct links or exchanges between Cyprus and Assyria, it is necessary to suppose the existence of intermediaries (in terms of both individuals and locations) playing the role of bridges between Cypriot resources, products, and people and Assyrian needs and demands. This role is likely to have been played by Phoenician and, more generally, Levantine cities and emporia, where Cypriot, Phoenician, and Greek merchants exchanged raw materials, products, technical skills and ideas, artistic motifs, and prototypes (one such place is Al Mina, on the northern Levantine coast, at the mouth of the Orontes River; Boardman 1999). This does not rule out the occasional dispatch of diplomatic gifts or tribute that established direct links between Cypriot vassals and the Assyrian king. But the formal episodes of tribute or gifts, the only ones related by the Assyrian sources, are likely to have been just the tip of the iceberg.

To return to Macartney's embassy to China, his objective in offering the most interesting British products to the Chinese emperor was to promote trade relations between the two countries, developing a commercial network under the auspices of the British crown. We know that Macartney's embassy failed in this point: the Celestial Emperor graciously accepted the tribute but did not show any interest in establishing trade relations with Britain. The result of the diplomatic exchanges between Assyria and Cyprus was, as far as we can appreciate it, different than Macartney's case. There was an economic reorientation within Cyprus, directed toward adapting the exploitation strategies of the kingdoms to the growing needs of their great eastern customer, the Neo-Assyrian Empire.

Assyria's most significant impact on Cyprus was thus economic, which also affected the island's political situation. This process has been argued persuasively by Maria Iacovou (2002, 2006, 2008, 2013), and it is perceptible from a *longue durée* perspective. Cypriot kingdoms, including many inland polities at the time of Esarhaddon (Chytroi, Ledra, Tamassos, Idalion), were led to reshape and recombine their territorial organization in order to concentrate under the control of the island's main harbor towns (Salamis, Kition, Amathus, Kourion, Palaepaphos, Soloi, joined sometime later by Marion and Lapethos) the entire process of the exploitation of copper, from extraction to export (Iacovou 2002, 2006, 2008, 2013) (figure 9.4). Starting at the time of Neo-Assyrian expansion in the Levant, this process culminated 300 years later with the annexation of Idalion by Kition around the mid-fifth century BCE.

This mainly economic reorientation and reshaping of Cypriot kingdoms' territories, starting during the Cypro-Geometric III Period, was accompanied by a substantial evolution in Cypriot civilization. Economic and political competition for territorial control and new exploitation strategies led to the development of more self-conscious, regionally differentiated material cultures that radiated from the main urban and political centers to the surrounding hinterland. We can appreciate them in the elaboration of distinct artistic styles (related to the production of pottery, terracottas, and sculpture; Fourrier 2007a, 2007b), as well as in the use of different languages and writing systems and the adoption of distinctive burial customs. By the Cypro-Geometric Period, the existence of regional stylistic distinctions in pottery production, with specificities in the selection of shapes, fabrics, and decorative motifs, was a clue to identifying emerging political and cultural identities (Georgiadou 2014). In addition, a network of extra-urban sanctuaries, some of them situated in the frontier zones, appeared beginning in the Cypro-Geometric III Period; these sanctuaries contributed to the negotiation of territorial strategies and

FIGURE 9.4. *Map of Cyprus, showing the main Archaic and Classical centers (©Anne Flammin, Yves Montmessin, Alexandre Rabot / UMR 5189 HiSoMA)*

established the boundaries of cultural and political influence on the island (Fourrier 2007a, 121–24; Papantoniou 2012; Fourrier 2013) (figure 9.5). Among the main extra-urban sanctuaries, Arsos (at the boundary between Salamis and Idalion) and Agia Eirini (in the stylistic area of Soloi) have provided extensive evidence for a renewed approach to the political and cultural influence of the capital cities on their territories (Fourrier 2007a, 35–36 [Arsos], 89–92 [Agia Eirini]). A great variety of cultural, economic, and political factors thus contributed to the reshaping of the Cypriot territory into a patchwork of territorial monarchies engaged for centuries to come in negotiating boundaries and areas of influence.

This is the time when the first Cypriot written evidence appears,[9] documenting from the seventh century BCE onward the existence of Cypriot kings, especially in the Paphos area. This evidence includes prestige items (gold and silver "Cypro-Phoenician" bowls, gold bracelets) inscribed in the local Cypro-Syllabic script and in Greek Arcado-Cypriot dialect. The names Akestor and Etewandros (the second one matching the king of Paphos in the lists of Esarhaddon and Ashurbanipal) are accompanied by the title "king of Paphos," *to-pa-po-pa-si-le-wo-se* (*tō Papō pasilewos*; ICS 180a and 176). Additional written evidence concerns a prince (Diweithemis, the *pasilewadas*, "the king's son"), possibly from Kourion (ICS 178), and an unnamed king represented in a sacred

FIGURE 9.5. *Map of Cyprus, showing the area of cultural influence of each kingdom according to terracotta stylistic analysis (after Fourrier 2007a, 113, fig. 9).*

banquet together with the Great Goddess of Cyprus, the Kypromedousa ("the one who reigns over Cyprus"; ICS 179; Hermary 2000) (figure 9.6).

Cypriot kings are the main actors in and beneficiaries of the transformations described above. They first appear in the archaeological evidence dated to the ninth–eighth centuries BCE (Cypro-Geometric III Period), in funerary assemblages (the rich royal tombs of Salamis, with parallels at Idalion, Tamassos, Amathus, Kition, and Kourion), and later in sacred contexts, which reveal the royal presence through massive offerings and royal iconography (Satraki 2013). The first known Cypriot royal palace, at Amathus, was also established in this period, at the end of the ninth–beginning of the eighth centuries BCE (Alpe, Petit, and Velho 2007). Cypriot kings appropriated a definite set of symbols, mainly of Egyptian origin (but mostly adopted through the Phoenician filter), to create a distinctive iconographic repertoire, which is particularly recognizable in the Archaic statuary but also on ivory and metal objects (Satraki 2013) (figure 9.7).

The impact of the opening of the Neo-Assyrian market to Cyprus is thus indirect but still important. It contributed to a substantial evolution of the Cypriot political and economic landscape and stimulated the transformation of Early Iron Age Cypriot polities into territorial kingdoms. Established since at least

FIGURE 9.6. *Silver bowl with incised decoration and Cypro-Syllabic inscription, said to be from Kourion, late eighth–seventh centuries BCE. Courtesy, Metropolitan Museum of Art, New York City, 74.51.4557 (© Metropolitan Museum of Art).*

the eleventh century, Cypriot polities went through a "foundation" process in the first centuries, characterized by a highly fragmented territorial pattern, a common material civilization, and the existence of competing local elites struggling for political power (Iacovou 2013). At the end of this obscure and poorly documented phase, thanks to the economic and political opportunities opened by access to the eastern markets, the now well-established Cypriot kings were able to impose their authority on the surrounding territories; develop new cultural, ideological, and religious agendas; and concentrate on and manage economic activities such as the exploitation of copper mines and building timber. The timber appears as a highly valued Cypriot good in Assyrian sources (Cannavò 2007), and it is mentioned as a precious material in the image of the merchant ship of Tyre found in Ezekiel 27. Incidentally, this confirms that Cypriot goods

FIGURE 9.7. *Limestone colossal head from Golgoi, late seventh–sixth centuries BCE. Courtesy, Metropolitan Museum of Art, New York City, 74.51.2857 (© Metropolitan Museum of Art).*

made it to Near Eastern markets through the Tyrian gateway (Ezekiel 27:6: "Of oaks from Bashan they made your oars, your deck they made with ivory inlaid in the cypress wood from the islands of Kittîm," author's translation).

CYPRIOT QARTHADASHT: THE HISTORY OF A NEW KINGDOM

Phoenician facilitation of Cypriot participation in Neo-Assyrian trade networks is clearly suggested by Assyrian and biblical sources; however, when looking for actual evidence of a Phoenician presence in Cyprus, we face an ambiguous, largely incomplete picture. As is well-known, the Phoenicians are credited with a widespread but limited presence on the island beginning in the ninth century BCE. That presence is scattered and without permanent settlements, with the notable exception of Kition, which is reputed to have been a Tyrian colony established around the end of the ninth century (Masson and Sznycer 1972; Gjerstad 1979; Aubet 2001, 42–45). Only in recent years has the "Phoenician colonization narrative" undergone substantial criticism and revision (Smith 2008, 2009; Fourrier 2013, 113–17; Iacovou 2014; Cannavò 2015b). As a result, we are now well aware of the difficulties facing those who try to identify a specific exogenous Phoenician material culture related to a presumed colonial movement in Cyprus. Not even in Kition is it possible to detect a distinctive material cultural assemblage related to the supposed Phoenician colonization of the late ninth century BCE, even if the progressive "Phoenicization" of Kitian civilization during the Archaic Period (750–475 BCE) is undeniable (Fourrier 2013, 113). Amathus is the only Cypriot site from the Archaic Period with evidence for separate, ethnically marked burial and cultural practices pointing to Phoenician presence, but its interpretation is far from straightforward (Christou 1998; Alpe 2007; Fourrier and Petit-Aupert 2007).

At the same time, several documents—a Cypriot Phoenician inscription of unknown provenance (CIS I 5, KAI 31, TSSI III 17; on the discovery of the inscription, see Masson 1985; on its chronology, see Matthäus 2010) and the aforementioned lists of Esarhaddon and Ashurbanipal—provide evidence for the existence of a Phoenician site named Qarthadasht, "New Town," in Cyprus, dated between the mid-eighth and mid-seventh centuries BCE. The *skn*, "governor" of this town, claimed to have been "a servant of Hiram, king of Sidon" sometime between 739 and 730 BCE (figure 9.8). By the time of Esarhaddon (680–669 BCE), Qarthadasht is mentioned as an independent kingdom. It disappears from the written evidence after the parallel mention in Ashurbanipal's list.[10] Various identifications have been proposed for Qarthadasht, the most convincing of them being with Amathus or Kition, but so far there are no conclusive arguments in favor of either of them (for Amathus, see especially Hermary 1996; Smith 2008, 272–74; for Kition, Gjerstad 1979, 234–37; Yon 2004, 19–22; Cannavò 2015b, 151–52).

Sennacherib's attack on Tyre in 701 BCE, and the subsequent weakening of the city in the economic and political landscape of the Levant, broke the bridge between Cyprus and Assyria. But Cypriot kingdoms were able to get over the shock and continue their profitable exchanges with Assyria through

FIGURE 9.8. *Phoenician dedication to Baal of Lebanon by the skn of Qarthadasht, found in Cyprus, 739–730 BCE. Courtesy, Bibliothèque nationale de France, Paris, Cabinet des Médailles, BB 2291 (after CIS I 5, pl. IV).*

other channels. It is highly probable that Qarthadasht obtained its independence from Tyre around 701 BCE. The Greek (or Greek-looking) name of its king in the lists of Esarhaddon and Ashurbanipal (Damusi) suggests that this Phoenician-named settlement was not entirely or exclusively Phoenician (Saporetti 1976, 86n30; Jas 1999).

The evidence concerning the political status of Kition in the same period is scanty. A passage of Menander of Ephesus quoted by Flavius Josephus (*Jewish Antiquities* 9.284) suggests that shortly before the end of the eighth century BCE, Kition was politically dependent on Tyre. Evidence is then lacking on this issue until the beginning of the Classical Period, when Kition began to strike coins under a powerful (possibly new) independent royal dynasty that soon conquered Idalion. Antoine Hermary (1996) argues that Kition obtained its independence from Tyre only after the Persian Wars, with substantial Persian support against its neighbors, Salamis and Idalion. For Maria Iacovou, too, Kition could not have been an independent kingdom during the Archaic Period since it lacked access to the inland copper mines. It probably functioned as a specialized second-level settlement (harbor) dependent on the inland royal capital of Idalion (Iacovou 2008). For Joanna S. Smith, Phoenician control of Kition was artificially maintained by Assyria; thus, Kition became an autonomous kingdom only after the downfall of the Neo-Assyrian Empire at the end of the seventh century BCE (Smith 2009; cf. Fourrier 2009). The definition of the political status of Kition and particularly of its relations with Tyre between the end of the eighth century and the fifth century BCE depends exclusively on the interpretation of a set of ambiguous and debatable data that emerge from analysis of the material evidence and provide no definite conclusions on the matter. These data, as we shall see below, are nevertheless essential to appreciate the pivotal role that town played in Cypro-Assyrian relations, as the erection of the stele in Larnaca and the history of the ethnonym Kittîm suggest.[11]

If it is correct that Kition controlled a remarkably reduced territory during the Archaic Period, particularly compared to Salamis, Idalion, and even Amathus, other elements suggest nevertheless that it was not a second-level settlement (Fourrier 2013, 114–16). Stylistically original Kitian products, even if few spread outside the main urban center, are detectable beginning in the eighth century BCE, combining the local Cypriot tradition with models from the Phoenician mainland (Fourrier 2007a, 53–61, 115–16). The "Phoenicization" of Kition's material culture proceeds throughout the Archaic Period, with the progressive affirmation of Phoenician as the main language and script and the adoption of Phoenician-type shapes, wares, and techniques in the local ceramic repertoire (Bikai 1981, 1987, 2003; Fourrier 2014). Some elite burials attest to the existence of an upper class imitating royal customs that were widespread all over the island (Hadjisavvas 2007, 2014, 1–33).

If Kition bears little resemblance to a second-level settlement (Fourrier 2013, 113–17), its progressive "Phoenicization" proceeding side by side with the elaboration of a distinctive cultural and political identity invites us to situate the acquisition of its independence, according to this evidence, fairly early in the Archaic Period, certainly no later than the seventh century BCE. Menander's text provides the relevant information that as early as the time of Lulî (whom he calls Eloulaios),[12] during the last quarter of the seventh century BCE, Kition had tried to revolt against Tyre's control. It thus seems reasonable to date Kition's independence from the years of Sennacherib's attack against Tyre, since the Phoenician motherland could hardly have controlled any rebellious territory after that date. Assyria's indifference to anything that happened "in the middle of the sea" does not support the assumption of continuous Assyrian backing of Tyre's claims over its possessions, especially after Assyria decided to diminish the restless Phoenician city by depriving it of the majority of its territory (Briquel-Chatonnet 1992, 193–200; Aubet 2001, 45–49, 68–74).

It appears, then, from our evidence that the two Cypriot settlements of Kition and Qarthadasht were both under Tyrian control at some time during the eighth century BCE and that they both threw off that control at the very end of that century. One would thus expect to find Kition named as an independent kingdom in the lists of Esarhaddon and Ashurbanipal. The fact that it is not so named might be because it had fallen under the control of Idalion, but this seems unlikely considering the emergence of its cultural and political identity and the Phoenician character of its material culture that increased throughout the Archaic Period. On the other side, Qarthadasht, after being registered in Esarhaddon and Ashurbanipal lists, does not appear in any later evidence.

It seems natural to identify the parallel and complementary Phoenician settlements of Kition and Qarthadasht with one another. Cypriot Qarthadasht was merely a Kition avatar, which lasted more or less as long as its dependence on Tyre and died out as soon as the Kitians recovered their autonomy and created their own kingdom—a Cypriot kingdom of (almost exclusively) Phoenician language and Cypro-Phoenician material culture. Kition, even when it was a Tyrian-controlled settlement in the eighth century, was never purely and exclusively a Phoenician "New Town." The Phoenicians, who had probably been entrenched there since the end of the ninth century BCE, had renewed a 500-year-old Cypriot site that had been in decline since the Late Bronze Age. There were monumental buildings still visible in the Kathari area and a local population documented by limited but concrete funerary evidence (Cannavò 2015b). The Phoenician renewal of the town and one century (or even less) of Tyrian control did not erase local Cypriot elements. Instead, Phoenician elements mingled with local elements to create a new Kitian-Phoenician material cultural assemblage that is fundamentally Cypriot and clearly perceptible in the Archaic Period.

An explanation for the kingdom's reduced territory in the Archaic Period can be found in the nature and history of the site. The relatively late formation of the politically autonomous polity and its geographic position between the two more precocious kingdoms of Salamis and Idalion make sense of the limits it encountered in establishing its territory. The essentially commercial nature of the settlement under Tyrian control, oriented toward the export of goods (copper, wood) coming from the island's interior and directed toward Assyria, encouraged a specialization of the newly born kingdom as a privileged gateway for the commercial flux directed toward the east.

In any case, regardless of whether one is disposed to endorse the proposed identification of Cypriot Qarthadasht with Kition, Phoenician involvement in Cypriot affairs during the Archaic Period appears strongly in both archaeological and textual evidence. Both Kition and Qarthadasht (either two distinct settlements or one and the same) constitute the bridgehead for the establishment of Assyrian (through Phoenician) penetration into the island and its economic and politic dynamics.

KISSING THE FEET OF THE GREAT KING: CONCLUDING REMARKS ON IDEOLOGY

The picture that emerges from the analysis of textual as well as archaeological evidence, both from Cyprus and from the Near East, is one of mutual discovery and ideological construction. For Assyria, Cyprus was the far western piece of a large and elaborate mosaic, a rich and almost fabulous country offering precious gifts and qualifying as one of the loyal servants of the empire. No matter how frequently and in which manner Assyria could claim its "tribute," the mere existence on the island of a monument representing Assyrian royal power (the Sargon II stele) ideologically extended the empire's territory far west beyond the sea. The occasional presence and collaboration of Cypriot vassals (or even just Cypriot products) at the imperial court was enough to justify the ideological representation of foreign kings, hands filled with gifts, kissing the feet of the Assyrian monarch.

On the Cypriot side, there is hardly any trace of that servitude. To the contrary, on Cyprus the period of Assyrian "control" is a phase of economic development, of political and ideological construction, of identity formation. The Assyrian royal ideology might have eventually inspired some of the Cypriot kings' iconographic and artistic choices (even if Phoenician mediation seems once again particularly important), but the process that transformed Cypriot Early Iron Age polities into territorial monarchies had more to do with internal economic strategies than with direct political Assyrian or Phoenician influence.

The history of Cypriot-Assyrian relations lasted less than a century and raised ideological, political, and economic concerns for the small polities on the island. While it had profound implications on the island, it had almost no repercussions for the empire, whose main concerns were far from a remote island floating in the middle of the Sea of the Setting Sun.

NOTES

I warmly thank Craig W. Tyson and Virginia Herrmann for their kind invitation to contribute to this volume, for their useful and stimulating remarks, and for the invaluable improvements to my English text. Thanks also to the two anonymous reviewers for their suggestions and commentaries.

1. The name seems to have survived in Cyprus itself, where it is still attested in some Greek and especially Phoenician documents of the fourth century BCE: the bilingual dedicatory inscription from Tamassos, ICS 216, for Apollo Alasiotas / *Ršp 'lhyts*, and a still unpublished ostracon from the archives of Idalion dating from "the year 1 of

Antigonos and Demetrios, in the year 1 of Alashiya," that is, at the very beginning of the Hellenistic Period (Hadjicosti and Amadasi 2014). The fact that the Neo-Assyrian texts use the new name Iadnana when referring to Cyprus instead of the second millennium name Alashiya suggests that the latter had been forgotten by that time.

2. As Antoine Hermary pointed out to me, a kudurru-stele of Marduk-apla-iddina II, also in Berlin (VA 2663, dating from 715 BCE), is said to have been found in Cyprus (André-Salvini 2008, 136, no. 93, bibliography), but I have not found any further information about this claim.

3. Among the studies reposing on this interpretation are Smith (2008); Radner (2010).

4. In the Assyrian texts, Lulî is invariably titled "king of Sidon," but in the passage quoted below, he is said to be fleeing from Tyre. On the long-debated identification of the kingdoms of Tyre and Sidon during the ninth and eighth centuries BCE, see Briquel-Chatonnet (1992, 65–66); Frahm (2001); Na'aman (2006); Radner (2010, 439–40n55); Boyes (2012). I maintain the assumption that Lulî, king of Sidon (and reigning over Tyre) in Assyrian sources, is the same as Eloulaios, king of Tyre in Greek sources.

5. Cf. the parallel passages that include some significant textual variants: Grayson and Novotny (2012, 63, no. 4, 32 ["Rassam Cylinder"], no. 22, 175, ii, 37–40 ["Chicago Oriental Institute Prism"], no. 23, 192, ii, 35–38); Grayson and Novotny (2014, 48, no. 42, 7–10).

6. See also Porter (2010) (on the literary construction of the passage); Cannavò (2007) (on the building material offered to Esarhaddon by Levantine and Cypriot kings).

7. Sennacherib had at his service Cypriot as well as Phoenician sailors from Tyre and Sidon (Grayson and Novotny 2014, 82, no. 46, 57–62).

8. Iaman, related to the biblical Yawan and the Greek Ionia, indicates in the Neo-Assyrian sources the land of western (mainly Greek) pirates, particularly active in Cilicia and the Levant (Brinkman 1989; Haider 1996; Mayer 1996; Bagg 2007, 123–24; Rollinger 2007;). In the building inscription on an alabaster tablet from Aššur, Esarhaddon claimed that "all the kings from the middle of the sea, from the land of Iadnana, the land of Iaman to the land of Tarsisi, threw themselves at my feet: I received their heavy tribute" (Leichty 2011, 134–37, lines 10–11; author's translation). The identification of Iadnana with Iaman, which are simply juxtaposed in the Akkadian text, is not certain, as stated in Muhly (2009, 26).

9. Even if the most ancient known Cypriot inscription in Greek dates from the tenth century BCE, its inclusion in the corpus of first millennium Cypro-Syllabic inscriptions has been disputed; after a two-century gap, the first inscriptions assuredly written in the Cypro-Syllabic script date from the eighth century BCE (Egetmeyer 2013).

10. The frequently evoked "Temple Tariff" from Kition-*Bamboula* (an ostracon with administrative records of a palatial nature; CIS I 86, KAI 37, TSSI III 33; see Yon 2004, 184–85, no. 1078), dating from the fourth century BCE, should not be included among the evidence documenting Cypriot Qarthadasht (Cannavò 2015b, 151).

11. Kittîm, literally the gentilic for the inhabitants of Kition, becomes in Hebrew a metonym for all Cypriots and later even Greeks and westerners generally, such as the Macedonians and Romans (Cannavò 2010, 180–88).

12. See note 4, above.

ABBREVIATIONS

CIS = *1881–1962. Corpus Inscriptionum Semiticarum. Parisiis: E Reipublicae Typographeo.*

ICS = *Masson, Olivier. 1983. Les inscriptions chypriotes syllabiques: Recueil critique et commenté. Études chypriotes 1. Paris: Éditions De Boccard.*

KAI = *Donner, Herbert, and Wolfgang Röllig. 1966–69, 2002. Kanaanäische und Aramäische Inschriften, 3 vols. Wiesbaden: Harrassowitz Verlag.*

TSSI = *Gibson, John C.L. 1971–82. Textbook of Syrian Semitic Inscriptions. Oxford: Oxford University Press.*

WORKS CITED

Alpe, Laurence. 2007. "La question du sanctuaire de Limassol-*Komissariato*: Modalités de la présence phénicienne dans le royaume d'Amathonte." *CCEC* 37: 265–82.

Alpe, Laurence, Thierry Petit, and Gilles Velho. 2007. "Sondage stratigraphique au palais d'Amathonte en 1997: Nature et chronologie du premier état." *BCH* 131 (1): 1–35. https://doi.org/10.3406/bch.2007.7454.

André-Salvini, Béatrice, ed. 2008. *Babylone: Catalogue de l'exposition.* Paris: Hazan and Musée du Louvre.

Aubet, María Eugenia. 2001. *The Phoenicians and the West: Politics, Colonies, and Trade.* Cambridge: Cambridge University Press. (Originally published in Spanish as *Tiro y las colonias fenicias de Occidente.* Barcelona: Bellaterra, 1987, 1994.)

Bagg, Ariel M. 2007. *Die Orts- und Gewässernamen der neuassyrischen Zeit, Teil 1: Die Levante.* Wiesbaden: Dr. Ludwig Reichert.

Barnett, Richard D. 1956. "Phoenicia and the Ivory Trade." *Archaeology* 9: 87–97.

Bikai, Patricia M. 1981. "The Phoenician Imports." In *Excavations at Kition IV: The Non-Cypriote Pottery*, ed. Vassos Karageorghis et al., 23–35. Nicosia: Department of Antiquities, Cyprus.

Bikai, Patricia M. 1987. *The Phoenician Pottery of Cyprus*. Nicosia: A. G. Leventis Foundation.

Bikai, Patricia M. 2003. "Statistical Observations on the Phoenician Pottery of Kition." In *Excavations at Kition VI: The Phoenician and Later Levels, Part II*, by Vassos Karageorghis, 207–57. Nicosia: Department of Antiquities, Cyprus.

Boardman, John. 1999. "The Excavated History of Al Mina." In *Ancient Greeks West and East*, ed. Gocha R. Tsetskhladze, 135–61. Leiden: Brill.

Borger, Rykle. 1996. *Beiträge zum Inschriftenwerk Assurbanipals*. Wiesbaden: Harrassowitz Verlag.

Boyes, Philip J. 2012. "'The King of the Sidonians': Phoenician Ideologies and the Myth of the Kingdom of Tyre-Sidon." *BASOR* 365: 33–44.

Brinkman, John A. 1989. "The Akkadian Words for 'Ionia' and 'Ionian.'" In *Daidalikon: Studies in Memory of Raymond V. Schoder, S.J.*, ed. Robert F. Sutton, 53–71. Wauconda, IL: Bolchazy-Carducci.

Briquel-Chatonnet, Françoise. 1992. *Les relations entre les cités de la côte phénicienne et les royaumes d'Israël et de Juda*. Leuven: Peeters.

Cannavò, Anna. 2007. "The Role of Cyprus in the Neo-Assyrian Economic System: Analysis of the Textual Evidence." *Russell Sage Foundation Journal of the Social Sciences* 35: 179–90.

Cannavò, Anna. 2010. "Between Iadnana and Kittim: Eastern Views of Archaic Cyprus." In *POCA 2007: Postgraduate Cypriot Archaeology Conference*, ed. Anna Satraki and Skevi Christodoulou, 169–96. Cambridge: Cambridge Scholars Publishing.

Cannavò, Anna. 2015a. "Cyprus and the Near East in the Neo-Assyrian Period." *Kyprios Charakter: History, Archaeology, and Numismatics of Ancient Cyprus*. kyprioscharacter.eie.gr/en/t/AL.

Cannavò, Anna. 2015b. "The Phoenicians and Kition: Continuities and Breaks." In *Transformations and Crisis in the Mediterranean: "Identity" and Interculturality in the Levant and Phoenician West during the 12th–8th Centuries BCE*, ed. Giuseppe Garbati and Tatiana Pedrazzi, 141–53. Pisa: Fabrizio Serra Editore.

Casabonne, Olivier, and Julien De Vos. 2005. "Chypre, Rhodes et l'Anatolie méridionale: La question ionienne." *RAnt* 2: 83–102.

Christou, Demos. 1998. "Cremations in the Western Necropolis of Amathus." In *Eastern Mediterranean: Cyprus-Dodecanese-Crete 16th–6th Cent. BC*, ed. Vassos Karageorghis and Nikolaos Stampolidis, 207–15. Athens: University of Crete and A. G. Leventis Foundation.

Desideri, Paolo, and Anna Margherita Jasink. 1990. *Cilicia: Dall'età di Kizzuwatna alla conquista macedone*. Firenze: Casa editrice Le Lettere.

Egetmeyer, Markus. 2013. "From the Cypro-Minoan to the Cypro-Greek Syllabaries: Linguistic Remarks on the Script Reforms." In *Syllabic Writing on Cyprus and Its Context*, ed. Philippa M. Steele, 107–32. Cambridge: Cambridge University Press. https://doi.org/10.1017/CBO9781139208482.007.

Fourrier, Sabine. 2007a. *La coroplastie chypriote archaïque: Identités culturelles et politiques à l'époque des royaumes.* Lyon: Maison de l'Orient et de la Méditerranée.

Fourrier, Sabine. 2007b. "La constitution d'identités régionales à Chypre à l'époque archaïque." *Pallas* 73: 115–24.

Fourrier, Sabine. 2009. "Review of *Art and Society in Cyprus from the Bronze Age into the Iron Age*, by Joanna S. Smith." *Topoi* 17: 591–601.

Fourrier, Sabine. 2013. "Constructing the Peripheries: Extra-Urban Sanctuaries and Peer-Polity Interaction in Iron Age Cyprus." *BASOR* 370: 103–22.

Fourrier, Sabine. 2014. "The Ceramic Repertoire of the Classical Period Necropolis of Kition." In *The Phoenician Period Necropolis of Kition, II*, by Sophocles Hadjisavvas, 135–81. Nicosia: Department of Antiquities, Cyprus.

Fourrier, Sabine, and Catherine Petit-Aupert. 2007. "Un sanctuaire phénicien du royaume d'Amathonte: Agios Tychonas-*Asvestoton.*" *CCEC* 37: 251–64.

Frahm, Eckart. 2001. "Lulî." In *PNA*, vol. 2, part II: *L–N*, ed. Heather D. Baker, 668–69. Helsinki: Neo-Assyrian Text Corpus Project.

Fuchs, Andreas. 1993. *Die Inschriften Sargons II: aus Khorsabad*. Göttingen: Cuvillier.

Gelio, Roberto. 1981. "La délégation envoyée par Gygès, roi de Lydie. Un cas de propagande idéologique." In *Assyrian Royal Inscriptions: New Horizons in Literary, Ideological, and Historical Analysis*, ed. Frederick Mario Fales, 203–24. Rome: Istituto per l'Oriente.

Georgiadou, Anna. 2014. "Productions et styles régionaux dans l'artisanat céramique de Chypre à l'époque géométrique (XIe–VIIIe s. av. J.-C.)." *BCH* 138: 361–85.

Gjerstad, Einar. 1979. "The Phoenician Colonization and Expansion in Cyprus." *RDAC*: 230–54.

Grayson, A. Kirk, and Jamie Novotny. 2012. *The Royal Inscriptions of Sennacherib, King of Assyria (704–681 BC): Part 1*. Winona Lake, IN: Eisenbrauns.

Grayson, A. Kirk, and Jamie Novotny. 2014. *The Royal Inscriptions of Sennacherib, King of Assyria (704–681 BC): Part 2*. Winona Lake, IN: Eisenbrauns.

Hadjicosti, Maria, and Maria Giulia Amadasi. 2014. "Το φοινικικό αρχείο του Ιδαλίου (To foinikiko archeio tou Idaliou)." Paper presented at the Cyprus Seminar of the Cycladic Art Museum, Athens, June 2.

Hadjisavvas, Sophocles. 2007. "The Phoenician Penetration in Cyprus as Documented in the Necropolis of Kition." *CCEC* 37: 185–95.

Hadjisavvas, Sophocles. 2014. *The Phoenician Period Necropolis of Kition, II: Nicosia*. Nicosia: Department of Antiquities, Cyprus.

Haider, Peter W. 1996. "Griechen im Vorderen Orient und in Ägypten bis ca. 590 v. Chr." In *Wege zur Genese griechischer Identität: Die Bedeutung der früharchaischen Zeit*, ed. Christoph Ulf, 59–115. Berlin: Akademie Verlag. https://doi.org/10.1515 /9783050072197-003.

Hermary, Antoine. 1996. "Le statut de Kition avant le Ve s. av. J.-C." In *Alle soglie della classicità: il Mediterraneo tra tradizione e innovazione: Studi in onore di Sabatino Moscati*, ed. Enrico Acquaro, 1:223–29. Pisa: Istituti editoriali e poligrafici internazionali.

Hermary, Antoine. 2000. "Déesse plutot que reine? À propos d'une coupe en argent de la collection Cesnola." *CCEC* 30: 67–78.

Iacovou, Maria. 2002. "From Ten to Naught: Formation, Consolidation, and Abolition of Cyprus' Iron Age Polities." *CCEC* 32: 73–87.

Iacovou, Maria. 2006. "From the Mycenaean *qa-si-re-u* to the Cypriote *pa-si-le-wo-se*: The Basileus in the Kingdoms of Cyprus." In *Ancient Greece: From the Mycenaean Palaces to the Age of Homer*, ed. Sigrid Deger-Jalkotzy and Irene S. Lemos, 315–35. Edinburgh: Edinburgh University Press.

Iacovou, Maria. 2008. "Cultural and Political Configurations in Iron Age Cyprus: The Sequel to a Protohistoric Episode." *AJA* 112 (4): 625–57. https://doi.org/10.3764 /aja.112.4.625.

Iacovou, Maria. 2013. "Historically Elusive and Internally Fragile Island Polities: The Intricacies of Cyprus's Political Geography in the Iron Age." *BASOR* 370: 15–47.

Iacovou, Maria. 2014. "'Working with the Shadows': In Search of the Myriad Forms of Social Complexity." In *Αθύρματα [Athyrmata]: Critical Essays on the Archaeology of the Eastern Mediterranean in Honour of E. Susan Sherratt*, ed. Yannis Galanakis, Toby Wilkinson, and John Bennet, 117–26. Oxford: Archaeopress.

Jas, Remko. 1999. "Damūsu." In *PNA*, vol. 1, part II: *B-G*, ed. Karen Radner, 375. Helsinki: Neo-Assyrian Text Corpus Project.

Josephus. 1926–65. Translated by Henry St. J. Thackeray et al. 10 vols. Loeb Classical Library. Cambridge: Harvard University Press.

Kaufman, Stephen A. 2007. "The Phoenician Inscription of the Incirli Trilingual: A Tentative Reconstruction and Translation." *Maarav* 14 (2): 7–26, 107–20.

Lanfranchi, Giovanni B. 2009. "A Happy Son of the King of Assyria: Warikas and the Çineköy Bilingual (Cilicia)." In *Of God(s), Trees, Kings, and Scholars: Neo-Assyrian and Related Studies in Honour of Simo Parpola*, ed. Mikko Luukko, Saana Svärd, and Raija Mattila, 127–50. Helsinki: Finnish Oriental Society.

Leichty, Erle. 2011. *The Royal Inscriptions of Esarhaddon, King of Assyria (680–669 BC)*. Winona Lake, IN: Eisenbrauns.

Lipiński, Edward. 1990. "Les Japhétites selon Gen 10,2–4 et 1 Chr 1,5–7." *ZAH* 3: 40–53.

Liverani, Mario. 2003. *Oltre la Bibbia: Storia antica di Israele*. Bari, Italy: Editori Laterza.

Luckenbill, Daniel D. 1914. "Jadanan and Javan (Danaans and Ionians)." *ZA* 28: 92–99.

Masson, Olivier. 1985. "La dédicace a Ba'al du Liban (CIS I, 5) et sa provenance probable de la région de Limassol." *Semitica* 35: 33–46.

Masson, Olivier. 1992. "Encore les royaumes chypriotes dans la liste d'Esarhaddon." *CCEC* 18: 27–30.

Masson, Olivier, and Maurice Sznycer. 1972. *Recherches sur les Phéniciens à Chypre*. Geneva: Droz.

Matthäus, Hartmut. 2010. "Die Weihung des Statthalters von Qarthadašt an den Baal des Libanon (CIS I Nr. 5)." *CCEC* 40: 125–40.

Mayer, Walter. 1996. "Zypern und Ägäis aus der Sicht der Staaten Vorderasiens in der 1: Hälfte des 1, Jahrtausends." *UF* 28: 463–84.

Merrillees, Robert S. 2016. "Studies on the Provenances of the Stele of Sargon II from Larnaca (Kition) and the Two So-Called Dhali (Idalion) Silver Bowls in the Louvre." *CCEC* 46: 349–86.

Muhly, James D. 2009. "The Origin of the Name 'Ionian.'" In *Cyprus and the East Aegean: Intercultural Contacts from 3000 to 500 BC*, ed. Vassos Karageorghis and Ourania Kouka, 23–30. Nicosia: A. G. Leventis Foundation.

Na'aman, Nadav. 1998. "Sargon II and the Rebellion of the Cypriote Kings against Shilta of Tyre." *Or* 67: 239–47.

Na'aman, Nadav. 2001. "The Conquest of Yadnana According to the Inscriptions of Sargon II." In *Historiography in the Cuneiform World*, ed. Tzvi Abusch, Paul-Alain Beaulieu, John Huehnergard, Peter Machinist, and Piotr Steinkeller, 357–63. Bethesda, MD: CDL Press.

Na'aman, Nadav. 2006. "Eloulaios/Ululaiu in Josephus, Antiquities IX, 284." *NABU* 6: 5–6.

Papantoniou, Giorgos. 2012. "Cypriot Sanctuaries and Religion in the Early Iron Age: Views from Before and After." In *Cyprus and the Aegean in the Early Iron Age: The Legacy of Nicolas Coldstream*, ed. Maria Iacovou, 285–319. Nicosia: Bank of Cyprus Cultural Foundation.

Porter, Barbara N. 2010. "Notes on the Role of the Kings of the Sea in Esarhaddon's Nineveh A Inscription." In *Gazing on the Deep: Ancient Near Eastern and Other Studies in Honor of Tzvi Abusch*, ed. Jeffrey Stackert, Barbara N. Porter, and David P. Wright, 181–87. Bethesda, MD: CDL Press.

Radner, Karen. 2010. "The Stele of Sargon II of Assyria at Kition: A Focus for an Emerging Cypriot Identity?" In *Interkulturalität in der Alten Welt: Vorderasien, Hellas, Ägypten und die vielfältigen Ebenen des Kontakts*, ed. Robert Rollinger, Birgit Gufler, Martin Lang, and Irene Madreiter, 429–49. Wiesbaden: Harrassowitz Verlag.

Reyes, Andres T. 1994. *Archaic Cyprus: A Study of the Textual and Archaeological Evidence*. Oxford: Clarendon.

Rollinger, Robert. 2007. "Zu Herkunft und Hintergrund der in altorientalischen Texten gennanten Griechen." In *Getrennte Wege? Kommunikation, Raum und Wahrnehmung in der alten Welt*, ed. Robert Rollinger, Andreas Luther, and Josef Wiesehöfer, 259–330. Frankfurt am Main: Verlag Antike.

Sahlins, Marshall. 1988. "Cosmologies of Capitalism: The Trans-Pacific Sector of 'the World System.'" *PBA* 74: 1–51.

Saporetti, Claudio. 1976. "Cipro nei testi neoassiri." In *Studi ciprioti e rapporti di scavo, fascicolo* 2:83–88. Rome: Edizioni dell'Ateneo.

Satraki, Anna. 2013. "The Iconography of *Basileis* in Archaic and Classical Cyprus: Manifestations of Royal Power in the Visual Record." *BASOR* 370: 123–44.

Smith, Joanna S. 2008. "Cyprus, the Phoenicians, and Kition." In *Beyond the Homeland: Markers in Phoenician Chronology*, ed. Claudia Sagona, 261–303. Leuven: Peeters.

Smith, Joanna S. 2009. *Art and Society in Cyprus from the Bronze Age into the Iron Age*. New York: Cambridge University Press.

Tekoğlu, Recai, André Lemaire, Ismet Ipek, and A. Kasim Tosun. 2000. "La bilingue royale louvito-phénicienne de Çineköy." *CRAIBL* 144 (3): 961–1006. https://doi.org/10.3406/crai.2000.16174.

Vermeylen, Jacques. 1992. "La 'table des nations' (*Gn* 10): Yaphet figure-t-il l'Empire perse?" *Transeuphratène* 5: 113–32.

Yon, Marguerite. 2004. *Kition dans les texts: Testimonia littéraires et épigraphiques et corpus des inscriptions.* Paris: Éditions Recherche sur les Civilisations.

10

Neo-Pericentrics

Bradley J. Parker[†]
(University of Utah)

The title of this book, which hinges on the phrase "imperial peripheries," betrays the fact that the present volume aims not only to examine two very important topics in the history of the ancient Near East but also to scrutinize the relationship between them. Empire is an important, if often illusive, subject that Carla M. Sinopoli (2001, 495) once characterized as an afterthought for most anthropologists. This, of course, is not the case for scholars of the ancient Near East who have been studying empire since the birth of the discipline (cf. Herrmann and Tyson, this volume). The difference here is that instead of focusing on specific details of Near Eastern empires, books like this belong to the growing body of literature that incorporates Near Eastern archaeology and history with what might be called the North American school of archaeological theory (cf. Trigger 1989). The literature that has sought to merge these fields has been very productive—first, because it has allowed Near Eastern scholars to come closer to understanding both the details of imperial histories and the larger processes that propel them and second, because it has made the ancient Near East more relevant to scholars specializing in other regions and time periods.[1]

By contrast, the study of peripheries has what might be considered a more sorted past. To begin with, the term itself still carries the baggage it picked up from two theories that are no longer central to

DOI: 10.5876/9781607328230.c010

anthropological thought: world-systems theory (Wallerstein 1974, 1980) and Central Place Theory (Christaller 1966). Both of these theories painted peripheries as the backwaters of history, ever subordinate, continually dependent, and always subject to the whims of the dominant metropol. Both of these theories were also taken up by archaeologists and adapted to fit a range of studies on the ancient world (e.g., Johnson 1972; Rowlands, Larsen, and Kristiansen 1987; Champion 1989; Chase-Dunn 1988; Chase-Dunn and Hall 1991, 1992, 1997; Algaze 1993). In spite of, or perhaps because of, the potential impediments to the use of this term, the current volume revitalizes the position of peripheries by coupling them with the study of empire. In this manner it is clear that this view, in effect, decenters empire by focusing on its edges rather than its heartland. In doing so it throws traditional views on the subject upside-down by highlighting the "centrality of the periphery." This is an important point because viewed in this way, peripheries are disassociated with their past and become a facet of the emerging literature on frontiers and borderlands. Unlike the study of empire, frontier theory is a relative newcomer not only to Near Eastern studies but also to archaeological theory (Rodseth and Parker 2005).

In summary, the literature on frontier theory sees zones of culture contact, which usually exist at the margins of complex polities, as the crucibles of historical change. In this light, "imperial periphery" does not simply refer to a group of studies that are not about the center of an empire. Instead, this title frames a group of studies that take areas outside or on the edges of empire as key to imperial dynamics, thus highlighting the role peripheries played in stimulating or even instigating processes of change.

In this short concluding chapter, I would like to continue down the path the present volume encourages us to follow by discussing three important, if unconventional, topics pertaining to imperial peripheries: *pericentrics*, *pathways of power*, and *imperial relationships*. In light of the case studies in the current volume, I end this chapter by proposing a new theoretical construct to decenter the study of ancient imperialism.

PERICENTICS

The current volume takes a unique stance both theoretically and geographically. Instead of reiterating imperial processes as they emanate from the imperial core, the chapters in this volume deliberately reorient the reader to consider ancient imperialism as a phenomenon that both affects political, social, and economic processes in the periphery and at the same time reverberates within and beyond the periphery to create a unique, important, and almost always overlooked dynamic—a dynamic Michael W. Doyle (1986) termed "pericentric." Pericentric forces are, simply put, events or processes that occur or emanate from the periphery of an imperial polity. According to Doyle (1986, 25), the pericentric approach "suggests that it is not in the metropoles but in the peripheries that the sources of imperialism can be discovered."

Pericentric views are intriguing if only because they force us to think about empire in a different way. However, one can also understand why pericentric histories are not easy to find, since such an orientation might completely alter what have become codified views of an imperial polity. Imagine, for example, what an uproar a pericentric rewrite of Grayson's famous chapters about the Neo-Assyrian Empire in the *Cambridge Ancient History* might cause (1991a, 1991b, 1991c).

Whether a particular scholar adheres to pericentric approaches, however, is not the point. The importance of this concept lies in the fact that pericentric phenomena can and often do have meaningful, lasting, and sometimes transformative effects on imperial cores. Numerous examples from various periods can be drawn from the literature on imperial frontiers and, in light of this volume, I dare say that many expansionist histories could (or should?) be rewritten as pericentric histories. Even Frederick Jackson Turner's original 1893 "Frontier Thesis," which was so instrumental in transforming the historiography of the American West, could be classified as a case study in pericentric imperial history. Indeed, many scholars have since acknowledged that in spite of its blatant ethnocentrism and underlying reliance on manifest destiny, the lasting value of Turner's thesis is that it reoriented American history away from the Atlantic World to the American West, that is, from the center to the periphery. A quick read of Turner's thesis can provide numerous examples of how pericentric agency shaped political processes, including, but not limited to, a long list of legislative actions that led Turner to the conclusion that "legislation with regard to land, tariff and internal improvements . . . was conditioned on frontier ideas and needs" (Turner 1938 [1893], 216).

Closer to home, in the Near East that is, one could easily cite Paul Zimansky's (1985) thesis that the formation of the Urartian state was largely a peripheral reaction to Assyrian expansion. An excellent example of pericentric phenomena, then, is the effect the rise of and competition with the Urartian state had on Assyrian history. This surprisingly resilient example raises the question of if or how much pericentric phenomena affected or even propelled Assyrian imperialism. Anyone familiar with the correspondence of Assyrian officials published by the State Archives of Assyria is well aware that a significant number of Assyrian letters concern the affairs of the Urartian state (Lanfranchi and Parpola 1990; Radner 2011). However, few Assyriologists have gone as far as to ask if the affairs of the Urartian state had a significant impact on the historical trajectory of the Assyrian Empire. A notable exception can be found in a rather obscure paper by Luis Levine. In this study, Levine (1977) argues convincingly that competition over the control of trade routes across the Iranian Plateau guided the military policies of Assyria, Babylonia, and Urartu during the first third of the first millennium BCE. The question is, is this an exception or the norm? How much of Assyria's foreign policy was shaped by events and processes taking place on the empire's peripheries, and did these phenomena significantly alter the empire's historical trajectory?

PATHWAYS TO POWER

Empires are often defined as expansive polities that impose various levels of control over the foreign peoples and landscapes they conquer. The problem is that it is very difficult to measure the degree or describe the type of control an imperial polity may hold over its subject territories. Furthermore, theorizing about the degree of control, even while acknowledging that imperial control may vary (D'Altroy 1992; Schreiber 1992; Sinopoli 1994, 2001; Parker 2001), leaves an almost insurmountable disconnect between theoretical constructs and the archaeological and historical data sets with which we all must contend. This situation stems from three fundamental flaws in the way we theorize about ancient empires. First, there is no clear definition of what we mean when we use the term *control* in reference to imperial systems. Second, the literature on ancient empires is not clear on what exactly it is that an empire aspires to control. And third, there is no clear discussion of how we might measure imperial control in the archaeological or historical records.

Issue 1: A Definition of "Control"

Generally speaking, most scholars would agree that control can be defined as "to influence, manipulate, or direct." This fits well with what we can observe in the archaeological and historical records. As umbrella organizations whose goal is to integrate and exploit diverse sociopolitical entities and natural landscapes (Parker 2011), empires assert control by influencing, manipulating, or directing events and processes that take place in subject territories.

ISSUE 2: WHAT AN EMPIRE ASPIRES TO CONTROL

If we agree that an empire aims to control the peoples and places over which it claims dominion by influencing, manipulating, or directing events and processes, the next question concerns *what* events and processes are influenced, manipulated, or directed.

It can be conclusively shown that empires intervene in the politics of subject territories; thus, one pathway to control is through the influence, manipulation, or direction of political institutions, events, and processes. In some cases it can be shown, for example, that the Assyrian Empire integrated existing political systems by coercing local elites, while in other cases indigenous political institutions may have been completely dismantled and replaced by a provincial administration. Imperial integration, especially as an empire moves into a consolidation phase (Schreiber 1987; Sinopoli 1994; Jennings and Alverez 2008), also means that empires attempt to assert social control. Some forms of social control, such as the abduction of cult statues, may not have had significant effects on the daily lives of imperial subjects (Cogan 1974). But others, like deportation and resettlement, for example, can be viewed as efforts to completely reorganize social systems (Postgate 1974, 1982, 2013; Oded 1979; Na'aman 1993; Wiggermann 2000; Rosenzweig 2016;). A second pathway to power is therefore a social pathway. Empires attempt to influence, manipulate, or direct the social systems of peoples over which they claim dominion. Finally, although integration is a key component of imperial systems, exploitation is equally, if not more, important (Liverani 1979; Parker 2011).[2] There is, in fact, widespread agreement among scholars that empires seek to influence, manipulate, or direct economic events and processes in subject territories. Examples of the economic exploitation of subject territories under Assyrian dominion are well documented. Thus, it can be conclusively shown that empires seek to control—that is, they seek to influence, manipulate, or direct political, social, and economic events and processes in their subject territories.

ISSUE 3: MEASURING IMPERIAL CONTROL

By clearly defining the parameters of our terms and then breaking them down into specific categories, we are in a much better position to define methodologies for measuring the degree of control an empire holds over its subject territories. It is my position that measuring the "degree of control" can best be achieved by considering what I call the "pathways" empires use to influence, manipulate, or direct events and processes in subject territories. Viewed from this perspective, it is not too difficult to imagine three pathways by which empires can assert control over conquered territories: political, social, and economic (Mann 1986; D'Altroy 1992). Empires exploit political pathways either by directly administering conquered groups or by co-opting local systems of government; empires employ social pathways by manipulating conquered peoples or by coercing potential subjects; and empires develop economic pathways through taxation, tribute, trade regulation, and the direct extraction of wealth or resources.

By breaking down the concept of "control" into specific pathways through which an empire might penetrate a subject territory, it becomes much easier to envision how a researcher might describe or measure the "degree of control" an empire holds over that territory. One might, for example, divide archaeological and textual data into political, social, or economic categories and then use those categorized data to theorize about the specific ways an empire controlled or attempted to control particular peoples or regions. In addition, focusing on particular pathways might also allow finer resolution within categories. Finally, such a system would also allow various, even relatively small, data sets to be included in the discussion and construction of theories about ancient empires.

IMPERIAL RELATIONSHIPS

Nearly every scholar who has written about ancient empires has, at one point or another, attempted to define the terms *empire* and *imperialism*. Interestingly, nearly all such definitions concentrate on what empires do. Empires expand. Empires conquer. Empires exploit. Empires control. Few definitions focus on what empires are or, more precisely, what empires are composed of. Empires are, as we know from nearly all the standard definitions, very complex polities. In spite of their complexity, at the most basic level empires are made up of relationships—complex overlapping relationships, but relationships nonetheless. From this point of view, one might say that empires are composed of multiple layers of interlocking political, social, and economic relationships imposed by an expansive polity on the myriad human and natural landscapes it encounters during the process of imperialism. I realize that this definition is vague and could be criticized on a number of fronts. However, I believe that beginning a discussion of empire from an unusual vantage point such as this might lead in some interesting directions.

So what does it mean to say that empire is a series of relationships? It is true that one could certainly view empire as a series of relationships between, for example, center and periphery, capital and provinces, emperor and subjects, or even between official and peasant. The key here, and where I think this definition veers off the path most traveled, is that we are considering the term *relationship* as integral to the definition of the polity we are attempting to study. This is crucial because regardless of whether one finds this type of definition useful, it focuses our attention in a very different way than more standard definitions do. The first observation that is brought to mind by this definition is the fact that relationships are reciprocal. Relationships are *between* things. Thus, if or when we focus on interactions between, for example, an imperial capital and one or more provinces, we are forced to consider both sides of the relationship. And second, viewing empire as a series of relationships highlights not just interactions between, for example, the capital and the provinces or the royalty and elites but also those between less celebrated actors or entities such as households, administrators, and colonists. Viewing empire from the vantage point of *imperial relationships* thus has the effect of both decentering our view of empire and encouraging us to include various types of analysis that might otherwise not be considered pertinent to the study of the imperial polity.

THE PATHWAYS AND RELATIONSHIPS OF PERICENTRICS

The chapters in the present volume both apply and challenge the original assumptions of the pericentric model and can thus be seen as new views on the pathways and relationships of pericentics. Avraham Faust, for example, argues that Neo-Assyrian conquest and annexation left large parts of the southern Levant devastated. However, the data suggest that in spite of the fact that these areas were incorporated into the Neo-Assyrian provincial system, they never became productive imperial holdings. Population remained low, and there was very little economic development. The opposite was true of the southern part of Faust's study area. This region, which remained outside the Assyrian provincial system, saw an economic boom. Although at least some of this new economic activity was likely propelled by markets in and tribute demands from the empire, it is interesting that the main source of economic stimulus appears to have come from the Mediterranean regional system—an economic system that largely skirted the edge of the Neo-Assyrian Empire.

This history could, of course, be viewed through a standard pericentric lens. In such a scenario political events and processes taking place in the north could be seen as precipitating the invasion and annexation of the region by the Assyrians; thus, pericentric forces could be blamed for the resulting dichotomy between the north and the south noted by Faust. However, one could also view this history through a more nuanced lens in which events and processes in Assyria's furthest and therefore most peripheral province in the Levant stimulated change in neighboring states, that is, in areas on the edge of but outside Assyria's direct control. Through such a lens, one could envision a complicated action and reaction in which peripheral events or processes drew in an imperial power and imperial action in the periphery resulted in a number of unforeseen and, until Faust's study, misunderstood consequences.

Guido Guarducci's chapter focuses on a particular geography in a detailed analysis of Assyrian intervention in the "Tigris Borderlands" (Parker 2006) of southeastern Turkey. Guarducci's contribution might thus be characterized as a study of the inner workings of pericentrics. Instead of addressing this area's relationship with the Assyrian heartland, Guarducci's chapter taps multiple lines of evidence to paint an intricate and elegant picture of the sociopolitical landscape of this volatile frontier region. In doing so, the author reconstructs the complicated constellation of ethnic, sociopolitical, and socioeconomic relationships and the actors that played them out in the Tigris Borderlands while at the same time highlighting the empire's motivations for expansion there.

Although most histories of the Tigris Borderlands emphasize Assyria's military exploits, Guarducci argues that the Neo-Assyrian officials were compelled to balance force (Parker 2014) and accommodation (White 1991) in their efforts to negotiate and manipulate local actors. Control of the Tigris Borderlands was indeed a complicated balancing act. This chapter is a great example of how categorizing data sets into what Guarducci calls "spheres of dynamics and interaction" can bring into focus relationships between, for example, the Assyrian administration and local communities and how an analysis of such relationships can be leveraged to assess socioeconomic landscapes of a periphery.

Megan Cifarelli's chapter, which reconsiders the data from the infamous site of Hasanlu in northwestern Iran, could be cast as a case study of the pathways and relationships of pericentrics. In it, Cifarelli challenges a long-standing interpretation of a peripheral center's relationship to a neighboring empire. For decades the standard interpretation painted this site within a classic dependency model in which local elites were portrayed as being in awe of Assyria's cultural, military, and political prowess (Dyson 1965; Dyson and Voigt 1989). Elites from Hasanlu were so drawn by the magnetism of Assyrian dominance that they emulated and propagated Assyrian tradition in their material culture. A similar propagation in modern scholarship of the model of Hasanlu's dependency led to this site being characterized by Cifarelli as "an exemplar of 'Assyrianization'" of the periphery. However, Cifarelli's study shows that if we reorient our view to give agency to peripheral actors, a very different picture emerges. Like peripheral actors in Cyprus (Cannavò, this volume), Edom (Brown, this volume), Ammon (Tyson, this volume), the southern Levant (Faust, this volume), and the Upper Tigris (Guarducci, this volume), elites in northwestern Iran were actors in broad regional networks that transmitted goods, ideas, and styles over long distances. In this light, the artifacts from Hasanlu do not betray cultural or ideological submission to Assyrian norms any more than Phoenician artistry of the same period betrays Egyptian dominance of the Levant (Winter 1976). Instead, the elites at Hasanlu were drawing on an artistic vocabulary in which art acted both as "interaction at a distance" (Winter 1982) and, paralleling the discussion in Düring's contribution to the present volume, as a link to an illustrious past.

Peripheries, semi-peripheries, far peripheries, and core-periphery hierarchies—a lot of ink has been spilled in an attempt to categorize peripheral variation (e.g., Chase-Dunn and Hall 1991, 1992, 1997). This situation is, in my opinion, a result of the fact that no two peripheries are alike. The preceding chapters underscore this observation. As we saw above, Guarducci highlighted peripheral variability in an Assyrian province, Faust drew a clear distinction between peripheral provinces and the states and societies that lay beyond, and Cifarelli highlighted a site well outside imperial hegemony.

Anna Cannavò, in turn, takes us into the far periphery in her analysis of the relationship between the Neo-Assyrian Empire and the island of Cyprus. Physically isolated by the vastness of the Mediterranean Sea, Cyprus was well beyond the reach of the empire. Yet at least one important pathway connected these two far-flung regions—economics. Although the Assyrians presented their interaction with Cyprus in ideological terms (cf. Smith 2005) and the relationship between Assyria and Cyprus was conditioned by geography, economic pathways appear to be the glue that (loosely?) bound these two unlikely partners together. Interestingly, this study both contradicts and complicates a key part of World System Theory that directly contributed to the stigma surrounding the concept of peripheries (see above). This key piece is the idea of peripheral dependency. Immanuel Wallerstein and even more so his followers who brought his ideas into ancient history and archaeology (especially Chase-Dunn and Hall 1991, 1992, 1997) envisioned a periphery's relation to its core as one of dependence. If dependence existed between Assyria and Cyprus, at the very least it was a codependence in which distance and geography leveled the playing field between a consolidated imperial polity and a much less complex peripheral zone.[3] Furthermore, this relationship was mediated by the Phoenicians, who were themselves a peripheral group that was anything but an underdeveloped dependency of Assyria. Such a situation changes the core-periphery hierarchy into a core-periphery codependence that is enabled or even enacted by a non-dependent, although at times unwilling, peripheral actor. This chapter thus highlights how the pathways and relationships of pericentrics can help explain peripheral variability.

Pericentric processes, as well as the pathways and relationships that interconnect peripheral actors, are complicated even more when we consider Bleda Düring's contribution to this volume. This chapter, titled "At the Root of the Matter: The Middle Assyrian Prelude to Empire," is, as the title suggests, about origins. In it, Düring interrogates the commonly held belief that Neo-Assyrian imperialism is a product of its time and that there is little or no connection between the Neo-Assyrian Empire and the earlier Middle Assyrian state. Although there are significant breaks in the archaeological and historical records between the Middle Assyrian Period and the Neo-Assyrian Period, Düring argues that precedents were set by the Middle Assyrian state that were used and elaborated upon by the Neo-Assyrian Empire. This chapter is therefore not so much about physical peripheries as it is about temporal peripheries. It thus represents a new and very intriguing type of pericentrism. By reorienting the reader to engage what is normally thought to be outside the "temporal center" of imperialism, we are forced to ponder how the Neo-Assyrian Empire's past shaped its ideology and the administrative systems it used. We are thus forced to consider how the direct application of imperialism in the historical present is both a product of and a construction made from historical memory (cf. Dodd 2005).

A number of recent studies of the Middle Assyrian state have highlighted specific tactics and characteristics that are also well-known in the Neo-Assyrian Period. These relatively obvious examples include social pathways such as deportation and resettlement (Wiggermann 2000; Postgate 2013), colonization (Akkermans and Wiggermann 2014; Tenu 2014), and intermarriage (Shibata 2014), as well as political pathways like the application of direct and indirect rule and the construction of military infrastructure (Düring 2014; Thareani 2016). However, the strength of this chapter for the present discussion is that it forces us to consider unusual types of relationships—not relationships between people or between people and things but those between people and time. That is, the relationship this chapter highlights is the relationship between the "ancient present" and the "ancient past." Neo-Assyrian monarchs sought to legitimize their expansion into the Upper Tigris, the Upper Habur, and the Balikh, for example, by claiming they were liberating lands formerly held by the Middle Assyrian state (Postgate 1992; Fales 2012), thus, as Düring explains, presenting expansion as a "*reconquista*" of former Assyrian holdings. This chapter brings up two questions we rarely consider: How do imperial actors relate to their past? And are these relationships enacted through pathways we have yet to consider?

Two of the chapters in the present volume address one of the most illusive yet also the most common imperial relationships—the relationship between the empire and the individual or household (cf. D'Altroy and Hastorf 2001). On a similar path to Cifarelli (this volume), whose raison d'être is to reassess a traditional historical interpretation, Erin Darby calls for a reexamination of the meaning and function of Judean pillar figurines (and by extension other types of artifacts of a similar class). She does so by interrogating the relationship between Judah's figurine tradition and the consolidation of the Neo-Assyrian Empire. Instead of seeing the introduction and spread of Judean pillar figurines as part of a centrifugal force emanating from the imperial core, Darby sees this phenomenon as a pericentric reaction to imperial expansion. She hypothesizes that imperial expansion, which caused widespread disruption of the preexisting social fabric, precipitated what amounted to a public health crisis. Local and perhaps regional reactions to epidemics that followed in the wake of imperial aggression included traditional healing rituals involving the use of votive objects such as these figurines. Through this lens, the spread of a particular type of artifact may be seen as part of a reaction reverberating along social pathways at the household level that was stimulated by events and processes occurring along larger political and military pathways linked to the imperial core.

A similar picture of domestic action and reaction can also be seen in Stephanie Brown's contribution. Brown begins by questioning the standard interpretations of the nature of Assyrian rule in the far-flung peripheral region of Edom in the south of modern Jordan. She then moves into the question of if or how the daily lives of local inhabitants of the region were affected by Assyrian hegemony. This chapter thus addresses a key question raised in the introduction to the present chapter, namely, how do the various pathways to power affect each other? If, for example, a peripheral state like Edom was under direct or indirect influence from the Neo-Assyrian Empire, such influence was likely expressed through political pathways. How does this type of interaction then affect social pathways? One way to address such a question is to examine changes and continuities that take place at the household level. As the smallest autonomous economic units in a society, households are the building blocks of society and the core ingredient of complex political formations (Chesson 2003, 2012; Souvatzi 2012). Households are thus ideal for researching the affects of imperialism on the everyday lives of imperial subjects.

Craig Tyson's chapter exemplifies all three of the themes I have highlighted in this chapter. To begin with, Tyson divides his data into various categories and uses those categories to measure pathways to power—that is, he uses the data to measure the degree to which local elites in the peripheral state of Ammon participated in the imperial enterprise. Highlighting the reciprocal relationships between Ammonite elites and the Neo-Assyrian and, later, Neo-Babylonian authorities and between the same elites and their local constituents, Tyson emphasizes the role imperial relationships played in the implementation of hegemonic rule. His analysis suggests that the rulers of Ammon acted as both a conduit and a filter for the dissemination of imperial norms to the local Ammonite population. However, while traditional core-focused approaches to imperial relationships might view the application of hegemonic rule in a peripheral state as one in which imperial authorities control local elites and use them as pawns to direct imperial interests, Tyson's pericentric view leads to a very different interpretation. In essence, Tyson argues that Ammonite elites manipulated their imperial overlords to heighten their own wealth and status. Tyson thus recasts Ammonite elites as active peripheral (imperial) actors who not only propagated imperial demands but, more important, affected the imperial system to their own advantage. This study therefore shows that Doyle's suggestion that events and processes taking place in the periphery can also affect change in the center is not the whole picture. Pericentrics can combine centrifugal with centripetal forces in a sort of reverberation that can affect change in both the center *and* the periphery.

NEO-PERICENTRICS

An examination of the case studies in the current volume through the lenses described in the first section of this chapter has brought a number of important observations into focus. To begin with, it is clear that the original definition of pericentrics set forth by Doyle (1986, 25) is far too rigid. Although the idea that the sources of imperialism should be sought in the periphery is certainly appealing, the case studies in this volume show that pericentrics is a bit more complicated than that. Doyle's observation is nevertheless germane in that it mandates a reconsideration of center-periphery relations. To aid in this endeavor, I propose the construction of a new analytical construct to examine pericentric phenomena. The small sample of studies of the imperial periphery contained in this volume makes it clear that a modern definition of pericentrics must take into account a number of important peripheral phenomena, including action and reaction, local agency, and multi-scalar relationships, as well as centrifugal and centripetal forces. That is, a new theory of pericentrics, what might be termed *Neo-pericentrics*, must be flexible enough to account for the fact that no two peripheral situations are the same.

With these observations in mind, we might define Neo-pericentrics as a theoretical approach for the study of ancient empires that is founded on the supposition that events and processes taking place in imperial peripheries constitute key mechanisms of historical continuity and change and that such events and processes both affect and can be affected by events and processes in or emanating from an imperial core. One of the key goals of Neo-pericentrics is to infuse peripheral actors with historical agency. However, this approach acknowledges that imperial histories are conditioned by dialectical interaction. Imperial agency and peripheral agency are therefore considered to have equal potential to influence historical continuity and change. Another goal of Neo-pericentrics is to illuminate continuity and change at various scales. Instead of studying empires as meta-phenomena, Neo-pericentrics seeks to break data sets into categories that might be indicative of specific pathways within and between imperial and peripheral actors and, in doing so, to isolate and analyze relationships between such actors at multiple scales. Ultimately, studies in Neo-pericentrics should aim to clarify the diversity that is both key to the imperial enterprise and specific to how that enterprise was experienced by imperial actors.

NOTES

1. Recent examples include Bagg (2013); Glatz (2009); Herrmann (2011); Harmanşah (2011); Parker (2011); Thareani (2016); Tyson (2014); and a number of studies in Areshian (2014).

2. Liverani (1979, 297) went as far as to say that empire is "the apex of all forms of exploitation."

3. See especially the "distance-parity" model in Stein (1999).

WORKS CITED

Akkermans, Peter M.M.G., and Frans Wiggermann. 2014. "West of Aššur: The Life and Times of the Middle Assyrian Dunnu at Tell Sabi Abyad." In *Understanding Hegemonic Practices of the Early Assyrian Empire*, ed. Bleda S. Düring, 89–124. Leiden: Nederlands Instituut voor het Nabije Oosten.

Algaze, Guillermo. 1993. *The Uruk World System: The Dynamics of Expansion of Early Mesopotamian Civilization*. Chicago: University of Chicago Press.

Areshian, Gregory E., ed. 2014. *Empire and Diversity: On the Crossroads of Archaeology, Anthropology, and History*. Los Angeles: Cotsen Institute of Archaeology Press.

Bagg, Ariel M. 2013. "Palestine under Assyrian Rule: A New Look at the Assyrian Imperial Policy in the West." *JAOS* 133 (1): 119–44.

Champion, Timothy C, ed. 1989. *Centre and Periphery: Comparative Studies in Archaeology*. London: Routledge.

Chase-Dunn, Christopher. 1988. "Comparing World-Systems: Toward a Theory of Semiperipheral Development." *CCR* 19: 29–66.

Chase-Dunn, Christopher, and Thomas D. Hall. 1991. "Conceptualizing Core/Periphery Hierarchies for Comparative Studies." In *Core/Periphery Relations in Precapitalist Worlds*, ed. Christopher Chase-Dunn and Thomas D. Hall, 5–44. Boulder: Westview.

Chase-Dunn, Christopher, and Thomas D. Hall. 1992. "World-Systems and Modes of Production: Toward the Comparative Study of Transformations." *HJSR* 18: 81–117.

Chase-Dunn, Christopher, and Thomas D. Hall. 1997. *Rise and Demise: Comparing World Systems*. Boulder: Westview.

Chesson, Meredith. 2003. "Households, Houses, Neighborhoods, and Corporate Villages: Modeling the Early Bronze Age as a House Society." *JMA* 102: 79–102.

Chesson, Meredith. 2012. "Homemaking in the Early Bronze Age." In *New Perspectives on Household Archaeology*, ed. Bradley J. Parker and Catherine P. Foster, 45–79. Winona Lake, IN: Eisenbrauns.

Christaller, Walter. 1966. *Central Places in Southern Germany*. Englewood Cliffs, NJ: Prentice-Hall.

Cogan, Morton. 1974. *Imperialism and Religion*. Missoula, MT: Scholars Press.

D'Altroy, Terence N. 1992. *Provincial Power in the Inka Empire*. Washington, DC: Smithsonian Institution Press.

D'Altroy, Terence N., and Christine A. Hastorf, eds. 2001. *Empire and Domestic Economy*. New York: Kluwer Academic/Plenum.

Dodd, Lynn Swartz. 2005. "Territory, Legacy, and Wealth in Iron Age Anatolia." In *Untaming the Frontier in Anthropology, Archaeology, and History*, ed. Bradley J. Parker and Lars Rodseth, 238–60. Tucson: University of Arizona Press.

Doyle, Michael W. 1986. *Empires*. Ithaca, NY: Cornell University Press.

Düring, Bleda, ed. 2014. *Understanding Hegemonic Practices in the Early Assyrian Empire: Essays Dedicated to Frans Wiggermann*. Leiden: Nederlands Instituut voor Nabije Oosten.

Dyson, Robert H. 1965. "Problems of Protohistoric Iran as Seen from Hasanlu." *JNES* 24 (3): 193–217.

Dyson, Robert H., and Mary Voigt. 1989. "East of Assyria: The Highland Settlement of Hasanlu." *Expedition* 31 (2–3): 3–11.

Fales, F. Mario. 2012. "'Hanigalbat' in Early Neo-Assyrian Royal Inscriptions: A Retrospective View." In *The Ancient Near East in the 12th–10th Centuries BCE: Culture and History*, ed. Gershon Galil, Ayelet Gilboa, Aren M. Maeir, and Dan'el Kahn, 99–120. Münster: Ugarit Verlag.

Glatz, Claudia. 2009. "Empire as Network: Spheres of Material Interaction in Late Bronze Age Anatolia." *JAA* 28: 127–41.

Grayson, A. Kirk. 1991a. "Assyria: Tiglath-pileser III to Sargon II (744–705 BC)." In *The Cambridge Ancient History*, vol. 3, part 2, ed. John Boardman, I.E.S. Edwards, N.G.L. Hammond, and Edmond Sollberger, 71–102. Cambridge: Cambridge University Press.

Grayson, A. Kirk. 1991b. "Assyria: Sennacherib and Esarhaddon (704–669 BC)." In *The Cambridge Ancient History*, vol. 3, part 2, ed. John Boardman, I.E.S. Edwards, N.G.L. Hammond, and Edmond Sollberger, 103–41. Cambridge: Cambridge University Press.

Grayson, A. Kirk. 1991c. "Assyria 668–635 BC: The Reign of Ashurbanipal." In *The Cambridge Ancient History*, vol. 3, part 2, ed. John Boardman, I.E.S. Edwards, N.G.L. Hammond, and Edmond Sollberger, 142–62. Cambridge: Cambridge University Press.

Harmanşah, Ömür. 2012. "Beyond Aššur: New Cities and the Assyrian Politics of Landscape." *BASOR* 365: 53–77.

Herrmann, Virginia Rimmer. 2011. "The Empire in the House, the House in the Empire: Toward a Household Archaeology Perspective on the Assyrian Empire in the Levant." In *Household Archaeology in Ancient Israel and Beyond*, ed. Assaf Yasur-Landau, Jennie R. Ebeling, and Laura B. Mazow, 303–20. Leiden: Brill. https://doi.org/10.1163/ej.9789004206250.i-452.92.

Jennings, Justin, and Willy Yepez Alverez. 2008. "The Inca Consolidation of the Cotahuasi Valley of Southern Peru." *Nawpa Pacha: Journal of Andean Archaeology* 20: 119–52.

Johnson, Gregory A. 1972. "A Test of the Utility of Central Place Theory in Archaeology." In *Man, Settlement, and Urbanism*, ed. Peter J. Ucko, Ruth Tringham, and G. W. Dimbleby, 769–85. Cambridge, MA: Schenkman.

Lanfranchi, Giovanni B., and Simo Parpola. 1990. *The Correspondence of Sargon II, Part II: Letters from the Northern and Northeastern Provinces*. Helsinki: Helsinki University Press.

Levine, Louis D. 1977. "East-West Trade in the Late Iron Age: A View from the Zagros." In *Le plateau iranien et l'Asie centrale des origines a la conquête islamique*, ed. Jean Deshayes, 171–86. Paris: Centre national de la recherche scientifique.

Liverani, Mario. 1979. "The Ideology of the Assyrian Empire." In *Power and Propaganda: A Symposium on Ancient Empires*, ed, Mogens T. Larsen, 297–319. Copenhagen: Akademisk Forlag.

Mann, Michael. 1986. *A History of Power from the Beginning to AD 1760*, vol. 1: *The Sources of Social Power*. Cambridge: Cambridge University Press.

Na'aman, Nadav. 1993. "Population Changes in Populations following Assyrian Deportations." *TA* 20: 104–24.

Oded, Bustenay. 1979. *Mass Deportation and Deportees in the Neo-Assyrian Empire*. Wiesbaden: Dr. Ludwig Reichert Verlag.

Parker, Bradley J. 2001. *The Mechanics of Empire: The Northern Frontier of Assyria as a Case Study in Imperial Dynamics*. Helsinki: Neo-Assyrian Text Corpus Project.

Parker, Bradley J. 2006. "Toward an Understanding of Borderland Processes." *American Antiquity* 71 (1): 77–100. https://doi.org/10.2307/40035322.

Parker, Bradley J. 2011. "The Construction and Performance of Kingship in the Neo-Assyrian Empire." *JAR* 67 (3): 357–86.

Parker, Bradley J. 2014. "Hegemony, Power, and the Use of Force in the Neo-Assyrian Empire." In *Understanding Hegemonic Practices of the Early Assyrian Empire*, ed. Bleda S. Düring, 287–99. Leiden: Peeters.

Postgate, J. Nicholas. 1974. *Taxation and Conscription in the Assyrian Empire*. Rome: Biblical Institute Press.

Postgate, J. Nicholas. 1982. "Ilku and Land Tenure in the Middle Assyrian Kingdom, a Second Attempt." In *Societies and Languages of the Ancient Near East: Studies in Honour of I. M. Diakonoff*, ed. Mohammed A. Dandamayev, I. Gershevitch, Horst Klengel, G. Komoróczy, M. T. Larsen, and J. Nicholas Postgate. Warminster, GB: Aris and Phillips.

Postgate, J. Nicholas. 1992. "The Land of Assur and the Yoke of Assur." *WA* 23 (3): 247–63.

Postgate, J. Nicholas. 2013. *Bronze Age Bureaucracy: Writing and the Practices of Government in Assyria*. Cambridge: Cambridge University Press. https://doi.org/10.1017/CBO9781107338937.

Radner, Karen. 2011. "Assyrians and Urartians." In *Oxford Handbook of Ancient Anatolia*, ed. Sharon Steadman and Gregory McMahon, 734–51. Oxford: Oxford University Press.

Rodseth, Lars, and Bradley J. Parker. 2005. "Introduction: Theoretical Considerations in the Study of Frontiers." In *Untaming the Frontier in Anthropology, Archaeology, and History*, ed. Bradley J. Parker and Lars Rodseth, 3–21. Tucson: University of Arizona Press.

Rosenzweig, Melissa. 2016. "Cultivating Subjects in the Neo-Assyrian Empire." *Journal of Social Archaeology* 16 (3): 307–34. https://doi.org/10.1177/1469605316667856.

Rowlands, Michael, Mogens Larsen, and Kristian Kristiansen, eds. 1987. *Centre and Periphery in the Ancient World*. Cambridge: Cambridge University Press.

Schreiber, Katharina. 1987. "Conquest and Consolidation: A Comparison of the Wari and Inka Occupations of a Highland Peruvian Valley." *American Antiquity* 52 (2): 266–84. https://doi.org/10.2307/281780.

Schreiber, Katerina J. 1992. *Wari Imperialism in Middle Horizon Peru*. Ann Arbor: Museum of Anthropology, University of Michigan.

Shibata, Daisuke. 2014. "Dynastic Marriages in Assyria during the Late Second Millennium BC." In *Understanding Hegemonic Practices of the Early Assyrian Empire*, ed. Bleda S. Düring, 235–42. Leiden: Nederlands Instituut voor het Nabije Oosten.

Sinopoli, Carla M. 1994. "The Archaeology of Empires." *ARA* 23: 159–80.

Sinopoli, Carla M. 2001. "Empires." In *Archaeology at the Millennium: A Source Book*, ed. Gary M. Feinman and T. Douglas Price, 439–71. New York: Kluwer Academic/Plenum. https://doi.org/10.1007/978-0-387-72611-3_13.

Smith, Stuart Tyson. 2005. "To the Supports of Heaven: Political and Ideological Conceptions of Frontiers in Ancient Egypt." In *Untaming the Frontier: Interdisciplinary Perspectives on Frontier Studies*, ed. Bradley J. Parker and Lars Rodseth, 207–37. Tucson: University of Arizona Press.

Souvatzi, Stella. 2012. "Between the Individual and the Collective: Household as a Social Process in Neolithic Greece." In *New Perspectives on Household Archaeology*, ed. Bradley J. Parker and Catherine P. Foster, 15–43. Winona Lake, IL: Eisenbrauns.

Stein, Gil J. 1999. *Rethinking World-Systems: Diasporas, Colonies, and Interaction in Uruk Mesopotamia*. Tucson: University of Arizona Press.

Tenu, Aline. 2014. "Building the Empire: Settlement Patterns in the Middle Assyrian Empire." In *Understanding Hegemonic Practices of the Early Assyrian Empire*, ed. Bleda S. Düring, 75–87. Leiden: Nederlands Instituut voor het Nabije Oosten.

Thareani, Yifat. 2016. "The Empire and the 'Upper Sea': Assyrian Control Strategies along the Southern Levantine Coast." *BASOR* 375: 77–102.

Trigger, Bruce G. 1989. *A History of Archeological Thought*. Cambridge: Cambridge University Press.

Turner, Frederick Jackson. 1938 [1893]. "The Significance of the Frontier in American History." In *The Early Writings of Frederick Jackson Turner*, ed. Everett E. Edwards, 183–229. Madison: University of Wisconsin Press.

Tyson, Craig W. 2014. "Peripheral Elite as Imperial Collaborators." *JAR* 70 (4): 481–509.

Wallerstein, Immanuel. 1974. *The Modern World-System I*. New York: Academic.

Wallerstein, Immanuel. 1980. *The Modern World System II*. New York: Academic.

White, Richard. 1991. *The Middle Ground: Indians, Empires, and Republics in the Great Lakes Region, 1650–1815*. Cambridge: Cambridge University Press. https://doi.org/10.1017/CBO9780511584671.

Wiggermann, Frans. 2000. "Agriculture in the Northern Balikh Valley: The Case of Middle Assyrian Tell Sabi Abyad." In *Rainfall and Agriculture in Northern Mesopotamia*, ed. R. M. Jas, 171–232. Leiden: Nederlands Instituut voor het Nabije Oosten.

Winter, Irene. 1976. "Phonecian and North Syrian Ivory Carving in Historical Context." *Iraq* 38: 1–22. https://doi.org/10.2307/4200021.

Winter, Irene. 1982. "Art as Evidence for Interaction." In *Mesopotamien und seine Nachbarn*, ed. Hans-J. Nissen and Johannes Renger, 355–82. Berlin: Dietrich Reimer Verlag.

Zimansky, Paul E. 1985. *Ecology and Empire: The Structure of the Urartian State*. Chicago: Oriental Institute.

About the Contributors

STEPHANIE H. BROWN is an archaeologist who has been excavating in Jordan since 2007. She completed her PhD, titled "Living on the Edge of Empire: Edomite Households in the First Millennium B.C.E.," at the University of California, Berkeley in 2018. Brown directed the Busayra Cultural Heritage Project (BCHP) from 2013 to 2016 and is interested in household archaeology, foodways, and postcolonial studies.

ANNA CANNAVÒ is a CNRS (Centre national de la recherche scientifique) researcher at the Maison de l'Orient et de la Méditerranée (UMR 5189 HiSoMA) in Lyon, France. She directs the French archaeological mission at Amathus and collaborates with the French archaeological mission at Kition. She is a specialist in the history of the kingdoms of Cyprus.

MEGAN CIFARELLI is professor of art history at Manhattanville College in Purchase, NY. Her recent publications include articles in the *Cambridge Archaeological Journal* and *Iran*, as well as a co-edited (with Laura Gawlinski) volume *What Shall We Say of Clothes: Theoretical and Methodological Approaches to Dress and Adornment in Antiquity* (Special Studies in Ancient Art and Architecture, vol. 3 [Boston: Archaeological Institute of America, 2017]).

ERIN DARBY is associate professor of religious studies at the University of Tennessee and co-director of the 'Ayn Gharandal Archaeological Project in southern Jordan. She is the author of *Interpreting Judean Pillar Figurines: Gender and Empire in Judean Apotropaic Ritual* (Mohr Siebeck, 2014). She is the recipient of a State Department Educational and

Cultural Affairs Research Fellowship (2007) and a National Endowment for the Humanities Fellowship (2016) for her work at the W. F. Albright Institute of Archaeological Research in Jerusalem. Most recently, she has begun work on the purported Edomite shrine at the site of 'En Hazeva in southern Israel.

BLEDA S. DÜRING is associate professor of Near Eastern archaeology on the Faculty of Archaeology at Leiden University. His research focuses on early Assyrian imperialism, prehistoric Anatolia and Cyprus, and the settlement history of southeastern Arabia.

AVRAHAM FAUST is professor of archaeology in the Department of General History, Bar-Ilan University (Israel). He specializes in the archaeology of ancient Israel during the Bronze and Iron Ages, especially from an anthropological perspective. He has published six books (as author) and well over 100 articles on these topics. He has excavated at a number of sites and is currently directing the excavations at Tel 'Eton in the southeastern Shephelah (lowlands), Israel, and conducting a survey in its surroundings.

GUIDO GUARDUCCI is co-director of the Center for Ancient Mediterranean and Near Eastern Studies (CAMNES) and supervisor of the Department of Ancient Studies at the Lorenzo de' Medici Italian International Institute, both based in Florence, Italy. He has participated in excavation projects in Italy, Israel, Syria, Cyprus, Azerbaijan, and Turkey. His research interests focus on the Late Bronze Age and the Early/Middle Iron Age material culture and socioeconomic dynamics of eastern Anatolia and the South Caucasus, as well as the effect of the Middle Assyrian and Neo-Assyrian Empires on these populations.

VIRGINIA R. HERRMANN is a junior research group leader in the Institute for Ancient Near Eastern Studies at the University of Tübingen (Tübingen, Germany) and co-director of the Chicago-Tübingen excavations at Zincirli, Turkey. Her research focuses on urban and household organization and Assyrian imperialism in the Iron Age Levant and Anatolia. She also works on the social role of mortuary cult and co-curated the 2014 Oriental Institute Museum exhibit *In Remembrance of Me: Feasting with the Dead in the Ancient Middle East*.

BRADLEY J. PARKER was associate professor of history at the University of Utah. At the time of his death (January 2018), he was director of the Nazca Headwaters Archaeological Project (NHAP) in Peru and recipient of a National Endowment for the Humanities (NEH) grant to study Inca and Wari imperialism. He was the founder and director of the Upper Tigris Archaeological Research Project (UTARP), which focused on southeastern Turkey, and author of several books and numerous articles on imperialism as well as the archaeology of the ancient Near East and Peru.

CRAIG W. TYSON is associate professor of religious studies at D'Youville College in Buffalo, NY. His research focuses on the history, religion, and culture of Transjordan; how empires affect peripheral societies; and historical-critical readings of the Hebrew Bible. He is part of a long-term excavation project at Khirbat al-Balua, Jordan, and has excavated at other sites in Jordan and Israel. He is author of *The Ammonites: Elites, Empires, and Sociopolitical Change (1000–500 BCE)* (London: Bloomsbury T&T Clark, 2014) and articles on the history of ancient Jordan.

Index

Page numbers in italics indicate illustrations.

Acco, 105
Adad-apla-iddina, 134
Adad-nirari I, 67
Adad-nirari II, 5, 183
Adad-nirari III, 152
Adana, 241
administration, 45, 50, 56; Amman Plateau, 192–93; imperial, 11, 51–52, 272, 274
Afghanistan, 18
Agia Eirini, 249
agriculture, 15, 16, 46, 80, 107; development of, 44, 45; estates, 53–54; intensification of, 55–56, 185–86; Upper Tigris, 72–74, 90(n9)
agro-pastoralists, 85
Ahazia, 133
Ahhiyawa, 241
Akestor, 249
Akhziv, 105
Alashiya, 240. *See also* Cyprus
alliances, Upper Tigris, 89
Al Mina, 247
Alzi, kingdom of, 69
Amathus, 248, 250, 253
Amīdu, 68
Amman, 153
Amman Citadel, 185, 189, 198(n6)
Amman Citadel Inscription, 183
Amman Plateau, 181, 185; during Iron Age, 182–83; religious changes on, 193–94; sociopolitical change, 188–93; trade networks, 187–88

Ammon, Ammonites, 25, 105, 106, *179*, 198(n3), 199(n13), 273; elite collaboration, 184–95, 276; figurines, 130, 131; Iron Age, 21, 181–84; socioeconomic changes, 194–97; subordination of, 97, 177–78
Anatolia, 71, 132. *See also various sites by name*
andurāru, 22
animals, 7. *See also* goats; sheep
Annals of Sargon II, 244
annexations, 19, 21, 44, 97, 271
apkallū, 132
Arabia, Arabs, 8, 18
Arabian Desert, 3, 16
Arad, 100, 159
Arameans, Aramaean states/kingdoms, 42, 197, 104, and Bīt-Zamāni, 68–69
Arcado-Cypriot dialect, 249
Archaic Period, on Cyprus, 253, 254–56
architecture, 225, 229, 256; Amman Plateau, 189–90; Hasanlu, *227*, 234(n28)
Armenia, 212
Aroer, 100
Arrapha, 47
Arsos, 249
art, 225, 229, 230; visual aspects of, 226–27
artifacts. *See* material culture
artistic internationalism, 227
Ashdod, 100
Asherah, 128

Ashkelon, 99; as trade center, 107–8, 109
Ashurbanipal, 8, 51, 134, 245; kings list, 254, 255, 256
Ashur-dan II, 82
Ashurnasirpal II, 5–6, 69, 220; and Upper Tigris, 82–83, 86
āšipu, 134, 139(n4)
assassins, in Šubria, 70
Aššur (god), 3, 6, 48; offerings to, 56–57
Aššur (place), 67, 134
Assur-dan II, 5
Assur-uballit I, 70
Assyria, Assyrian Empire, 12, 43–44, 51, 227, 268; and Bīt-Zamāni, 68–69; as changing concept, 20–21; and Cyprus, 253–54, 257; and Hasanlu, 210–11, 221–22; and Levant, 112–15; warfare, 67–70; as world-empire, 3–4
Assyrianization, 16, 20; at Hasanlu, 211, 230, 231(nn2, 3), 272–73
Assyrian Palace Ware, 163
Assyrians: in Šubria, 69; at Ziyaret Tepe, 74
Assyro-Aramaic *koine*, 20
Assyro-centric bias, of Hasanlu excavations, 210, 213
asû, 134, 139(nn4, 5)
Augustan threshold, 18

Baal-zebub, 133
Babahaki, 80
Babylonia, 22, 47, 133; hegemonic practice, 180–81; rulers in, 7–8
Babylonian Chronicles, 180–81
Babylonians, in Assyrian courts, 133
Balikh Valley, 46, 52, 56, 79, 81; Middle to Neo-Assyrian transition, 42, 274; settlement pattern changes, 53–54, 55
Banquet Stele, 5–6
Bashan, 252
Beersheba, 100
Beersheba Valley, 107, 159
Beit Aryeh, 103; olive oil production, 110, *111*
belts, 233(n17); copper-alloy, 215, 227, *228*
Benjamin Region, 102
Bennett, Crystal M., 158
Bethel, 103
Bethsaida, 104
Beth Shean, 104
Beth-Shemesh, 100

Beth Zur, 100
Biainili, 70
Bible (Hebrew Bible), 70, 182, 242; magico-medical ritual in, 133, 135, 140(n11)
Birkleyn Çay, 72
Bīt-Zamāni, 68–69, 70, 88, 89
Bohtan Valley, 56
Boqe'ah valley, 102
borderlands, 66–67
bottom-up processes, 22
Bowl K, 162–63, 172(n5)
Boztepe, 53, 73, 85
British School of Archaeology, in Iraq, 212
Bronze Age, artistic imagery, 228. *See also* Late Bronze Age
Building DD (Busayra), *164–65*, 168–69, 170, *171*
burial traditions, 49, 85; at Hasanlu, 217–18, *219*, 228, 229
Busayra, 151, *152*, *157*; ceramics from, 165–68, *169*–71, 172(n4); Edomite pottery from, 158–60, 161–63; excavations at, 163–65; monumental architecture, 153–54
Busayra Cultural Heritage Project (BCHP), activities of, 163–68

Calah, 5–6. *See also* Nimrud
canals, 6, 45, 46, 56, 186
capitalism, 12, 13
caravan trade, 16
Carchemish, 225
Caucasus, 224, 232(n11)
Çayirlik Tepe, 80
cedar, from Lebanon, 107
center-periphery model, 4, 44, 198(n3), 221, 276–77
Central Place Theory, 266
ceramics, 49; from Ammon, *189*–90; from Busayra, 165–68, *169*–71, 172(n4); East Greek, 111–12; Edomite, 154–55, 158–63; at Hasanlu, 214, 227, 233(n26); Upper Tigris region, 74–77, 84, 85, 86, 90(n5)
cereal grains, grain production, 71, 109
Chaldeans, 7
Choga Zanbil, 220
Chytroi, 248
Cilicia, 241, 258(n8)
Cimmerians, 70
Cisjordan, client kingdoms in, 98–102

cisterns, Upper Tigris, 73
civil service, Neo-Assyrian, 84
client kingdoms, in southern Levant, 98–102, 107–9, 117
client states, 105
Coastal Plain: economic integration, 107, 108–9; Philistine cities in, 98–100; Sharon, 103–4
coffins, anthropoid, 182
collaboration, by elites, 184–95
collecting, as elite activity, 215–16
colonization, colonists, 46, 49, 253, 274
Çöltepe, 80
commemorative practices, at Birkleyn Çay, 72
communications networks, 52
communities, in Upper Tigris Borderland, 68, 84–85
compromise, 65; Upper Tigris, 69
conflict, 65; Upper Tigris region, 67–70. *See also* military campaigns; warfare
conquests, 7–8, 14, 159, 184; in Levant, 97, 113–15, 271; Neo-Assyrian, 42, 70, 274–75
contact, and culture change, 155–56
control, 15, 97; Assyrian state, 9, 89; of conquered territories, 52, 56–57; imperial, 178–80, 268–70
cooking vessels: from Busayra, 165, *167*; Edomite, 161
copper production, 71, 152, 155; Cyprus, 248, 251
core and periphery model. *See* center-periphery model
craft production, 21; Local Style, 220, 224–25, 227–29, 234(n27)
cremations, Upper Tigris, 85
cults, 132, 172(n2), 193
cult statues, removal of, 10
cultural changes, 45; contact and, 155–56; foodways and, 156–57
culture: "high" and vernacular, 49; imperial, 45
culture of empire, 49, 50
cuneiform tablets, 80
customs, Assyrian, 49–50
cylinder seals: at Hasanlu, 213, 214, 215, 216, 220, 229; iconography, 190, *191*, 192, 199(nn13, 14)
Cypro-Geometric III Period, 248–49
Cypro-Syllabic script, 249, *251*, 258(n9)
Cyprus, Cypriots, 18, 130, 240, 245, 246, 257, 258(n9), 259(n11); and Iadnana, 241–42;

Kition's status on, 254–55; Phoenicians and, 247, 252–53, 273–74; Qarthadasht, 253–54; Sargon II stela on, 242–44; socioeconomic changes on, 248–52

Damdamusa, 69
dams, Upper Tigris, 73
Dan, 104
Danaoi, 241
Danunians (Rhodians), 241, 242
David, City of, healing rituals in, 135
debt remission, 22
Deir Daqla, 103, 110
Deir es-Sid, 102
demographic changes, 45
dependency theory, 12, 13
depopulation, 14, 114
deportations, 9, 11, 14, 27(n15), 45, 46, 73, 88, 274
Dhiban, 153
dimtu, 47. *See also dunnu*; estates
diplomatic gifts, 244–45
division of labor, 17
Diweithemis, 249
Diyarbakır, 68
Dodanîm (Rhodanîm), 242
Dor, fortification of, 103
dry farming, Upper Tigris, 72
dunams, 99, 101
dunnu, 42, 53–54, 87, 90(n6); Middle Assyrian, 79–80
Dur-Katlimmu, 46, 55
Dur-Sharrukin, 7, 45
dynasties, 47, 48–49

Early Iron Age (EIA), 68, 69; Cyprus, 250–51; luxury goods, 218–19; pottery production, 75, 76; Upper Tigris region, 81–82, 85, 88
East Greek pottery, in southern Levant, 111–12
East of Assyria, 212
economies, 23; Ammon, 186–88; Cypriot, 248–52; pre-modern, 17–18; of southern Levant, 106–12
Edom, Edomites, 24, 97, 105, 106, 156, 171, 273, 275; figurines, 130, 131; Iron Age, 150–55; pottery, 158–63
Edomite Plateau, 105, 152
Egypt, Egyptians, 8, 47, 107, 133, 180, 182, 250; figurine styles and use, 130, 132, 136; and Philistia, 98, 99

INDEX 289

'Ein el-Ghuweir, 102
'Ein et-Turaba, 102
Ein Gedi, 102
Ekron, 14, 99; and Assyrian policy, 112–13; olive oil production, 108–9, 110
Elam, Elamites, 8, 220, 227
el-'Id, 100
Elishah, 242
elites: Ammonite, 45, 88, 183, 196–97, 269, 276; Assyrian, 22, 50; co-optation of, 49, 57; exotic goods collection by, 215–16; grave goods of, 217–18; at Hasanlu, 214–15, 223–24, 229, 230, 272, 273; identity of, 10, 27(n15); imperial collaboration by, 184–95; local, 24, 25; and state propaganda, 50–51
Eli-Tešup, 69
Eloulaios. *See* Luli of Tyre
empire(s), 19, 52, 265, 275; Asian, 10–11; incorporation into, 184–85; periphery and, 20–23, 266–68; power and control by, 178–80, 268–70; relationships, 270–71
emulation, of Assyrian objects, 220
En Gev, 104
entanglement, 156
epidemics, 114, 140–41(n12), 275; and healing rituals, 136–37
Erzurum-Kars region, 75
Esarhaddon, 8, 70, 134, 244, 245, *246*, 258(n8); kings list, 248, 254, 255, 256; treaty with Tyre, 115–16
estates, agricultural, 42, 47, 53–54, 85. *See also* *dunnu*; *kapru*
Etemenanki Cylinder, 180
Etewandros, 249
exchange, 17. *See also* trade networks
exiles, return of, 22
exotic goods, 16; at Hasanlu, 213–15, 216–17, 227
exploitation/extraction, imperial, 14, 269
exports, Amman Plateau, 186

Fajer-South, 100
families, Middle Assyrian role of, 50
famines, 70, 114
farming. *See* agriculture
farmsteads, Southern Levant, 100, 101, 102, 107
faunal remains, 187
female trope, 136; naked, 132–33

figurines, 275; magico-medical rituals and, 133, 134–35; regional traditions, 131–32. *See also* Judean pillar figurines
Flavius Josephus, 254
foodways, 150, 159; at Busayra, 166–68, 170; cultural change and, 156–57; ethnic identity and, 160–61
forts, fortifications, 44, 46, 90(n6), 100, 103, 229; Upper Tigris region, 78, 80–81
free born villagers, as *dunnu* labor, 80
French Hill, 101
frontier theory, 266
Fum, 69

Galilee, 104
garrisons, 9, 78. *See also* forts, fortifications
Garzan Valley, 56
Gedaliah, 181
Gezer, 102–3
Gezer Region, 102–3
Gibeon, 102
Giizānu, 6
Gilead, 97, 105, 106
Gilzānu/Gilzanu (Meshta), 6, 221, 233(n22)
Giricano, 42, 53, 78, 80, 85, 90(n6)
Givat Homa, 101
glyptic objects, 226
goats, Amman Plateau, 187
goddesses and gods, 53, 128, 134, 194, 250; integration of, 9–10
gold, 187; at Hasanlu, 215, 216, 224
Golgoi, 252
grain production, Judah, 109
graves, Hasanlu, 217–18, *219*
grazing areas, Southern Levant, 109
Gre Amer, 75
Gre Dimse, 53, 77, 84
Greece, 134; pottery from, 111–12
Gre Migro, 69
Grooved pottery, Upper Tigris production of, 75–76, 86
Gula, 134
Gurgumu, 6

Habur region, 42, 52
Hakemi Use, 53, 77, 80, 83; pottery from, 74–75
Hamath, 73
hamlets, 84

290 INDEX

Hanigalbat, 52
Har Gillo, 100
Harran Stele II, 180
Hasanlu, 25, 231(nn2, 3), 232–33(nn14, 22), 272; Assyrian culture and, 210–11; burials at, 218, *219*; elites at, 223–24, 273; interaction network, 226–27, 232(n11); Local Style craft production at, 220, 224–25, 227–29, 234(n27); material culture at, 212–19, 225–26, 230, 232(n13), 233(nn15, 17, 26), 234(n28); Urartian control of, 222–23
Hasanlu Expedition, 210, 212
Hasanlu Gold Bowl, 215, 216, 224, *225*
Hasanlu Period, 210
Hasanlu Silver Beaker, 224, *226*
haserim, 100
Hatti, 6, 87, 246
Hazor, 104
healing rites, healers, 133, 134, 135, 136, 139(n4), 140(n11), 275
Hebrew Bible, 10
Hebron, 100
hegemony, 52, 179–80, 275; types of, 44–45
Ḥeṣban, 185, 187, 192
Hindānu, 6
Hirbemerdon Tepe, 53, 75, 76, 77
Hittites, 47, 53, 133, 227
Horbat Avimor, 103
horse trappings, with female decorative tropes, 133
Horvat ʻEli, 103
Horvat Malta, 104
Horvat Radum, 100
Horvat Rosh Zayit, 104, 110
Horvat Uza, 100
households, 22, 136, 156, 275
houses, 49; Aramaean, 68; Middle Assyrian, 84
Hubušku, 6
Hurrians, 47, 74; and Hasanlu, 224, 226, 227; in Šubria, 69–70
Hu-Tešup, 69
hydraulic technology, Upper Tigris region, 73

Iadnana, Neo-Assyrian reference to, 240–42, 257–58(n1)
iconography, 11, 141(n14), 224, 250; Amman Plateau art, 190, *191*, 193–94, 199(n13); of figurines, 128, 130–31, *132*
Idalion, 248, 250, 254
identity, 68; Assyrian, 19, 49; elite, 10, 27(n15), 50; foodways and, 160–61; Judean pillar figurines as, 137, 138
identity formation, 22–23
ideology, 4, 20; imperial, 44, 50–51
Ik-Tešup, 69
ilku obligations, 80
imagery, visual, 51
imitation Assyrian Palace Ware, 161–62; at Busayra, 167–68, *169*, 170, 171
imperialism, 3, 4, 12, 270–71
Inner Coastal Plain, economy, 108–9
inscriptions, 10, 11, 51
Iran, 7, 25, 215
Iraq, 12
Irbid, 105
Iron Age, 42, 51, 57, 66, 102, 106, 110, 141(n13), 171–72(n1); Ammon, 21, 181–84, 185, 198(n4); in Edom, 150–54; figurines, 130, *132*; magico-medical traditions, 133–34, 135–37; pottery production, 75–76
irrigation systems, 73
islands of power, in Upper Tigris, 78
Israel, 113, 130, 160; kingdom of, 24, 97, 106, 116; Southern Levant provinces, 102–5
Istanbul Prism, 180
ivories, at Hasanlu, 213, 214, 215, 220, 225, 227, 233(n26)

Jalul, 183, 185
Jazirah, 14
Jericho, 102
Jerusalem, 14, 101, 107, 109, 131
Jokneam, 104
Jordan, Iron Age, 150–55, 171–72(n1), 275
Jordanian Plateau, 155, 159
JPFs. *See* Judean pillar figurines
Judah, kingdom of, 100–102, 106, 110, 118(n10), 194; Assyrian subordination of, 97, 113; economic integration, 107, 109; magico-medical rituals in, 135–37; pillar figurines, 130–31
Judean Desert, 102, 109
Judean Highlands, 100
Judean pillar figurines (JPFs), 24, 132, 140(n10), 275; characteristics of, 128–30; contexts of, 135–36, 137–38; regional styles, 130–31
Judean sites, 159

Kadashman-Enlil, 215
*kapru, i*n Upper Tigris, 84, 88
Karashamb, 224
Karm er-Ras, 104
Karmir Blur, 212
Kar-Tukulti-Ninurta, 45
Kassites, 47, 215, 227
Kathari area, 256
Kavuşan Höyük, 53, 77, 84, 85
Kedesh, 104
Kenan Tepe, 53, 75, 85
Ketef Hinnom, 101
Khabur Triangle, 42
Khirbet abu et-Twein, 100
Khirbet Abu Shawan, 100, 101
Khirbet Abu Tabaq, 102
Khirbet al-Jariya, 152
Khirbet 'Alona, 101
Khirbet Anim, 100
Khirbet Dawwar, 103
Khirbet el-Maqari, 102
Khirbet el-Qatt, 100
Khirbet er-Ras, 101
Khirbet en-Nahas, 152, 154, 155, 171–72(n1)
Khirbet esh-Shajra, 103
Khirbet es-Samrah, 102
Khirbet Hilal, 100
Khirbet Jarish, 100
Khirbet Jemein, 103
Khirbet Kla, 103, 110
Khirbet Marjameh, 103
Khirbet Mazin/Qast el-Yahud, 102
Khirbet Rabud, 100
Khirbet Shilhah, 102
Khorsabad, 7, 153
kidinnūtu, 22
Kilokki Rabiseki, 76
kings, 5, 67; Amman Plateau, 192–93; Cypriot, 244, 247(table), 249–50, 254; divinity of, 9–10
Kinrot, 104
kinship, and Aramaean identity, 68
Kition (Kittim), 242, 244, 248, 250, 253, 256, 259(n11); political status of, 254–55
Kourion, 248, 249, 250
Kullimeri, 69, 70, 89
Kul Tarike, burials at, 217–18
Kulushinas (Tell Amuda), 46
Kumme, 70

Kummu, 6
Kurdistan, Assyrian materials in, 217–18
kur land, 71–72, 90(n4)
Kushites, rebellion, 8
Kypromedousa, 250

labor, 80; on water control systems, 73–74
Lachish, 100
landscape, symbolic, 71–72
landscape engineering, 54
land tenure, 11; Upper Tigris, 73, 84
Lapethos, 248
Larnaca, Sargon II stele from, 242–44, 255
Late Assyrian Period. *See* Neo-Assyrian Period
Late Bronze Age (LBA), 42, 51, 53, 57, 68, 75, 87, 132, 181, 227; luxury goods, 218–19
Lebanon, cedar from, 107
Ledra, 248
Lenin, Vladimir, on imperialism, 12
Levant. *See* Southern Levant
literacy, Ashurbanipal's, 51
livestock, in Judah, 109
Lower Habur canal, 46
Lower Habur valley, 55
Luli of Tyre, 244, *245,* 258(n4)
Luwians, at Ziyaret Tepe, 74
luxury goods, 13, 212; on Amman Plateau, 190, 192; Bronze and Iron Age, 218–19; at Hasanlu, 213, 225–26; visual aspects of, 226–28

maceheads, at Hasanlu, 213, 215
magico-medical traditions, 133–34; Judaean rituals, 135–37
Malatya, 225
Malidu, 6
Mallowan, Max, 212
Manahat, 101
Mari, Land of, 55
Marion, 248
markets, Amman Plateau, 186
marriages, 274; dynastic, 49
material culture, 52, 183, 232(n10); on Amman Plateau, 186–87, *189*–90; Assyrian, 42, 49–50, 153–54; Assyrianizing, 220–29; Hasanlu, 210, 212–19, 231(nn2, 3), 232(n13), 233(n15); spread of, 49–50; Upper Tigris region, 74–77
medicine. *See* magico-medical traditions

Mediterranean, 3, 16, 109. *See also* Cyprus; Phoenicia
Megiddo, 97, 104, 153
Memphis, 8
Menander of Ephesus, 254
mercenaries, Greek pottery and, 111
Mesopotamia, 99, 215; figurine styles and uses, 130, 132
metals, 16, 196. *See also* copper; gold; silver
metalwork, at Hasanlu, 220
Metropolitan Museum of Art, and Nimrud, 212
Mevasseret Yerushalayim, 101
Mezad Michmas, 102
Middle Assyrian Period (MAP), 23, 24, 41, 46, 45, 48, 49, 50, 56, 274; pottery, 74–75; scale, 42, *43*; in Upper Tigris Borderland, 65, 68, 70, 71, 78–81, 87
Middle Bronze Age, 80, 224
middle ground theory, 66
Middle Iron Age (MIA), 69, 86; pottery production, 75–76
military, 9; social mobility, 21
military campaigns, 159, 244, 253; in Levant, 97, 103–4; in Nairi lands, 67, 69, 71, 87
Milkom, 194
Mitanni Period, 53, 87
Mitanni state/empire, 47, 69, 88, 226, 227
Mizpah (Tell en-Nasbeh), 102
Moab, 97, 105, 106, 130
money, monetization, 12, 187
monuments, 11; art, 132–33; construction of, 44, 153
Musasir/Musasiru, 6, 70
Muški, 70
Müslümantepe, 53

Na'aman, 133
Nabonidus, 180, 181
Nahal Zimri, 101
Nairi lands, 89(n2); military campaigns against, 67, 69, 87
NAM.BÚR.BI- ritual, 134
Nebi Samuel, 102
Nebuchadnezzar II, 180, 181
Negev, 100, 109, 170; Edomite pottery in, 159, 160, 161
Neo-Assyrian Period (NAP), 41–42, *43*, 45, 48, 113, 133, 223, 274; agricultural production,

56, 185–86; and Ammon, 177, 195–96; hegemonic control, 180–81; state propaganda, 50–51; Upper Tigris, 24, 65, 69–70, 71, 81–86, 87
Neo-Babylonian Empire, 5; and Ammon, 177–78, 195, 196; hegemonic practices, 180–81
Neo-Hittites, 241
neo-pericentrics, 25, 277
Niḫrija, 53
Nile Delta, 8
Nile Valley, 3
Nimrud, 5–6, 11, 153, 154, 212, 220
Nineveh, 7, 46, 134, 153, 244
nomads, 8–9, 71, 73; Upper Tigris region, 81, 85, 88
Northern Coastal Plain, 104–5
North Syria, monumental art in, 225, 234(n28)
Northwest Palace (Calah/Nimrud), 5–6
Nubia, 18
Nuzi, estates in, 47

offerings, to Aššur, 56–57
officials, 9, 26(n6), 181, 199(n14). *See also* administration
Old Assyrian Period, 71
olive oil production, 24; Southern Levant, 108–9, 110, *111*, 128(n9)
orthostats, 51
ostraca, 192
Ottoman Empire, 10

palaces, 5–6, 11
Palace Ware, 76
Palaepaphos, 248
Paphos, 249
papyrus, administrative use of, 193
Patinu, 6
patronage, royal, 21
Patti-hegalli, 6
Pax Assyriaca, 22, 117, 199(n10)
pericentrics, 25, 266–68, 271–72, 274; redefining, 276–77
peripheries, 4, 25, 198(n3), 211, 273, 276; archaeological study of, 265–66; Assyrian identity/influence, 20–23; imperial control, 178–79
Persian Gulf, 3
Persian Period, Ammon, 196

Persian Wars, 254
Petra, Edomite pottery and, 161
Philistia, Philistine city-states, 16, 106, 110, 111, 109; as client kingdoms, 98–100; figurine styles, 130, 131; subordination to Assyria, 97, 113
Philistines, trade, 18
Phoenicia, Phoenicians, 18, 104–5, 107, 109, 131, 240; and Cyprus, 244, 247, 252–54, 255–56, 273–74
Phoenician cities, 56, 97
Phoenician ports, 16
Phoenicization, of Kitian, 253
Pisgat Zeev A, 101
Pisgat Zeev D, 101
plagues. *See* epidemics
podiums, at Busayra, 153
population(s): changes in, 14, 114; movements in, 46–47; resettlement/redistribution of, 44, 45, 185, 186
Pornak, 76, 78
pottery. *See* ceramics
power, imperial control, 268–70
prestige goods, 17; on Cyprus, 249, *251*. *See also* exotic goods; luxury goods
prisoners of war, as agricultural labor, 73, 80, 85
propaganda, Neo-Assyrian Period, 50–51
provinces, 9, 12, 42, 44, 48, 98; Assyrian rule, 23, 106, 271; in Levant, 97, 102–5, 109–10, 117
publications, on Transcaucasia excavations, 212–13

qanats, 73
Qarney Hittin, 104
Qarthadasht, 253, 254, 259(n10); and Tyre, 255, 256
qīpu officials, 9
Qumran, 102
quotidian meal, 156–57
Quwe, 241

Raghdan Royal Palace Tomb, 182
raiding, by Assyrians, 222
Ramat Beit Ha-Kerem farmstead, 101
Ramat-negeb, 159
Ramat Rahel, 100
Rambam Cave, 101
Ramot farmsteads, 101
rank, negotiating, 215

Ras el Karrûbeh, 102
raw materials, access to, 13
rebellions, 8, 178, 180, 194
reciprocity, 66
reconnaissance survey, Upper Tigris region, 52–53
relay systems, 45, 47
religious imperialism, 16
religious traditions, Amman Plateau, 193–94
resettlement, 274
resins, 71
rituals, magico-medical, 133–37
ritual specialists, 21; magico-medical, 134–35
road systems, 45, 47
rock monuments, iconography, 11
Rosh Ha'ayin, 102
royal house, dynastic linkages to, 48–49
R.P. 1618/1239, 100
Rujm al-Kursi, 190, *191*, 193–94
Rujm el Bahr, 102
Rujm esh-Shajra, 102
rulers: Ammonite, 183–84; and gods, 9–10

Ṣafuṭ, 185
Saḥab, 182, 185
Sais, 8
Salamis, 248, 250, 254, 256
Salat Tepe, 53, 75, 85
salvage archaeology, 12
Samaria, 97, 102–3
Samsi, 9
sanctuaries, Cypriot, 248–49
sandstone, Nubian, 161
Sargon II, 7, 69, 70, 90(n10), 97, 134, 244; stele to, 242–*43*, 257
scholarship, Assyrocentric bias, 25
scribes, 136
sculptures, 190, 220
seals. *See* cylinder seals
semi-nomadic peoples, Upper Tigris region, 85–86
semiotic system, Assyrian, 11
semi-precious stones, from Upper Tigris, 71
Sennacherib, 7, 70, 134, 244, 258(n7); military campaigns, 100, 159, 253
serving vessels: from Busayra, 166–68; Edomite, 24, 161–62
settlement systems/patterns, 52, 53, 113–14; Ammon, 184–86; Kingdom of Israel, 102–4;

Kingdom of Judah, 100–102; Middle Assyrian Period, 78–79; modification of, 44, 45–46; Philistia, 98–100; Phoenicia, 104–5; of subject territories, 23, 105–6; Upper Tigris, 78–79, 84, 85–86
shadouf, 73
Shalmaneser I, 67, 80–81
Shalmaneser III, 5, 7, 69, 72, 183, 222
Shalmaneser V, 97, 134
Shamshi-Adad V, 7, 222
Sharon Coastal Plain, 103–4
Shechem, 103
sheep, on Amman Plateau, 187
Shephelah, 100, 107, 108
Shilṭa of Tyre, 244
Shiqmona, 105, 110
shrines, figurines in, 132, 140(n10)
Sidon, 6, 258(nn4, 7)
siluhlu, 47
silver, 16, 18, 71, 187, 224
Sinabu, 69, 81, 83
Sînmuddameq, 53
Sin of Harran: images of, 190, *191*; worship of, 172(n2), 193–94
slaves, 14, 85
social engineering, 48, 54
social mobility, 21
social stratification, 12, 192, 229
socioeconomics: Ammonite, 194–95; Upper Tigris region, 78–86
sociopolitical change, 24; Amman Plateau, 188–93
Soloi, 248
Southern Levant, 8, 12, 14, 16, 22, 47, 56, 73, 97, 117, 141(n13), 153, 154, 163, 170, 187, 199(n10), 225, 244, 258(n8), 273; client kingdoms in, 98–102; economy of, 106–12; figurine styles and uses, 24, 132–33; provinces in, 102–5, 270–71; textual information on, 115–16
Southern Transjordan-Negev Pottery (STNP), 159–60
sovereignty, Assyrian, 20–21
Spain, 18
specialization: and imperial control, 185; and social mobility, 21
springs, Upper Tigris, 73
starvation, Southern Levant, 114
state embedding, 18–19
state formation, 71

states, 13; competing, 7–8
stelae, 11; on Cyprus, 242–43, 257
STNP. *See* Southern Transjordan-Negev Pottery
stone slabs, from Upper Tigris region, 71
storage pots, from Busayra, 165–66
storerooms, at Hasanlu, 227
straw, from Upper Tigris region, 71
subjugation, 4; Bīt-Zamāni, 69
Šubarû, Subartu, 69–70
Šubria, 69–70, 88
Suhu, 6
Šurpu-style rituals, 134
Susa, 8, 215
Suteans, 81
symbolic capital, 17
Syria, 12, 68, 99, 130, 215

Table of Nations, 242
Talavaş Tepe, 85
Talesh, 215; excavations in, 212–13
Tal-i Malyan, 220
Tall Jawa, 183, 185, 187, 189–90
Tamassos, 248, 250
Tan-Ruhuarater, 215
Tarshish, 242
taste, 156
Taurus Mountains, 3
Tawilan, 150, 153, 154, 158, 169
taxation, 11, 14, 18, 22
Tell (Tel) Abu Hawam, 105
Tell (Tel) Ahmar, 14
Tell (Tel) Amuda (Kulushinas), 46
Tell (Tel) Barri, 42, 55
Tell (Tel) Batash. *See* Timnah
Tell (Tel) Beersheeba, 159
Tell (Tel) Beit Mirsim, 100, 110
Tell (Tel) Brak, 46
Tell (Tel) Chuera (Ḫarbe), 49
Tell (Tel) el-Farah, 103
Tell (Tel) el-Ful, 102
Tell (Tel) el-Hammah, 104
Tell (Tel) en-Nasbeh (Mizpah), 102
Tell (Tel) 'Eton, 100
Tell (Tel) Fekheriye, 42, 55
Tell (Tel) Gath Hefer, 104
Tell (Tel) Hadar, 104
Tell (Tel) Hadid, 102, 108, 109–10, 118(n8)
Tell (Tel) Halaf, 42, 225

Tell (Tel) Halif, 100
Tell (Tel) Hefer, 103
Tell (Tel) 'Ira, 100, 159
Tell (Tel) Jemmeh, 99
Tell (Tel) Keison, 105
Tell (Tel) Malhata, 100
Tell (Tel) Masos, 100
Tell (Tel) Michal, 103
Tell (Tel) Qasile, 103
Tell (Tel) Qiri, 104
Tell (Tel) Rehov, 104
Tell (Tel) Rumeith, 105
Tell (Tel) Sabi Abyad, 47, 49, 53–54, 79, 81, 90(n6)
Tell (Tel) Šeh Hamad (Dur-Katlimmu)/ Tell (Tel) Sheikh Hamad, 14, 42, 115
Tell (Tel) Sera', 99
Tell (Tel) Shioukh Fawqani (Bûr-marîna), 115
Tell (Tel) Taban, 42, 55
Tell (Tel) Yin'am, 104
Tell (Tel) Zeror, 103
Tell (Tel) Zira'a, 105
tenant farmers, 73
Territorial-Hegemonic Model, 15, 179–80
territories, 19, 53; conquered, 44, 49, 113–14; incorporation of, 56–57
textiles, textile production, 71, 187–88, 199(n9)
texts: administrative, 115–16; archival, 10, 11; diagnostic and prognostic, 133–34
Tidu, 69, 80, 81, 83
Tiglath-pileser I, 67
Tiglath-pileser III, 5, 7, 8, 9, 23, 69, 73, 97, 134, 152; military campaigns, 177–78, 184
Tigris River, 72. *See also* Upper Tigris region (Borderland)
Til Barsip, 46, 153
timber: from Cyprus, 251, 252; from Upper Tigris region, 71
Timnah (Tel Batash), 99, 107, 108, 110
tombs, 86, 189, 250
trade, trade networks, 7, 12, 15, 16, 18, 215; Amman Plateau, 187–88, 196–97; Cyprus-Tyre, 251–52; Southern Levant, 98–99, 107–12, 118(n10)
trade colonies, in Anatolia, 71
Transcaucasia, 212; copper alloy belts from, 215, 227
Transjordan, 24, 105, 170, 198(n1)
treasuries, Hasanlu, 214, 215, 216, 233(n15)

treaties: with Tyre, 115–16; Upper Tigris region, 69, 89
Trialeti, 224
tribal lineages, Aramaean, 68
tribute, 11, 13, 14, 16, 69, 180; Amman Plateau, 186, 187, 196; diplomatic gifts as, 244–45; Edomite, 154–55; from Hasanlu, 221–22; from Levant, 97, 114
Tukulti-Ninurta I, 67
Tukulti-Ninurta II, 5, 86, 183
Turkey, 7, 12
Tušhan. *See* Ziyaret Tepe
Tuššum, 70
Tyre, 6, 104–5, 258(nn4, 7); and Cyprus, 244, 246, 251–52, 253, 254, 255–56; treaties with, 115–16

Üçtepe, 53, 75, 76, 78
Ugarit, 47, 136
'Umayri, 185, 187, 192
Umm al-Biyara, 151, 158, 169
Upper Euphrates, 75
Upper Habur, 42, 274
Upper Khabur, 56
Upper Mesopotamia, 5, 15
Upper Tigris region (Borderland), 24, 42, 65, 66, 87–89, 185, 272, 273, 274; agriculture in, 46, 56, 72–74, 84–85, 90(n9); archaeological data from, 52–53; Middle Assyrian socioeconomics, 78–81; Neo-Assyrian socioeconomics, 81–84; pottery in, 74–77; semi-nomadic settlements in, 85–86; symbolic landscape, 71–72; warfare and conquest, 67–70
Upper Zab River, 6
Uppumu, 69, 70, 89
Urartians, 69, 216, 222
Urartian state/empire, 7, 69, 86, 212; as pericentric phenomenon, 267–68
Urartu (Ur[u]atri), 70, 83, 88, 220, 232(n10), 233(n22); and Hasanlu, 222–23
urbanism, 14
Urmia, Lake, 7, 222, 223
Ushnu-Solduz Valley, 210
Ushpinu, 222

Van Basin, 75
vassals, 12, 13, 18, 26(n5), 180, 193; Ammonites as, 177–78; integration of, 9–10; tribute and, 14, 187

Vered Yericho, 102
villages, 84, 100
violence, at Hasanlu, *211*

Wadi Arabah, 159
Wadi Faynan, 154, 155, 171–72(n1); survey around, 151–52
Wadi Fukin, 100
Wadi Qelt, 102
Wallerstein, Immanuel, 13, 273
warfare, 53; in southern Levant, 113–14; Upper Tigris Borderlands, 67–70
water control systems, Upper Tigris region, 73
wealth, proto-capitalist creation of, 14
western provinces, settlement systems in, 53–55
wheat, trade in, 107
wine production, 100, 107, 108, 109

wool production, 71, 187–88, 196, 198–99(n8)
world-empire, 3–4, 18
world-systems theory, 25, 266, 273; influences of, 12–16; intersocietal networks, 17–18

Yahweh, 194
Yareaḥ, representations of, 194
Yawan, 242, 246

Zagros Mountains, 222; in symbolic landscape, 71–72
Zamua, 222
Zeviya Tivilki, 76
Zincirli, 153, 225
Ziyaret Tepe, 14, 46, 53, 69, 70, 77, 218; burials at, 85, 218; displaced people at, 73–74; Grooved pottery production, 75, 76; Middle Assyrian Period, 78, 80; Neo-Assyrian Period, 82–83

www.ingramcontent.com/pod-product-compliance
Lightning Source LLC
Chambersburg PA
CBHW070909030426
42336CB00014BA/2347